CLASS UNKNOWN

CULTURE, LABOR, HISTORY SERIES
General Editors: Daniel Bender and Kimberley L. Phillips

The Forests Gave Way before Them: The Impact of African Workers on the Anglo-American World, 1650–1850
Frederick C. Knight

Class Unknown: Undercover Investigations of American Work and Poverty from the Progressive Era to the Present
Mark Pittenger

Class Unknown

Undercover Investigations of American Work
and Poverty from the Progressive Era to the Present

Mark Pittenger

NEW YORK UNIVERSITY PRESS
New York and London

NEW YORK UNIVERSITY PRESS
New York and London
www.nyupress.org

References to Internet websites (URLs) were accurate at the time of writing.
Neither the author nor New York University Press is responsible for URLs that
may have expired or changed since the manuscript was prepared.

Library of Congress Cataloging-in-Publication Data
Pittenger, Mark.
Class unknown : undercover investigations of American work and poverty from the
progressive era to the present / Mark Pittenger.
p. cm. — (Culture, labor, history series)
Includes bibliographical references and index.
ISBN 978-0-8147-6740-5 (cl : alk. paper) — ISBN 978-0-8147-6741-2 (pb : alk. paper) — ISBN
978-0-8147-2429-3 (ebook) — ISBN 978-0-8147-2430-9 (ebook)
1. Social classes in mass media. 2. Social classes in mass media. 3. Investigative reporting—
United States—History—20th century. 4. Social classes—United States—History—20th
century. 5. Working class—United States—History—20th century. 6. Poverty—United
States—History—20th century. I. Title.
HN90.S6P58 2012
305.50973—dc23   2012008071

New York University Press books are printed on acid-free paper,
and their binding materials are chosen for strength and durability.
We strive to use environmentally responsible suppliers and materials
to the greatest extent possible in publishing our books.

Manufactured in the United States of America
c 10 9 8 7 6 5 4 3 2 1
p 10 9 8 7 6 5 4 3 2 1

For Rachel and Benjamin

CONTENTS

ACKNOWLEDGMENTS

In the house where I grew up in postwar suburban Indianapolis, books served as doorways into other worlds. This book was born in that house's sunwashed living room, a welcoming sanctuary of words, ideas, and images that introduced me to other places and people—people who were not like us. One could find there, somewhere above the row with *Kidnapped*, *The Double Helix*, and the old hardbacked Oz books, and across the mantle from the shelves that held Shakespeare and Richard Halliburton's globe-trotting *Seven-League Boots*, a thin paperback by John Howard Griffin called *Black Like Me*. On the day I pulled Griffin's book from the shelf, the gestation of this work began. Here was a book about a man who changed his racial identity in an effort to learn what it meant to be oppressed and despised as a black man in the United States of the late 1950s. I learned in that living room that books opened out not only into long-gone and imaginary worlds, but also into the one that we were all coming to inhabit in the twentieth century's second half. As for so much else, I have my parents—Suzanne Masters Pittenger and the late Robert C. Pittenger—to thank for that.

I haven't literally been writing the book from that day to this, although it probably feels that way to some of the patient people around me. Patience and considerable help from others carried me through, and my thanks go out to the National Endowment for the Humanities, the American Council of Learned Societies, and, at the University of Colorado, the Council on Research and Creative Work and the Eugene M. Kayden Research Committee, all of whom provided time and material support for research and writing. The Interlibrary Loan team at the University of Colorado's Norlin Library was unfailingly efficient and helpful in large and small ways, and I received excellent research assistance from Jennifer Hammond, Colin Church, and Rachel Pittenger, all of whom brought not only energy and skill but ideas and judgment to their work. As the project developed, I benefited from a barrage of suggestions, criticisms, leads, and encouragement, for which I thank Peter Boag, Jim Bright, Lee Chambers, Constance Areson Clark, George Cotkin, the late Jim Denton, the late Nora Faires, Bob Ferry, Leon Fink, Toby Higbie, David Hollinger, Dan Horowitz, Padraic Kenney,

Eric Love, David Papke, Eric Rauchway, Dorothy Ross, Kristine Stillwell, and David Wrobel. My colleagues in the CU History Department made a lively and discerning audience for one of the first papers that I presented on this topic. They also generously rallied to render aid during a time of personal difficulty—for which I especially thank Susan Kent and members of the department in the late 1990s—and have continued to provide an ideal academic home. I am grateful for the intellectual stimulation and sustenance that I received from Erika Doss, Martha Gimenez, Julie Greene, Rickie Solinger, and the many other members who passed through CU's American Studies reading group. Stan Thurston and the late Marion Thurston were always warm and reliable sources of support. And, as readers of this book will know, there is nothing academic about the friendships we forge in the academy: to Fred Anderson, Virginia Anderson, Bob Hanna, and Martha Hanna, my thanks for our years of abundant food and drink, camaraderie, and intellectual work and play, as our families have grown up together while our working lives advanced.

Parts of the first three chapters have been published previously, and I am grateful for permission to make use of material from "A World of Difference: Constructing the 'Underclass' in Progressive America," *American Quarterly* 49 (March 1997): 26–65; and "What's on the Worker's Mind: Class Passing and the Study of the Industrial Workplace in the 1920s," *Journal of the History of the Behavioral Sciences* 39 (Spring 2003): 143–161. I also appreciate the suggestions and guidance of editors Lucy Maddox and Raymond E. Fancher, respectively, and the perspectives offered by readers for those journals, all of which helped me to sharpen my arguments and exposition. Thanks to Dan Bender and Kim Phillips, who believed in this book and moved it along the path toward publication in NYU Press's Culture, Labor, History series; to Salwa C. Jabado, Gabrielle Begue, and Constance Grady who answered questions and kept the process moving; and to Deborah Gershenowitz, my editor at the press, who saw to it, with great patience and consummate professionalism, that the job got done.

Books would be written faster if historians didn't have families, but life, as well as departmental social functions, would be less rich and interesting. This book is dedicated to my children, Rachel and Benjamin, who helped it along by regularly demanding to know how I was progressing on the dedication. They probably did not expect to grow up with the book, but so they have, and magnificently. I hope it proves worthy of them. But without Sharon, so much would have been missing—including them. Although the words "for better or for worse" did not appear in our homemade wedding ceremony, they might as well have. Thanks to Sharon, for everything, again.

In 1902, Bessie and Marie Van Vorst—sisters-in-law, writers, and avowed "gentlewomen"—changed their clothes and took up factory work, promising to reveal to readers the world of the "unknown class," for whom they intended to serve as a "mouthpiece" in the struggle to inaugurate a more just and egalitarian society. In undertaking this project, they joined an American tradition of undercover investigation that had begun to take shape in the late Gilded Age, flourished from the Progressive Era through the 1930s, shifted in focus and method during the postwar decades, and persists to the present, constituting a distinctive ongoing commentary on the development of class society in the age of industrial capitalism. The Van Vorsts shared a conviction with other journalists, social scientists, novelists, and intellectuals who went "down and out," to use the term later coined by George Orwell: The only way to understand life across the class line was to live it. Over more than a century, a mass of such investigators fanned out through American steel mills, coal mines, construction sites, hotels, department stores, paper-box factories, taxi-dance halls, restaurants, hobo jungles, hop fields, and lumber camps. They hoped to learn what it meant to work hard and to be poor. They wanted to know what it meant not to be—and perhaps by extension, what it did mean to be—"middle class." Most writers shared with the Van Vorsts a suspicion of grand theory, favoring instead a homespun epistemology of experience. Their books and articles characteristically foregrounded two perspectives: a sometimes shrewd critique of the official knowledge obtainable from self-interested employers, sentimental philanthropists, and abstractly minded economists; and an often naïve and condescending conviction that, through class masquerade, they might "discover and adopt" their subjects' viewpoint, and thereby contribute to resolving "the social problem."[1] For most, going undercover was both an empirical task and an existential dare—a mission, and an adventure. This book tells their story.

The Van Vorsts' coinage of the "unknown class" implies two things about the undercover tradition. First, these investigators went beyond tourism or slumming to immerse themselves in what the restaurant investigator Frances Donovan called "a new world" replete with "life, new and strange": a world of difference. In that world, they worked and lived among people who shared traits and practices (later sometimes called "cultures") that were strikingly different from their own. Their task as writers became especially to represent difference, if also to seek commonalities that might foster cross-class solidarity. In describing from the inside how "the other half" lived, they often revealed why and how they believed class differences had arisen, and to what extent they seemed fixed and permanent.[2] Second, "unknown class" implied how class, as a category applicable to U.S society, remained vague and troublesome to investigators and to their audiences.[3] When most down-and-outers described the working-class other, they tended to emphasize appearance, behavior, language, and social practices, while paying less attention to the structural factors and power relations that produced harsh working conditions, unemployment, and poverty. Many echoed the American narrative of social mobility, fluidity, and classlessness; indeed, their stories of class switching suggested such fluidity, as could their well-meaning efforts to make the poor seem less alien than their readers might expect.

This is a multigenerational story, but not one in which the same gestures were endlessly repeated. Writers' perspectives on class, labor, and working-class people shifted in concert with particular historical contexts, as will be evident in the chapters that follow. I will track the tradition from its Progressive Era origins and proliferation (chapter 1) through a sequence of distinctive stages: into a "New Era" of postwar labor militancy and 1920s industrial psychology, personnel management, and romantic vagabondage (chapter 2); through numbing defeats and redemptive struggles in the wastelands of the Great Depression (chapter 3); across wartime renegotiations of gender and national identity in a reborn industrial economy, and onward to celebrations of postwar affluence that merged with Cold War fears of communism to cast class into the shadows (chapter 4). The story's contours and key themes change markedly in the later 1940s and 1950s, with the increasing prominence accorded to race in social thought and public discourse during the rise of the civil rights movement (chapter 5). John Howard Griffin's undercover classic *Black Like Me* (1961) serves as a marker for those shifts, and it signifies a turning point in the nature of the tradition and its discourses.[4] The final chapter briefly charts the undercover tradition's persistence in postmodern America, when the very definitions of borders and identities underwent seemingly constant reconsideration.

My goals are twofold. First, I will reconstruct the story of a little-known mode of producing social knowledge that proved influential in both popular and academic realms. By "social knowledge," I mean not what Americans today would acknowledge as verifiable truth statements, but I refer to ideas and images that earlier historical actors took to be accurate when explaining their society. Bearing an authority that seemed undeniable, undercover investigators worked to establish knowledge about the unknown class in a nation that largely denied the very relevance of class to its historical experience. These investigative accounts tell us much about how earlier Americans thought about work, poverty, and class, and about how modern understandings of those categories were created. I will also consider how class passers' personal, professional, gender, and class identities were at stake in this enterprise. Because their truth-telling method relied on sustained deception and masquerade, their stories illuminate how less-flexible Victorian understandings of identity gave way to modernist conceptions of malleable selfhood. In attempting to do this story justice, I will range beyond conventional nonfiction print sources to interweave discussions of short stories, novels, plays, and movies that drew from and commented on the undercover tradition.

Second, I wish to demonstrate the role of cross-class passing in the genesis and development of something much larger: the common view of the poor that was once associated with terms such as "dangerous classes," and more recently with debates about a "culture of poverty" and an "underclass."[5] Labels in this lineage have typically connoted a social stratum whose members' values and practices are believed to be entirely separate from those of people in mainstream society, and whose undesirable traits appear to result from a vague congeries of environmental and hereditary influences. Because undercover investigators claimed a unique authority to speak of and for the poor, and because they often portrayed their subjects as beings of a radically different order, we must ask about their contribution to this genealogy. How did such essentialist representations comport with the emphasis on environmental causation that was supposedly ascendant from the Progressive Era onward? What role did undercover writers play in advancing an alternative view that conflated class with race and culture—a conflation often understood to have degenerative or devolutionary implications—which can be identified in popular and academic discourse throughout the same period? I believe that this tradition of conflating categories coexisted with, and even infiltrated, the better-known countertradition associated with the anthropologist Franz Boas and his students, who stressed cultural and historical factors over biological explanations of difference.[6] Variants on the Boasian culture concept that emerged in the social sciences could prove just as deterministic as biology had proven in older formulations about human development. Such determinism often reflected the persistent legacy of Lamarckian biology, which had long linked environment with heredity through its emphasis on the inheritance of acquired traits.[7] Down-and-outers usually saw themselves as friends of the poor, but many did meld class, race, and culture to articulate degenerationist, quasi-Lamarckian theories of poverty. Yet their texts often proved internally contradictory, because many of the same investigators also emphasized the positive ways in which poor people sought work, struggled to survive, and found meaning in those endeavors. Thus, down-and-outers intended to serve as tribunes of the poor, even as they also helped to lay the foundations for the concept of an underclass—a concept later attacked by critics for similarly conflating race with class and culture.[8]

This study is marked by some anomalous features. First, although what I call a "tradition" was demonstrably continuous and productive, it was not always overtly self-conscious. Writers and reviewers did sometimes allude to previous undercover texts. But perhaps to underscore the audacity of their approach, authors often ritualistically described achieving the supposedly unprecedented realization that they must live a working-class life in order to write authentically about it. "Why not be a waitress," Frances Donovan asked herself in 1917, as if such a thought had never struck anyone before—when it obviously had, as anyone with Donovan's graduate training in sociology should have known.[9] Comparable declarations of originality remained common at the twentieth century's end.

Further, most participants in this tradition had no set name for their method. Reviewers sometimes called it "slumming"—an appellation that down-and-outers routinely rejected because it implied sensationalism and exploitation—and sometimes it was referred to as the more academically respectable "participant observation." But neither label precisely describes the practice of purposefully deceiving others about one's class standing in order to write about the resulting experiences. Therefore, I have used the terms "down-and-outers," "undercover investigators," and "class passers" more or less interchangeably. The last term, suggesting an analogy with racial passing, is the trickiest. Racial passing in the United States has usually meant moving upward on the scale of societal power and privilege. But class passing, in which downwardly mobile writers proclaimed themselves uniquely qualified to represent those below them on that scale, was itself an exercise of power. It could also lead to further accretions of power through professional advancement, public notoriety, and book sales. But if the analogy is not exact, the term still seems appropriately descriptive. Clearly, the makers of this tradition will not solve the problem of nomenclature for us. Some simply called it spying, or worried that it might be seen that way.[10] Reviewers have always been of mixed mind about the practice's legitimacy, regarding its results either as uniquely valuable and insightful, or as inauthentic, unscientific, and redolent of undemocratic attitudes. However warranted such praise and blame may have been, I believe that this tradition's history is uniquely revealing about the construction of social knowledge of work and poverty in modern American history.

I should also emphasize that I have not attempted to write social history. I will not argue that these writers' narratives did or did not match up with some verifiable social reality, that they can or cannot show us "how it was" to be a hop picker or a hobo. Rather, I have tried to reconstruct how investigators entered a world that was not their own, and why they represented that world and its inhabitants as they did. To accomplish this, I have sought to establish connections among these individuals, and to link them to the contexts—intellectual, cultural, social, economic, political—in which they operated. Drawing on the evidence of their texts and on available biographical information, I have put those texts in dialogue with each other to ask certain basic questions about each generation of investigators. Why did they go undercover, and what were they looking for? What intellectual equipment and cultural preconceptions did they bring to their tasks? How did their often-contradictory mix of motives and emotions—idealism, daring, desire, fear, voyeurism, revulsion—shape their efforts to forge experience into ideas and images? How did their class, gender, and racial identities affect their representations of the other? How did they change, or not change? How did their texts fit within, challenge, or just ruffle the surface of ongoing discourses about class, work, and poverty?

Finally, assessing this tradition is not a simple matter. Other scholars who have touched on it tend to highlight the investigators' elitism and self-delusion.[11] In a thoughtful analysis of the subject, the literary scholar Peter Hitchcock concludes that undercover texts arise out of writers' class-based "reflex or duty" to understand the conditions of their own class's superior position, and that they always reaffirm the permanency of class distinctions and shrink from suggesting any effort to abolish them. This perspective has not been limited to the academy, because class passing has also been a popular journalistic genre. Reviewing the stage version of Barbara Ehrenreich's undercover study *Nickel and Dimed* (2001), a critic complains that the play is mainly about the middle-class narrator's "liberal guilt" and offers no "authentic voice" for the poor.[12]

This approach bears a certain sort of fruit, but such readings strike me as unduly limited. Undercover texts are only inconsistently egalitarian and cannot offer a transparent window on reality, but they are not reducible to exercises in middle-class condescension. In highlighting the complex interplay between democratic aspiration and elitist objectification in these works, I will argue against Hitchcock's contention that a "cultural logic of slumming" operated to consistently confirm an invidious sense of difference and to rein-scribe the class line.[13] While most down-and-out texts were not avowedly revolutionary, they were produced because middle-class authors situated themselves amid some of the worst ravages of the emergent capitalist order, struggled to grasp the origins and nature of class difference, and groped toward a critical, independent, modern consciousness of self and society. They are better understood, as Hitchcock also suggests, in terms of "position" and "identification." Beginning from my best understanding of each writer's consciousness of self and class, I ask how class passers positioned themselves with regard to their subjects, to their imagined audience, and to structures of power and authority; and I ask to what extent they identified themselves with their subjects, and sought to represent—however imperfectly—their points of view. It is too easily asserted that describing the working-class other serves solely to define the middle-class self and that crossing a border serves only to reinscribe it.[14] We should also recognize that neither the border nor those on either side of it will necessarily look the same to a writer or an audi-ence after the crossing has occurred. This was what set undercover investiga-tions apart from more conventional modes of studying American work and poverty. Whatever their blindnesses and limitations—and I will not under-state them—down-and-outers from the Progressive Era to our own time have repeatedly demanded that Americans open their eyes to the willfully unseen and that they confront the persistent, pressing, and still-unanswered question of the unknown class.

PART I

A World of Difference

Constructing the Underclass in Progressive America, 1890–1920

1

Writing Class in a World of Difference

From the early stirrings of social and political reform in the 1890s through the progressive heyday of the 1910s, journalists, social scientists, novelists, and the occasional unemployed college graduate chose to live and work in disguise among factory laborers, clerks, waitresses, beggars, and tramps, in order to observe and to write about them. Most produced texts that embodied the contradictions of Progressive Era American thought, which was riven by tensions between democracy and egalitarianism on one hand, and elitism, racism, nativism, patriarchy, and a drive for social control on the other. Most also offered a characteristically progressive mix of science and sympathy when describing their subjects: They proclaimed their scientific faith in the primacy of facts over opinion and mere sentiment, yet their pages pulsed with the authors' efforts to sympathize and identify with their coworkers and neighbors. Most hoped that their hard-won knowledge might contribute to a progressive reshaping of the U.S. social order.[1]

Jack London's *People of the Abyss* (1903) is the best-remembered chronicle of such experiences,[2] but I will address an array of less familiar figures who contributed to this discourse. While charting their practice's prehistory, reconstructing their motives and methods, and examining their texts, I also consider how tightly stretched were their intellectual and cultural commitments between a waning Victorian culture and the subversive attractions of modernity. These social explorers belonged to that founding generation of young American moderns who from the 1890s onward confronted the jarring but exhilarating transformations of America's economic organization, its sex and gender roles, its ethnic and racial makeup, and its international posture; who navigated between capital and labor through settlement-house work, political reform, and radicalism; who sought to live experimental lives, and, in myriad ways, attempted to "capture the new." But when older evolutionary and racial preconceptions shaped their encounters with social difference, investigators could find the border zone between class identities to be a shadowy and liminal realm, disconcerting to those still imbued with an orderly Victorian worldview that depended on fixed categories and borders. Many worried that their project might entail more than temporarily adopting a new persona—a modernist performative strategy typical of a "culture of personality" in which they had not been raised. What might become of the eager explorer cast adrift in that nether region where middle shaded into lower, whiteness into color, and human into subhuman? Indeed, going down-and-out might result in going native, becoming addicted to tramping, or disappearing forever into the teeming urban "underbrush."[3] The risks were real and the stakes were high as this first generation of undercover investigators began its descent into the abyss of American poverty.

Origins

Fin-de-siècle social investigators had precedents aplenty for their project of dwelling as natives in unknown worlds. From colonial-era captivity narratives, to Richard Henry Dana's ordeal before the mast, to the Civil War–era deluge of stories about cross-dressing women's military adventures,[4] American readers enjoyed a steady stream of opportunities to imagine life on the far side of various lines. In the 1880s, Mark Twain constructed fictional adventures in downward mobility to shock his aristocratic characters into realizing their submerged democratic tendencies: After trading places with the pauper, the young prince would become a more caring king; after traveling in peasant garb with the Connecticut Yankee and enduring the horrors of slavery, King Arthur would abolish the evil institution. But when Edward died too young to affect social conditions, and the Yankee's plans for reform foundered on the rock of Arthurian Britons' "training"—deeply ingrained, quasi-hereditary cultural values and assumptions—Twain's tales presaged similar confusions among progressive social investigators who also grappled with environment and heredity, free will and determinism, and elitist pessimism and democratic hopefulness.[5]

British and Continental students of poverty provided Americans with more precise models for undercover social investigation. Peter Keating has identified a British tradition of such explorations, generally intended to stimulate reform through state action, which he dates from the journalist James Greenwood's 1866 account of "A Night in a Workhouse." Charles Booth's monumental studies of London poverty (1887–1903) marked a shift within the British tradition from Greenwood's brand of individual journalistic and humanitarian impressionism to Booth's efforts, as a Comtean positivist and self-styled sociologist, to achieve a more detached and scientific standpoint. But here, too, complexities arose. As Judith Walkowitz points out, once Booth went to live among the impoverished, both his personal identity and his scientific determination to construct a taxonomy of the urban poor continually wavered and collapsed in the face of his multiplicitous experiences.[6] The example of Booth's scientific aspirations proved important to American investigators, even as they faced similar issues of conceptualization and identity.

Continental exemplars of undercover investigation came especially from Germany during the 1890s. American students of industrial conditions encountered the works of a theology student, Paul Göhre, and of Dr. Minna Wettstein-Adelt, both of whom published studies of Saxony workers. Wettstein-Adelt's book, which came out in 1893, remained untranslated and unreviewed in the United States, but academic writers sometimes cited it together with Göhre's *Three Months in a Workshop* (1891) when reviewing American down-and-out texts. Göhre's book, translated in 1895, had a much broader American effect. The reform-oriented economist Richard T. Ely contributed a prefatory note for American readers, and the book was widely and well reviewed in both learned and popular opinion journals.[7] Göhre offered Americans their first example of a book-length down-and-out study, and he introduced many of the questions and themes that would characterize the American discourse over the ensuing decades: the methods and ethics of undercover investigation; the tensions between science and sympathy (between amassing data and empathizing with the objects of study); the propriety of investigators speaking for their "less fortunate brothers"; the labor question considered in its moral and intellectual, as well as its economic and social, dimensions; and the possible roles of the state, the churches, the unions, and the socialist movement in addressing workers' conditions and

concerns. Richard Ely noted the "profound sensation" the book had produced in Germany and urged American readers to embrace its lessons, as
all industrial nations could be expected to develop according to the same
evolutionary model.[8] The German investigators quickly made their mark in
the United States. The sociologist Annie Marion MacLean, who published
down-and-out studies between 1899 and 1923, acknowledged in 1903 her
debts to Wettstein-Adelt and Göhre. Ely's promotional efforts also bore fruit
closer to home: His daughter, Anna, a Wisconsin Ph.D. student, expanded
her education by working at a Milwaukee tool manufacturing shop, and
then at a New York cannery where she toiled along with Alice Van Hise, the
daughter of the university's president.[9]

American undercover investigations seem to have begun as a means to
investigate crime and labor activism (often seen as roughly synonymous
by the owning classes). From the beginning, issues of personal identity and
social utility were both salient. John Kasson found that Pinkerton detectives
who entered the underworld in disguise sometimes grew so inured to duplic-
ity and so alienated both from their own "true sel[ves]" and from the society they purported to protect that they led lives "more radically fragmented,
isolated," and "theatrical" than did their quarry. Just such a fate would have
threatened the Springfield, Massachusetts, police detectives who marched
for a month in the ranks of the New England tramp "army" during the 1877
national railroad strike. Chief Detective Stephenson reported that his fellow
knights of the road stood "ready for pillage and destruction," but, like the
social revolution feared by that era's middle class, Stephenson's tramp upris-
ing failed to materialize.[10]

The novel *Murvale Eastman: Christian Socialist* (1890), by the lawyer and
social critic Albion Tourgée, served as a harbinger for the growing number of
cross-class passing accounts that appeared in the 1890s. Tourgée's protagonist
temporarily assumes the identity of a streetcar driver to learn about the labor
question from the inside, and he finds that his "month of strange experience"
as a worker reshapes his life and vocation.[11] Many of his real-life counterparts
could have said the same. Their endeavors must be understood in light of two
emergent phenomena: an expanding discourse on class relations and poverty, and mounting middle-class anxieties about the stability of class identity
and privilege. Cities served as foci for both developments, as cities increasingly became the sites of concentrated wealth and poverty. Several notable
down-and-outers tramped through rural and small-town America, but
nearly all eventually explored "the hidden city of the poor"[12]—the gloomier
side of a harshly dichotomized urban realm. For the better-off who withdrew
to comfortable downtown enclaves or to the expanding suburbs, the poor

became literally less visible—except to participants in slumming tours—and increasingly were a construction of newspapers, magazines, and books. Just as Londoners had been taught for decades by the reform and sensational presses to see their city as sharply divided between savage, poverty-stricken East London and civilized, prosperous West London, so also did Americans come to understand their cities in radically binary terms.[13] Already by mid-century, a lurid genre of urban exposé had evolved. Newspapers, magazines, and guidebooks conducted illustrated "gaslight" tours through the "lights and shadows" of metropolitan poverty, penetrating realms that were rife with immanent dangers and forbidden pleasures. More serious Gilded Age readers could also peruse Charles Loring Brace's analysis of *The Dangerous Classes of New York* (1872), and, by the 1890s, the sympathetic but still touristic explorations of Jacob Riis and others into the lives and lairs of the "other half," now lavishly illustrated with photographs.[14]

This variegated literature offered consumers a peculiar mix of stern Victorian moralism and furtive enticement. Readers' responses might range from sympathy, to quasi-pornographic stimulation, to fear of falling from their own positions of privilege. As early as the depression of the 1870s, middle-class readers of *Frank Leslie's Illustrated Newspaper* began to see faces and bodies that looked all too much like their own in wood-block engravings of tramps and vagrants. Such images portrayed once-respectable casualties of unemployment, now among the familiar degraded types who were assumed to have merited their fate. During the deeper depression of the 1890s, middle-class Americans might increasingly perceive their perch in the social hierarchy as precarious. The very meaning of "middle class" was rendered uncertain by the chaotic industrial changes that incessantly eroded existing social boundaries.[15] Recurrent assertions that the "embers of social hatred" had for years been "smoldering in the vagrant class" (as one student of tramps put it) fed those middle-class insecurities, even as they sharpened readers' curiosity about the unknown world of the poor. As the reform impulse quickened in the nineties, armchair explorers found this other world graphically represented for their private consumption in a burgeoning variety of formats.[16]

By the 1890s, reformers and social scientists were conducting interviews, mapping neighborhoods, and gathering statistics about poverty and the poor.[17] But these individuals generally did not represent themselves as members of the class they were investigating. Neither did those whose sojourns among the poor were undertaken for therapeutic purposes but included no element of deception, or were simply unintended and involuntary.[18] Progressive Era down-and-outers' most exact American predecessors were the sensational "stunt girl" newspaper journalists such as Nellie Bly and her many imitators, who escaped the confines of the women's page by writing about their brief experiences as flower vendors, beggars, and ballerinas. Nellie Bly wrote "Ten Days in a Madhouse" for Joseph Pulitzer's *World* in 1887, and she spawned this fad for female writers, which subsided in the early 1890s when such assignments came to be seen as overdone and trivial, and also as demeaning exercises imposed by male editors who resisted female reporters' efforts to broaden their domain.[19] Just as the genre was waning in the United States, Elizabeth Banks, an American expatriate journalist, carried out a series of stuntlike investigations in London where she passed as a domestic servant, a crossing sweeper, a flower girl, and a laundry worker. Billed as the work of "an American Girl in London," Banks's articles made a great splash in that city, and many were republished in New York papers. On returning to the United States in the later 1890s, Banks parlayed her newspaper notoriety into a few years' lucrative work as a yellow journalist. But her 1894 book *Campaigns of Curiosity*, based on her London adventures, did not sell well and was little noticed in this country, perhaps reflecting the decline of the stunt genre.[20]

As the novelty and luster of stunt journalism ebbed in the early nineties, the related mode of undercover social investigation began to take shape. Henry George had formulated in 1879 the besetting conundrum of Gilded Age America—the simultaneous advancement of "Progress and Poverty"— giving voice to a rising concern that poverty was expanding across a nation that had imagined itself immune to Old World class divisions. In that context, the writer Josiah Flynt and the seminarian Walter Wyckoff (later an economist) put Albion Tourgée's fictional strategy to work and embarked on their expeditions into the world of tramps. In 1891 Wyckoff disguised himself and began an eighteen-month cross-country tramp, which he described in a series of magazine articles and two books over the next ten years. In the same year, Flynt distilled from his tramping experiences the first of eighteen articles and a book that would appear over the ensuing decade.[21] Others quickly followed their lead. Between 1893 and 1896, as books by Wettstein-Adelt, Banks, and Göhre reached American shores, Stephen Crane's New York flophouse nights provided the raw materials for his newspaper story "An Experiment in Misery" in 1894,[22] and Alvan Francis Sanborn, a settlement house resident, published two articles and two books on his explorations of Boston lodging-house and street life in 1895–1896.[23] C. W. Noble wandered the "border land" of Michigan "Trampdom" in 1896.[24] During the decade's final years, Wyckoff's and Flynt's books (published in 1897–1898 and 1899, respectively) garnered considerable attention, while the Chicago sociologist Annie Marion MacLean's research on department-store work saw print, and *Henry*

Worthington, Idealist, an 1899 novel by the Wellesley literature professor Margaret Sherwood, offered a literary-intellectual manifesto for undercover investigation and social activism.[25] The 1890s investigators thus pioneered, and to some extent even theorized, the undercover method.

Flynt's tramp articles and Crane's urban sketches marked the beginning of investigators' purposeful efforts to justify their method and to position themselves as unorthodox authorities. As Flynt explained it, he had studied irregularly at the University of Berlin, and he still hoped that sociologists would read his articles in popular magazines. However, he portrayed himself as having gradually abandoned the academy's approved yet "fruitless" approach to gathering information through sketchy statistics and interviews with unreliable informants.[26] Crane announced to readers of the *New York Press* that he would eschew the stance of the pitying omniscient observer and cross the gulf of class to "discover" the Bowery bum's "point of view." As Alan Trachtenberg pointed out, what distinguished Crane from novelists such as William Dean Howells, who had written about the poor with mixed concern and condescension, was Crane's determination to achieve an "exchange of subjectivities" with the impoverished other, to make the reader a temporary denizen of the underworld: "an experimenter in mystified space." When Crane's shabby protagonist reaches scruffy Chatham Square, he feels relieved to have arrived "in his own country" and enters fully into the experiment: "He aligned himself with these men, and turned slowly to occupy himself with the flowing life of the street." Unlike most social investigators, Crane wrote not to spur reform or to serve up slices of raw truth, but to render the city aesthetically from the viewpoint of its most marginal inhabitants.[27] Subsequent investigators with reformist or social-scientific goals would typically subordinate Crane's aesthetic agenda to the task of properly presenting data, while novelists such as Margaret Sherwood and Marie Van Vorst would deploy both approaches.[28]

Stephen Crane was neither the first nor the last reporter to conduct an experiment in misery; the method became so common that it gave rise to parodies. By 1909, one of O. Henry's New York stories would describe a park-bench bum repelling the overtures of an undisguised newspaperman: " 'Oh, no, no,' said he. 'You ain't a reporter. . . . They pretend to be one of us, and say they've just got in on the blind baggage from St. Louis. I can tell a reporter on sight.'"[29] When Crane's 1894 newspaper story was reprinted nationally in 1898, its author bridged the worlds of local journalism and national publication. Crane also served as a bridge between contemporary and later undercover investigators, and perhaps not only because he operated in the milieu already established by Nellie Bly and her acolytes. One biographer suggests that Crane's experiment may have been inspired by the proletarian wanderings of Walter Wyckoff, but as Wyckoff had not yet begun to publish in 1894, it also may be that Crane's story inspired Wyckoff to publish the record of his earlier experiences—or even to echo Crane's title in his own book's subtitle: *An Experiment in Reality*.[30] Whether or not there was any actual connection, Crane and Wyckoff certainly shared the desire of an emergent generation of writers to experiment with their lives, and to entice readers to journey with them into novel realms of reality. From the 1890s through the end of the Progressive Era, many an explorer with similar ambitions would follow their lead.

A "Little Body of Adventurers"

What sorts of people became undercover investigators, and what motivations and preconceptions did they bring to the experience? Faith in the following generalizations must be tempered by the fact that information on these individuals is scarce at best. Still, a combination of solid information about some of them, fragmentary evidence gleaned from others' writings, and familiarity with the broader progressive reform milieu does warrant certain claims. First, most were young—in their twenties or thirties during the Progressive Era—and prepared to confront what could be extremely harsh conditions.[31] In their backgrounds, down-and-outers resembled the social welfare activists studied by the historian Linda Gordon. Predominantly of native-born, white, Northern European, Protestant stock, most hailed from prosperous families and were well educated. Several counted ministers among their forebears, and most of that group also pursued theological studies before veering off into social reform, social science, or both. Some adopted the stance of the modern, secular, scientific investigator, but many combined an allegiance to science with religious faith or with a vaguely religious moralism. In bending inherited religious commitments to the cause of social betterment, many corresponded roughly to Robert Crunden's description of progressives as "ministers of reform." They were also part of a much larger progressive and radical milieu in which settlement workers and bohemian intellectuals sought out cross-class experiences to obtain what some called "vital contact" with the poor.[32]

In seeking such contact, down-and-outers resonated strongly with the progressive mentality emerging in the 1890s, as seen in Jane Addams's distinctive compounding of commitment to the scientific method with insistence on an expansive human sympathy. In her famous 1892 speech on "The Subjective Necessity for Social Settlements," Addams called on college-educated women to join a settlement-house movement that would "demand from its residents a scientific patience in the accumulation of facts and the steady holding of their sympathies as one of the best instruments for that accumulation." Addams's generation commonly used the word "sympathy" to suggest the erasure—even if temporarily—of barriers between otherwise-different people, as when the novelist Margaret Sherwood described the "tingling sympathy" that bridged the class gulf between two of her characters. But Sherwood's Annice Gordon also recognized that a "vague, wistful sympathy" was not enough—that she must do something practical with the knowledge that she gathered.[33] Precisely how the people whom we now call progressives balanced their commitments to science and sympathy has been the stuff of endless historiographical debates.[34] Science could imply elite imposition of efficiency and social control, while sympathy could suggest condescension and mere charity. Achieving what Linda Gordon calls "egalitarian empathy" between social workers and their clients was never a simple matter. But what is crucial for the present study is Addams's insistence on the two approaches' interconnectedness: Only genuine, democratic, cross-class sympathy could foster the gathering of that social-scientific knowledge that most progressives believed must undergird serious social reform. This was the point of Sherwood's novel, which brought together in a politically charged romance a male economist, whose statistics and interviews with workers are the typical tools of "masculine" scientific inquiry, and a female investigator, who expresses and expands her "feminine" sympathy through undercover explorations. Real-life investigators garnered praise from reviewers when their work interwove both elements. Thus the *Outlook* attributed Walter Wyckoff's ability to produce significant sociological work to his "fine brotherly sympathy" with tramps, and the *American Journal of Sociology* noted that Francis Donovan's "sympathetic point of view" toward waitresses had enabled her to gather the wealth of empirical data which gave her study its "reality" and "scientific worth."[35]

While concerns about science and sympathy were typical of progressives, a distinctive set of motives impelled certain individuals into the underground. Walter Wyckoff saw before him a "new, unoccupied, inviting field," ripe for exploration by an ambitious young scholar. As incipient or established professionals, down-and-outers sought the authority of authentic experience to break the bonds of insular middle-class life and to justify their social generalizations. Reality was their quarry, and investigators were well aware that they operated in an intellectual milieu that increasingly valued empirical data over airy speculation. If few literally compared their approach to the "laboratory method," as did Alvan Sanborn, most believed themselves embarked on a fact-finding expedition that would come to rest on the rock of verifiable truth.[36] Some investigators also hoped to bridge the divide between intellectuals and workers—a task that Cornelia Stratton Parker argued would not likely be undertaken by academic social scientists, who were too often "worked to death under the present university system" and therefore lacked "practical contact" with working people.[37] Others were executives bent upon learning about the lowest ranks of their own workplace hierarchies, or journalists eager to participate in a popular, widely discussed genre.[38] A few explored specific issues such as the ethics of alms-giving or "the servant problem," and some sought material for their fiction.[39] Certain female investigators evinced a feminist-inspired interest in women workers, or they searched for an antidote to Jane Addams's plaint about the dearth of outlets for educated women's energies.[40] Many—both male and female—hoped to grasp the worker's supposedly distinctive psychological makeup: to learn, as one entitled his book, "what's on the worker's mind."[41] All hoped to add to the still-slim stock of social knowledge. Charlotte Perkins Gilman, who later wrote a novel with an undercover protagonist, argued in her 1905 review of a down-and-out study that the "scientific sociologist" should preface the traditional reformer's litany (" 'Agitate! Educate! Organize!' ") with a new term: "Investigate!"[42]

Beyond this mix of professional and political concerns, many down-and-outers showed an idealistic willingness to shoulder the same burdens as the poor, and even to take serious physical risks in order to gather knowledge that might advance the causes of social justice and societal reconstruction. Annie Marion MacLean, a strong partisan of the Consumer's League, counted herself "enthusiastic" about "endur[ing] the hardships of the saleswoman's life" in order to amass evidence about child labor and forced overtime.[43] Others who were less self-consciously idealistic clearly feared the rebellious potential of the disinherited and hoped that it might be defused through expanded knowledge and interclass understanding.[44] More prosaically, some were simply unemployed college graduates and would-be writers who turned necessity to the purposes of research. In their autobiographies, the journalists Elizabeth Banks and Rheta Child Dorr were candid about their need for copy; this had been especially true for Dorr, who at the time of her research was a single mother supporting a young son. Finally, for some, there was the sheer pleasure of the experience. Cornelia Stratton Parker jumped at the chance in the 1920s to resurrect "Connie Park," the working-class identity that she had inhabited for an earlier book. Freed from other obligations, she wrote, "I knew exactly what and who I wanted to be. I had been waiting seven years for the chance."[45]

To take on a new identity could thus serve both public and private ends. Besides understanding and transforming society, some down-and-outers also sought to transform themselves. Many Progressive Era intellectuals who feared the degenerative effects of encroaching overcivilization became acolytes of the cult of strenuous, authentic experience that was embraced by figures as diverse as Theodore Roosevelt and William James.[46] Writers who established the broader intellectual context for down-and-out investigations often articulated the truism that a raw, unmediated vitality was both the gift and the curse of poverty. Charles Loring Brace observed that poor boys lived in thrall to a universal, atavistic desire to "gratify 'the savage in one's blood,' and lead a wild life in the woods." Brace took this inclination to be the norm among his imagined audience, save that most middle-class readers presumably benefited from a civilizing super-ego, which checked the "Indianlike propensity" that so dominated the lives of his street urchins.[47]

This longing to plunge into a simple, savage existence also figured in the ideas of William James, who was particularly attuned to the potentials and pitfalls of modernity and for whom "experience" became a central philosophical category and a talismanic term. Though no down-and-outer himself, James was fascinated by the idea, and he used Walter Wyckoff's proletarian sojourn to show how the unremarkable daily experiences of an unskilled laborer might achieve the highest heroic significance. Such individual heroism could have profound regenerative implications for a softening society; thus private needs pointed the way back to public concerns.[48] Contemporaries of James and of John Dewey who studied the lives of the poor used personal experiences as the epistemological bedrock for their truth claims about the tangled social realities they encountered. In this regard, their method comported with the empiricist bent of the modernizing social sciences, and they were true believers in the progressive faith that Truth would spring naturally from experience and data. But down-and-outers would not always live up to James's insistence that they regard all people unlike themselves as fully human (as James himself did not consistently do), and they would not always honor his caution that no one could finally speak authoritatively about the experience of another.[49] In the quest for truth, the perceived power of experience often overrode such caveats.

According to many who did it, the best way to gather foundational experiences was to explore America "from the bottom up," as Alexander Irvine entitled his 1910 autobiography. In an era when Chicago sociology students, muckraking journalists, social-realist painters, and reform politicians such as Theodore Roosevelt all pursued American reality in strenuous excursions through the social depths, down-and-outers achieved a special status.

Writing in the *Nation*, the literary critic Stuart Pratt Sherman dubbed such investigators a "little body of adventurers who have been in forbidden lands and have brought back something strange at the cost of their lives."[50] But for what they gained, most down-and-outers seemed not to consider the personal cost excessive. Like Roosevelt among the cowboys, Paul Anderson became an apprentice tramp both to heal a frail physique and to seek adventure. The historian Cecil Fairfield Lavell urged socially concerned readers to undertake a down-and-out experience, not just to "learn the truth" about labor and poverty, but also to feel "a curious mental and physical exhilaration, a purgation of the soul." College students ought to enter the proletarian ranks, according to one young woman, to achieve "a new adjustment of values," to pierce through the rampant "shams" of collegiate life, and to reach the core of genuine experience. The just-married Stuart Chase, confronted by pressing questions about class identity and masculine independence, wanted above all "to see what I was good for."[51]

The results could be edifying. For Walter Wyckoff, reducing life to an elemental struggle for survival brought one "to marvelous intimacy with vital processes." At the uttermost reaches of physical exhaustion, renewal awaited: "It is as though you were a little child once more, and your moods obedient to little things." Alvan Sanborn found that Boston's abyss was not such a bad place and that having survived there would enable him to approach his other life with greater élan. Annie Marion MacLean felt herself uplifted by the rough democratic camaraderie that prevailed among her fellow Oregon hop pickers—especially among the women. And to Frederick C. Mills in California, if posing as a member of the Industrial Workers of the World was "playing with fire all the time," it was nonetheless "a great game to have a hand in."[52] The historian George Cotkin has linked the curse of *tedium vitae* that afflicted late-Victorian intellectuals to the motives that impelled down-and-outers into voyeuristic and parasitical efforts to renew themselves at the well of working-class vitality—efforts that Cotkin characterizes as "passive" and "pathetic but understandable."[53] While there is certainly truth in this sketch, I would insist that these investigators' motives were far more complex. Further, theirs was both an active endeavor (one might even say strenuously so) and a constructive one: down-and-outers constructed their subjects, for better and for worse, rather than passively parasitizing them.

Yet Cotkin was right to suggest that there were questions of identity in play. For men, an explicitly rugged, masterful style of masculine identity was sometimes at issue. Walter Wyckoff, who was said to be a person of "limited physical strength and unusually sensitive tastes," announced himself initially "unman[ned]" by poverty. The two thick volumes that followed may in part be read as chronicling the physical reconstruction of that emasculated male self—a self already made precarious by the softening conditions of his privileged academic life, and then further reduced to the ignoble states of (unmanned) woman and "little child."[54] Wyckoff derived psychological benefits by immersing himself in a man's world from which he still preserved a certain psychic separateness. Perhaps not incidentally, the growing self-confidence that Wyckoff portrayed over the course of his two tomes coincided with a renewed faith in America's possibilities as he moved westward across the continent, finally assimilating his own hardening body to a "body politic" that he had come to believe was maturing both in "industrial achievement" and in "personal character."

Women down-and-outers were less liable to describe or justify their experiences in the language of a discourse of authenticity, which typically posited a male subject struggling to reconstitute his subjectivity as an autonomous, rugged American actor. While some female investigators alluded to issues of authenticity and personal identity, usually entwining those themes with expressions of desire to be of use or to improve the lot of their working-class sisters, others adopted the more neutral idiom of a professionalizing social science that sought only to cast light on a little-studied realm. Thus Frances Donovan, a high school teacher with graduate sociological training, asserted her right to enter the domain of academic sociology by offering only "a truthful, sober, and exact statement" about the conditions of waitressing, with "no other purpose than that of making a certain situation intelligible." Ironically, this was to claim an objectivist rhetoric, identifiably both "scientific" and "masculine," that itself signified a growing movement to displace women from the academic social sciences by distinguishing between sociology and social work, between male knowers and female do-gooders.[55] Issues of personal, gender, and professional identity were thus inextricably intertwined.

The down-and-outers' quests for experience introduced tensions into what is usually seen as progressives' characteristically hopeful environmentalism. As Miles Orvell writes of Stephen Crane, undercover investigators worked "at the epistemological intersection of experience and preconception." At that conflicted crossroads, attraction to workers' perceived vitality and concern for their condition were frequently cross-cut by disgust and repulsion that stemmed from actual contact. It was one thing to consider from a distance the heroic possibilities of workers' lives, and it was quite another to lie awake in a fetid flophouse gasping for oxygen in a roomful of men snoring "like stabbed fish."[56] Thus it was often self-defined friends of the destitute who provided the raw materials for the idea that these were a separate people—sometimes effectively a separate race or species. The very poor seemed mentally, physically, and morally different from middle-class white Americans, and they were becoming more so all the time under the impact of a self-reinforcing combination of environment and heredity.

To explain such perceptions, many down-and-out writers deployed a Lamarckian view of human evolution, arguing (or simply assuming) that traits willfully acquired for survival in a horrific environment would be inherited by later generations. While Lamarckism was once thought of as having been vanquished in scientific circles by the early twentieth century, there is considerable evidence for its persistence both within and outside of formal scientific thought, especially because its emphases on will (what Lamarck called the "*sentiment intérieur*") and adaptation fulfilled philosophical needs for those who were disturbed by the determinism that seemed inherent to the emergent field of genetics.[57] Not surprisingly, reform-oriented social investigators who hoped to preserve a role for human will in confronting oppressive conditions were especially prone to this sort of thinking. While Lamarckism underwrote much reform thought—it was easily assumed that acquired traits would be progressive ones—and is usually remembered in that optimistic light, it could also explain downward-spiraling degeneration among those trapped in a degrading environment. It is no coincidence that the notion of a "cycle" or "vicious circle" of poverty emerged in this period, when an embattled Lamarckism was retaining its influence by receding into vaguer, more attenuated forms. As the reform journalist Helen Campbell observed in 1891, the "human beasts" of the tenements had become so through "reflex action": The "tenement pulls them down, but they also pull down the tenement."[58] To those who submerged themselves in the world of the poor, such a perspective held grim implications—both for the subjects under investigation, and for the investigators themselves.

In the end, diverse and mixed as their motives often were, nearly all down-and-outers shared three convictions. First, they believed that Henry George had raised the great and compelling question of their time—Why did poverty exist amid American abundance?—and that he had been right to look for answers not in providential design, but in human social arrangements.[59] Second, they thought that only by going undercover could they gain the knowledge they needed: "How else," asked an undercover domestic servant, Lillian Pettengill, "am I to learn what I would know?" Third, like the newlyweds Margaret and Stuart Chase, most wanted to "shake off" the "superfluous" niceties of middle-class life in order to foster both personal growth and greater social equity. At some level, all of them resonated with Jane Addams's call to conjoin science with sympathy in advancing the struggle against poverty and injustice. It was in that spirit that this "little body of adventurers" renounced—however briefly—the comfortable and the familiar in order to join the sweated and the powerless.[60]

Going Down

The genre had its conventions. Down-and-outers typically prefaced the accounts of their adventures in the netherworld of poverty with an assertion that only by joining the lower class could they fully understand its point of view, and they often justified—sometimes at considerable length—their deceptive means. In an apologia that ran on for four pages, the sociologist Frances Kellor argued that her team was driven to deceive by the dishonest employment agencies they investigated. Elizabeth Banks clearly had in mind her own experiences when she praised Kellor's book in a *New York Times* review: Powerful employers would not offer up the truth voluntarily, so Kellor and her "gallant little band of seekers after truth" had made the only justifiable choice.[61] But there was more than one side to the issue of power. What usually remained unsaid in the investigators' self-justifications was that middle-class truth-seekers also possessed the power to make working people into the objects of their attention, the raw materials of their professional advancement, and the stuff of their readers' imaginative experiences. Martha Bensley Bruére offered a rare and perhaps unconscious note of candor on this matter. Bruére had worked undercover as a governess for *Everybody's Magazine* and had coauthored a play about a "sociological maid," but she complained that when she tried to study a higher rank in the social scale, "compulsion" no longer sufficed: "You can't investigate the middle-class, as you can the poor, without its free consent."[62]

Having explained and justified their method, few investigators seemed to doubt that they could become conduits for the unmediated truth, for the "true picture" of conditions, in the words of the sociologist Annie Marion MacLean. To comprehend "all that life meant to" the homeless worker seemed a reasonable project to Edwin Brown, a retired businessman and journalist. To then serve as a "mouthpiece" for the workers' viewpoint was also a goal that many down-and-out writers shared with self-described gentlewomen Bessie and Marie Van Vorst. Of course, it was a frightening prospect to undertake such an endeavor, which entailed the willful erasure of one's overt identity and the abandonment, if only temporarily, of what Walter Wyckoff called his "frictionless" privileged existence. But it also promised to liberate the overcivilized college graduate from the chains of mere book learning by offering access to the "vital knowledge" of life beyond the library walls.

Wyckoff concluded that he must supplement his "slender, book-learned lore" on the labor question, and he therefore launched an "experiment in reality."[63]

Down-and-outers typically underwent certain rituals of divestment and disguise as they prepared to enter the social abyss, and describing these changes became another convention of the genre. Clothing was the most obvious emblem of class, and most accounts offered some description of the clothes removed and those put on, sometimes to the extent of including prices, as Marie Van Vorst calculated: from a sealskin coat ($200) to gray serge ($3.00); from a black cloth dress ($150.00) to a flannel shirtwaist ($1.95). The total value of clothing removed was $447; of clothing put on, $9.45. Such sartorial cost accounting struck one reviewer as bespeaking "a certain naïve snobbery" on the part of Van Vorst.[64] Snobbery there certainly was, but the clothes-changing ritual was only one stage in the highly self-aware process by which down-and-outers tried to analyze the signs and symbols of class and to divest themselves of the stigmata of respectability. They attempted to suppress their well-bred weakness for proper grammar and fortified themselves with book-learned slang (though none admitted to competence with language any saltier than a "mild but passable profanity").[65] They professed sensitivity to class differences in bearing, even in body type. If a female investigator felt that she lacked the reserved demeanor and the short, stocky build of what Rheta Childe Dorr called "the average peasant type," she might compensate by cultivating a manner "timidly reserved, unobtrusive and monosyllabic" and by practicing "a hang-dog position of the head," as did Lillian Pettengill and Annie MacLean. Men accustomed to the office and classroom worked at developing a "swinging drawl of a gait" for the mill, or an appropriately "shiftless" appearance for the roadside.[66] Women gave themselves names like "Louise Clark" and "Connie Park," which they thought rang with "proletarian simplicity."[67] And they tried to adopt working-class habits, as when Cornelia Stratton Parker approached a New York City newsstand and brazenly "demanded a package of—chewing gum. And then and there got out a stick and chewed it, and chewed it on the Subway and chewed it on the streets of New York." Having been raised by intensely pious small-town schoolteachers, Parker found public gum chewing sufficiently outré to make her feel herself to be "someone else."[68]

Down-and-outers' texts sometimes displayed before-and-after photographs of the authors, providing graphic evidence for the investigator's authority to speak about an alien culture. Such contrasting images could make questions of authorial identity and stance seem simple. Upon changing her clothes, Marie Van Vorst reported: "My former personality slipped from me as absolutely as did the garments I had discarded. I was Bell Ballard." By her account, she became the comfortable companion of people from whose physical presence she would normally have shrunken. But others reported a metamorphosis that was less smooth and comfortable. As Jack London reconnoitered London's East End by cab before subjecting his soft skin to an abrasive "hair shirt" and his feet to inflexible brogans, he was seized by a paralyzing fear of the crowd. The neighborhood's degenerating masses appeared to him as a literal force of nature, a "vast and malodorous sea" that threatened to engulf and strangle him. Like the suicidal sailor of his novel *Martin Eden* (1908), London later slipped down voluntarily into the sea of the lumpenproletariat. But unlike Martin—an alienated individualist cut off from his working-class origins—London survived his de-evolutionary descent into the primordial slums, and he eventually embraced a socialist analysis that condemned capitalism for rending London society into two distinct "races."[69]

Accounts of the initial descent ranged widely in tone and content, but they were generally calculated to give readers the feeling that they were entering a strange and partly hidden world. The experienced tramp Josiah Flynt, who clearly relished displaying his expertise, explained that one began by approaching a "town bum" for information about where the "moochers hang out." Flynt described such a scene in road language so arcane as to require constant parenthetical translations to help the bewildered reader. Lacking such guidance, the novice investigators Stuart and Margaret Chase failed at first even to find the class line, which they anxiously hunted across Rochester by trolley; apparently the city had so benefited by progressive movements for municipal reform and beautification that its slums had become invisible.[70] Still other writers emphasized the inherent drama of crossing over. Margaret Sherwood depicted a distinct line, embedded in the elaborate geography of class that gave shape to her fictional Southern college town of Winthrop:

> North Winthrop means tenement-houses, small grocer-shops, pawn-brokers' establishments, and a life of work at hammer and anvil, sewing-machine, or shuttle and loom. South Winthrop means the scholarly calm of the Library, the Gothic structures of St. Cuthberts, the beauty of shaven lawn and diamond-paned windows. Between the two cities stretches the long bridge across the river where electric cars go, trailing light.[71]

That liminal, half-lit zone of the bridge figures frequently in Sherwood's plot as a place where characters pause to consider their position in the town's class system, and to contemplate their next move in challenging or supporting it.

As Jack London discovered, the process of descent into proletarian life could prove disjunctive and frightening. Walter Wyckoff reported a heady mixture of fear and excitement on beginning his tramp, but for many, the dominant initial sensation was simply fear. Alvan Sanborn at first distanced himself from his newly adopted identity by affecting an ironic, detached tone and professing the "genuine artistic pride" he took in his carefully constructed bum's outfit. Similarly, Stephen Crane's narrator in "An Experiment in Misery" enlists the help of an "artist friend" to assemble a proper set of ragged clothing.[72] But if Crane's concern lay with aesthetically constructing the real, Sanborn's clothes served as an expression of his playful and cultivated sensibility, a work of art to armor the invader against his strange new surroundings. Nervously postponing the impending descent, a sardonic Sanborn called himself "underbred" for mixing in the social world of the poor. He paced endlessly in front of a cheap lodging house before frigid conditions overrode fear and forced him to enter.[73] As his apprehension abated and he came to feel himself a part of lodging-house society, his tone modulated from irony and self-mocking to empathy—even respect—for his fellows.

Fear was, of course, a natural response to entering strange and sometimes dangerous environments. Jessie Davis described one of the woolen mills where she worked as a gloomy medieval fortress, and another as a prison. Charles Rumford Walker forced himself to appear calm, but he "walked with excessive firmness" in the "violent environment" of the steel mill. A terrified Frances Donovan, trying to dress for her first waitressing job in a dank basement locker room, felt as though she were emerging from anesthesia; to the "dizzy" and "stunned" novice, the musty room held "an air of evil and of horror indescribable" (this from one of the less fastidious of down-and-out investigators). And fear was often spiced with humiliation. Lillian Pettengill, an applicant for domestic work, reported being inspected by a potential employer "as if [she] were a prize cow up for sale," and eliciting the enthusiastic judgment that she was " 'a nice *looking* girl; yes, a *very* nice looking girl.'" Indignantly reporting a similar encounter, the sociologist Frances Kellor insisted that "any American girl of poor but good family" with the requisite training and sensibility to be a maid would be equally ashamed and outraged. No doubt Kellor was right, but a distinct whiff of class resentment emanated from Pettengill's pages, which pointedly informed the reader of the author's status as a "college woman."[74]

To pass successfully was no simple matter. Alexander Irvine reported that it took only "a gesture, a look, a word, to betray" his class origins. Inadequate preparation could prove costly, as Willard Straight discovered when failure to have invented a plausible personal history barred him from the comforts of a suspicious farmer's barn. On the other hand—Horatio Alger to the contrary—downward-mobility narratives raised no suspicions. Margaret and Stuart Chase found it "alarmingly" easy to convince others with their typical tale of abrupt unemployment and dispossession.[75]

The bohemian Chases, like many investigators, professed feelings of liberation when they sloughed off their privileged identities. But such emotions were not uncomplicated. Most down-and-outers were so deeply stamped by feelings of class difference that some were actually chagrined by their success at being impostors. Wyckoff reported ruefully that he had been taken for a drunkard and for a detective, but never for a gentleman down on his luck; sometimes, he reflected, his disguise worked too well. Frances Donovan was delighted to be mistaken for a customer instead of a waitress upon arriving at a new job, having been distressed at how easily she deceived others by merely donning an apron. From a different angle, Jack London's fears reflected the fact that he was plunging back into a class milieu from which he had earlier raised himself, and against which he had constructed a new identity as a self-educated, successful writer. London dreaded the possibility of sinking back into the abyss of his own origins.[76] Thus, fear of failure and ambivalence about success racked many down-and-outers as they set about to declass themselves.

For all investigators, there was the enticing possibility of understanding working-class psychology and life, but they were disturbed about the potential of being drawn fully into it—of going native among a population often seen as primitive or as devolving toward savagery. Walter Wyckoff developed such empathy for his fellow construction workers that he began to write of them as "we": "We are grown men, and are without a trade. . . . You tell us" that "our" interests are identical with those of the boss, who assumes that "we" are lazy thieves who will cheat him if possible; "You" tell us, in the end, "that degradation as men is the measure of our bondage as workmen." Amy Tanner, a restaurant worker, adopted not only the viewpoint but the habits of her subjects, finding that thirteen-hour days and seven-day weeks dulled both the body and the mind and made of her a "typical shiftless servant." She stole food and hairpins, ceased to bathe regularly, and found that her "ethical tone" had deteriorated. As her mind became increasingly fixed on the moment and less capable of focusing on the past or future—a trait typically attributed to the poor, and later a prominent feature of the "culture of poverty" literature—all thoughts of friends, family, and books receded and "lost their tang." Befuddlement closed in, and she "became a creature ruled chiefly by sensations."[77]

Wyckoff and Tanner escaped all this, thanks perhaps to the protective armoring of postgraduate educations, and returned to civilization to publish their stories and to teach at universities. But there was always the danger that whatever virus infected those at the bottom of the pit could be catching and permanently debilitating. The economist Frederick C. Mills, who passed as a hobo in 1914 while investigating rural labor conditions in California, noted cheerfully in his diary that he had just lunched sumptuously on six stolen oranges: "The virus of the life must be getting into my veins, as I felt absolutely no compunctions [sic]." Young men who stayed on the road long enough, Mills noted, inevitably succumbed permanently to its lure—an assertion commonly made by hobo and tramp autobiographers, who tended to believe that tramping was literally addictive. This idea stemmed from the German quasi-scientific concept of compulsive *Wanderlust*, a notion widely discussed by scholars and popularized by Josiah Flynt, who believed he had inherited the affliction from his mother. Unable to conquer the call of the road, he finally turned it to the legitimate end of undercover investigation.[78] Urban mendicancy was equally dangerous, noted Theodore Waters, a magazine writer who spent six weeks as a beggar in 1904–1905. Although primly incapable of begging at first, Waters eventually became adept at the practice and made a good living at it, admitting finally that he did indeed feel the lure of the begging addiction. Waters was among the journalists who repeated the twice-told tale of a prosperous fruit-stand owner who one day inadvertently left home without carfare, successfully solicited it from a passerby, and ended by selling his shop to take up full-time begging.[79]

Even as down-and-outers came to identify with their fellow denizens of the social pit, they found ways to inoculate themselves against the danger of infection and to remind themselves of who they "really" were. This was no small matter to Wyckoff, who found that wealthy friends encountered by accident seemed to look right through him, "as through something transparent, [at] the familiar objects on the roadside." Such disconcerting invisibility gave him "an uncomfortable feeling of unacquaintance with myself"—a feeling shared by Bessie Van Vorst, who worried that she had disguised herself so successfully as to deceive "not only others but myself"; the erstwhile gentlewoman now felt herself "with desperate reality a factory girl, alone, inexperienced, friendless." The anonymous author who spent "four years in the underbrush" claimed that she never intended to stay submerged for so long.[80] How was one to avoid becoming what one appeared to be?

Whatever their professions to having become someone else, down-and-outers necessarily lived with a tensely divided consciousness and drew on the resources of their middle-class origins to resist the threat of going native.

For some, salvation lay in the fact that a genteel education had struck deep roots. A defiant Mills wrote in his diary that no matter how taxing the work, "Lay on Macduff, and damned be he that first cries 'hold, enough.' " Mills found that silently quoting Shakespeare, thinking about poetry, alluding to the classics—shielding himself behind a wall of high culture—became a way to preserve his identity against erosion in the "hive" of toilers. Similarly, Wyckoff was occasionally tempted by a public library, where he indulged in day-long orgies of reading when he should have been looking for work. On being ejected by the janitor, he would emerge blinking in the twilight to find that he was still "a proletaire out of a job," and he would then hurry to his boardinghouse to lose himself, as so many of his destitute brethren did, in sleep. If their downfall had been cheap liquor, his had been free books.[81]

The most useful preventative against a permanent slide into the pit was work itself: the "real" work of writing that the investigators carried on surreptitiously, keeping their minds engaged and their faculties supple. Mills incessantly sought out secluded spots to take notes, while Rheta Childe Dorr and Frances Donovan wrote up their days' experiences in the evening before they collapsed with exhaustion. But perhaps down-and-outers' most powerful method for holding themselves apart from the world they investigated was to attack its inhabitants. Fellow mission stiffs and tenement neighbors who appeared benign and helpful on one page could prove depraved and dangerous on the next. One temporary slum dweller joined the clamor for immigration restriction, declaring the influx of "foreign riffraff," especially of Irish "scum," to be a national emergency. Most called for harsh penalties against tramps and beggars, arguing that such parasites found it entirely too easy to ply their trade and constituted a serious threat to the American social and moral order.[82] Overall, these investigators retained and reinforced the idea that the poor were indeed different from themselves.

This is not to say that down-and-outers remained unchanged by their experiences. Certainly they gained new insights about class. Just as Twain's King Arthur was nearly trampled by a heedless knight, Jack London learned that street traffic was now a threat: "My life had cheapened in direct ratio with my clothes."[83] Tales of harsh treatment by representatives of the established order or of kindly support by other workers accompanied professions of new sympathy for labor organizations, in an era when unions remained anathema to many middle-class Americans.[84] Such accounts often smacked of the formalized conversion narrative. It became something of a discursive convention to announce oneself a former disciple of classical economics or a onetime believer in the inherent unfitness of working people who had now converted to pro-reform views.[85] But while down-and-outers routinely acknowledged that they could not fully enter the consciousness of those whom they studied,[86] the identities they established through encountering the working-class other were more than cardboard constructions. Investigators protected their real identities, and they sometimes referred to their working-class incarnations in the third person rather than the first.[87] But they inhabited those identities to the point that, as Alvan Sanborn expressed it, "Living does away with the necessity of playing at living." When Walter Wyckoff resisted the temptation to quit prematurely and resolved instead to "try it a little longer," he wrote of his worker self as a near suicide who had drawn back from the brink of self-destruction. Like Cornelia Stratton Parker, who returned periodically to her Connie Park identity, some never quite seemed to come all the way back. Although Lillian Pettengill had ceased to "live out" after a year as a servant, she still felt herself to be, in some sense, a "living-out girl."[88]

In the end, to define and shore up their own identities was a secondary task. The down-and-outers' principal job was to constitute an image of the poor for their readers. To accomplish this, they worked in shoe factories, department stores, textile mills, warehouses, and logging camps. They labored on farms and at construction sites. They stood on breadlines, they begged for handouts, they stole rides on freight trains, and they tramped. They slept in cheap lodging houses, police stations, doorways, parks, unlighted brick ovens, haystacks, and hobo jungles. They took notes, they remembered, and they wrote.

Writing Class: "To Set the Stamp of Difference on It All"

As middle-class writers, down-and-outers had power—the power to define difference, to specify who and what the other might be, and, ultimately, to return to a world of comfort and plenty. In exercising those prerogatives, many reaffirmed their own positions as representatives of a higher civilization and a superior culture. They made laundry workers, road builders, waitresses, and the drifting unemployed into the objects of their discerning middle-class gaze. Their stance toward their subjects might vary drastically with circumstances: To a desperate, homeless, and hungry Walter Wyckoff, Chicago's skyscrapers were "prison walls" behind which teemed "hiving industry, as if to mock you in your bitter plight"; once Wyckoff was steadily employed as a road builder, he commented loftily on the jobless riffraff as weak-willed "victims of the gregarious instinct" who embraced squalor and failure due to an "incapacity for the struggle for existence." If down-and-outers blurred the border between "us" and "them" through the rituals of disguise and descent, they often reestablished it when reconstituting their experiences as texts. Many wrote, as Cornelia Stratton Parker later put it, "to set the stamp of difference on it all."[89]

It should be recognized that if the class passers' project was sometimes about affirming the superiority of their own class, it was also sometimes about criticizing and subverting existing structures of authority and ideas of class identity. Their texts were often internally inconsistent; like progressives generally, many investigators were governed by a contradictory consciousness in which the democratic and the elitist, the scientific and the sympathetic, and the Victorian and the modern jostled uncomfortably together. On the positive side of this dialectic, most down-and-outers saw themselves as friends of labor and sought to convey the fundamental dignity of all forms of work: from machine tending, to domestic service, to some of the more inventive forms of begging.[90] They sometimes highlighted workers' focused and intelligent engagement with labor processes in ways that cut against conventional social-scientific assertions about proletarian laziness and limited or degenerating mental capacities,[91] and they recognized workers' uncredited abilities by recounting their own serial firings for incompetence.[92] They showed that even intellectual pursuits need not be foreign to the lowest orders, as Josiah Flynt and Alvan Sanborn demonstrated in their descriptions of economic, political, philosophical, and literary debates among lodging-house men and tramps.[93] Down-and-outers could balance science with sympathy in ways that were neither authoritarian nor condescending, portraying workers and the poor as ordinary human beings—and, perhaps more shockingly, as the stuff of good democratic citizens. When the statistically minded Stuart Chase saw the world anew through proletarian eyes, the always-occupied park bench became no longer a site of shiftlessness, as many readers might have seen it, but "a barometer of unemployment." Margaret Chase applied for ninety-two jobs, held six, and never earned a living wage. She came to see her fellow female workers not just as the suffering objects of exploitation, but as people of strength and possibility such as "no amount of previous 'sympathy' had ever suggested to me." It was not the repulsive otherness of the benighted poor but the "true democracy of the motley crowd" that Annie MacLean experienced among Oregon's migrant hop pickers. And for all of middle-class society's superior comforts, Alvan Sanborn did not see its "hypocrisies and chicaneries and velvet sins" as the standard against which to measure the neighborly "village communism" of Boston's Turley Street.[94]

Yet even considering such examples, the people down-and-outers depicted for the popular and muckraking magazines and for academic journals were typically marked by the stigmata of difference. The very placement of Bessie and Marie Van Vorst's articles in *Harper's* and *Everybody's Magazine* gave notice of exotic and bizarre subjects. *Everybody's* featured sensational muckraking tales of urban political malfeasance, of shocking conditions in mining towns, and of the equally shocking lives of "the unemployed rich."[95] *Harper's* offered a range of exotica leading up to Bessie Van Vorst's article on women factory workers: A short story featured an insane narrator who apparently willed her imaginary lover into existence; "A Strange People of the North" displayed photographs of a Siberian tribe hitherto unvisited by whites; a travel story set in mysterious Constantinople offered the photograph of a turbaned, bearded, and berobed man above the caption "The man by your side may be a spy." Bessie Van Vorst's own spy story followed, beginning with the revelation that "psychologically, [female factory workers] are practically and morally unknown" to those outside their sphere. The next article moved to another sphere entirely, as it recounted the arcana of "photographing the nebulae with reflecting telescopes." Could there have been a more appropriate setting for the Van Vorsts' explorations into the mysterious world of the "unknown class" than these magazines, with their panoply of other peoples, other worlds, and certified experts to guide the wide-eyed reader?[96]

In an era of deepening urban segregation by class, ethnicity, and race, the sense that readers were being introduced to strange beings and alien worlds was enhanced by the common conceit that the American poor inhabited a domestic "Dark Continent" whose denizens were effectively a primitive and "unknown race," as the social gospel leader Walter Rauschenbusch called them. Perhaps such creatures were not even entirely human. Owen Kildare, a New York journalist, found Bowery dwellers impossible to place firmly, relative to apes and cannibals, on the evolutionary scale.[97] Many undercover investigators shared such perceptions: Benjamin Marsh, the son of missionaries, decided against teaching in Africa when he discovered that one "need not cross the ocean to work in a Dark Continent."[98] Reviewers also routinely compared undercover narratives to African explorations.[99] Preconceptions that linked Africa, race, and class were significant for both readers and writers of undercover narratives. The tropes of primitivism have often mediated white Westerners' concerns about the fragility of identity, so for down-and-outers to represent the poor as an uncultured, primitive, devolving race was in part to insist on their own antithetical qualities. To Bessie Van Vorst, who had worried about deceiving even herself with her disguise, knitting-mill workers exhibited a distinctively "primitive love of ornament." Frances Donovan reflected the tendency to ascribe vitality as well as degradation to primitives when she observed that waitresses shared the "vulgarity and robustness of primitive life everywhere."[100]

The strange world of the primitive poor could seem both remote and unnervingly near. It was a world, Jack London noted, that the estimable Cook's Tours did not even know how to find. Hence, down-and-out investigators would explore and interpret that realm for their readers. They would decipher its signs and its languages, categorizing types of beggars and producing lexicons of tramp and panhandler lingo. To evoke such self-contained and often racialized worlds was doubly powerful given that they actually lay, as London wrote, "barely a stone's throw distant" from familiar landmarks. James Clifford notes that, in the hybridized cultural context of our own times, "the exotic is uncannily close" and self-other relations are perpetually in flux.[101] If the geographical and psychical gaps were somewhat wider in Progressive America, down-and-outers intended to close them long enough to shake their own and their readers' complacency. "Oh, you don't know anything about this life . . . and I can't tell you," protested a servant acquaintance of Lillian Pettengill's.[102] So Pettengill and her peers crossed into that other country to explore it for themselves.

The images they produced of that country's inhabitants often reinforced an overwhelming sense of otherness. Unskilled laborers, tramps, and street people looked, talked, thought, felt, and (it was more than once remarked) smelled differently than "we" did. They were frequently described as subrational and animal-like, and sometimes as sliding more or less helplessly down the evolutionary scale toward utter bestiality. Undercover taxonomists collated apparently generic physical traits—often thought to be expressed physiognomically—and reified them in arrays of photographs or drawings as distinctive "types" of tramps, steelworkers, lodging-house dwellers, and textile-mill laborers. To Marie Van Vorst, commenting on a tableau of millworkers' faces, "The Southern mill-hand's face is unique—a fearful type, whose perusal is not pleasant or cheerful to the character-reader."[103]

Investigators often filtered their efforts to frame the poor through nativist and racialist assumptions. Those who saw themselves as old-stock Americans whose forebears had fought in rank with General Washington were prone to perceiving mass immigration as a new invasion by inferior hordes.[104] The "stagnant scum of other countries" that "floats here to be purified" occasioned considerable concern. The Irish and Italians were seen as especially unpromising stock, and there was much contrasting of Italian and Greek immigrant workers with "white [American] men."[105] In such characterizations, ideas about nationality, race, color, class, physicality, and mental competence flowed together and fused, through the Lamarckian hereditary transmission of environmentally acquired traits, into a suffocating devolutionary matrix.[106] And investigators' concerns were not limited to immigrants. Many dwellers in the abyss were native-born white Americans who had been dislodged from their proper station by a bout of unemployment, and they were no less susceptible than the foreign-born to declining into permanent degradation. To thus racialize and naturalize class, ethnicity, and national identity was to powerfully reinforce a perception of unbridgeable difference. It was also to reiterate the superiority and stability of the investigators' own white, middle-class American identities, and to militate against the likelihood of going native.

Down-and-outers often found that only the most extreme metaphors of Dark Continent savagery and animality sufficed to describe their discoveries in the urban "underbrush." Thus, the world of New York City tenements was "a jungle abounding in treacherous quicksand and infested by the most venomous and noisome creatures of the animal kingdom—a swamp in which any misstep may plunge you into the choking depths of a quagmire or the coils of a slimy reptile."[107] Such language reminds us of why the American reformer Charles Loring Brace, like Karl Marx, wrote nervously of a "dangerous" class.[108] The threat posed by the very poor might take the form of communicable diseases that spread like a stain from filthy shops to respectable, middle-class consumers, or of roiling masses "in whom discontent has bred the disease of riot, the abnormality, the abortion known as Anarchy, Socialism."[109] And such dangers grew ever more acute: In the "jungles of civilization the evolution is always downward—from man to beast, to reptile, and to that most noisome of living creatures, the human worm." By contrast, in the city's wealthy districts, the favored individual might "grow to perfection— the superman." Enfolding the reader within their language of evolutionary bifurcation, the Van Vorsts observed that "our bodies grow accustomed to luxury" while "theirs grow hardened to deprivation and filth," that "our souls" expand toward the ideal while "their souls diminish under the oppression" of the struggle to survive.[110]

Such descriptions were usually framed by a progressive reformer's focus on the social origins of this socio-biological disaster: Dangerous, ill-paid toil turned miners into "human moles" and their calloused hands into "claws or talons"; owners' greed produced the tenements that incubated the "forced decivilization" of their inhabitants; economic defeat reduced men on a breadline to being " 'dumb, driven cattle' " and left paupers happy in their squalid conditions, wishing for nothing better.[111] It was the grim, inexorable logic of the daily unrequited pursuit of work that degraded the "unemployed" into the "unemployable."[112] But such socially conditioned physical and moral decline had lasting biological implications: If a single day in a mine could drive an investigator down to "a level with the grossest," damaging or perhaps eradicating his "finer instincts," then what fate awaited the just-hired textile worker fresh from the South Carolina hills? Surely she would soon lose her "womanly sentiment" and "coarsen to [become an] animal" like those around her, no longer fit to bear children—embodying the spectre of race suicide evoked by Theodore Roosevelt in his preface to the Van Vorsts' book.[113]

Among the many striking features of this literature is the common assertion that no basic biological or psychological differences distinguished poor people from their social superiors. Indeed, these texts abound with positive assessments of laborers' courage and solidarity, tramps' and beggars' native wisdom and ingenuity, and saloons' and unions' societal utility. Yet the authors' actual descriptions of the poor often absolutely contradicted their stated egalitarianism. Jack London gloried in the change from "sir" to "mate," yet he was quick to label his mates a "new race" of degraded human beasts. Maud Younger and Frances Donovan, posing as waitresses, stressed their coworkers' positive, cooperative, and relational traits: a cheerful, unsentimental determination to survive and get ahead, a ready sympathy toward the novice worker, and a sisterly solidarity against abusive customers and bosses.[114] Yet Younger also described a lowly scrubwoman as "always squirming, squirming backwards, her tentacles swaying from side to side, like the horrible slugs that come out in California after a heavy dew." Similarly, Donovan showed great affection for the other waitresses but detested the "scum"—mainly homeless men and lodging-house dwellers—who worked in the kitchen.[115]

These judgments in part reflected common intraclass distinctions between the "respectable," regularly employed wage worker and the casual laborer who could find only the dirtiest, least-skilled jobs. But even respectability could mask incipient degeneration. Bessie and Marie Van Vorst, who sampled a range of women's employments in both the North and South, seemed eager to find evidence that they shared a common humanity with their subjects. Marie noted gladly that her fellow South Carolina mill girls' spirited pursuit of pleasure and lively dancing showed that they were still "human beings" and were "*not yet crushed to the dumb endurance of beasts.*"[116] Yet just a few pages later she characterized her comrades in the spooling room as "degrading to look upon and odourous to approach."[117] If the mill hands were by nature a kindly and courteous people, their "unlovely environment" was driving them downward, mentally and physically, toward an animal-like state. Describing a similar dynamic among unemployed Northern city

dwellers, Margaret and Stuart Chase posited a "vicious circle" of reciprocally reinforcing unemployment and personal degeneration. They stopped
just short of declaring that such acquired degeneracy might be passed on
through biological heredity.[118]

Josiah Flynt took that further step. Flynt began his landmark *Tramping
with Tramps* (1899) with a long and fervent refutation of the hereditarian
school of criminal anthropology associated with the Italian criminologist
Cesare Lombroso, insisting that criminals and tramps were no different from
members of other social classes. Then in the following chapters Flynt divided
tramps into "classes," "species," and "sub-species" like an entomologist por-
ing over his specimens. He began with a long chapter on the "Children of
the Road," who were represented as mentally, physically and morally stunted
by their amoral vagabond life. Flynt waxed explicitly hereditarian when he
described the "gipsy [sic] character" the children had acquired, and which
would require generations to breed out of their progeny. Culture phased subtly into nature as acquired traits became permanent ones. For Flynt, as for
the eugenicist George R. Stetson—whose 1909 *Arena* article drew on the Van
Vorsts' and Wyckoff's work—"environment [was] the architect of heredity."[119]

Walter Wyckoff also recorded contradictory perceptions of the heredity/
environment dialectic. On the western leg of his two-thousand-mile trek,
recorded in Volume II of *The Workers* (1898), he praised the "intelligent,
industrious, God-fearing people" who did America's work. Flushed with
incipient Boasian antiracialism, he noted with approval that the Iowa-born
children of immigrants were said to be "los[ing] certain physical characteristics" of their "alien ancestry" and to be gaining features of "recognized American types."[120] Wyckoff's journey ended in California with a jubilant evocation of boundless American opportunity. But he began this volume with a
sequence of scenes set in teeming and claustrophobic Chicago that graphically depicted the hideousness of the vagrant other. Wyckoff first described
men sleeping on the police-station floor, men "widely severed from all
things human," whose physiognomies were "unreclaimed by marks of inner
strength and force" and revealed "in plainest characters the paralysis of the
will." The writer's eye then fell with relief on a respectable worker who was
only temporarily on the bum, whose face evinced "the open frankness which
comes of earning a living by honest work." And finally, Wyckoff silently reasserted his own private, privileged identity, completing this excursion up the
evolutionary scale from subhuman vagrant to temporarily displaced man of
leisure: "I lie thinking of another world I know, a world of men and women
whose plane of life is removed from this by all the distance of the infinite. . . .
What living link," he wondered, could join these sundered worlds and vivify

the Apostle's words "We, being many, are one body in Christ, and everyone members of one another?"[121]

Wyckoff himself might logically have provided that link. Instead, he reasserted his difference and maintained an essential separateness from his noisome, snoring comrades, even as they shared the same jailhouse floor. Down-and-outers such as Wyckoff and the Van Vorsts tended to be more sympathetically environmentalist when describing the regularly employed respectable working class, and were more prone to lurid essentialism when describing the lowest social strata. And because so many workers were poised more or less constantly on the border between uncertain employment and vagrancy, they were always susceptible to the downward evolutionary pull of the abyss. Wyckoff's optimism about the children of immigrants in the West was based on their inheritance of new traits acquired in an open and promising environment. Such a Lamarckian assumption could, of course, cut two ways. Inhabitants of a sordid environment such as the Chicago slums could only be expected to devolve over succeeding generations.

That these texts so regularly subverted themselves on questions of human unity and difference suggests that their authors harbored a contradictory consciousness typical of an era in which environmental explanations of poverty were supplanting, but had not vanquished, moral and hereditarian ones. Through the mechanism of a usually implicit Lamarckism, authors could argue that negative traits acquired in a debased environment would be passed on to the poor's progeny. Degeneration, therefore, was initiated by environmental forces but fixed in place by heredity. Thus, Robert Hunter argued in *Poverty*—a book that cited Flynt, Wyckoff, and the Van Vorsts— that the evils of destitution were "not barren, but procreative" and that the dregs of society produced "a litter of miserables whose degeneracy is so stubborn and fixed that reclamation is almost impossible."[122]

Here we find a characteristic image of the impoverished as sliding helplessly down the evolutionary scale—a degenerating "litter"—together with a characteristic ambivalence about the finality of their fate: Their downward trajectory was "fixed," yet only "almost impossible" to arrest. The social origin of their plight was simply unemployment. But sinking into pauperism, which Hunter compared to biological parasitism, brought on a "disease of character" that also led to physical degeneration. Transmitted across generations, that disease produced children who were congenitally unable to work. Predestined to become aimless, drunken drifters, they happily subsisted on charity and garbage, spawning more generations of children who were born "debilitated, alcoholic, idiots, and imbeciles, as a result of their heritage." Like the notorious Jukes family of R. L. Dugdale's 1877 study, these degraded hereditary products of a hellish environment would never even enter the struggle for existence, in which they were foredoomed to failure.[123] Had the down-and-out writers set out to verify Hunter's thesis and to carry forward nineteenth-century ideas about hereditary degeneration and criminality, they could hardly have done a more effective job. Although they denied such deep-lying differences, they ended up graphically representing them.

Dorothy Ross articulated a characteristic problematic for Progressive Era thinkers that applies with special force to the subgroup of undercover investigators: She argued that progressive social scientists operated "at the intersection of history and nature, seeking to capture both the concrete particularities of experience and universal natural forms, both the changing shape of modern society and an unchanging dynamic at its core."[124] The down-and-out literature suggests that from a street-level perspective, although culture gradually supplanted biology in twentieth-century social explanation, essentialism need not disappear. In these investigators' eyes, nature often contained or outstripped the contingencies of experience and history. During the later years of the Progressive Era, images of degeneration and otherness did appear less frequently in down-and-out writings. But while the early-twentieth-century social sciences were gradually rejecting Lamarckism and embracing culture as a determinative category, Lamarckian-derived essentialism, with its inner histories of conflating environment with heredity and of variously conflating class, race, ethnicity, and nationality, could simply migrate from biology to culture.[125] Eventually, culture and values would be used to explain poverty much as congenital immorality and lassitude had previously done. And for social scientists who drew on the emergent concept of "social heredity," culture itself could loosely be seen as heritable.[126] The groundwork for this strategy is discernible as early as 1891 in an article written by the progressive sociologist Lester Frank Ward and published in the reform magazine *The Forum*. In "The Transmission of Culture by the Inheritance of Acquired Characters," Ward argued that mental capacities that were acquired, exercised, and strengthened through education and training were "clearly hereditary," and might even be ethnically and nationally specific: He cited the Italian proclivity for sculpture and the German mastery of music.[127] Such reasoning, intended to promote a progressive agenda of democratizing education, ironically laid the basis for a tradition of hereditarian and essentialist explanation that would persist in the face of the assault by the anthropologist Franz Boas and his followers on biological determinism and racial formalism— an assault that triumphed in academic circles by the early 1920s, gained popular notice in the 1930s through the works of Margaret Mead and Ruth

Benedict, and reached fruition in the 1940s with the Boasian underpinnings of Gunnar Myrdal's *An American Dilemma*.[128]

But despite the apparent apotheosis of the Boasian tradition, the essentialist, culture-based, hereditarian counter-tradition would continually reemerge in different guises and to different ends, both in further undercover investigations and elsewhere, through much of the twentieth century. The looming fact of the Boasian paradigm shift[129] cannot obscure the equally obvious fact that varieties of class and racial essentialism did not disappear from popular journalistic and academic discourse. That crucial conflation of evolution with class, culture, and race had its roots partly in Progressive Era undercover excursions into the shadowed world of that day's "underclass."

Conclusion: Progress and Poverty

World War I did not put a stop to undercover investigations, but the pace of publication had already begun to slow after the great burst of activity during the century's first decade, and it then declined to a trickle.[130] Between 1914 and 1918, only two significant down-and-out books appeared: Margaret and Stuart Chase's *A Honeymoon Experiment* about their time in Rochester, New York, and Upton Sinclair's *King Coal*, a novel about the 1913 Colorado coal miners' strike.[131] Sinclair's book summed up (in fictional form) most of the Progressive Era genre's conventions. The wealthy protagonist Hal Warner, like his Shakespearean predecessor, mingles with the peasants while struggling to get the accent right. His venture into the mines is partly a collegiate "lark" (11) and partly an exercise in "practical sociology" (158) reminiscent of Wyckoff or MacLean. As in Jack London's undercover story "South of the Slot," the hero's class allegiance is tested by his conflicting romantic attractions to an ornamental daughter of the haute bourgeoisie and to a budding proletarian heroine.[132] Living as a miner, Hal gradually develops working-class psychological and political perspectives and eventually becomes a heroic, Londonesque strike leader—a better proletarian than the real workers—before returning to his own class. Meanwhile, the reader learns a great deal about capitalism and conditions in the mining West. Hints of the undercover genre's future were visible less in Sinclair's novel than in the Chases' book.

A Honeymoon Experiment is at once the most romantic and the most incipiently technocratic of the undercover studies. The bohemian Chases had flouted convention to pursue the experimental life in a spirit of "utter equality and comradeship," building for themselves "a half-exhilarating, half-tragic memory" that would powerfully shape their later lives—first as suffrage activists, and then as converts from Fabianism to the Socialist Party, whose bare, drafty halls felt closer to their recently discovered "reality" than did the Fabians' cozy, tea-drinking conclaves. Embodying Margaret Sherwood's call to combine undercover with objectivist methods, they characteristically balanced science with sympathy in constructing a book that interspersed numbers and tables with a narrative that lent dramatic human meanings to the raw facts. The authors delighted in describing their hard-scrabble days, and in deploying the sharp-edged power of "first-hand data which cut into the arguments and the theories like a knife into soft cheese."[133]

Enchanted by evidence, the Chases hinted at a trend toward objectivism and a growing cult of expertise that were evident elsewhere in the post-1910 literature—especially in texts by investigators affiliated with advocacy groups or universities—and that presaged a rising social-scientific debate in the 1920s and 1930s over the legitimacy and scientific efficacy of deceptive and subjective research methods. As early as 1911, Sue Clark and Edith Wyatt, investigators from the Consumers League, largely relegated themselves to the background when they wrote a hard-hitting, fact-filled article for *McClure's* on their investigation of women's labor conditions in New York. More starkly, when the sociologist Frances Kellor published a much-expanded version in 1915 of her 1904 *Out of Work*, she presented some of the same information but expunged all trace of the down-and-out method that she had so ardently defended in the earlier edition and that had attracted reviewers' attention and praise.[134] And in his 1917 Columbia Ph.D. dissertation on theories of unemployment, former down-and-outer Frederick C. Mills briskly relegated Josiah Flynt and Walter Wyckoff to the past: Although they were pioneering "investigators of reality," their approach had been superseded by the "more intensive methods of study" in use.[135] Because he had become an accredited academic, Mills made no mention of his own adventures among the California harvest hands.

Stuart Chase made no such attempt to cover his tracks. In the longer term, Chase's career as a popular economist would constitute a lifelong effort to come to grips with the issues he had faced as a footsore job hunter.[136] More immediately, looking back from the 1920s, he honored his youthful honeymoon adventure with a certain wistfulness; but, adopting the hardened tone of that decade's ex-sentimentalists, he also saw their experiment as a crucial step toward the managerial, technocratic socialist position that he had come to embrace.[137] What loomed largest in the intellectual autobiography that he traced from 1911 to 1924 was his ongoing struggle with the nature and uses of "facts"—the empirical grail in which all investigators believed—beginning with the facts that he and Margaret had gathered in Rochester.[138] Their sympathy-charged search for scientific reality eventually led Stuart down the path to the twenties' hard-boiled brand of realism.

The war did not bring to America the widening industrial rebellion that Sinclair—and, to some degree, Chase—had hoped for. What it did bring to Chase, as to many other veteran progressives, were a belief that the government's wartime coordination of production offered a model for postwar "social control" of industry; a faith in the Veblenesque cult of the engineer; and a fascination with the mutability and manipulability of human psychology. Stuart Chase's plan to serve labor's cause while searching out the wellsprings of human behavior[139] suggested a signal line of continuity from the Progressive Era to the 1920s. The search for the "worker's mind," in the supposed service of both egalitarianism and efficiency, would be one of the principal paths explored by undercover investigators during the decade of Normalcy and the Big Money. Meanwhile, the tide of investigations that had begun in the 1890s with Flynt and Wyckoff, and which had crested in the century's first decade, was now receding around Upton Sinclair and the Chases. They had carried the endeavor as far as it would go in that setting. The Progressive Era had seen the establishment of a popular genre of investigative literature with distinctive conventions, and the framing of a societal discourse on poverty and class as experienced from the inside. Those projects would go forward during the ensuing decade, but their economic, social, and intellectual contexts would be transformed—as would their outcomes.

PART II

Between the Wars, 1920–1941

2

Vagabondage and Efficiency

The 1920s

In March of 1925, *Collier's* weekly magazine featured a two-page tableau of photographs under the title "They Know Real Toil." While some of the pictures illustrated the familiar American upward-mobility narrative—James J. Davis's trek from an iron puddler's assistant to Secretary of Labor, and the aptly named Robert Dollar's rise from lumberjack to shipping magnate—the article's reference to living "in two worlds" applied quite differently to Fannie Hurst and Whiting Williams, whose temporary trajectories had been downward, rather than up. Hurst had sought material for short stories by waitressing and sales clerking, while Williams had built his résumé as a personnel manager by wielding a miner's pick and a steelworker's shovel. The *Collier's* tribute reminds us that while the 1920s was an era of anti-union backlash, the decade also featured a tremendous outpouring of popular and academic writing on work and its place in modern life. Catalyzed by postwar class conflict, antiradical hysteria, and concerns about the future of class relations, this discourse demonstrated that the old rags-to-riches tale could no longer accomplish its accustomed cultural work. "Modern civilization is industrial," observed the historian Charles Beard in 1923, yet the worlds of wage labor and "real toil" remained largely unknown territory to vast numbers of literate, middle-class Americans. In a decade that Americans self-consciously called a "New Era," audiences embraced explorers such as Hurst and Williams who promised to reveal not only workers' daily experiences, but also—as Williams put it—"what's on the worker's mind."[1]

Williams's phrase named one of the new themes that ran through the decade's undercover discourse. In addition to working-class psychology, investigators addressed the persistence of poverty and the specter of class conflict amid the decade's prolonged economic boom, the shifting balance between science and sympathy in social discourse, the rising impact of the anthropological culture concept, and persistent questions about class identity and personal transformation. Like their Progressive Era predecessors, down-and-outers of the 1920s begged, hoboed, and worked. Their genre remained popular and identifiable—book critics often compared a work under review to others of its type[2]—and their books were widely and well reviewed. But the context was shifting: Old issues were reframed in new ways, and new issues came to the fore.

Undercover in the New Era

The economist Don D. Lescohier's 1919 study of *The Labor Market* showed how knowledge produced by the previous generation's investigators was redeployed to suit the new decade's needs. Lescohier relied heavily on earlier undercover investigators' work to describe and explain the modern laborer.[3] Those older texts had mixed Victorian moralism with modernist scientism in typically progressive fashion, and Lescohier carried forward that mode of thinking when he argued that unemployed or idle workers were often "feeble-minded," were burdened by physical, mental, or moral "defects," or simply were suffering from the "wrong sense of values."[4] But Lescohier's interest in the casual worker's debased mental state presaged the concerns of a new generation of investigators who reflected the emerging focus on working-class psychology in the 1920s, as seen in the growing fields of industrial psychology, industrial sociology, and personnel relations. He argued that working-class minds could be jarred from their lethargy by the attractions of an expanding culture of consumption, foreshadowing employers' efforts during the prosperity decade to increase productivity by instituting training and welfare programs that would further socialize workers into that culture. As Lescohier insisted, "*People must know how to live if they are going to know how to work.*"[5]

Down-and-outers shared some of the economists' questions, but not always their answers. For Lescohier, knowing how to live meant learning to desire the fruits of the era's abundance. But to Whiting Williams, who had jockeyed barrels and shoveled mud in an oil refinery, causation ran the other way: The nature and quality of workers' domestic lives and the extent of their participation in the public sphere hinged first of all on the conditions of their labor. As Williams saw it, in the keyed-up atmosphere of modernity, abused and exhausted workers with little hope for advancement would naturally forego conventional matrimony for heated temporary liaisons, and they would reject respectable consumerism for the fervid masculine pleasures of the cockfight, boxing match, and saloon. When Williams thus deployed the Victorian ideals of civilization, domesticity, and productive labor against the enticements of modern consumer culture, he balanced his Progressive Era roots in divinity school, the Social Gospel, and settlement work against his more recent management experience and commitments. In this case, the interests of workers seemed to him paramount. To one who had lived on both sides of the class line, the "sophistries of leisure" could offer no compensation for inhumane conditions of work.[6]

Sociologists' emphases of the 1920s are evident in the *American Journal of Sociology*'s review of Nels Anderson's landmark 1923 study *The Hobo*. Anderson's monograph was not technically an undercover study, but it had many affinities with the tradition, and its author—an experienced down-and-outer—would stand at the center of the decade's discourse. If earlier investigators had struggled to balance science with sympathy while reaching both popular and scholarly audiences, Anderson's generation would confront a growing tilt toward scientific objectivism, and those who sought professional acceptance would increasingly adopt objectivist tones and narrative strategies.[7] The reviewer, A. J. Todd, writing in his still-young discipline's flagship journal, praised *The Hobo* for spurning the unscientific method and penchant for exoticism that had marred earlier studies, including those by Josiah Flynt, Walter Wyckoff, and Jack London. Todd was impressed that Anderson's empirically rich but unsentimental book— a revised version of his University of Chicago master's thesis—bespoke its author's formal sociological training through its organization of fragmented firsthand observations and its establishment of causal relationships. Ironically, when Todd praised Anderson for clearly classifying "the varieties of the [hobo] species," he could have been describing Flynt's scientistic approach. And despite Todd's obvious commitment to disciplinary professionalism, he also correctly predicted that the book would reach "a reading public far beyond the student compound"—just as its unscientific predecessors had done.[8] Still, the review mainly pointed ahead rather than backward, both in its preference for the credentialed, professional investigator and in its highlighting of Anderson's reliance on "culture" as an analytical tool. In arguing that Chicago's "Hobohemia" was "a city within a city—a distinct culture," Anderson reflected the rising influence of the Boasian culture concept within sociology and within the broader public discourses to which the discipline connected. From the twenties onward, whether in the hands of undercover investigators or of mainstream social scientists, culture—Lamarckism's successor idea—would prove to be a double-edged sword: a tool for combating scientific racism, as Franz Boas had intended; but also a means to sequester the poor into a separate, self-perpetuating conceptual preserve.[9]

Undercover journalistic texts of the 1920s were also shaped by the decade's distinctive concerns. Postwar red scare fears were manifest in *Inside the I.W.W.*, Frederick Wedge's lurid but little-noted exposé, in which undercover investigation and the psychologizing of radicalism converged with labor spying on the notorious Industrial Workers of the World.[10] Closer to the mainstream, some investigators tentatively accepted boosters' ebullient expectation that poverty might soon be swamped by the decade's expansive economic boom. In 1920, two such journalists spent a few nights in disguise on the Bowery: George L. Moore reported for the Methodist *World Outlook*, while Cloudsley Johns, who had corresponded with Jack London on undercover methods, wrote for *Collier's*. Moore found that the happy conjunction of prosperity with Prohibition made it easier and more profitable to work than to panhandle, elevating many Bowery denizens to relative respectability. The more circumspect Johns found similar improvements, but he wondered how long the boom would last, and whether the subjects of his article would ultimately go "up—or down?" But by 1926, when the *Saturday Review of Literature* reviewed an undercover study of life entitled *In Darkest London*, the American critic dismissed "stark poverty" as "one of the far-off half forgotten things." Similarly, a reviewer for the *New York Times* thought the book was true enough for the unfortunate British but would hold little interest for American readers who basked in the pleasures of their seemingly permanent prosperity. That the New Era's riches were neither universal nor permanent would become obvious by the decade's end, as down-and-outers registered the swelling ranks of unemployed who inhabited New York's subway tunnels and repopulated the Bowery.[11]

But throughout the twenties, even amid the ballyhoo's din, a determined corps of investigators provided a steady stream of corrective narratives. Reviewers nearly wore out the words "real," "realism," and "reality" in describing the works of the numerous privileged imposters who crossed the class line to labor in mines, mills, factories, and stores.[12] In texts that exemplified the decade's clipped and economical literary aesthetic, writers told hard truths about twelve-hour shifts, brutal foremen, aching feet, strained backs, abdominal ruptures, sexual predation, bone-weary exhaustion, and short wages. When Charles Rumford Walker distilled his experiences into a novel that acknowledged the copper mill's "terrible night beauty" as well as its deadening oppressiveness, reviewers compared his style to Hemingway's, and they praised the book for inaugurating a new kind of modernist fiction that critically embraced the industrial landscape "instead of revolting futilely against it." Nonfiction writers likewise produced straightforward narratives that eschewed the florid in favor of the telling detail. Powers Hapgood, a Harvard graduate and Pennsylvania coal miner, wanted readers who lived "in the sunlight and freshness" to know what went on beneath that most mythic of American scenes, a farmer plowing his sunlit field:

> All during the hours when the sun is shining brightest on the meadows and fields of that green hill, the miners, hundreds of feet below, are working with their backs bent at right angles from their waists, hewing at the black coal by the dim light of the lamps on their caps, shoveling coal in the stinging white smoke of the powder, or straining against cars which are heavy and stiff.[13]

Like their forebears, the investigators of the twenties hoped that a dose of reality would not only enlighten their audiences but would also revitalize their own lives. In a decade that prized possessions, style, and status, the grail of authenticity still beckoned. Their constructions of reality could ring with naïvete and condescension, as when Alfred Bingham, scion of a prominent academic and political family and later a well-known social critic, wrote to his parents about working in a rivet shop: "The masses are very real, and I find that I can appreciate for the first time their reality." While Bingham felt his experiences nudging him toward "the democratic ideal," he also saw himself as an anthropologist—somewhat like his father, a Yale historian and explorer of South America—and he intended to learn from the working class without merging with them. In a different key, Powers Hapgood was a son of privilege who sought a more thorough personal transformation. Upon taking his union membership oath, Hapgood felt himself to be no longer a mere student of the workers but a genuine working-class man. The change proved permanent, and he continued to work as a miner and organizer in the United Mine Workers of America.

But it was the steel and copper worker Charles Rumford Walker, in his thoughtful novel *Bread and Fire* (1927), who most fully acknowledged the complex impact of "reality" on his fragmented modern identity. Harris Burnham, Walker's autobiographical narrator, finds that his mill experiences have "shown me reality," even as they have "numbed my power of knowing it" (289). For Walker, Burnham is befuddled by capitalist economic relations, just as the real workers are every day. Later, far from the factory and involved with a circle of New York City radicals, Burnham continues to strain against his class identity; he wants somehow to eradicate all comforts "that got between me and suffering" (122). The anguished narrator finally strips off his "artificial-silk socks" (121) and returns to the mill's fierce reality in order to escape his talkative comrades' "pallid revolution" (140). Charles Walker struggled similarly in the twenties with his class and political identities, moving leftward from the position he had occupied in 1922 when writing his objectivist memoir *Steel*. In the 1930s he navigated the contradictions of reality by the compass of Trotskyist Marxism.[14]

Down-and-outers began the New Era by appreciating both its perils and its possibilities. Cornelia Stratton Parker saw that "the labor problem" was pressing but that few who wrote about it had any industrial experience, and so she set out to work "with the working woman." On the practical side, Parker was also a recently widowed mother who hoped to carve out a niche for herself as a labor relations consultant. In Whiting Williams's troubled view—shaped by his work in the steel industry, both as personnel man and as laborer, on the eve of the great national strike of 1919—this was a moment when labor relations were "worse than at any time in history." But to Charles Walker, a Yale graduate and Army veteran, as well as to many postwar intellectuals, it was also a moment pregnant with possibilities for far-reaching social reconstruction: "It was impossible not to feel that the civilized structure had shaken and disintegrated a bit, or to escape the sense of great powers released. I was unable to decide whether the powers were cast for a role of great destruction or of great renewal."[15]

Walker chose to "enlist in steel" because it seemed an opportune moment to observe how capital and labor were going to function in postwar America: whether in "the breaking-up or the making-over of society."[16] With such fears and hopes, Parker, Williams, Walker, and others would plunge into the world of poverty in search of reality, renewal, and the worker's mind.

Persistent Progressives

One category of New Era investigators looked remarkably like old-fashioned progressives. Progressivism contracted drastically during and after the war years; the context that had produced the original down-and-outers no longer existed by 1920. So for the recently demobilized Walker, this was a world "never convertible quite to the one that had kindled the war," and it was one in which all previous political and social ideas had been thrown into doubt. Stuart Chase, writing in his chastened ex-sentimentalist mode, would pronounce himself "chary of creeds" after the war, disdainful of sympathetic humanitarianism and interested strictly in the scientific, expert-led restructuring of society.[17] Still, if the new decade's undercover investigators embraced no broad movement for social betterment, a considerable proportion did share at least some of their predecessors' characteristics and concerns.

A few were actually veterans of the earlier era. Since 1909, Edwin Brown, a retired Denver businessman, had been tramping and going to jail for vagrancy to promote the establishment of municipal lodging houses. Brown was well past his mid-sixties in 1925 when the *Literary Digest* anointed him the "Most Arrested American" for his street exploits. The sociologist Annie Marion MacLean, by then in her early forties, offered a sharp critique of welfare capitalism after her four-month sojourn in a "model factory," and she worked both sides of the picket line in a bitter collar-factory strike. Consumers League investigators continued to infiltrate the work forces of hotels and canneries, exposing unsafe conditions and promoting labor-law reform. And Frances Donovan, a Chicago schoolteacher who used her graduate training in sociology to research restaurant labor in 1917, closed out the 1920s with an account of her work as a department-store saleswoman.[18] Proworker sentiments and reformist motives continued to animate these experienced investigators.

Some among the newer faces were also lit by the old progressive fire. Many were idealistic college students or graduates who chose, as the magazine *New Student* put it, to "try work" in industry, hoping to fill gaps that college had left in their education. Their numbers included Roger Baldwin and Powers Hapgood of Harvard (1905 and 1920, respectively), Charles Walker and Alfred Bingham of Yale (1916, 1927), Joseph Vogel of Hamilton (1926), and Alice Kimball of Smith (ca. late 1910s), among many others. In the early twenties, *New Student* organized "summer-industrial groups" and printed enthusiastic reports by Hapgood and other veterans. In a 1923 article for the reform periodical *The World Tomorrow*, Hapgood urged progressive college graduates to take up industrial work. This special issue on labor showcased undercover investigation: It featured Alice Kimball's account of working in the New Jersey silk mills, as well as a review by Roger Baldwin of Charles Walker's *Steel*.[19] Clearly, the undercover method had attracted a new generation of practitioners.

These were serious young people who had not been rendered cynical by the postwar deflation of idealisms, and they saw the labor question as the compelling issue of their time. Alice Kimball reported matter-of-factly that she "naturally" chose to work for three years in the mills after learning about the class divide from a stint in social work. Hapgood and Baldwin were equally earnest; both were described by the writer Joseph Freeman as deeply committed individuals who bore the "austere, willful, thoughtful face of the New England Puritan." Similarly, Alfred Bingham traced his social commitment to the stern New England Calvinist and missionary residues in his upbringing.[20] The twenties, then, also had its ministers of reform, although this era's saving remnant was certainly smaller and more embattled than its earlier counterpart.

Students and graduates in the twenties echoed earlier investigators' complaints that college had taught them little about class and labor, leaving them without the knowledge and conceptual tools they needed for social activism.[21] New Haven's railroads and factories went unmentioned in Bingham's Yale economics course, and he learned that "poverty, like death, was something well-bred people did not talk about." Baldwin found that working in a Missouri lead mine and a Pennsylvania steel mill taught him things that Harvard had not. But to those who were still students, much seemed changeable. Mildred Meeker found "Christ-like" patience and sisterly "sympathy" among her coworkers in a Kansas cracker factory. If few of her privileged classmates demonstrated such qualities, Meeker returned to campus convinced that class differences sprang only from environment and that even the collegiate environment was transformable. Similarly, Fern Babcock predicted that "when more students have become workers, many of the shams of . . . college life will disappear."[22] Roger Baldwin was two decades past graduation when he reviewed Walker's *Steel*, but he did not hesitate to recommend that fresh alumni follow Walker's path: It would "help them recover from college," in addition to equipping them for a life of useful service. And while the rhetorics of manliness and strenuosity had long appealed to down-and-outers, they took on a strikingly new tone when used by Charles Fitch, a dishwasher in Colorado. Gassed in the Argonne campaign and partly disabled, Fitch urged students to "come out and try it," because "it will make men of [them]."[23]

Certainly some 1920s collegiate vagabonds took to the road in a lighthearted, bohemian spirit; little interested in labor, they would hardly buttress the case for progressivism's continuity. Such romantic "bohoboes," as the hobo writer Thomas Healy disdainfully dubbed them, sought only a modicum of mild adventure during a summer's hiatus from classes and family life. One who left an account of such vagabondage was Glen Mullin, a self-styled "scholar-tramp" on a break between college and art school. Reveling in reverse snobbery, Mullin felt pleasantly superior to the awed undergraduates in Harvard Yard, where he aired his knowledge of Leibnitz and casually rolled a cigarette before ambling off to the freightyard. His book offered little evidence of social insight but was prettily decorated with literary allusions to remind the reader of its unshaved author's cultivation.[24]

Few undercover investigators' motives were entirely unmixed with romanticism, and their time in labor's harness was limited by definition. Almost always, they did go home again. The exceptional figure was Powers Hapgood, who found his vocation among the workers. Even Roger Baldwin, Hapgood's politically serious friend, fit the more common model. After three months of the hardest and dirtiest labor, Baldwin returned to his wife in New York City, let his union memberships lapse, and hired a maid. But if part of Baldwin's motivation had been just as romantic as Mullin's—he confessed to harboring a temperamental affinity for rebels and underdogs—the important part had been getting to know workers' lives in order to provide legal defense for embattled organizers and radicals, as he would soon be doing after helping to found the American Civil Liberties Union.[25]

Persistent progressives went undercover for familiar reasons and addressed familiar themes. Consumers League investigators chose the method because it offered the "truest picture" of working conditions. College students discovered reasons for hope and models for social justice. Alfred Bingham found "real zest" in the experience.[26] The down-and-outers' vivid descriptions of the work they did, whether bent double in a coal mine or standing endlessly upright in a department store, could leave readers stunned and vicariously exhausted. They offered positive images of solidarity and mutuality among workers, and they typically insisted that workers were regular human beings, "of like mind" with management—and, by extension, with middle-class readers.[27] They saw this similarity as the basis for knitting up tattered postwar class relations.

Like earlier progressives, most sympathized with moderate unionism[28] and saw workplace reform as a way to reduce class conflict and prevent the growth of radical movements. Edwin Brown hoped that decent lodging houses could curb radical disaffection among transients, who were widely seen as potential IWW recruits. Frances Donovan observed that belligerent supervisors and long work hours drove embittered saleswomen toward class consciousness and labor militancy. Hapgood, Williams, and Walker all investigated their industries on the eve of major strikes in mining and steel, and they wrote with a sense of urgency about their hopes for heading off bloodshed. Williams urged his audience (which included the biggest steel manufacturers) to heed the comments of the radical organizer William Z. Foster: "Sure, where the men are getting good wages, right hours, good conditions, and are generally happy, we organizers can't do nothin' with 'em." Foster reciprocated when he reviewed Williams's book, praising its portrayal of conditions while blasting its class-reconciliationist political analysis.[29]

Progressive ideas and hopes did not end altogether, then, with the transition to the twenties. But they were certainly less in evidence and were sometimes subordinated within discourses that foregrounded science while reducing sympathy to a by-product, or even casting it as a threat to the investigator's objectivity. Persistent progressives who investigated work and its discontents in an age of growing affluence hoped to advance workplace reforms and to improve class relations. But as the visibility of the bohoboes suggests, another trend of the 1920s concerned a group that most Americans—however inaccurately—believed were defined by not working. The popularity of Nels Anderson's *The Hobo* attested to the broad and growing importance of this discourse, while scholarly reactions to the book suggested how the social sciences were struggling to come of age.

Hoboes and Scientists

When Nels Anderson dropped from a freight car onto the Chicago yard in September 1921, he was headed not down, but up. Back for his second year of graduate study after a summer of stealing rides and dodging police, Anderson had just covered some 2,200 irregularly routed miles between Salt Lake City and Chicago. He had spent nothing on fares or lodgings and had gathered data on some four hundred hobo workers, which he stored on index cards tucked away in hidden vest pockets.[30] But Anderson had not descended into the hobo world to study it. He was working his way up and out of that life, and into the very different world of academic sociology at the discipline's American capital, the University of Chicago. Meanwhile, studying hoboes was a way of "getting by," in Madison Street parlance: of squeezing out a living from opportunity and chance. For hoboes, that could mean odd jobs, picking pockets, rolling drunks, or writing sociology. The trip from Salt Lake would be Anderson's last without a ticket. But the hobo days that preceded it would be his ticket to the scholarly niche that he would occupy, sometimes unwillingly, for the rest of his long career.[31]

Anderson's book *The Hobo* inaugurated the university's series on urban sociology, made Anderson's name, and led many to call him a pioneer of participant observation—a term not yet used in 1923, and an honorific that he rejected. Although he had "faithfully followed the method" as it later came to be understood, his experience had meant something different to him than it would mean to his more privileged peers in the sociology department.[32] It was perhaps in part to honor his own past as a migratory harvest hand and laborer (and that of his father, "a real hobo worker"), as well as his scholarly obligation to be specific and truthful, that Anderson protested: He had not descended into the social pit to encounter an unknown class. As a boy, Anderson had sold newspapers on West Madison Street. As an adult, sitting on curbs and lounging in flophouse lobbies, he chatted easily with homeless men about shared experiences of work and travel.[33] He had not brought to his research an alien subjectivity or a malleable middle-class identity to be remade through encounters with the exotic other. Knowing well the world of homeless and transient men, he made it his study even as he was making his exit. But despite his oft-repeated desire to be freed from the label of hobo sociologist,[34] Anderson maintained an interest in how others studied the world of workers, both itinerant and settled, during the 1920s. He labored at the fringes of undercover investigation, reviewed undercover books for reform magazines, and contributed to the methodological literature that helped to define what did and did not count as legitimate research in the social sciences.

Anderson's connection to the down-and-out method began with his first undergraduate sociology class at Brigham Young University, when Professor John C. Swenson assigned him the task of reporting on Josiah Flynt's *Tramping with Tramps*. Flynt's interest had been in "the voluntary vagrant," not the seeker of work. Anderson wrote later that while Flynt may have accurately described the eastern "Weary-Willie" types who were moved by a "romantic passion" for travel, he found this emphasis misleading—and probably a little insulting—in light of his own midwest and western hobo-worker background. Indeed, when Anderson drew the assignment to report on Flynt, he had just spent the Christmas holiday re-roofing a railroad roundhouse in a snow-swept Utah canyon. Yet he failed to persuade a skeptical Swenson or his snickering classmates that he knew more about road life than the famous Flynt, and Anderson never forgot this early academic setback. As he wrote some sixty years later, recalling how he had sent a copy of *The Hobo* to his old professor, "*The Hobo* was my answer to Flynt"—and also, it would seem, to Swenson.[35]

As the twenties proceeded, Anderson typically reviewed undercover studies positively, while his theoretical work warned against the superficialities produced by touristic slumming expeditions among the poor. His perspective on research grew from his hobo roots. During his summer trek through western freight cars and hobo jungles, Anderson found that he could efficiently obtain information only by disguising his purpose. When approached openly, his fellow hoboes generally distrusted and shunned him. Once he fully assumed their role, none appeared to suspect him. Such "informal interviewing," as he later called it, seems also to have been the method he employed—with his advisor Ernest W. Burgess's encouragement—to research hobo life in Chicago.[36] Although Anderson did not write from the viewpoint of a down-and-outer, he certainly believed in the method's legitimacy for social science research. For the report on his summer trip, he distilled his findings into standard sociological tables that profiled his four hundred tramps according to a series of categories including occupation, years on the road, military service, voting activity, and "position on the I.W.W. question." Some of these data eventually found their way into *The Hobo* and into a scholarly article. For Anderson, as for his mentors who engineered *The Hobo*'s publication, the undercover method clearly could produce raw materials for conventional scholarship.[37]

Anderson's book gained currency partly because the twenties saw an explosion of hobo discourse, most of it in the vein of romantic vagabondage, and very little of it done by serious undercover investigators.[38] Hobo writers were something of a magazine fad, and Anderson found his book valorized in the *New Republic* by Harry Kemp, a tramp poet who praised its portrait of the hobo as wandering worker, rather than as the pathological figure portrayed by many a "half-baked sociologist."[39] But for Anderson, who felt keenly his own shortcomings as an academic sociologist, what mattered most was establishing himself as a rigorous scholar, not solely as a commentator on hoboes. Reviewing undercover books was one way to assert his authority. Believing that journalistic accounts could provide the raw material for social scientists interested in labor and urban sociology, he praised Charles Walker's *Steel*, as well as his novel *Bread and Fire*, both of which resonated with his own memories of itinerant industrial experiences. The latter he pronounced not only a good novel, but also a useful sociological "document." Anderson also lauded William Edge's undercover novel *The Main Stem* (1927) as an unsentimental portrait of hobo workingmen, written in their genuine idiom, whose authenticity would recommend it both to true hoboes and to "the parlor folks." His affinity for the book may have stemmed partly from its scrupulous sociological underpinnings: Edge's description of Chicago's Hobohemia, down to the four barber colleges on West Madison Street, appears to have been drawn directly from *The Hobo*.[40] Like many Progressive Era down-and-outers, Anderson believed that the undercover journalist, sociologist, and novelist could sometimes operate in a common, mutually invigorating context.

But Anderson had no patience with what he called "slumming." Without clearly defining the term or naming its practitioners, he condemned slumming on several occasions in his writings of the late 1920s when he was completing his New York University dissertation on the history of Manhattan's slums. Anderson associated slumming not only with the spectatorial urban tours of the Gilded Age and Progressive Era, but also with contemporary expeditions of thrill-seeking university students—some led by sociology professors—which produced little cross-class empathy, but tended to overemphasize the slum dwellers' otherness and the slum environment's supposed disconnection from the rest of the city.[41] Still, Anderson acknowledged the continuing value of the "method of personal contact," which he associated especially with sociology's infancy—and, by implication, with the immature labors that had produced *The Hobo*. This method's potential was now being realized through the "scientific approach," which would move the discipline beyond social description to explanations and quantifiable generalizations.[42]

In sociology's interwar battles over scientific objectivism, which had implications for the assumed reliability of undercover data, Anderson occupied a centrist position. He was happy to see that "crusading and slumming are yielding to science," and he could sound quite positivistic when calling on his colleagues to deploy the "methods of the clinic and the laboratory." But he also insisted that the physical sciences could not serve as their sole model and that urban sociologists must draw on a range of informational sources. Anderson trusted serious, systematic observers, including the "realist" journalist who "alternates between art and science," to gather information covertly and to report it in the first person.[43] He clearly did not see Frances Donovan's undercover research in department stores, or Stanley B. Mathewson's work in factories, as "slumming," and he reviewed both of their books positively. That he praised Donovan for putting the saleswoman's world under the "sociological microscope" and also made favorable reference to her earlier study of waitressing attests to Anderson's catholic vision of social science. That he published these reviews in the reform magazines *Survey* and *New Outlook*, while reviewers for professional journals were far less kind to Donovan's *The Saleslady*, points to the narrowing range of methods and sources deemed acceptable in the social sciences by the end of the New Era. Reviews of *The Saleslady* in popular and reform magazines were generally positive, but reviews in scholarly journals ranged from mixed to terrible, the worst of them scoring Donovan—a high school teacher, despite her graduate training in sociology—for her "impressionistic jottings" and superficial attempt at participant observation. Yet scholarly reviewers agreed that while the book was flawed, it would provide good raw materials for some serious sociologist to plumb and analyze. This was as much as members of a professionalizing discipline would concede to an uncredentialed methodological outlier. In light of such responses, it seems unsurprising that Nels Anderson—first known for consorting with hoboes—did not find a full-time academic position before he had turned seventy-four.[44]

What Anderson also found troubling about slumming was its unscientific tendency to separate analysis of the slum from that of the city as a functioning whole: to see the slum as both a world of difference and a world apart. On its face, Anderson's perspective would seem to delegitimize earlier down-and-outers' tendency to consign the poor to a category of inherent and unredeemable otherness. But latent in his thinking, informed as it was by the rise of the culture concept in social-scientific thought, lay the potential for reproducing just such images of hierarchy and separateness. With George A. Lundberg and Read Bain, Anderson coedited and contributed to a 1929 volume on *Trends in American Sociology* that highlighted the work of younger American sociologists. The book demonstrated the ubiquitous impact of the culture concept, including its laudable critique of racial determinism, on that group.[45] But culture was a double-edged sword. Any slum, as Anderson had earlier written of Hobohemia, had "its own social values, its own universe of discourse; in short, culture patterns of its own." Drawing on Gestalt ideas that were also being deployed by the Boasian anthropologist Ruth Benedict in her studies of Native American cultures, Anderson insisted that slum cultures needed to be studied internally and then linked to the broader workings of the city: They should be seen as "a functioning part," not as a "disease."[46]

Yet understanding cultures holistically could easily slide into seeing them as hermetic enclaves of otherness. Even Anderson had called Hobohemia an "isolated cultural area." For sociologists, culture would prove increasingly detachable from social and economic structures, taking on a determinative life of its own. As the discipline became further professionalized in the 1920s, it shifted focus from reform-oriented analyses of structural conditions to ethnographic portraits of the poor and their cultures. Culture could then sometimes perform the labor of other categories, such as race and class, that it had effectively subsumed and effaced.[47] The *Trends* index listed only two references to "class"—one to "social class" and one to "class struggle"—but "poverty," one essay noted, was the second most-taught subject (behind crime) in U.S. applied sociology courses. And while race was clearly of great interest to sociologists, the category was also meldable: Bain noted that "race 'problems' almost always dissolve into cultural problems when they are approached scientifically."[48] Anderson and his colleagues had helped to lay the foundations for a culturalized reconstruction of poverty, and for the idea of an isolated, savage, self-perpetuating underclass, that would be advanced by undercover social scientists and others in the 1930s.

Anderson's deployment of the culture concept, viewed in light of the decline of Lamarckian hereditarianism, marked one way that key ideas from the earlier undercover discourse were reoriented in the 1920s. Hereditarian ideas about poverty were certainly still in circulation; indeed, one critic of *The Hobo* complained that Anderson had overlooked the eugenic solution to the hobo "problem." But Anderson was skeptical of eugenics, and his colleagues in the *Trends* volume generally rejected hereditarian and racial determinisms.[49] Read Bain argued that scientists had convincingly refuted the hypothesis that acquired traits could be inherited, disposing of a view that had once been central to down-and-outers' explanations of poverty. Yet Bain left open the door to a cultural version of Lamarckism—much like the one earlier advanced by Lester Ward, but now given a stronger scientific cachet—when he argued that "acquired characters may exert a *non-specific* influence upon offspring." It was this sort of thinking that underlay Cornelia Stratton Parker's undercover study of working women. Parker concluded her book by insisting that workers and bosses shared common desires and were in most ways basically similar. But in the fourteen pages preceding that assertion, she characterized "the great body" of American workers as "unfit physically, mentally, nervously," their normal endowments of intelligence and industriousness having atrophied in brain-numbing jobs and in the "discouraging environment" outside the workplace. To Parker, working-class culture was shaped by a "vicious circle" of degenerative home and workplace conditions that trapped and degraded workers and their families, producing a working class that was culturally, if not biologically, unfit.[50] If the culture concept had helped to free social thought from racist, hereditarian, and degenerationist ideas, it had also cleared a space where new forms of determinism could take root.

Ten years after his last free freight-car ride landed him in Chicago, Nels Anderson published what he hoped would be his farewell to the hobo genre. Trying to exorcise an identification with hoboes that he felt was holding him back professionally, Anderson paradoxically chose to pass in print as Dean Stiff, a hobo writer who reproduced many of the stereotypes that Anderson had tried to puncture. He would later write that this parody of hobo discourse had been an effort to dispel the personal and scholarly "complex" that had come to bedevil him.[51] He hoped it would enable him to consign his outdated first book to the past and to establish a long-sought identity as a professional academic sociologist, moving on with other, more carefully designed studies of migration and labor in the changing conditions of the 1930s and 1940s.

Yet forty-four years later, Nels Anderson's autobiography appeared under the title *The American Hobo* (1975). Getting by as Dean Stiff had not helped Nels Anderson to get out from the shadow of *The Hobo*. That book had been an unusual form, neither undercover investigation in the older mold nor participant observation as that term was coming to be used. But its method and popularity had legitimized its author as a thoughtful commentator on undercover discourse, and the book would remain an important reference point for down-and-out investigators in the coming Depression decade. It had grown from its author's unique relationship to two worlds: his hobo past and his professional academic future. Despite his concerted efforts, Anderson never fully made the transition from one to the other.

"What's on the Worker's Mind": Studying the Industrial Workplace

While other class passers of the 1920s focused on the older progressive agenda or on the social-scientific study of hoboes and slums, Cornelia Stratton Parker found herself drawn less to investigating conditions than to understanding minds: What and how, she asked, did working women think? Parker's concern with the worker's mind reflected the interests articulated by the psychologist Arland D. Weeks, who wrote in 1917 that workers' "actual mental attitudes" were "among the more elusive, yet among the most important conditions of society." It was in this spirit that Whiting Williams, a personnel director for a Cleveland steel company, wrote *What's on the Worker's Mind* to recount his adventures during the first seven months of 1919, when he passed as an unskilled laborer in steel mills, coal and iron mines, shipyards, and oil refineries. With twenty-five dollars in his overalls and the determination to survive on whatever jobs he could find, Williams set off to experience the "long turn" in a steel plant and the long wait for work outside the factory gate. He told his readers how it felt to stand outside a plant gate with a crowd of hungry men, most of them "negroes and foreigners," desperate but stolid under the gaze of police guards who looked "as though they thought we were so many hogs threatening to rush in and eat up the place." Yet he insisted that, on the whole, his experiences demonstrated the rationality and "fundamental humanness" of both workers and bosses. Rejecting theories of inevitable social conflict, Williams intended his experiment to serve the interests of labor, management, and the general public, while also advancing his own career in the postwar movement of social scientists and corporate managers to reform the industrial workplace.[52]

The war years and the 1920s saw the emergence of a new tone and intellectual substructure in texts produced by undercover investigators such as

Parker and Williams. Amid sharp postwar economic dislocations and proliferating strikes, progressive intellectuals who had been drawn to the wartime
focus on massive economic mobilization now concerned themselves with the
peacetime need to maintain efficient production while mending increasingly
frayed class relations. Some investigators reflected this shift by downplaying prewar muckraking and social reform emphases and by embracing the
New Era focus on restructuring the workplace. This was to be accomplished
through some combination of welfare capitalism and limited "industrial
democracy," with prominent roles for personnel management and a gentler
version of Frederick Winslow Taylor's scientific management, all underpinned by insights gleaned from the emergent fields of industrial psychology
and sociology.[53] By the end of the 1920s, many investigators had abandoned
the authorial stance of the outraged muckraker/moralist for that of the
detached and open-minded observer; some even cast themselves as "objective" social scientists whose distinctive narrative voices largely disappeared
from their written accounts and whose sympathies lay with those "truly scientific managers" who could best be trusted to run American industry.[54]

These postwar down-and-outers especially carried forward that scientific
aspect of progressive thought that had always stressed expertise, order, and
top-down administration over sympathy and democratic participation. What
they retained of Progressive Era reformist optimism was expressed mainly in
their commitment to a generalized ideal of science.[55] Hence, when Ordway
Tead, a teacher of personnel relations at Columbia University and an admirer
of Whiting Williams, surveyed the progress of industrial psychology by the
decade's end, he found that salvation from the "futilitarian view of life," then
fashionable among literary intellectuals, lay with the progress of science, and
especially of psychology, which promised to redeem the workplace by revealing (to management) the mysteries of human motivation. To Tead, once a
socialist and still a union sympathizer, firsthand evidence provided by investigators like Williams would help to reconcile democracy with efficiency in
industrial relations. And as Williams frequently insisted, because work was
the central factor in modern human experience, the benign effects of steady
work in a well-run workplace would soon spread to the larger social and
political order.[56] It now appeared that earlier progressives' hopes of building
a more just and efficient society might be achieved by changing the workplace from within, rather than by regulating it from without.

Such thinking flourished in this period when a nexus was developing
between academia and business, and psychologically inflected academic
studies of industrial relations were gaining influence.[57] From a bottom-up
perspective, the undercover investigators recognized that any attempt to

transform the workplace must begin with a sophisticated understanding of the worker's mind. When Williams and other contemporary class passers became interested in exploring proletarian psychology, they diverged from the tradition of Frederick Taylor, who had famously characterized a typical manual laborer as mentally akin to an ox.[58] They took seriously the concept of the worker's mind as a distinctive functional entity, and they believed that they had gained access to workers' psychology through their own shop-floor and boardinghouse experiences. They tried to devise an alternative portrait of the worker's mind, freed from the abstractions of classical economics and also from the strictures of hereditarian and scientific racist thought, which they recognized as obstacles to the establishment of a harmonious multiethnic workplace. As Lamarckism lost credibility in the 1920s, the way opened for a more positive, more optimistically environmentalist understanding of class differences. While social scientists designed studies of industrial relations, class passers gathered their own evidence; contextualized it by drawing on a range of intellectual resources from economics, sociology, psychology, and philosophy;[59] and offered their own contributions to that new understanding of the worker's mind.

Down-and-outers saw themselves as interclass mediators: as conduits to scholars, corporate managers, and the reading public for truths about working-class experience. In this effort they achieved considerable success. They lectured widely, published innumerable articles and well-reviewed books, and helped to shape popular and academic debates on labor. But despite their generally pro-labor sentiments, their formulations of the worker's mind were shaped by their own backgrounds and biases and by those of the authorities on whom they relied, and they were also mediated through the complexities of their efforts to pass across the class line. In the conservative, antilabor atmosphere of the 1920s, their work lent itself less to the purposes of industrial democracy and reform than to managerial deployments of the rising schools of personnel relations, industrial psychology, and what came to be called the "human relations" approach.[60] Thus, their story suggests one way that an elitist construction of progressivism's scientific impulse largely eclipsed the sympathetic, reformist strain that had also been part of the prewar investigative tradition.

The first flurry of 1920s industrial passing texts was based on research beginning in or after 1918 and had been published by 1925, although further works saw print throughout the remainder of the decade. These studies were shaped by the contexts of war, postwar economic downturn, and industrial turbulence. The great steel strike that began in September 1919 drew particular attention to Whiting Williams's and Charles Walker's accounts of their lives as steelworkers during the months leading up to the stoppage. This period of intensive down-and-out industrial investigation coincided with the years when workers, managers, and the state all struggled to reshape the contours of the American industrial order. Despite some progressives' expansive hopes for postwar reconstruction, labor's fortunes fell rapidly. According to David Montgomery, capital's triumphs on the industrial and political fields and its "consolidation of scientific management" by 1922 left "beleaguered unions clinging to minority sectors of their industries, surrounded by a hostile open-shop environment and governed by ruthless suppression of dissent within their own ranks."[61] In such an atmosphere, intimidated workers learned not to hope for much more than a job and a paycheck.

The intellectual contexts in which class passers did their work also posed challenges as they sought to demonstrate that workers were normal, rational human beings with legitimate social and economic concerns. The intelligence tests administered to all Army recruits during the war were widely interpreted in the early 1920s to show that many Americans—but especially working-class immigrants and African Americans—were of below-normal intelligence. Despite public controversy over the tests' reliability, industrial psychologists throughout the decade made vocational testing a key tool in their field, and they often used instruments based directly on the Army tests.[62] A considerable literature that relied heavily on ethnic stereotypes to construct scientific guidelines for job placement also developed.[63] At the same time, the industrial researcher Elton Mayo presented to popular and scholarly audiences his view that most workers' complaints arose not from unsafe or unjust conditions, but from irrational, "primitive" mental processes that were exacerbated by the monotony of modern industrial labor. In Mayo's view—influential through the students he trained at the Wharton School and Harvard, and through his association with the famous studies at Western Electric's Hawthorne plant (1924–1933)[64]—studying the worker's mind meant analyzing the operations of "psychopathology" in the workplace. Sharing with Williams and Walker the fear that modern society might be on the verge of disintegration, Mayo reached far more authoritarian conclusions: Because workers were incapable of exercising any rational say about their future, they could hope to escape maladjustment and sickness only by submitting to the paternalistic rule of a therapeutic administrative elite.[65]

This was hardly the outcome that the class passers advocated. None directly addressed the intelligence tests, which provoked public debates during and after 1922, when Parker's, Walker's, and Williams's books had already appeared. Nor did any of them attack Mayo's ideas, although Williams was aware of his work.[66] But when investigators criticized older class and ethnic stereotypes that the tests and Mayo reinforced, they implicitly contested newer scientific assertions that immigrants and workers were subintelligent, psychopathological creatures. Williams's argument that "abnormal beliefs and attitudes" were rooted in "abnormal conditions" in and around the job[67]—that is, not in the worker's unbalanced brain—might easily have served as a rejoinder to the tests' advocates or to Mayo. Against the prevailing winds of thought, the down-and-outers clearly saw it as their task to demonstrate that the worker's mind was rational and capable.

Class passers also saw themselves as offering a third way between militant labor and repressive capital during the early 1920s, when owners had not yet won the battle over the workplace. They reported straightforwardly about atrocious working conditions, surly plant police, and bullying foremen, but they still insisted on management's honorable intentions and on the possibility for industrial harmony if both sides would simply get to know each other. Sharing earlier progressives' faith in data and information as tools of class reconciliation, they believed with Cornelia Stratton Parker that what industry most needed was not reformers but "translators—translators of human beings to one another." When Whiting Williams urged Powers Hapgood, then in search of a vocation, to serve as the workers' neutral interpreter to the middle class, Hapgood rejected such a stance as too detached and uncommitted. But this was just what most industrial class passers tried to be. Like Parker, they believed that once they had done their work, " 'reforms' [would] follow of themselves."[68]

Armed with this faith, these "intellectual[s] in overalls," as Williams was later dubbed by an admirer, prepared to "walk the plank off the good ship 'White Collar' " and to plunge into the "rough seas of 'Common Labor.' "[69] Down-and-outers practiced fracturing their syntax and ransacked secondhand shops for clothes, resisting puzzled proprietors' efforts to sell them apparel that was "too clean, too new," and altogether too "respectable."[70] While a ragged and unkempt Williams did not relish frightening children and feared that he would lose the capacity to think and speak grammatically, he shared with Parker the conviction that they were better people for their experiences in the underground. For Parker, sloughing off the bonds of genteel womanhood resolved the gendered vocational dilemma articulated by Jane Addams, and it led to a delightful dose of authentic experience:

> Packing chocolates, thumping a footpress in an unspeakably mismanaged brass factory, thumping an ironing machine in a huge New York laundry, running my legs off daily as errand girl for a fresh owner of a wholesale dress factory and his skilled workers, packing two thousand pillow cases a

day in a bleachery up the Hudson, pantry girl in a big New York hotel—I could hope that every girl or woman of my own "sheltered" class might have something of the same necessary and enriching, confusing, and enlightening experience the winter of 1920–21 meant to me.[71]

If life across the line offered rewards, it also imposed burdens that passers happily abandoned at their sojourn's end. On returning, they would have much to say about fatigue, repetitive labor, restriction of output, unions— and, above all, how all such factors were refracted through and molded the worker's mind.

Industrial class passers in an age of scientism found new ways to establish their authority to speak of the other. Writing in the era of the culture concept's emergence, some took on an anthropologist's persona. Thus Frances Donovan analyzed the culture of a department store, while Charles Walker— an amateur, but later the president of the Society for Applied Anthropology—represented himself as a "foreigner" studying the "natives" in a steel mill.[72] Down-and-out writers typically assumed the pose of the plainspoken empirical investigator, lacking ideological or theoretical preconceptions and invoking the authority of experience to justify their claims. Williams framed his blank-slate empiricism in photographic terms: He intended to make himself into a "camera." In contrast to the professorial Mayo's penchant for citing Freud, Piaget, and Malinowski, Walker asserted that he had no thesis to propound, and he expressed the hope that his observations would "weather theorists, both the hard-boiled and the sentimental, being compounded of good ingredients—tools, and iron ore, and the experience of workmen." Similarly, Williams invoked a down-home Deweyan pragmatism in commenting that "a fact just isn't a fact until it has operated—has got up out of its bed of ink and proceeded to walk into life by becoming a part of our experience."[73] Yet both were also clearly eager to establish their intellectual credentials, and they sprinkled their texts with references to William James, Walter Lippmann, Thorstein Veblen, and other contemporary sages.[74]

In so relying on empiricism and experience, class passers set themselves against popular and scholarly discourses that had long offered a priori pronouncements on the innate inferiority and degenerative tendencies that were supposed to characterize proletarian mentalities.[75] Such views were further reinforced during the 1920s by the results of the Army intelligence tests and by the dissemination of ideas such as Mayo's. By contrast, down-and-outers typically deplored the persistence and popularity of such thinking,[76] and they argued that mental degeneration and "savage" behavior—which they often identified with hoboes or members of the IWW—resulted from the repression and misdirection of natural human instincts that could not express themselves normally in oppressive working and living conditions.[77] The foundations for this view had been provided by the labor economist Carleton Parker and his undercover investigators among California fruit pickers. Like Parker, class passers acknowledged that class-based psychological differences could arise. But most also agreed with Parker that far from being primitive or stupid, workers were not much different from themselves—which was to say, from the broad middle classes, and ultimately from management, with whom workers would cooperate if given a fair shake.[78]

If the worker's mind was primarily shaped by experience, then the authority of these texts lay largely in their authors' ability to evoke the particularities of life on the factory floor for an audience who saw that environment as alien terrain. Williams's insistence on the primacy of feelings over thought—an idea he probably owed to William James, whom he frequently cited[79]—suggests not only how he thought workers' minds were shaped in the workplace, but perhaps also how he thought readers' minds might be changed. Class passers' restrained, realistic prose could prove powerfully affecting. Having committed himself to a descent into hobodom if work eluded him, Williams convincingly conveyed his genuine fear when slack times in steel left him indefinitely unemployed: "Every hollow-chested derelict you see is a human sign-board which says: 'Where I have been there is no work.' . . . And it scares you." In a different key, his furious diatribes against autocratic plant cops, slimy labor spies, and condescending "pompadoured" clerks also enhanced his authority to speak as one who thought "worker thoughts" and felt "worker interests." And convincing in yet another way were his occasional modernist paeans to the pleasures of working with machinery: the thrilling locomotives that "breathe power as they pant"; the sturdy steam shovel that bit into a hillside, its "exhaust singing joyously."[80] Such passages marked Williams as a true man of modern industry, fully knowledgeable and believable on its best and worst aspects.

If readers were engaged by Williams's accounts of how the steel around them was made, they were surely jolted by his graphic descriptions of the harsh forces besetting the steelworker: heat, noise, danger, friction with coworkers and foremen, and, especially, the deadening fatigue of a twelve-hour day—or worse, a twenty-four-hour turn. Williams had been a personnel manager and would be one again, as would other class passers,[81] and their books sometimes spoke the language of class reconciliation through paternalistic recognition of "the human factor" in industrial relations. But these texts were ideologically riven: Abstractions about maximizing efficiency paled before blunt descriptions of men who gave "the only thing these 'boys' have to give . . . their physical strength" and who could hardly be blamed for guarding their sole "capital" when they could get away with resting. Walker thought he made good money at a bad job on an open hearth furnace near Pittsburgh, but when he asked the Italian third helper's opinion as they neared the end of a twenty-four-hour turn, he got a memorable response: "He looked up, and the veins swelled out on his forehead. His cheeks were inflamed, and his eyes showed the effects of the twenty hours of continuous labor. 'To hell with the money!' he said, with quiet passion; 'no can live.' The words sank into my memory for all time."

The helper's phrase became a recurring motif in the book, a way to strip the blinders from readers' eyes. It was seized upon by reviewers, who also recognized its brute power.[82] In previous decades, an occasional socialist novel had offered a comparably detailed portrayal of industrial work processes and their effects, but never with the cachet of unmediated authenticity that distinguished these books. Reviewers attested that no one could read them unmoved, nor without gaining something like a shop-floor perspective on issues such as long hours, restriction of output, technological alienation, the roles of plant police and foremen (often rendered by the authors as brutal thugs), and unions (usually seen with at least a modicum of sympathy, if not openly embraced).[83]

The environmental forces that affected workers, so vividly rendered by undercover authors, were then taken to explain the development of the worker's mind. But because of tensions within investigators' ideas, and because of the intellectual and institutional contexts that framed their work, their efforts could sometimes produce unintended consequences. While class passers usually sought to establish the fundamental similarity between working-class and middle-class mental functioning, images of essentialized difference still sometimes surfaced. Investigators' depictions of the worker's mind could then be deployed by social scientists and practitioners of the emergent "human relations approach" to labor relations—sometimes including themselves in later incarnations[84]—to push for accommodation and harmony over worker autonomy and reform. Although Williams had used the term as early as 1918, what came more generally to be called the human relations approach grew out of the Hawthorne studies in the 1920s and generated much of the key early literature for personnel management. This approach stressed that management must gain worker support without giving up real control in the workplace and that they could improve shop-floor relations through counseling of workers and better training of supervisors. It was to these ends that Elton Mayo, Fritz Roethlisberger, and others involved in the Hawthorne experiments emphasized workers' psychological difference and need for therapeutic intervention.[85] Class passers of the early 1920s had already been using the language of "the human factor" or "element" in the workplace.[86] As the decade progressed, these terms became catchphrases denoting industry's newfound sensitivity to workers' concerns. These terms proved to be potentially powerful for reducing issues of collective power to individual psychological problems. Thus class passers helped to build the prehistory and set the intellectual terms for the post-Hawthorne rise of the human relations approach, in which many of them became prominent figures.

How then did class passers of the 1920s construct the worker's mind? First, they eschewed overtly essentialist constructions of workers' psychology as inherently different. When Cornelia Stratton Parker said she wanted to know workers' minds, she used terms that applied to members of any social class: "What did the girls think" about their jobs, about work, about life? According to Williams, too many companies ignored the fact that workers resembled anyone else in wanting more than good wages. They shared a universal "desire to 'be somebody' and to 'count,' " especially by deriving their identity from work: "to show ourselves men by virtue of showing ourselves *work-men.*" Cornelia Parker expressed similar ideas about female workers, who needed "independence" and "new callings," especially given the "nonproductiveness of most home life to-day."[87] In stressing workers' noneconomic motivations, Williams and Parker contributed to the assault mounted by industrial psychologists on Frederick Taylor's portrait of the worker as a bourgeois self-seeker, the abstractly rational "economic man" then under fire from so many quarters.[88] On this point Elton Mayo would agree. But in the end, Williams's strategy both humanized the worker's image and laid it open to charges of primitivism and irrationality that also resonated with Mayo's work.

Williams and Walker sharply revised popular views of immigrant workers' limited mental capacities. In an era when racialist views of immigrants who were not yet deemed "white" had considerable scientific standing,[89] and when workers were often assigned to jobs believed to accord with their fixed "racial" traits and capacities, they insisted upon the possibility of a democratic, multiethnic, multiracial workplace and society. Like the Boasian anthropologists who wielded ethnographic evidence against abstract racial formalisms,[90] Williams and Walker relied on the authority of their daily experiences to deny that Poles, Italians, Mexicans, and African Americans were mentally inferior or something less than fully human. Thus Walker's "Hunky" mates struck him not as men of "lower intelligence" but as repositories of untapped mental "voltage." And against frequent references to foremen who wanted no "head work" from their subordinates, Williams described the African American and Spanish workers who taught him the tricky operation of a power chisel, and the Polish miner who showed him how to work around a dangerous roof area and then used a bar to bring down several tons of loose rock into a coal car: "a very good piece of head work," the grateful Williams pointed out. Williams worried about the prospect that immigration might soon be curtailed—as indeed it would be—because this would result in fewer Slavic "buddies" to work beside him in American mines and factories. Williams and Walker were not immune to the temptations of ethnic stereotyping, but they constructed difference mainly in order to reassert a broader commonality. In doing so, they offered shop-floor contributions to the conversation about ethnic pluralism, cosmopolitanism, and national identity that is usually associated with Jane Addams, Randolph Bourne, and Horace Kallen.[91]

Beyond their critiques of racialist nativism, class passers disputed the conventional wisdom that repetitive or unskilled work necessarily reduced any worker's mind to flabby incapability. None would have denied that work processes could be reformed to lessen danger and monotony and to draw more on workers' mental resources.[92] But the textile worker Alice Kimball, like the itinerant factory laborer Henri DuBreuil, insisted that "machine craft" required skill and hard-learned "mental processes," while Williams and Walker highlighted the unexpected complexities of "pick-and-shovel work." Williams found that shoveling coal on a locomotive required considerable knowledge about engines, coal, and fire. Walker discovered that shoveling hot slag called for "judgement and knack, and he is a fool who says that 'anyone can do the job.'" He saw that his fellow workers cultivated distinctive styles with their tools, that they moved with grace, wielded their shovels with a "smart snap," and enjoyed showing off for each other.[93] Such images of the unskilled ran counter to much contemporary discourse, both hostile and sympathetic, about the worker's naturally inferior or environmentally reduced mental capacities.[94]

If workers did not meet middle-class standards of education and deportment, class passers insisted, it was because they lacked the time and energy, not the capacity, for study and self-improvement. Parker recounted how the rigors of a day spent packing chocolates were capped by "the crowning agony of all—standing up on the Subway going home." And in two dramatic exercises in "physical arithmetic," both Williams and Walker calculated how few free hours remained each week to a steelworker: Walker found two hours out of every twenty-four for all activities and functions outside of eating, sleeping, and working; using a different calculus, Williams found just four free hours per week.[95] Were it not for the narrowing effects of such conditions, Williams and Walker would not have been obliged to insist on the "fundamental humanness" of labor. Yet that humanness still emerged, even in the crucible of the industrial workplace. After his sojourn in mine and mill, Williams professed to find workers so utterly "normal" that he now smiled at the "air of mystery and 'differentness'" with which he and most of his "white-collared friends" had invested them.[96]

To counter such assumptions of "differentness," class passers presented the worker's mind as a fully rational one. Thus Williams explained that the limited attractions of a miserable company town might well prompt a worker to choose a twelve-hour job over a ten-hour option, even though the wage advantage was slight; this choice would indicate not a dull or irrational mind, but a reasoned decision to avoid the filthy and overcrowded boardinghouse.[97] Likewise, against the common perception that workers lacked the capacity to think ahead, Walker and Williams both learned to understand—and practice—restriction of output (or "soldiering," as Frederick Taylor had called it) as a reasoned and reasonable strategy to save precious physical energy and make jobs last longer. Elton Mayo saw nothing reasonable in soldiering, which he believed stemmed from a "mental conflict" that could be resolved through "an intelligent interview technic [sic]." Walker might have agreed at first, because he felt anguish over his own soldiering, and imagined himself assaulted by furious authors from the *Quarterly Journal of Economics* whom he had read as a student. But like Williams, he soon gave way to the conviction that the "work-rhythm" defined by his mates possessed its own "inward reasonableness." To the less-sympathetic Stanley Mathewson, another class-passing personnel man, soldiering workers were seldom truly overworked; but they were still, in his view, fully rational actors.[98]

Williams and Cornelia Stratton Parker both argued that workers often appeared ignorant because they lacked a broad understanding of the industrial enterprise that employed them[99]—an understanding, according to Williams, that companies willfully withheld from their operatives. This expropriation of rationality from individuals by bureaucratic institutions, as C. Wright Mills would later describe it, was an aspect of Taylorism in its original incarnation, and it became a target of the class passers' criticism in the names of both industrial democracy and true scientific efficiency. Where Taylor had wanted to concentrate knowledge at the management level, Parker and Williams insisted that workers possessed a great fund of knowledge and ability that ought to be made available through democratic participation in company affairs—an idea also promoted by academic allies such as Ordway Tead.[100] Williams claimed to have learned far more from his buddies (who taught him not only how to work, but also how to avoid working) than from foremen who often and abrasively expressed their absolute indifference to his mind.[101]

Williams also resented the foreman's ability to monopolize the dignity and satisfactions of honest labor, with the attendant associations of fully realized gender identity.[102] Only the foreman experienced "a satisfactory sense of manliness and personal worth-whileness through the solving of the real problems and the overcoming of man-sized obstacles." To restrict "manliness" to those who used intellect and ability to affect their environment was to locate a desirable ideal beyond workers' reach. Walker likewise complained that the rigors of a twelve-hour day "put a premium on [apparently feminine] timeserving and drudgery, in lieu of the more masculine qualities of adventure and initiative." As an American-born employee in a heavily immigrant workforce, Williams was well aware that bosses sometimes gave him choice assignments that entailed more responsibility, greater satisfaction, and the chance to prove himself a man by proving himself a "work-m[a]n." Sounding what would become a central theme in 1920s industrial relations, Williams called for an end to the old-fashioned, authoritarian foreman who hired, fired, and abused his charges. But he would be replaced not by workers' democratic participation, but by counseling, personnel work, and the human relations approach—or what Mills would later call "a new universe of management and manipulation."[103]

Management's efforts to analyze and shape the worker's mind suggested a persistent belief, despite the evidence proffered by class passers, that workers' psychology was indeed "different" and required some degree of control. Such control would certainly have to come from management, not from organizations created and led by workers themselves. And despite their overt thrust to the contrary, down-and-out texts sometimes supplied fuel for this viewpoint. That this happened should prove no surprise. Most class passers evinced at least some sympathy for unions.[104] But the new fields of personnel relations and industrial psychology—the milieu in which Williams, Walker, and Parker all hoped to work—always had as part of their agenda to obstruct the advancement of unions and radical organizing. According to Thomas G. Spates, a Yale professor of personnel administration, corporate executive, and fervent admirer of Whiting Williams, workers "prefer good personnel administration to unionism." Thus, personnel work came to be seen as an alternative to unionism, not as a supplement to it. Walker hoped to enter the personnel field as an honest broker of class interests, but he recounted a discussion with his plant's employment manager in which he was warned never to bring up unions, for "they won't stand for that sort of thing."[105]

At the same time, like their Progressive Era forebears, these investigators generally rejected radicalism and saw it as part of their task to reduce the likelihood of violent revolution.[106] To sidestep the specter of class conflict, class passers and those who appropriated their ideas often dissolved political and economic issues into psychological ones, as when Williams asserted that the problems of labor relations ran "as deep as human nature—and no deeper." It was here that down-and-outers' ideas could dovetail with the primitivist and irrationalist perspectives of researchers like Elton Mayo. In Williams's view, workplace tensions and dissatisfactions were not inherent to the system but had arisen from "a lack of proper adjustment to certain requirements of human beings," especially in an ethnically mixed workforce. Working conditions and authoritarian management were not irrelevant, but neither was psychological adjustment. Williams observed hopefully that "practical psychology" was now playing an ever-greater role in the workplace; managers would soon outstrip radical agitators in their ability to shape group psychology. Trained shop-floor leaders—no longer the hated autocratic foremen of earlier days, but now "the conservative guide[s] of excited men"—would relay information and soothe discontent among unhappy workers. Such thinking led logically to Elton Mayo's assertion that workers could simply "talk out" their often-irrational concerns in therapeutic interviews.[107]

While management had long tended to see workers as dull, dissipated, and less than fully human, class passers offered a view of the worker's mind that was generally more positive, yet sometimes internally contradictory. There was no linear progression from Progressive Era investigators' tendency to essentialize class differences to a straightforward, democratic environmentalism in the 1920s generation. The possibility that workers' psychology was not simply distinctive but actually inferior still lurked behind generalizations such as Cornelia Stratton Parker's (that the most oppressed American workers lacked the capacity even to see that they were oppressed), or Walker's (that he found little evidence of ideological thinking among steelworkers), or Williams's (that rank-and-file unionists often presented irrational demands to their more reasonable and conservative leaders).[108] Just how different was the worker's mind, and how had it become so?

Whiting Williams quoted William James's famous essay "Of a Certain Blindness in Human Beings" to underscore the difficulty of gaining access to others' thoughts, especially to those of "creatures and people different from ourselves." To cross that chasm was of course precisely the down-and-outers' goal, but they did not downplay the differences between themselves and their subjects—sometimes to the point of blurring the line between culture and biology, much as their predecessors had often done. Thus Williams tolerated a twelve-hour shift partly because he "had more in [his] mind" to occupy it as he painted numbers on barrels, while most workers had little "worth thinking about" unless they were distracted by a company-sponsored movie or a lunchtime singalong.[109] Williams implied here that workers' minds could be seized by such stimuli because they were essentially empty vessels, while his own mind was a dynamic and functional tool—undercutting his insistence elsewhere upon workers' capacity for independent, rational thought.

Williams also fell in with common stereotypes when he characterized transient workers as "degenerating," and when he opined that African American and Slavic workers were less sensitive than he to "bathroom-stable smells" while being "driven more surely than [he]" to the seductions of the saloon.[110] Yet overall, Williams was far less inclined than Progressive Era class passers to cast difference in hereditarian or racist frameworks, emphasizing instead the effects of fatigue, job insecurity, and the disorienting difficulty of understanding one's role in the bigger industrial picture. While he agreed with Carleton Parker that the blocking of workers' instinctive drives produced pathological results, he also decried the tendency to emphasize the shaping power of "physiological and primitive inheritances" over "the influence of our complex present-day relationships with our neighbor"—that is, to emphasize heredity over culture.[111] When difference did loom larger, both for Williams and for Cornelia Stratton Parker, it was often because they refracted it through the lens of instinct theory, which they tended to apply to those workers whom they regarded as the most marginal and degraded.[112] Here their practice converged with that of earlier investigators such as Walter Wyckoff, who also saw the bottommost layer of casual and transient laborers through a hereditarian lens, and likewise suggested the emergence of a socially detached, hereditary underclass.

Industrial investigators rejected the socialist argument that an inevitable conflict divided workers from management, and they believed that they could serve as mediators, helping each side to know and understand the other. Yet just as they had not entirely dispensed with negative portrayals of the worker's mind, they also tended to drift toward management's perspective. Cornelia Stratton Parker concluded regretfully that organized labor, having been shaped psychologically by its emergence in a context of bitter business hostility, could not play a constructive role in industrial relations. For Williams, a past and future manager, the inclination toward management was strengthened by his Jamesian emphasis on "feelings" over "thoughts." While he resisted the tendency to label the worker as a creature of emotion and the boss as an avatar of intellect, he did emphasize in practice the need to convey the worker's feelings upward through the corporate hierarchy in order to affect the distinctly downward flow of ideas. To say that management relied too much on practical reason without accounting for workers' feelings presumed that reason was indeed principally the prerogative of managers. Ultimately, both the feelings and the ideas that truly counted for steelworkers originated "deep down inside Mr. [U.S. Steel chairman Elbert H.] Gary" and his colleagues. Thus Williams's feelings/thoughts distinction, while theoretically applicable to all people, served as a convenient way to downplay worker rationality and leave the head work to the bosses—just as Frederick Taylor had advocated.[113]

If images of difference continued to arise among class passers despite their professions to the contrary, Charles Walker reached more unusual and creative conclusions about his own subjectivity and the worker's mind. In *Steel*, Walker had written forcefully of the untapped potential in those immigrant workers commonly supposed to be of " 'lower intelligence.' " At the end of *Bread and Fire*, the novel that Walker based largely on his later undercover sojourn in a copper mill,[114] the recently fired narrator prepares to leave town in search of other factory work. No longer simply a middle-class man passing as a worker, Harris Burnham struggles to articulate just how he has changed. Lying on a hillside above the mill, Burnham reflects that "it was curious how full and moving I felt the life inside me. Like an even river, I had a sense of knowing something through the whole of my body, not one part only, not my brain" (300). This passage suggests that an alternate mode of rationality—one that merges reason and emotion, mind and body—might arise from factory experience. Yet this distinctive way of knowing is neither inferior nor somehow inherent to the working-class immigrant other; despite his Exeter-to-Yale training, Burnham feels it within himself. Here Walker differed from Williams, who also counted himself transformed in mind and body, "with arms and shoulders stronger and huskier, head saner, and heart . . . wholesomer than before." But for Williams, when mind, body, and spirit achieved fruitful integration on the job, then class harmony reigned, the "agitator" went unheard—and the investigator went home.[115] Harris Burnham, reflecting Walker's developing leftist politics, feels both "terrified and comforted" that he will never entirely leave the mill, nor will it fully leave him (302). Permanently marked by his proletarian experiences, he now "knows" in this new way—through his body—that his future is tied to the fortunes of labor. Far more than Williams, Walker became a worker and took a side.

The industrial class passers' legacy was complex. Because of their investigative method, their texts carried special authority in many contexts. When these authors insisted on the full humanity of workers and on the rational resources of workers' minds, they helped to elevate the worker's image in public discourse and in management literature. As both popular and scholarly reviewers noted, their powerful evocations of working-class experience contributed to the debates on long hours and the long turn, technological alienation, welfare capitalism (which they generally rejected), and industrial democracy (which they generally supported).[116] By focusing attention on workplace experiences during a decade more notably devoted to the pleasures of spending, they insisted that it was on the job—not in some compensatory realm of leisure and mass consumption—that solutions to broader societal ills must be sought.[117] If their arguments could not prevent immigration restriction, textbooks citing Williams would increasingly reject hiring and job-assignment practices based on particular ethnic groups' supposed racial traits.[118] And for some observers, their work validated the undercover method: When Ordway Tead reviewed the third volume of the Hawthorne studies in 1940, he criticized what he called the latest inquiry into " 'what's on the worker's mind' " for relying too heavily on interviews and observation, implying that Williams's down-and-out method would have produced more reliable results.[119]

Although Williams, Walker, and Parker were thoughtful observers and not mere "servants of power," in Loren Baritz's narrowly opprobrious term for social scientists who worked in industry,[120] they were nonetheless limited by their belief that managers and workers could simply get to know each other, respect each other's feelings, and talk out their differences. When Williams humanized the worker and made that person an individual like any other with common needs and desires, he also dismissed the very idea of class, or of any consciousness beyond the self. Passing was, of course, a distinctly individual experience, understood by the investigator through a consciousness first formed far from the precincts of proletarian life and always aware of its otherness. Perhaps then it is not surprising that the class passer so readily prescribed individual, psychologically informed solutions for the problems of class. Thus, for Williams, the labor leader would be happier exercising leadership capacities—fulfilling a basic human drive for distinction, for a sense of self-worth—within the plant, as a member of the team, much as the boss gained satisfaction from membership in the Chamber of Commerce (an organization that apparently did not advance the boss's class interests). All conflict, including strikes, boiled down to hurt feelings, not to systematic oppression or exploitation—though readers could certainly find in these texts plenty of evidence for what looked like oppression and exploitation. Even so strong an academic supporter as Ordway Tead criticized Williams for overpsychologizing his subjects, noting tartly that one might become a labor leader for material reasons, not because of "infantile fixations" or "chronic fears."[121]

Class passers of the 1920s carried forward the Progressive Era tradition by transporting their middle-class readers across the class line to show them something of the worker's world and, more than their predecessors had, something of the worker's mind. At the same time, they channeled many of their conclusions toward the needs of management, which were equated with the needs of society, because social harmony originated with the job and a happy worker made a good republican citizen. What, then, was on the worker's mind? According to Annie MacLean, a persistent progressive who preferred the "plain honesty" of open class antagonism to the subtle manipulations of the "model factory," it was self-expression through work and a genuine voice in determining work's conditions.[122] Yet the scientistic remains of progressive reform, now embedded in the discourses of personnel management and industrial psychology, would mediate the outcomes of experiments like MacLean's.

In the end, it seemed that class passers had assumed proletarian trappings and stigmata in order to obliterate class itself and to elevate the individual as the unit of social betterment. Thus in 1930, Ordway Tead invoked the authority of Whiting Williams when reflecting that most labor-management issues were now understood as at least partly psychological in origin. Likewise, Elton Mayo concluded by 1931 that irrational workers' grievances could be talked out of existence rather than addressed through workplace reform.[123] If earlier industrial psychology had been explicitly but narrowly racialist, by the 1930s the human relations approach had become far more committed to a view of the worker, of whatever ethnic or racial origin, as a primitive and childlike being in need of the expert's gentle ministrations. These would seem to be ironic outcomes indeed of the decisions taken by Parker, Walker, Williams, and their fellow adventurers to pass into the workers' world—to cast themselves adrift on the "rough seas of 'Common Labor' "—as the New Era of the 1920s dawned.

Conclusion

Down-and-outers pursued older agendas and advanced new ones during the prosperity decade. But changes loomed. Alfred Bingham, while a law student, spent the summer of 1929—for him, "the last of the glorious 1920s"—following the wheat harvest through Oklahoma, Kansas, and Nebraska. Ominously, he found little work, and it was only in places where the increasingly ubiquitous combine had not yet rendered his muscular frame unnecessary. Bingham had set off in search of the frontier, but, instead of sturdy yeoman farmers who embodied the American agrarian myth, he encountered unemployed harvest stiffs, "gaunt men who sat silent and dusty on the curb-stones." When he did get work, he found himself "appalled" by the "bleak-ness and ugliness of these dung-encrusted farm homes, the 'backbone of America.'" His frontier illusions blasted, a battered and road-weary Bingham sought sanctuary with rich friends in the Montana Rockies; he knew he was back among his "own kind" when a wary maid ordered him to report to the service entrance.[124]

Another decade passed before Alfred Bingham distilled the lessons of his undercover experiences into a new social analysis for a nation stricken by the Great Depression. After returning east in the fall of 1929 for his final year of law school, he at first paid little attention to the October stock market crash. Talk of growing unemployment seemed unconnected to his summer experiences among brass workers and farm laborers. But it gradually became apparent—to Bingham, as to other investigators who were then on the road—that the "glorious 1920s" had come to a painful and inglorious end. In the months before the crash, an aspiring writer named Paul Peters left New York's artistic bohemia in search of authentic working-class experience, and he tellingly entitled a report for *Harper's* "I'm Hunting for a Job." To Peters, the vaunted "prosperity" that was still being trumpeted was only a mirage.[125] As this recognition spread, earlier down-and-outers such as Walker and Wil-liams turned their attention to the transformed conditions of the 1930s. And Paul Peters would figure among the new generation of undercover wander-ers, along with a new group of fellow traveling journalists, novelists, and social scientists, who would emerge during the Depression decade. Tougher-talking and more politicized than their predecessors, animated above all by an acute awareness of social crisis, they would take the down-and-out dis-course in new directions.

3

Finding Facts

The Great Depression, from the Bottom Up

When the sociologist Robert S. Lynd reviewed an undercover study of hobo youths in 1934, he found that however horrifying the subject matter, it was nonetheless "a hopeful sign when academic folk 'take to the road' " and get their hands dirty addressing the current crisis.[1] The Depression lent down-and-out texts a worrisome immediacy as the focus of undercover writing shifted from work to unemployment. Journalists' undercover accounts of transiency and breadlines became a recognizable subgenre of the downward-mobility narratives that filled popular magazines with familiar images of physical, mental, and moral degeneration. Sociologists hopped freight cars and choked down flophouse fare to study the emergent cultures of the unemployed. Tensions over objectivity among social scientists continued to shape the reception of their work, and the culture concept increasingly supplanted biological determinism in explanations of difference—although it could also serve as the vehicle for more subtle forms of determinism. Meanwhile, novelists and playwrights garnered positive critical attention by forging undercover experiences into art. Even Hollywood got into the act: In *Sullivan's*

Travels (1942), the writer-director Preston Sturges created an undercover epic that summed up and commented on the 1930s discourse, ostensibly concluding that the industry should forswear "message movies" in favor of providing escapist entertainment.[2]

Sullivan's Travels shared with most Depression-era undercover texts—whether popular or academic, fictional or nonfictional—a narrative structure of crisis and resolution. Always characteristic of the undercover genre, this structure took on new implications in the 1930s context. Even as Depression down-and-outers recounted harrowing stories of descent into hopeless poverty and identity slippage, they simultaneously offered hopeful narratives of re-emergence from the abyss that presaged the rebuilding of middle-class identity and national prospects. If the Depression revealed a crisis of class in America, the emphasis on happy endings paradoxically meant that class as a structural feature of American society could ultimately be deemphasized. The appearance and behavior of poor people were especially cast in the spotlight; class was increasingly subsumed by culture.

Downward Mobility, Class Anxiety, and the Fate of the Nation

Images of downward mobility and poverty permeated 1930s print culture, from the reportage of intellectuals like Edmund Wilson to the innumerable magazine articles of the "We Live in the Slums" variety.[3] My concern here is with individuals who passed, as distinct from social explorers who were animated by the broader and much-discussed "documentary impulse," and who produced a plethora of "on the road" books, photographs, documentary films, and novels.[4] But undercover investigators' analyses reflected a tendency that historian Terry Cooney also finds within the documentary impulse: They imposed a comforting discursive order on uncertain times by gathering and presenting the "social facts."[5] In particular need of reassurance was the vast and nebulous middle class—a group to which, according to various polls, a substantial plurality of Americans from every economic and occupational group seemed to think they belonged.[6] For such Americans, the specter of downward mobility fostered anxiety not only about their own futures, but also about the very survival of their putatively middle-class nation. It was reason for concern when the journalist Matthew Josephson, touring New York City's shelters for the *New Republic*, found that the clients were increasingly "a very good class of people"; fully half were "not bums at all." Josephson fretted that the erstwhile "vigorous, optimistic American," now succumbing to the lethargy and hopelessness of flophouse life, was fast becoming a "citizen of the Other Nation."[7] This combination of class anxiety with fears about national fragility established the broader context and swelled the audience for undercover studies of poverty in the Great Depression.

Why did some writers take the dramatic step of going undercover to study poverty in the thirties? To some extent, they went for the same reasons that had motivated their predecessors: to confront reality and to fortify their identities with authentic experience. But they did so in the strikingly new context of a nationwide depression, which provoked new questions and concerns. So in the "terrifying" days of 1932, Maury Maverick, a San Antonio politician and eventual Texas congressman, set out by Ford and by freight car on a series of hobo expeditions around his region to "find out what it was all about" and to report on conditions to the state's governor. Social scientists also found that the down-and-out approach uniquely suited their efforts to explore Depression conditions. The sociologist Donald Roy claimed that he gathered better data by living in Seattle's Hooverville than he would have gotten by remaining "one who snoops and quizzes as an outsider." Both Roy and Thomas Minehan found that tramps volunteered more information during informal conversations than in conventional interviews. And sometimes that information conflicted sharply with the official version of reality: The undercover social worker Herbert W. McCanlies's report to the state of California about the treatment of transients exposed numerous untruths that had been mouthed by officials of the San Francisco Community Chest, the YMCA, and the Los Angeles Police Department.[8] All such investigators tended to share Minehan's reasons for passing into the world of the poor: "to experience their life, study their problems, and to acquaint the American public with the facts." Like Minehan, who taught sociology at the University of Minnesota and became a state official focusing on youth issues, they blended the down-and-outer's faith in the epistemology of experience and the earlier progressive's drive to educate the public with a New Deal–era conviction that expanding state agencies would put their findings to public use.[9]

One notable change in the down-and-out discourse was that female participants were far less common in the 1930s than in previous eras. Earlier investigators had explored all areas of women's labor, from urban domestic service to Southern textile mills. But the Depression reinforced older gendered assumptions about work, mobility, and danger. The economic slump was widely seen as a crisis of the male breadwinner, and with widespread unemployment, undercover accounts of actual work were largely supplanted by dramatic chronicles of hobo odysseys and shelter sojourns that explored the lives of transient "forgotten" men in search of jobs. Even though far more dispossessed females—from teen refugees to mothers with families—appeared in road narratives than had shown up in previous decades, female investigators did not seek them out. Women writers such as Lorena Hickok and Martha Gellhorn stayed in the safer and more conventional aboveground realm when they documented the Depression. The exceptions, such as Lauren Gilfillan's account of retail and lunch-counter work, were rare.[10]

Writers of fiction took to the road in search of raw materials and new social roles. Paul Peters, a radical college graduate, followed the advice of Mike Gold, the editor of the left-wing literary magazine *New Masses*, that young writers submerge themselves in the "lost continent" of working-class America. Why voyage to Africa or Asia, Gold asked, when there was plenty of "primitive material" available in the nearby world of the wage slave? Peters duly embarked on a five-year voyage of discovery through proletarian America, seeking authentic experiences to forge into art.[11] Fleeing the "padded isolation" of life among New York aesthetes and intellectual radicals, he went looking for authenticity: "for rough-and-tumble experience, for wholesome dirt and hard work." He found plenty of the latter at the bottom layer of the job hierarchy, as it became apparent that his unmanly lack of skills did not recommend him to foremen. He wrote, "I cannot do *anything*. I was brought up on books. . . . Actually I'm nothing." Reversing the imagined arc of American social mobility, Peters concluded that any son he might have—potential daughters were not mentioned—must learn a trade.[12]

Such reversals and blurrings of class identity had always been part of the undercover discourse, and they remained so in the 1930s. Minehan was initially appalled when he joined his first breadline: The men struck him as "strange night creatures" issued from "caves and water holes." But within a paragraph, he had become one with them, and it was "we" who "inched down the alley" toward the promise of a moldy sandwich and vile coffee. Paul Peters carefully constructed a steelworker identity, but he sometimes struggled to maintain it: When he let slip some evidence of his educated background, he had to fight off a suspicious superior's efforts to elevate him from furnace work to an office job. Like Walter Wyckoff, Peters also shored up his older identity by taking refuge in free library books. Similarly, John Kazarian, a reporter, bracketed his grim account of life on the highways in the "Starvation Army" with bracing quotations from Seneca and Shakespeare.[13]

After changing clothes and class affiliation, what did Depression-era investigators find? Many were shocked by the variety of class origins represented among the dispossessed, as the unknown class had come to include so many recent victims of the downward slide. Exploring the jungles, jails, and flophouses, Texan Maury Maverick mixed with onetime farmers, businessmen, lawyers, and doctors, and with veterans of the Great War, the Bonus Army, and the federal prison system. In the packed waiting room of the Sacramento shelter, Herbert McCanlies's near neighbors were a teenaged Southern black freight-hopper, a white former businessman of middle age, and a one-armed, octogenarian migrant laborer who picked body lice from his shirt while telling McCanlies his story.[14] The stunning breadth of downward mobility was also flattened and caricatured in popular culture representations such as the successful novel and movie *My Man Godfrey* (1935, 1936), in which a New York City Hooverville houses a former Boston patrician driven downward by a failed romance, an ex-banker who went broke protecting his depositors, and similarly good-hearted but ill-starred aristocrats. The movie infuriated the *New Masses* critic Edward Newhouse, a radical novelist with hobo experience, who called it "a slap in the face" of every true Hooverville dweller. *Godfrey* effectively satirized "the witless wealthy," as Graham Greene put it when he reviewed the film. The movie also did far less justice than Maverick and McCanlies did to the true range of origins among the American dispossessed.[15] In their renditions, the future of the middle and respectable working classes—and therefore, of the nation itself—seemed in jeopardy.

In undercover Depression narratives, the world had gone awry in unprecedented ways and all social norms were apparently at risk. Minehan's account showed the American family facing a crisis as children and youth left home to relieve their parents' burdens, descending into the primitive "tribal" life of hobo gangs. Conventional lines of gender and sexuality were shown to waver dangerously on the road. Minehan, McCanlies, and Roy reported male homosexual encounters with greater frankness than had their predecessors, provoking fears about the moral futures of respectably born boys.[16] Investigators also depicted girls and women donning male garb to ride the rails, a practice that was dramatized in popular accounts such as the movie *Wild Boys of the Road* (1933) and in the hobo physician Ben Reitman's fictionalized portrait of *Box-Car Bertha* (1937). Female tramps were portrayed as serially domestic, licentious, and feral; they cooked for the tribe, enjoyed sexual liaisons within it, prostituted themselves for its benefit, and fought the police side by side with the boys.[17] The line between middle-class respectability and the abyss seemed so permeable that *Life* magazine published a photo essay instructing its middle-class readership on how to safely hop a freight train complete with helpful "do's" and "don'ts" that the photographer, Louis Van Dyke, had learned while in hobo guise. He instructed aspiring hoboes to stand with feet straddling the coupling between cars and to firmly grasp the brake rod, and not to hide from cops in open-topped cars or take shortcuts under trains. The essay ended with the cautionary image of a tramp lying dead by the tracks, his legs sliced off due to improper technique. On the same page, as if to illustrate a world gone thoroughly out of joint, that grisly final photo was weirdly juxtaposed with an advertisement that featured simpering Victorian matrons introducing a hapless young homemaker to the virtues of Fels-Naphtha laundry soap.[18]

The Depression discourse was also notable for more expansive attention to race than earlier down-and-outers had demonstrated, as investigators commonly noted that hard times appeared to be lowering traditional racial barriers. During two years of investigations in the Midwest, Thomas Minehan found that hobo youth of all backgrounds freely intermixed: "Swede and Italian, Protestant and Catholic, white and black are brothers on the road," and sex between black boys and white girls was commonplace. Donald Roy called Seattle's Hooverville "an ethnic rainbow." He observed there a broad tolerance among whites, blacks, Filipinos and Mexicans, including eleven instances of shared living quarters and an "utter absence" in the black population of "feelings of resentment or inferiority toward the whites." Below an embankment in Sacramento, Herbert McCanlies shared jungle stew and conversation with two black men and two whites, all of them Southerners, united for the moment in a "brotherhood born of hunger." And in Houston, Maury Maverick "jungled up" with two whites and three African Americans on land where Texans had once fought the forces of General Santa Anna: "Historic ground, indeed; once for heroes, now for bums." Maverick reported a complete collapse of racial barriers in the jungles as people of different origins struggled with the same disaster. Speculating in his report to the governor that such a shift was probably happening all over the South, he was even moved to suggest that the black teenaged transients accused in the famous Scottsboro case of raping two white girls on a freight train had probably been framed—a view that Minehan's findings on consensual interracial sex among hobo youth would have supported. By the decade's end, Theodore Caplow, a hobo sociologist at the University of Minnesota, found not only that racism was "markedly low" among Northern hoboes, but also—concurring with Maverick—that "a relative decrease" in such sentiments was discernible in the South.[19]

This is not to say that all down-and-outers foresaw the imminent emergence of an interracial utopia or that they had reason to. Seven of the eight black hoboes Caplow met intended not to return to their Southern birthplaces. And Maverick's progressive sentiments probably shaped the conclusions he drew from his experiences; as a congressman who supported black civil rights, he would operate at the far-left periphery of New Deal Democrats. In Chicago, the sociologists Edwin Sutherland and Harvey Locke led an undercover study that found "intense prejudice" in municipal shelters against black and foreign-born shelter men, with whom white residents had a long history of competing for jobs as dishwashers and stevedores.[20] Racism and ethnic prejudice may have been less common in the more fluid populations studied by the hobo investigators. Nonetheless, in a decade marked by a rising level of black civil rights consciousness and activism, down-and-outers did identify promising new models of interracialism—if Depression-bred and largely transient. Conditions forced these investigators to pay greater attention to race than had their predecessors, which suggested a shifting emphasis in American social thought that would come to fruition in the 1940s and afterward.

As the stability of all social categories was thrown into question by the Depression, radical alternatives were one possible response. Similar to down-and-outers of the 1870s who feared a tramp-led insurrection, Depression-era investigators looked for, and sometimes found, evidence of revolutionary sentiments brewing among the dispossessed. When John Kazarian, a writer for *The Nation*, concluded a national freight-hopping tour in 1933, he warned that "rumblings of rebellion" were rising wherever the transient unemployed gathered. Minehan found expectations of revolution among St. Paul shelter men, as well as rapidly growing communist convictions among young hoboes who lacked their elders' persistent faith in the American dream of success, and sought other avenues for engagement and hope. The down-and-out experience could itself prove radicalizing, as in Edward Newhouse's novel *You Can't Sleep Here* (1934). The narrator—a radical newspaper man and, like the author, a veteran of several hobo excursions—tells his editor that to understand the communists' appeal for the unemployed, he should don hobo garb, hop a freight to Detroit, and live undercover for six months. From a different perspective, the unsympathetic reviewer of another leftist novel with undercover themes recommended the book for readers who wanted to know "why red terror lifts its ugly head."[21]

Most down-and-outers hardly saw their subjects as a likely revolutionary vanguard. Donald Roy would have agreed that most of his Hooverville neighbors favored "some form of socialism," but aside from several Communist Party members, most were largely passive and, for the short term, despaired of finding work again. Charles Rumford Walker reported hopefully that an unemployed friend had resisted pauperization and, impressed by the communists, had joined the Unemployed Council; but an organizer for the Council told the Chicago sociologist Robert W. Beasley that they didn't "give a damn" for any man who had spent more than six months in a flophouse. The experience drained away from an unemployed man all capacity for collective action: "It does things to him. . . . He forgets who he used to be." Sutherland and Locke found similarly that Chicago shelter men—or "linesmen," as they were also called, because they spent so much time standing in lines—were wont to attack capitalism in the name of socialist or communist alternatives, but willful group action was rare among men whose every move was programmed and regimented. In California, Herbert McCanlies heard radical criticisms of the "whole godamned system," but he also rediscovered what predecessors such as Stuart Chase had well known: Being unemployed and homeless was an enormous amount of work, entailing endless trips—on foot, in freight cars, or hitchhiking—within and between towns to seek jobs, relief agencies, and shelters. Unable to find work or to qualify for relief, McCanlies described a day spent panhandling without result, a night endured in the back room of a cheap café with fifty-two other men, another day of fruitless bumming, and ultimately, his return to the highway after twenty-four hours without food. Of such utter exhaustion and despair, militant resistance was not easily roused.[22]

When it came to assessing the radical potential of the lower classes, some undercover investigators probably found what they went looking for. Paul Peters and Whiting Williams were among the few Depression-era investigators who wrote more about workers and class than about drifting hoboes and flophouses. Their conclusions about class politics were clearly shaped by their own political perspectives. The leftist Peters's five years of proletarian experience straddled the end of the New Era and the early Depression years. In an *American Mercury* article blasting the oppressive wastefulness of ten-hour days in a New South cotton mill, his acknowledgment of soldiering—of learning "to spare myself, to stall, to sneak off and hide" when fatigue overcame him—sounded surprisingly like Williams's 1920s critique of the twelve-hour day in steelwork. But Peters was "hot-footed after a vision" and put his faith in the millworkers, a long-faced, freedom-loving mountain folk who were commonly reviled as "hill-billies." He shared none of Williams's affinity for the tweed-suited personnel man, who complacently avowed to Peters that "most of our people are local people and they're satisfied." Torn between his socialist commitment and his ability to escape from the "knitting-mill hell," Peters took solace in revolutionary teleology: "What will happen when they stop being satisfied? . . . Already they begin to chafe." If the "savageness" of these poverty-stricken mountain folk were to be released, Peters foresaw a sanguinary revolt unrivaled in human history.[23]

But Whiting Williams would have none of this. As he wrote in a 1933 *Saturday Evening Post* article, his undercover adventures of the early 1930s left him remarkably sanguine about the prospects for "the hopeful American worker." Over the decade, he became increasingly a defender of Hooverian individualism and a harsh critic of the New Deal, the Congress of Industrial

Organizations (CIO), and "European" communist agitators. Williams was convinced by his own experiences as a working man that workers built identities not through class solidarity, but through the personal satisfactions of productive workplace participation. He saw no likelihood of revolution, and he remained confident that the personnel management movement, which he had consistently championed, was fostering a positive national "*psychology*" of class interdependence that would trump the grim "*arithmetic*" of mass unemployment. Although he took the crisis seriously and worried that the "demoralized loafer" might degenerate into a floating criminal "yegg," he expected better times if government could only be restrained from inordinate interference in the economy. Meanwhile, Williams was almost certainly unique among down-and-out writers in praising the "meaty but palatable" fare to be enjoyed in urban shelters. Former President Hoover, with whom he maintained a long-running friendship, urged him in 1934 to continue his investigations; Hoover volunteered to provide the overalls.[24] If Williams in the 1920s had exposed oppressive conditions and management practices, he became in the thirties a paragon of positive thinking.

Undercover investigators shared no single political perspective, offered no single solution, in an era that threatened to drive so many Americans down into the unknown class. Thomas Minehan captured the moment's confusions when he wrote of the "feeling of insecurity and unrest that permeates all classes" as the country shifted uneasily away from "the old securities of free competition and individualism, which turned out to be so insecure," toward the "promised security of planning in the social order," which had not yet proven itself. If Minehan, as a reformist state official, shared anything with the radical Peters and the conservative Williams, it was the same faith that had long linked the projects of down-and-outers: a modernist faith that science, whether Peters's scientific socialism or Williams's scientific management, held answers to the day's great social questions. Similarly, Maury Maverick—a lawyer, businessman, and politician who wore the mask of a simple man, a plain-speaking radical populist—put his hopes in scientific expertise. Disclaiming any effort to make his Depression memoir a "professorial volume" and offering no footnotes or references, he still devoted two chapters to praising a Brain Truster, Rexford Tugwell, for applying the fruits of research to federal policy making. Maverick urged Americans to "follow science, and not taboos." America's crisis would be solved by heeding Tugwell's advice: Professors should broaden their "practical" and "human" experiences, while politicians must absorb more "scientific" understanding.[25] This was effectively a recommendation that policy makers learn from the work of social scientists who were going down and out in the Depression.

Science and Subjectivity: Social Science Goes Undercover

Social scientists, and especially sociologists, made considerable use of the undercover method to investigate the Depression's impact. Their work typically corroborated popular downward-mobility narratives such as the movie *Wild Boys of the Road*, which chronicled the descent of a middle-class teen-aged boy into transiency after his father's unemployment. But while they unavoidably took note of the structural causes of poverty, Depression-era investigators resembled their predecessors in foregrounding behavioral and cultural attributes of the poor, now framed in social-scientific language. By the decade's end, an informal canon of undercover and related works had been established, as sociologists cited older exemplars such as Josiah Flynt and Carleton Parker, as well as recent predecessors and contemporaries. Most acknowledged the influence of Nels Anderson's *The Hobo*, and as the Depression wore on, they built upon his and each other's work.[26] The chain of influences ran especially through the Universities of Chicago and Minnesota. Edwin Sutherland had encountered sociology through a Chicago correspondence course with Annie Marion Maclean, and he eventually earned a Ph.D. (1913) under her mentor, Charles R. Henderson, who had also taught Frances Donovan and Frances Kellor. Sutherland and his colleague Harvey Locke cited Minnesotan Thomas Minehan's study of young tramps in their monograph on Chicago public shelter life, while their work in turn inspired Jesse Walker Dees as a Northwestern graduate student to investigate the same city's private flophouses, as well as its shelters and missions. Theodore Caplow—another product of Minnesota training—cited Anderson, Minehan, and Jack London in a study based on a 1939 hobo trip across much of the United States. Graduate students seemed to find the down-and-out method especially inviting, perhaps because they were generally young enough to tolerate working in roadhouses, traveling by foot and by freight car, and sleeping in flophouses, Hoovervilles, and hobo jungles. Seasoned scholars such as Sutherland and Locke were more inclined to supervise.[27]

While the down-and-out method hardly dominated the field, it did gain legitimacy during the 1930s as one approach for conducting social research. Debates over scientific objectivism had agitated social scientists since the 1920s, and Chicago sociology, to which so many down-and-outers bore a connection, was never committed to a single method. But under Robert Park's leadership, the Chicago school did consistently emphasize not only the ideal of science, but also the importance of personal, empathetic contact with those being studied, and the consequent generation of "subjective data." In a 1928 manual for students that attempted to codify the Chicago approach,

Viven M. Palmer discussed the utility of subjective data for gauging attitudes and motivations. Palmer acknowledged that such data were often disparaged as "unscientific," but she cautiously endorsed Nels Anderson's "informal interview" method while expecting that researchers would ensure reliability by developing further techniques for cross-checking data. Park and his colleague Ernest W. Burgess took a similar tack in essays for a state-of-the-field volume published in 1929, in which they reaffirmed the importance of subjective data but also pictured the city as a "social laboratory" for systematic scientific study. Yet even as they established a context in which undercover studies could be taken seriously, the Chicago leaders showed a curious amnesia about earlier practitioners of the method such as their own Annie Marion MacLean and Frances Donovan—both of whom went unmentioned by Palmer, Park, and Burgess, even though Park had just written the introduction for Donovan's *The Saleslady*. While calling for the pursuit of subjective data, the field's leaders distanced themselves from the practice's unscientific—often female and reformist—origins in their own social laboratory.[28]

The undercover method also gained status by its resonance with the Chicago tradition of participant observation, which similarly relied on subjective data. But while reviewers sometimes called down-and-outers "participant observers," the two were not synonymous.[29] The latter term was coined by Eduard Lindeman, a Columbia social work professor, in the 1920s, but it did not gain much currency until after World War II and did not entail the degree of deception inherent to full-blown passing. For Lindeman, participant observation did not mean (as it came to mean later) an investigator's undisguised immersion in the group or environment to be studied; rather, the investigator was to enlist a recruit from within that milieu who would furnish data from an insider's perspective—biases and distortions included. Lindeman saw subjective data as useful for fine-tuning the principal investigator's conclusions while the investigator provided the detached, ordering voice of science.[30] The roles of insider and outsider were not, as in undercover investigation, to be merged.

Closer in spirit to the down-and-outers' cause were Read Bain and Paul G. Cressey. Bain was later commonly identified with objectivism, but early in his career he saw a role for subjective material obtained through first-person encounters. Thomas Minehan would cite Bain's 1925 article "Impersonal Confession and Social Research" to support his own deployment of the undercover approach. Bain drew on Werner Sombart's "sociology of the stranger" to argue that sociologists who developed a knack for empathetic conversation could elicit valuable "confessions" from targeted "specimens" encountered in seemingly casual circumstances. Citing Nels Anderson's example,

Bain asserted that disguised interactions could garner not just "facts" but "attitudes," which must then be treated "in an objective, impersonal, professional manner." Paul G. Cressey, a Chicago graduate student, cited Bain and Anderson in an influential study of taxi-dance halls that combined undercover encounters with conventional case studies and data from social agencies.[31] In the book that followed, Cressey only briefly adopted the voice of the down-and-outer to offer a generic description of the halls investigated, and while he occasionally interpolated evidence that he cited as "records of an investigator," he did not distinguish between material gathered anonymously and data obtained from "casual acquaintances" struck up by members of his team.[32] But Cressey's blending of undercover data with more conventional sources exemplified the approach that Depression-era class passers would follow. In an age of ardent debate over the scientific status of sociology, practitioners often split the difference between impersonal scientism and streetwise subjectivity, leaving open a space for professional sociologists and their graduate students to cross the class line.

Thomas Minehan exemplified young sociologists' efforts to balance the competing claims of science and subjectivity by calling for a "new technique in sociology" that would combine scientific data with an experiential "literary" narrative. After completing his more orthodox 1933 master's thesis—in which he utilized the passive voice or called himself "the investigator"—he adopted in 1934 the first-person narrative voice of a hobo sociologist who placed himself within the story of *Boy and Girl Tramps of America*. Minehan framed his richly anecdotal account of road life with chapter titles that posed sociological questions ("Why Did They Leave Home?"), which were then answered by the youthful tramps' own voices in the text and by data aggregated into a series of nineteen tables in an appendix.[33] Popular reviewers were uniformly impressed—and suitably horrified—by the book and its method, while sociologists were only slightly less positive, occasionally demurring that Minehan's sample population was only "presumably representative" or that his picture of conditions might be "too extreme." Least convinced was Nels Anderson, who suspected that Minehan had written with one eye on Hollywood (perhaps thinking of the recent success of *Wild Boys of the Road*); Anderson also complained that Minehan had "[broken] faith with the scientific spirit" by exaggerating the importance of young tramps at the expense of the far more numerous older men on the road. While Anderson's scientism may have reflected his continued struggle with the yoke of *The Hobo*, he was not alone in arguing that the undercover method's current legitimacy might be Depression-related and, therefore, short-lived. For the moment, however, Minehan's strategy of combining a first-person undercover narrative with objective sociological data exemplified the disciplinary practice of the 1930s.[34]

What did social scientists find when they plunged into shelter life, joined demonstrations of the unemployed, and swung themselves up into rolling freight cars? Two intersecting intellectual and cultural currents shaped their interpretations: the anthropological culture concept, and national fears of degeneration among the downwardly mobile. Beginning with Robert Park and W. I. Thomas, Chicago sociologists had largely absorbed the nonhierarchical, nonevolutionary view of culture as an interlinked set of lived practices and ideas that had been pioneered by Franz Boas and his students. Paul Cressey's investigation of the taxi-dance hall's distinctive "cultural world" reflected the assumption underlying numerous undercover studies that hoboes, casual laborers, and shelter men also inhabited separate, self-contained cultures.[35] Although the Boasian culture concept was conceived as a tool to combat evolutionary and racialist models of human society, researchers did not always automatically shed the notion of linear cultural evolution, and culture could have quite deterministic implications when it came into tension with socioeconomic explanations of poverty.[36] In an era when scientific distinctions between environmental and hereditary influences remained murky, the culture concept could legitimize the sorts of behavioral explanations for poverty that had underwritten earlier formulations such as "pauperization," and that would sustain later interpretations of the "culture of poverty" and the "underclass." With the decline of Lamarckism's credibility, culture sometimes interwove environment with heredity to perform a similar explanatory function.

Understood this way, culture—seen rather vaguely as both learned and inherited—was a powerful force that could drive communities downward into collective degeneration. Edwin Sutherland's articles leading up to the 1936 undercover study *Twenty Thousand Homeless Men* showed him moving toward culturalist explanations. As he separated sociology from biology and rejected hereditarian theories of crime and intelligence, he also foregrounded culture as one causal factor explaining crime in urban ethnic communities. Sutherland and Locke never dismissed socioeconomic factors when explaining homelessness, but they did confess their inability to weigh the influence of individual "hereditary" traits, such as "defective intelligence" and "psychopathies," against social and environmental factors stemming from Depression conditions.[37] However unclear remained the relationship between heredity and environment, their graduate students' experiences with shelter life convinced Sutherland and Locke of that culture's deterministic thrust, and even of its dangers to the investigator. The man whose personality was shaped by the "reciprocally reinforcing tendencies" of casual labor and shelter life had little chance of escape: "His world closes in on him and the lock snaps shut."[38]

Not only were individuals and subcommunities of the poor under threat, but the fate of the nation was at stake as well. The broader American concern that a generation of downwardly mobile Americans was at risk of degeneration was common coin among Depression-era social scientists. For undercover sociologists, the deterministic dangers of flophouse culture fed the fears of working-class and middle-class decline into lassitude and incapability. As increasing numbers of formerly middle-class transients populated the shelters and freight cars, students of the unemployed echoed the old Lamarckian language in asserting that occupational skills would "deteriorate through disuse," while physical deterioration would follow from the ravages of hunger and the dangers of life on the road or in the slums.[39] Thomas Minehan worried that the boy and girl tramps—many of them refugees from "good homes"—whose distinctive culture he had studied would sink permanently into trampdom. Nels Anderson questioned whether the unemployed, condemned for their "parasitism, shiftlessness and lost morale, together with their isolation" into a separate culture, would come to be defined as a subordinate "caste" within American society.[40] The influence of the culture concept and broader fears of degeneration merged dramatically in the Chicago investigators' concept of "shelterization," a new variation on the notion of going native.

Sutherland and Locke, who introduced the idea of shelterization, ushered their readers through the shelter's door so they could experience the world within "from the point of view of the [shelter] men," not that "of the police, the social worker, or the tax-payer." Similarly, readers joined Jesse Dees in taking "the pauper's oath" and crossing the flophouse threshold. Once inside, they saw, smelled, and tasted the investigator's version of shelter life.[41] But the reader's ride could be a bumpy one. Unlike most earlier undercover narratives, these books offered a peculiar mix of shocking first-person experience and detached social-scientific analysis. Such contrasting voices sometimes jarred the reader by appearing in the same sentence: "*One* was shocked," wrote Dees, by the "barbaric and 'hoggish' way" the men ate their meals.[42] Perhaps equally shocking was the fact that Dees, the newly initiated shelter man, would soon "assume the same piggish, shoveling habits" as the veterans.[43] This degradation of table manners was but one indicator of the sinister process that was clearly under way: the descent into shelterization.

What Sutherland and Locke identified as shelterization—a concept that reviewers both professional and popular found compelling—was first a psychological and then a physical process. For some downwardly mobile individuals, entering the municipal shelter was a delaying action until work could be found. For many others, it was an admission of final defeat. To face the fact of "total destitution," declared Sutherland and Locke, was to suffer "social death" and to recognize that only the shelter's "culture" was now accessible. Such clients underwent the intake process in "a trancelike state," anesthetized by the shock of admitting indigency. They eventually regained consciousness in a new identity: that of a thoroughly acculturated "shelter dependent"—that is, one who was shelterized. The cultural divide that had distinguished Hobohemians from outsiders was erased by psychological and physical deterioration. Middle-class refugees, once-respectable workers, and confirmed bottom-dwellers were melded into a single, homogeneous subclass of shelter men. As those from a "higher cultural background" succumbed to hopelessness, they adapted themselves to the lower local culture and were finally reduced to "just hogs, even to the grunting." Thus shelterization assimilated the downward devolutionary tug of biology to the degraded culture of the shelters.[44]

First-person accounts of shelterization could be chilling. In the "Shelter 'Client's' Diary" included in Sutherland and Locke's book, a researcher described his own experience, which the other investigators were also said to have undergone. Worn down by months of regimentation and hopelessness, he felt no need to use his brain and lost track of time: "After a few months, his independence is broken down, his individuality disappears, his identity is lost, his personality becomes reorganized, and he becomes shelterized." Jesse Dees recounted a similar descent into the mental pathologies associated with shelterization: "With each succeeding day one feels himself pushed down into a hopeless maelstrom—getting farther and farther from the outer edge, into the middle of the vortex from which there will be no escape."[45] Both books described shelterization as a process of cultural adaptation, of "reorganizing" the personality to suit local norms. Dees, who called himself "somewhat 'shelterized'" by his experiences, felt the culture's tug when he was surprised by a touring group of former college classmates. Craving the anonymity of the other "beaten men," he found himself trying to recede into the sad, mumbling mass. In the private flophouses that Dees also patronized, he identified an "institutional disease" comparable to shelterization that he called "flophouseitis": a pseudo-medicalization of the same process of cultural devolution that left once-rational residents capable of nothing but sitting, lining up, and going to bed. Spreading like a disease, infecting both older hoboes and the newly destitute, the flophouse culture, Dees wrote, "finally gets under the skin."[46]

Dees equated shelterization with the older term "pauperization," with its similar devolutionary connotations.[47] Shelterization would be used by sociologists into the 1960s, and it functioned in the historical discourse of American poverty as a mediating term between pauperization and the 1960s idea of a "culture of poverty," which would in turn foreshadow the emergence of the "underclass" discourse of the 1980s and 1990s. In that later context, the concept of shelterization would be resurrected to identify what was seen as a characteristic affliction of the underclass. As the anthropologist Anthony Marcus described this more recent usage, the shelter came to be seen "as a site of social contagion that recast the character and sense of self, restructured residents' behavior, prevented the development of healthy habits in dysfunctional people, or threatened to infect functional people with dysfunctional values." The persistence of shelterization as a vehicle for suggesting a vague but sinister confluence of cultural and biological degeneration in the very poor—a usage quite comparable to that of Sutherland and Locke, or Dees—is striking.[48] Although none of the Depression-era sociologists would have denied the social and economic origins of poverty, they did confuse the behavioral with the socioeconomic when they grafted terms such as shelterization and flophouseitis onto the Boasian culture concept to ground deterministic explanations of dependency and degeneration. It certainly seems ironic that the culture concept, usually seen as having helped to liberate American thought from racialist and hierarchical assumptions, should also have functioned to frame the impoverished as a primitive and degenerating breed apart.

Like the broader Depression-era downward-mobility literature, the down-and-out discourse on poverty offered not just realism but also reassurance. Although undercover investigators presented distressing portraits of class instability, degeneration, and even of their own shelterization, they found ways to somewhat soften the effects. First, there was the reassuring display of the facts: In each text, the investigators supplemented and balanced their personal narratives with a proliferation of charts, tables, statistics, and glossaries. They imposed elaborate typologies, replete with categories, subcategories, and further subcategories, upon the inchoate and teeming materials of Depression poverty, in ways that may have exerted the reassuring "ordering power" attributed by Terry Cooney to the documentary impulse. For example, Sutherland and Locke divided "bums" (as distinct from "home guard casuals," "migratory laborers," and several other categories) into "mission stiffs," "drunkards," and "beggars," the last of whom they further subdivided into "main stem stiffs," "moochers," "house cats," and "peddler panhandlers." This almost entomological rage to classify had always been characteristic of undercover poverty investigators.[49]

The dialectic of shock and reassurance was completed most effectively by the very presence of the book in the reader's hands. However grimly deterministic the ideas might seem, one message of that material object, of those pages sewn into bindings, was that the author had made it back. If culture was powerful, perhaps—as in classic Lamarckism—it was still malleable, and never finally divorceable from economic and social conditions. And the latter were beginning to seem at least somewhat susceptible to human intervention, with the onset of the so-called Second New Deal shortly after Sutherland and Locke's book appeared. By the decade's end, undercover investigations of trampdom by the sociologist Theodore Caplow and of unemployed workers' communities by the economist E. Wight Bakke would offer far more positive, if not exactly cheerful, assessments of the poor, of their cultures, and of American society and its prospects.

Finally, it is only fair to note that if these writers sometimes objectified the poor, they also tried to act as their advocates. Dees angrily decried the fact that American capitalism had required a mobile, low-wage labor force in its early phases, but now it easily relegated such formerly indispensable men to the ranks of the vagrant and indigent. Sutherland and Locke wrote that because the homeless had been denied any voice in policies affecting them, one purpose of their book was to point out the inadequacies of current policies and to propose better ones: in particular, jobs programs of the sort that the federal government would shortly undertake. Likewise, when Dees emphasized the degrading aspects of shelterization, he did so in the service of advocating "outdoor" cash relief as a more dignified and productive alternative to shelters and flophouses.[50] And whatever the relative success of such political initiatives, it is also true that in these books—which were principally about looking at and talking about the poor—the voices of the poor sometimes did make themselves heard. "They don't give a damn about us," one man told an investigator. "What if a few men do die, who in hell cares?" What was a social scientist to do? As a shelter man said to Jesse Dees, "If there was a short story writer ever came down here and stayed for two weeks he'd have enough material to write a hell of a good book."[51] Whatever their failures and distortions, the sociologists tried to do just that. Others of their era whose métier truly was the writing of stories would also try their hands at the task.

Experience as Art: Radical Reportage and Theater

Since Albion Tourgée and Margaret Sherwood, American novelists had written about undercover investigation. In January 1930, the *New Masses* echoed

Mike Gold's call for the American writer to "attach himself to one of the industries" in order to "write like an insider, not like a bourgeois intellectual observer." Much leftist 1930s writing sprang from this impulse, though it would spawn few undercover narratives.[52] Jack Conroy, Robert Cantwell, and Albert Halper would make art from working-class experience in their promising proletarian novels, but these were not undercover accounts. Nelson Algren and Tom Kromer initially went on the bum in search of work, only later finding that they had the raw materials for novels that would briefly bring them acclaim. All resembled Nels Anderson in that writing was their means to move up and out of a lower-class world into which they had plunged of necessity, and not primarily as class explorers.[53] Purposeful undercover investigation did play a role in some Depression writing. Part of John Steinbeck's research for the newspaper articles that became *Their Blood Is Strong* (1938), the pamphlet on California farmworkers that prefigured *The Grapes of Wrath* (1939), may have been done undercover, but the resultant pamphlet was a conventional first-person exposé of conditions in the camps and fields. The radical novelist Edward Newhouse, who prided himself on having covered some twenty thousand miles by freight train in response to Mike Gold's call to explore the proletarian world, later made use of what he learned in *You Can't Sleep Here* and two other books with hobo elements. Lauren Gilfillan would engage to a limited degree with the undercover tradition in her novel *I Went to Pit College* (1934), and more fully in "Weary Feet" (1933), a fine piece of undercover reportage for the *Forum* about her work as a salesgirl and lunch-counter attendant in two New York City five-and-dime stores.[54] But the decade's most fully realized artistic expression of the undercover tradition would not be a novel; it would be the successful radical play *Stevedore* (1934), coauthored by Paul Peters, a wandering worker and aspiring revolutionary writer.[55]

"Paul Peters" was itself a pseudonymous mask assumed by a University of Wisconsin graduate, radical journalist, *New Masses* staffer, and would-be playwright named Harbor Allen. Peters drifted through the American labor market for five years between 1926 and 1931. He logged time in Eastern steel plants and Southern textile mills, and he also worked on an oil boat in the Canal Zone, at a California dam project, and on a Wisconsin farm. Inspired to submerge himself in the proletariat by the leftist writers Mike Gold and Joseph Freeman—the latter a close friend of earlier down-and-outers Powers Hapgood and Roger Baldwin—the doubly masked Peters described episodes from his undercover life in articles for *Harper's* and *American Mercury*.[56] In "I'm Hunting for a Job," he penned a classic undercover account of hunger, insecurity, and the contradictions of industrial labor: Peering through padlocked gates of a New Orleans Ford plant "into the twilight of the factory," he and his fellow outcasts—the jobless "we" constructed by Whiting Williams and so many others—felt "like convicts waiting for a cell. Still we were all anxious to get in." In these texts, Peters distanced himself from the abstractions of New York communism, as Charles Walker had done in his undercover novel *Bread and Fire*. Peters declared himself to be unsentimental about workers, disdaining the "grandeur which the *New Masses* exhales about them like a cloud of gold." But despite the tough-talking front, he still unearthed heroism among the poor. The next paragraph found him quoting Walt Whitman, laureate of the interwar literary left, on the " 'strong uneducated persons' " who—for Peters, too—were the "flower of the nation."[57]

By the article's end, the penniless and desperate narrator had fallen back on exploiting personal contacts and presenting himself to men of influence as a "promising young writer," which netted him a job on the New Orleans docks as a freight checker. Peters would have his greatest impact by channeling his undercover experiences among the black dockworkers into a successful play about Southern racial tensions and labor organizing. In the article "Dockwallopers," which appeared in the *American Mercury* in 1930, Peters first explored the material that he would reshape by 1934 into *Stevedore*. The article introduced most of the African American dockworkers who would appear in the play, in most cases using the same names (which presumably Peters had already changed for the article, to protect his former fellow workers).[58] Vivid scenes of the black workers joking and singing snatches of improvised blues lyrics while lounging in the sun at lunchtime, or pacing themselves with rhythmic work chants as they unloaded freight in the floodlit midnight glare, would draw much praise from critics when they were incorporated into *Stevedore*. In the article, the white narrator was ever-present to frame the scene and mediate the reader's experience. Thus, Peters describes his escape from the dull lunchtime company of the white workers in their squalid, restricted café to join his livelier black workmates and to chronicle their doings in the free air of the dock. In the play, the audience observes this scene directly, their eyes fixed on the strong black protagonist and his crew, with Peters's viewpoint quietly embedded in the script.

His viewpoint in the article was that of a left-wing, antiracist white man who worked mainly in a black world, who was happiest on days when he saw no other whites, and who congratulated himself that his coworkers eventually "almost forgot I was 'white folks.'" Reviewers of *Stevedore* would lavishly praise Peters for having brought to the stage what they took to be authentic black working-class language.[59] But the article narrator's whiteness inevitably set him apart: both as a freight checker rather than a muscle worker, and as an outsider privileged to critique and contextualize in print the racism that was rife among white management and workers. As a worker, Peters was awed by the "vital" and vigorous black bodies that surrounded him, and he acknowledged the shame of his physical weakness in a way that echoed earlier down-and-outers' feelings of intimidation in the face of (traditionally white) working-class physicality and competence. But Peters's descriptions also recalled Alvan Sanborn celebrating his fellow bums' intelligence and creativity: It was not just the dockwallopers' physical dominance, but also their ability to "lash each other with their wit," that impressed and delighted Peters. By contrast, the "cheap and small" whites on the wharf guffawed at the blackface comedians Amos and Andy but remained deaf to "the real Negro wit everywhere about them."[60]

Just when such constructions bordered on minstrel-show essentialism, Peters drew back to insist that the vast popular literature on the "'elemental joy of the African'" amounted to nothing but "volumes of tripe." Black vitality, he argued, grew from the fact that those relegated to the bottommost layer of the social heap had no reason to embrace the "putrid national lies" about opportunity, and no alternative to authenticity: "Here is one man forced to be himself." For Peters, racial distinctiveness was ultimately grounded in class position, and the story of the dockworkers was a story of how capitalists exploited racial divisions to achieve class victories. There had once been a union on the wharf, but in Peters's telling, racist white workers had collaborated with management in the name of a spurious white solidarity to ensure that blacks would remain the cheapest of cheap labor. Peters related this unhappy history near the end of his article.[61] With the help of his coauthor, George Sklar, he wrote a new dénouement to that history's most recent chapter—to the racial and class standoff depicted by "Dockwallopers"—in *Stevedore*'s triumphalist narrative of black and white workers uniting and fighting.

In response to the Depression, the early 1930s saw the emergence of a lively left-wing theater movement that would take various organizational forms throughout the decade. As the Marxist playwright John Howard Lawson wrote in 1934, the 1933–1934 season had seen "the first flowering of revolutionary plays." Lawson especially praised the three offerings from the left-wing Theatre Union, which presented radical politics in sophisticated, professional productions. Most successful among these three, both with the critics and at the box office, was *Stevedore*, which powerfully combined the characteristic communist emphases on labor organization and racial justice.[62] In developing *Stevedore*, Peters drew together his longtime interests in race and labor. As he demonstrated in an interview with the *Daily Worker*,

he commanded an extensive knowledge of the history of interracial organizing since the 1880s. He put that knowledge to use by modeling particular
events in the play on aspects of the 1917 and 1919 riots in East St. Louis and
Chicago, the latter of which he had witnessed while studying at the University of Chicago. Peters also had considerable experience working within left-
wing interracial circles. After his stint on the docks, he served for a year as
the publicity director for the International Labor Defense at the Scottsboro
trial in Alabama, writing a series of dispatches to the *Daily Worker*. In the
resulting pamphlet, *8 Who Lie in the Death House* (1933), Peters described
the defendants not as fearsome racial others, but as young men riding the
rails in search of work—a world about which he knew something.[63]

Building on historical sources and his own experiences, Peters drafted a
play that he initially called *Wharf Nigger*. The Theatre Union rejected the
play on the ground that it overemphasized the race issue at the expense
of a Marxist focus on class—an odd criticism, given that class had hardly
been a missing category in "Dockwallopers." But the veteran down-and-
outer Charles Rumford Walker—like Peters, a founder of the Theatre Union
and an aspiring playwright—saw the play's potential, and Walker enlisted
the writer George Sklar to collaborate with Peters on improving the work's
structure and sharpening its class politics. The two worked well together and
cowrote what the director-producer John Houseman later remembered as
one of "the thrilling theatrical events" of the 1930s. Thus Paul Peters realized,
far more fully than Charles Walker ever did, the latter's ambition to turn
undercover experiences into politicized art. Fittingly, *Stevedore* was dedicated to Charles Rumford Walker, without whom "there could have been no
Theatre Union"—and likely no *Stevedore* either.[64] The play opened at New
York's Civic Repertory Theatre on April 18, 1934.

Stevedore was an act of revolutionary imagination, a rewriting and an
extension of the history that Peters had studied and whose results he had
observed firsthand while undercover on the docks. In the play, past defeats
and present oppression have rendered the characters introduced in "Dockwallopers" variously wary, cynical, detached, and hopeless. For political and
dramatic purposes, the playwrights add two new figures: Lonnie Thompson,
a militant African American stevedore interested in unionization, and his
acquaintance Lem Morris, a white radical union organizer. Fusing class with
race issues, the authors use the timeworn device of an accusation that Lonnie
has raped a white woman to introduce motion into the static situation that
Peters originally chronicled. The bosses frame Lonnie for the rape and launch
an armed attack on the black neighborhood; hired thugs and a swelling racist mob, bent on lynching the fugitive, take over the streets. The assault is

intended both to stanch the threat of interracial unionization and to remind those blacks who survive the lynching-bee of their proper place in the local hierarchy. But the black dockworkers and their community shake off the pre-scribed role of passive victims and fight back against the mob, in concert with Morris's white union men, who arrive like the cavalry to help defend the barricaded black neighborhood. Lonnie is martyred, but his resilient friend Blacksnake takes up the torch and leads the rout of the thugs as the curtain falls. In his 1929 "Cotton Mill" article, Paul Peters had contemplated a revolt by exploited white Appalachian workers; he had made far more vivid and consequential use of his experiences when he reimagined the future of his black coworkers in "Dockwallopers."

In its electrifying effect on audiences, *Stevedore* restaged Peters's earlier boundary crossings in multiple ways. The Theatre Union had challenged Broadway's class barriers and invited in a working-class audience by keeping ticket prices low and by selling discounted blocks to unions, peace groups, and political, cultural, and fraternal organizations. African Americans from across New York and its environs turned out to see many of the day's best black actors playing parts and speaking lines that had almost never been seen or heard on the American stage. Black actors were paid and treated on an equal basis with whites, and blacks were seated throughout the theater, in defiance of the segregated seating that prevailed on Broadway. The line between the real and the theatrical also eroded at performances of *Stevedore*; audience members of both races were noisily demonstrative, and the tradi-tional distinction between actors and audience weakened. The results were explosive. In laudatory reviews, the *New York Times* and the *Nation* called the play "April's liveliest theatrical bomb" and "an incitement to riot of the very first order." As Mike Gold described one performance, the heightening tension during the final scene nearly impelled the viewer "to climb over the footlights" and join the struggle. In a famously dramatic moment during one performance, as the racist mob began its final assault on the black neigh-borhood's protective barricade, a black audience member leapt from his sec-ond-row seat, charged onto the stage shouting "Let's get 'em!" and joined the fray, hurling bricks at the attacking thugs. He turned out to be Bill "Bojan-gles" Robinson, the famous tap dancer, who later said he had "no conscious notion" of what he had done, but he nonetheless took a curtain call with an elated cast. A comparable event occurred in Seattle when a 1936 production by the Federal Theatre Project's Negro Unit coincided with a longshoremen's strike, and union members charged the stage to help build the barricade.[65] Performance merged with reality in these left-wing theatrical spaces. It was only appropriate that *Stevedore*—the product of an investigator's boundary transgressions, and the vehicle for radical assaults on racial and class lines—should instigate its viewers to cross normally insurmountable barriers. Michael Denning has argued that the left-wing theater established a model for artists' collective engagement with social issues; it certainly carried Paul Peters beyond the isolation of undercover labor, and beyond the limited audiences of small magazines.[66] From such beginnings, Peters forged experience into popular art.

Stevedore was a substantial hit with audiences and critics, with 175 performances in New York before moving on to Philadelphia, Washington, Chicago, Detroit, and eventually London, where Paul Robeson played the role of Lonnie. George Sklar argued that the play re-legitimized an older tradition of socially critical theater for the 1930s. Its success encouraged Harlem intellectuals, artists, and *Stevedore* actors to found the Negro People's Theatre in 1935 and, in 1937, Langston Hughes's Suitcase Theatre, in which Paul Peters was a collaborator. As the play continued its run, Peters defended *Stevedore* against the complaint by some "bourgeois critics" that it was "melodramatic": What he and Sklar had portrayed, Peters insisted, was simply reality. With a confidence grounded in the authority of his undercover experiences, Peters could attest that the struggle to survive was rife with such "melodramatic" elements as clubbings, beatings, and occasional acts of heroic resistance. Indeed, he argued, the recent battle of an interracial group of unionized sharecroppers against sheriffs seeking to seize their mules proved "the authenticity" of *Stevedore*'s final act.[67]

In general, however, reviewers were full of praise for the play's fresh characterizations and subject matter, lively pacing, and above all, its tang of reality. Mike Gold must have seen in *Stevedore* the fruit of his advice that writers submerge themselves in the proletariat—advice that Peters had followed to the letter. Brooks Atkinson of the *New York Times* wrote that Peters's "roving career in the ranks of labor reads like a modern odyssey" and gave his work "a ring of authenticity." Variants of "real," "factual," and "authentic" appeared as laudatory terms in the mainstream *Times*, the liberal *Survey Graphic*, and the radical *New Masses* and *New Theatre*. To Mike Gold, although the dialogue sometimes lapsed into a drab "photographic realism," the work chants that Peters had brought from the wharf were the stuff of a new proletarian poetry. To Atkinson, the author of the lunchtime dock scene necessarily "had been there and had relished what it represents in the elemental saga of the Negro race."[68] *Stevedore* had written an end to what Gold called the "stale Belasco realism" of the bourgeois stage. To have seen this play, he effused, would be "something to tell your Soviet grandchildren."[69]

Much of what critics found distinctive and appealing about *Stevedore* lay less in its politics than in its exploration of what Chicago sociologists would have called culture. Although the word did not appear in Peters's writings, he was in fact exploring the intersections between class (as a connection to the means of production) and culture (as a set of everyday rituals and practices that invested the mechanics of life with meaning). Having spent time at the University of Chicago, Peters may have imbibed the conventional anthropological idea that culture was particularly embedded in language, and it was especially his rendition of the black workers' highly expressive language that impressed critics. But black and white critics did not necessarily register their praise in the same key. J. A. Rogers, a black critic, persuaded by the play's call for interracial labor unity, wrote in the *New York Amsterdam News* that "for the first time, Negroes are given the opportunity on stage to talk back to white people and say what's on their minds."[70] These characters spoke a language that grew from their material circumstances, and that expressed their experiences and concerns.

White critics, on the other hand, tended to see the language, and black culture in general, as the natural products of an essential Negro character. Peters had sharply distanced himself in "Dockwallopers" from essentialist and primitivist constructions of African Americans' supposed "nature," but reviewers of the play commonly wrote of the black actors' "exoticism and strangeness"; of their "directness, credulity, and simplicity"; and of the white director's wise decision to leave these "lively instrument[s]" "unconfused" by excessive direction or "discipline." More generally, critics were wont to mention the race's "good nature and simple humanity," characteristic "animal enthusiasm," and general inclination toward a state of mindlessly jocular "ecstasy."[71] For the *Times*' Atkinson, it was Peters's special virtue to have captured these native qualities for the stage. But for Peters, the glimpses that the play afforded of African American culture—the religious rituals that follow a man's murder by the mob, or the workers' gatherings in Binnie's restaurant to joust, joke, argue about unionizing, and plan the next move—showed how men and women, when relegated by color and class to society's bottom layer, adjusted themselves to the working life and its limits. Marxist critics such as Granville Hicks and Eugene Gordon praised the play for thus connecting class with race and with what could be called culture; to most other white critics, *Stevedore* was mainly about who the dockwallopers seemed to be, rather than about what they did.[72]

Whatever the playwrights' intent, many critics essentialized race and downplayed class dynamics in much the same way that earlier down-and-outers and their commentators had often essentialized class, while largely ignoring questions of racial equality. Yet there were also hints—both from Peters and from the critics—that crossing the class line might connect in new ways to crossing the race line. The Peters of "Dockwallopers" had liked to believe that his fellow workers could almost forget that he was white: By working in isolation from other whites, he could almost become black. The *Saturday Review* suggested that the playwrights had realized this hope aesthetically, observing that Peters and Sklar had actually managed to think like blacks when writing for black actors, so that "the beneficent influence of the Negroes" had "warmed the lines" they produced.[73] Something new was afoot. African American writers had often explored the dynamics of racial passing from their side of the line, but for white writers and critics to imagine appropriating blackness in a context other than minstrelsy was less common.[74] The Theatre Union's priority on class over race notwithstanding, Peters's experiment in crossing the class line to speak for the racial other, and the resultant play's enthusiastic reception, marked a moment in the rise of race to greater prominence in American social thought and politics. The same incipient shift was visible in the greater notice of race taken by other Depression down-and-outers such as Thomas Minehan and Maury Maverick. Even during a decade when social class seemed to be the preeminent and unavoidable issue, Peters participated in the intellectual and cultural shift that would eventually de-emphasize class in favor of race as the key analytic for American society. By 1960, one outcome of that shift would be a decline in white people who passed as poor, as well as the rise to public attention of a white man who passed as black.

Sullivan's Travels: Make 'Em Laugh?

Marxist drama was not the only vehicle that brought undercover images to the Depression-era public. In January 1942, as the nation's focus shifted from the Depression to World War II, Paramount Pictures released *Sullivan's Travels*, a movie that seems to participate in the down-and-out discourse while simultaneously mocking its pretensions and denying its validity. The contradictions singled out for lampooning by the writer and director, Preston Sturges, were typical of the undercover tradition, although Sturges chose to frame them as unique to this project's plot: as problems of art, not of theory and politics. Like other undercover Depression texts, *Sullivan's Travels* was internally riven. It presents grim portraits of poverty, identity slippage, and national disaster; at the same time, it offers a reassuring narrative of hope for American middle-class identity and national prospects.

Sullivan's Travels concerns the Hollywood director John L. Sullivan's decision to renounce the fluffy comedies that made his reputation (*Hey, Hey in the Hayloft*; *Ants in Your Plants of 1939*) in order to make a hard-hitting, socially significant picture about the desperate poverty that afflicts so many Americans in the 1930s. Against the strenuous objections of his studio bosses and his butler, Sullivan determines to pass as a tramp in order to research the movie. By stepping off from his lifelong path of privilege, he will get to know what "trouble" really is. Like previous undercover social scientists and writers, he will explore the "sociological" as well as the "artistic" possibilities of a medium. The picture is to be called *O Brother, Where Art Thou*, adapted from a novel by one Sinclair Beckstein: a name obviously compounded from those of socially significant authors Upton Sinclair and John Steinbeck, both of whom worked at the margins of undercover investigation when writing their best-known novels.[75] Sullivan, played with stolid earnestness by Joel McCrea, meets and travels with a would-be starlet known only as "the Girl" (Veronica Lake). Together, they endure the down-and-out experiences that had been written about by so many before them—riding in jolting boxcars, choking down mission food, sleeping in packed and reeking flophouses—many details of which are presented with what seems like considerable fidelity to the earlier written texts. When Sullivan thinks he "knows enough," he makes a final tour through the slums, munificently distributing cash to the astonished transients—one of whom knocks him on the head, steals his money, and shoves him into a departing freight car. This incident and the ensuing scenes realize earlier investigators' worst fears about going native. Awakening in a Southern freightyard, Sullivan is stricken with temporary amnesia; his condition recalls the "trancelike state" that Sutherland and Locke's beaten men often developed when beginning a descent into shelterization. Sullivan is brutally handled by a tough yard man, recalling one of Minehan's young tramps who similarly "folds up like a camp chair" when slugged by a police detective. Sullivan fights back, but he winds up in a prison camp straight out of *I Am a Fugitive from a Chain Gang* (1932), a picture that Sturges screened while working on *Sullivan*.[76]

When the convicts are invited to attend a "picture show"—a Disney cartoon—at a nearby African American church, Sullivan finds himself laughing uproariously along with the rest of the audience. The moment prompts a conversion experience, and Sullivan comes to comprehend his true vocation. After getting himself released and returning to Hollywood, Sullivan announces that he now believes light comedies to be more therapeutic for anxious audiences than social realism. He abandons *O Brother, Where Art Thou* in favor of another installment of what is now becoming the *Ants in your Plants* franchise. In the movie's final moments, Sullivan observes that "there's a lot to be said for making people laugh. . . . It isn't much, but it's better than nothing in this cockeyed caravan." As the film closes, a montage of laughing Americans of all classes and types, backed by swelling symphonic music and booming tympani, frames the bemused visages of Sullivan and the Girl. The message, as one of Sullivan's producers has earlier insisted, is that movies should not "stink with messages."

Since its release, *Sullivan's Travels* has perplexed both critics and historians. Because it interweaves witty verbal comedy, slapstick, and romance with elements of the thriller and the 1930s social drama, the movie's content can seem seriously at odds with its message. One critic found it nightmarish and "literally incomprehensible."[77] What could be called the "face value" interpretation of the picture started with Sturges himself and relies on the fact that, as Hollywood's first true writer-director of talking pictures, Sturges exercised complete control over the production. He saw himself as what later critics would call an "auteur," and he is seen that way by those who hold the face-value view: Sturges authored the picture, and it everywhere expresses his stated intentions. Sturges laid the basis for this view well after the fact, in the 1959 manuscript for his posthumously published 1990 autobiography: "After I saw a couple of pictures put out by some of my fellow comedy-directors [Frank Capra and Leo McCarey, for example] which seemed to have abandoned the fun in favor of the message, I wrote *Sullivan's Travels* to satisfy an urge to tell them that they were getting a little too deep-dish; to leave the preaching to the preachers."[78]

This literalistic view has been perpetuated by many commentators, and it commonly leads to the criticism that the movie is "politically evasive."[79] *Sullivan's Travels* does pull back from Sullivan's social-realist project and presents itself as a self-consciously intertextual comedy: a Hollywood movie about making Hollywood movies, with a somewhat strained happy ending. But to acknowledge this does not exhaust the film's potential meanings. Embedded in the picture are many suggestions—both verbal and visual— that it participates in a more serious discourse that goes beyond Hollywood talking about itself.

A different reading of the film starts with Morris Dickstein's argument that 1930s popular culture was not reducible to "escapism": The impulses to confront and to escape were linked, and "mere entertainment" was very often, and necessarily, about "real life."[80] Much of the complexity and appeal of *Sullivan's Travels* arise from its many connections, if not exactly to "reality," then at least to other discursive forms beyond Hollywood that did assert such a connection. Those forms included texts arising from the Depression-era documentary impulse (reportage, photographs, fiction, movies), which prominently featured representations of class slippage and poverty, as well as the downward-mobility narratives that so commonly appeared in popular periodicals. Further, the plot of *Sullivan's Travels* had organic links to the discourse of undercover investigation that had developed since the 1890s, and it both culminated and commented on that discourse's extension through the 1930s. While the movie may be analyzed in terms of its engagement with other, entirely unrelated genres (screwball comedy, movies about movies), it should also be analyzed in terms of its relation to the undercover discourse. Preston Sturges may have seen himself as the author of his own movies, but *Sullivan's Travels* is something more than a director's sardonic riposte to his earnest peers' deep-dish pretensions.

There were precedents in Sturges's earlier career for his decision to explore the cinematic possibilities of an undercover odyssey. He wrote an adaptation of *Imitation of Life* (1933), a best-selling novel of racial passing by the one-time down-and-outer Fannie Hurst, for the 1934 film version; little of what he wrote was ultimately used, but he clearly gave some thought to the dynamics of passing.[81] Identity switching and social mobility were also at the heart of *The Great McGinty* (1940), Sturges's debut effort as a writer-director, which followed a bum's rise from the streets to the governor's mansion and back down again. And Sturges must have been familiar with many titles from the substantial list of 1930s films that explored downward mobility, hobodom, poverty, and cross-class romance.[82]

But most strikingly, in discussions of *Sullivan's Travels* it is seldom mentioned that the list of 1930s undercover investigators apparently included Preston Sturges himself. According to the Sturges biographer Diane Jacobs, Sturges may have gotten the idea for *Sullivan's Travels* when he went undercover for two nights in the Los Angeles slums sometime in the early 1930s. With his Hollywood friends John Huston and William Wyler, who were researching a movie about young transients in the Depression, Sturges prowled the hobo districts and slept in a flophouse. Jacobs cites this experience as evidence of Sturges's lifelong concern about poverty and the poor, despite his pose of detached cynicism on political matters.[83] So there may after all have been something of the earnest wanderer John Sullivan in Preston Sturges. The best evidence for this may lie in the movie itself, and especially in the stunning seven-minute silent sequence—a remarkable intrusion into a typical Sturges talkfest—in which the camera follows Sullivan and the Girl through slums, breadlines, and flophouses. Audiences see the protagonists showering with caustic soap in a mission fumigation room, a sign encouraging inmates to write to their mothers, a midnight mission preacher haranguing an exhausted congregation, Sullivan losing his shoes to a thief while the two sleep packed in a press of bodies on the mission floor, a shoe that may contain a severed foot falling by the railroad

tracks: All of these were standard images in down-and-out books and articles, which bespeak either Sturges's familiarity with the genre or a careful
observer's eye—if not both.

That Sturges had a brief down-and-out experience helps to locate the
movie in connection with the undercover tradition, and to account for
some of its specific features—including the much-debated ending. Sturges
acknowledged reviewers' dissatisfaction with the ending, and he framed it
as an artistic failure: "I didn't know how to solve the problem, which was not
only to show what Sullivan learned, but also to tie up the love story."[84] But the
film's primary contradiction is not between "what Sullivan learned" (about
the importance of comedy) and the love story. Rather, the central contradiction is the juxtaposition of stark realism through much of the picture against
the forced comedic ending. This shows something more than the director's
failure to resolve a narrative problem. It also mirrors the form of the 1930s
down-and-out discourse, whose texts shared a similar structure of crisis and
resolution whether they were produced by a novelist, a magazine writer, or
a sociologist. All such authors shocked their readers by confronting them
with "the facts," with a reality so horrifying that it seemed unlikely to admit
of any positive outcome. Yet because these were personal narratives, they
simultaneously reassured the audience by confirming that the investigator
did not go native, did not become permanently shelterized, and had made it
back to write the book that was spread across the reader's lap. Further, writers such as Thomas Minehan and Maury Maverick also returned to join the
state apparatus—the Minnesota welfare bureaucracy, the U.S. Congress—
which would, at least in theory, actually do something about the situation.
Ultimately, these texts suggested, the crisis would be resolved and America
would survive. Perhaps, as that final scene of *Sullivan's Travels* promises, it
would even laugh again. The movie may be read, then, as both participating
in and commenting on the undercover tradition.

When Sullivan tells his producers that he wants to realize film's potential as a "sociological and artistic medium," he echoes Thomas Minehan's
1934 call for a "new technique" in sociology "that unites scientific and literary methods." Minehan found that truth stubbornly refused to emerge from
conventional case histories, and he argued that by living with tramps for two
years "under conditions of social equality," he had transcended the incom-
plete and finally "untrue" nature of mere statistics. Similarly, the sociologist Theodore Caplow insisted in 1940 that his undercover sojourn among
tramps produced reliable knowledge, and he claimed that he found it unnecessary to revise the original draft of his study even after consulting the "available statistics." The very nature of social science was at issue: For Minehan,

to truly explore American poverty, "an artist—not a scientist—was needed."[85] John Sullivan may not have been that artist. But perhaps Preston Sturges was.

Sturges presents his movie to the audience as a book. It begins with an image of hands unwrapping a package, revealing a book's cover that reads "*Sullivan's Travels*, by Preston Sturges." The book is illustrated with a picture of Sullivan and the Girl towering over the suffering masses, evoking Gulliver among the Lilliputians. Sturges may have chosen this opening because he was angry at having been denied story credit for his previous project, *The Lady Eve* (1941); thus he was probably trying to emphasize his authorship.[86] But *Sullivan's Travels* is also a movie about making a book into a movie, as well as a movie that routinely disparages the authority of books. The putative author of *O Brother, Where Art Thou?* is Sinclair Beckstein, a joke that depends on the audience's familiarity with two established authors whose books are made to seem earnestly pretentious. Sturges complained in his autobiography that his mother had subjected him to an overly rich diet of high culture, and he claimed to delight in the fact that "the writer-director never has to read anything" to do his work.[87] But if this deprecation of books and authors seems to harmonize with the movie's anti-deep-dish message, it does not comport well with the picture's substance.

In the film, it is clear that somebody has been reading. Burrows, Sullivan's butler (Robert Grieg), warns Sullivan against undertaking his adventure by eloquently criticizing the "caricaturing of the poor" by "rich people and theorists." Because "the poor know all about poverty," he contends, "only the morbid rich would find the topic glamorous." These were common criticisms of down-and-out books. Common also were Burrows's doubts that the poor would appreciate Sullivan's efforts on their behalf, and his conviction that they would rightly "resent the invasion of their privacy."[88] Further, to point out the danger of such an enterprise, he recalls a "gentleman" for whom he worked in 1912 (evoking the tradition's high tide during the Progressive Era) who went undercover and never returned. Although Burrows speaks of poverty in an impeccably upper-crust British accent, it is clear that he knows his subject firsthand. To Sullivan's comment that he seems "to have made quite a study of it," he replies, "Quite unwillingly, sir."

It would be easy to see this exchange simply as Sturges deflating Sullivan's pretensions, and it is certainly that in part. But it is also recognizably a set piece, some version of which may be found in many undercover narratives. Its purpose is to enhance the writer's authority to speak of the other by forcing him or her to strive for a higher level of methodological self-consciousness. The encounter usually takes one of two forms: Either a friend or acquaintance—often someone from the lower class—warns the investigator, or the latter engages in an internal debate.[89] Most down-and-out writers were far from naïve about their undertaking; rather, they commonly asked themselves what it meant to go undercover, what they could truly learn, how fully they could inhabit a working-class identity, and what dangers they might face. The movie evinces such self-consciousness, both in its comical and condescending view of Sullivan's efforts to shed his privileges—he is relentlessly drawn back to Hollywood during his first, failed efforts to get on the road—and also in the serious documentary and going-native narratives within the film. Burrows's speech is well constructed to provoke a similar self-consciousness in the viewer, who might leave the theater laughing but is still unable to suppress those images of hunger, fear, and violence that also run through the movie.

Burrows's warning fails to deter Sullivan, who comments to his valet (Eric Blore) that the butler tends to get "gruesome." The valet attributes this quality to the fact that Burrows is "always reading books, sir"—a comment made with an obvious distaste for the practice. Burrows is someone, then, who has been poor and who knows the undercover tradition—by the experience of his former employer, and by having read books—and, for those reasons, he strongly distrusts it. This theme of books' unreliability recurs throughout the film. When Sullivan first takes to the road, another character asks why, if he wants to learn about poverty, does he not just read a book? As we know, as Burrows knows, and as Sturges probably knew, there was a long list of books available that had already used Sullivan's method to seek the same sort of knowledge. But the movie's concluding message against messages seems to deny the usefulness of such knowledge, especially as embodied in books. Movies that make audiences laugh are said to be more useful than books or movies that try to represent reality. And yet traces of the written discourse that preceded *Sullivan's Travels* continue to surface within the movie.

Sullivan's Travels is full of visual and narrative elements that show a solid knowledge of hobo life and language. Sturges's script specifies that the crowd of transients joined by Sullivan and the Girl should include men of "all nationalities, including Chinese, Filipino and Negro," like the groups that Maury Maverick and Herbert McCanlies observed in their travels.[90] The script directions are sprinkled with hobo lingo of the sort contained in the lexicons appended to undercover articles: an experienced hobo who hops a freight car "flips on board expertly,"[91] the language showing Sturges's familiarity with the term "to flip" (or catch) a freight. More subtly, the homosexual liaisons between men and boys, which had long been documented by undercover authors, are suggested visually by the scenes of growing intimacy between Sullivan and the short, boyishly attired Girl. Cross-dressing female hoboes had been chronicled by Minehan and dramatized in *Wild Boys of the Road*, but Sturges staged his couple in ways that heightened the sense of sexual ambiguity. Veronica Lake was known for her blond tresses and peek-a-boo bangs, and in nonhobo scenes her hair and her femininity burst forth in dazzling display. But in hobo drag, she covers what *Life* called her "celebrated hair" with a boy's confining cap. Shot from behind, arm in arm before a glittering moonlit river, Sullivan and the Girl manage simultaneously to evoke Dick Powell and Joan Blondell about to break into song, as well as a jocker caressing his punk.[92] More sinister is the way Sturges flavors hobo otherness with a hint of homosexuality: When a pair of grizzled trainhoppers dismiss the protagonists as "amateurs" on observing their incompetent efforts to flip their freight car, the Girl then observes that they make a "very interesting couple." The hoboes quit the car in disgust over the unwanted company, but it is one of these apparent degenerates who later assaults and robs Sullivan after a harrowing nighttime pursuit sequence. Such scenes evoke subtextually the fears raised by Minehan's and others' work about the Depression's unsettling of gender and sexual norms.

Sullivan's Travels dramatizes numerous other elements familiar from the down-and-out discourse. The movie is unflinching about the brutal class violence often witnessed and sometimes experienced by undercover investigators, as when Sullivan is shoved and hit from behind by the railroad yard man, and then arbitrarily beaten and remanded to the "sweat-box" by the prison warden. Anxieties about identity slippage and permanent disappearance into the social pit are vividly represented in the prison scenes: in the other cons' dismissive laughter, punctuated by a blow from the warden's blackjack, when Sullivan asserts his "rights"; and in his efforts to convince a skeptical con that he is really a "famous movie director" and therefore not properly subject to imprisonment. Racial issues, which received considerable attention in the down-and-out discourse of the 1930s, are also strikingly conveyed in the movie. Racist stereotyping of a black cook in an early slapstick segment contrasts sharply with the dignified portrayal of a black minister and his congregation during the prison sequence near the end. Sturges constructs a scene more paradoxical and poignant than anything Sullivan might have accomplished in making *O Brother, Where Art Thou* when he shows lines of shackled prisoners, most of them white, shuffling into the fog-enshrouded church while the congregation sings "Let My People Go." The stately song's evocation of unjust servitude and hope for liberation resonates behind dramatic images of solemn-faced convicts and the foregrounded sounds of clanking leg irons, with Sullivan's presence reduced to a brief shot as he seats himself. When the minister admonishes his congregation not to "act high-toned" before these "neighbors less fortunate than ourselves"—to remember that all are "equal in the sight of God"—Sturges's symbolic inversion of conventional race and power relations could hardly have been lost on audiences.[93] It was here that *Sullivan's Travels* made its most subversive comment on the state of American society.

A consideration of the picture's conclusion raises again the questions of how this movie presents itself as a book and how it functioned as a text in a larger discourse. The script directions for the final scene locate Sullivan, the Girl, the producers, and most of the other characters on an airplane flying back to Hollywood. The group is gathered around a table laden with "glasses, whiskey, cigarettes and ashtrays"; in addition, "on the table are several copies of *O Brother, Where Art Thou?*"[94] The movie thus ends as it began, with the camera focused on a book. The scene opens with a close shot of the novel, a tome that looks worthy, at least in bulk, of Sinclair or Steinbeck. Everybody is there, and as usual in a Sturges picture, everybody is talking—in effect, drowning out the book's potential voice in the conversation. As both producers clutch copies of the Beckstein volume, Sullivan announces that he will return to making comedies instead of filming *O Brother, Where Art Thou*, in part because he has not "suffered enough" and never will. This decisive moment in the movie's plot is also another convention from the down-and-out genre: Investigators typically announced near the end of their texts that they had failed to fully inhabit their adopted working-class identities; they could never truly know what Sullivan calls "trouble" because of their relatively privileged backgrounds and their indelible awareness that they could always go home again. Hence, the time had come to head back to the study and write. The reader was encouraged to admire the author's modesty, who ended by gaining greater authority to speak for and about others.

The movie bends this convention in a different direction. Not only does Sullivan abandon Beckstein's book in the name of comedy, but in a passage from the script that does not appear in the final cut of the film, he further claims reluctance to make *O Brother* because "it's already been done . . . they made it a couple of thousand years ago and I don't believe in remakes."[95] Here the director—Sullivan, Sturges, or both—affirms the original Book and disclaims any ability to match or surpass it. This may be too sanctimonious for the astringent Sturges, but not for Sullivan. Why, then, was it cut? Like the Bible, the movie's aesthetic politics affirm that the poor are always with us: They are subjects to our sympathizing gaze, but are not actors in transforming their condition. Unlike Paul Peters, Sturges possessed no ideology of transformation. As a director, he surely preferred not to return poverty and suffering to the center of the story, which might remind the audience that these were matters too serious to be laughed out of existence. This would create too much of a narrative tangle in what was already a confused ending.

The movie's conclusion wants to close the book on books as purveyors of serious information and drama; it wants to negate the discourse of which it is a part and a partial culmination. Just before Sullivan's announcement, one of the producers talks excitedly about the prospects for a book-and-movie tie-in, to feature a paperback edition with an initial press run of a million copies.[96] For a moment, the movie and its print context are seen as united. But Sullivan puts an end to that idea: There is no book without the movie. In effect, he (or Sturges) proposes to stop the discourse in its tracks, to silence the book by making a different movie. Books make people "gruesome" like the butler Burrows, and they are not to be trusted. Movies will go on, but there will be more *Ants in Your Plants* instead of hard-hitting social drama.

Still, this attempt to wrench *Sullivan's Travels* from its larger contexts and to deny the discourse in which it participated would not entirely succeed, regardless of Sullivan's proclamation and regardless of Sturges's message. A discourse does not stop because a movie director—fresh from perpetuating it—says that it should. The audience had seen the down-and-out scenes, whose power was inextricable from the broader cultural discourses on poverty and class and which made their claim based partly on those associations. Critics who disliked the ending still commented on the indelibility of those images.[97] Mildly successful in its day, the movie would come to be seen as a classic. Meanwhile, Sturges's prescription notwithstanding, undercover investigations of work and poverty continued, taking other forms in the 1940s and 1950s.

Conclusion

If class could not remain entirely unknown during the Depression, the dramatically swollen unknown class could mainly be comprehended not as a structural feature of American society, but as the by-product of a crisis that Americans would survive through their characteristic grit and resourcefulness. Down-and-outers finally did little to change this perception. Undercover sociologists did not neglect the economic origins of their subjects' troubles, but it was especially the powerfully depicted cultural dimensions of flophouse and transient life that provoked strong responses from reviewers, adding to culture's momentum as a growing emphasis in the social sciences. Despite Paul Peters's recasting of *Wharf Nigger* into *Stevedore*, the play was received and celebrated more as a racial than as a class drama. And if *Sullivan's Travels*—the principal popular representation of class passing—did confront its audiences with dramatic images of poverty and dispossession, it never asked where such conditions came from; it offered solace through shared laughter, not through hopes for structural change. As if to seal the case, the popular economist and onetime down-and-outer Stuart Chase announced in 1941 that traditional conceptions of class were obsolete. Marx's shrinking proletariat was rapidly being replaced by an expanding class of service and professional workers who were deeply imbued with a middle-class psychology. This, argued Chase, would certainly ensure the "twilight of communism in the U.S.A."[98]

On a similar note, investigators who descended into the pit of unemployment and transiency near the decade's end brought back better news than had their counterparts of the earlier thirties. E. Wight Bakke, a Yale economist whose research team used undercover methods for his eight-year study of New Haven working-class life, argued in 1940 for the existence of a distinctive working-class culture, but he rejected the degenerative implications that earlier investigators had attached to the concept. Bakke's own undercover encounters convinced him that government policies mandating adequate unemployment compensation, work relief, and direct aid would enable workers to remain "geared in" to that sustaining culture through the fraternal, political, religious, and social groups from which they derived their identities. Workers who benefited from governmental support and vigorous labor unions would not decline from individualism into dependency; rather, they would participate in advancing a broader cultural transition "from individual to collective self-reliance."[99]

The mixture of fear and fascination about hobo life that had been heightened by the Depression also showed signs of waning. Reporting on his 1939 hobo trek around the United States, Theodore Caplow corroborated other recent studies' assertions that because of governmental and social agencies' efforts, along with improving economic prospects, child tramps and female transients of all ages had nearly disappeared from the road. Having dampened the social anxieties about gender, youth, and family that had especially been spurred by Minehan's earlier work, Caplow went on to frame the hobo's world in cultural terms that were functional rather than degenerative, as with Bakke's analysis of more settled working-class cultures. Caplow normalized the adult male hobo as a traveling worker belonging to a loosely organized vagabond culture. Uprooted by a combination of economic conditions and wanderlust, he was not inherently antagonistic toward organized society and was usually expected to re-enter it soon. Caplow did portray his fellow hoboes as hostile toward coercive social institutions, such as the police and the Salvation Army, and as waging "open warfare" against railroad cops. But far from being pathological degenerates, they were participants in an alternative "cultural pattern" that might someday be recognized as "an expected phase" in the lives of younger Americans, as transiency was already understood in some European countries.[100]

Thus down-and-out investigators did their part to enact the rituals of reassurance that especially characterized the end of the Depression decade. Disturbing images of class instability and cultural degeneration that had typified investigators' reports during the early years of the slump were increasingly displaced by reassuring portrayals of working-class cultural adaptation, the naturalization and decline of transiency, and, in the case of *Sullivan's Travels*, the transcendence through mass culture of poverty's stubborn material realities. None of these newer images entirely effaced those of the early 1930s, as the nation did not return to full employment until well into the war. But however terrible had been the poverty and dispossession uncovered by Depression-era investigators, those images could increasingly be understood as the results of a world only temporarily turned upside down, and not as the inevitable outcomes of a pernicious class system. A wartime culture would further consolidate images of class solidarity and stability, as massive industrial mobilization opened new paths to the undercover investigator.

PART III

The Declining Significance of Class, 1941–1961

4

War and Peace, Class and Culture

"Good-bye, white collar," jauntily proclaimed the former car salesman Alan McCone in a 1942 *American Magazine* article that described his metamorphosis into a boilermaker's helper at a Sun Oil refinery.[1] World War II provoked a new variation on the 1930s downward-mobility narrative, now refigured as an invigorating, patriotic plunge into a realm of hardening muscles, honest sweat, and national service. A few curious adventurers took that plunge for undercover investigative purposes. But with the return of peace and rising postwar prosperity in the later 1940s and 1950s, the number of classic undercover investigations declined. The worlds of skid row, hobohemia, and itinerant labor that had nourished them were shrinking. Industry could have provided fertile ground, and some anthropologists and sociologists continued to argue in favor of the undercover technique. But it is clear from this period's methodological treatises that scientific objectivism was pushing subjectivist approaches out to the disciplines' margins, where they were viewed with growing skepticism. In addition, from the 1950s through the century's end, periodic crises over professional ethics would increasingly delegitimize deceptive research practices. Finally, the central concerns of social science were also shifting decisively away from a real if limited Depression-era emphasis on class—a term to be avoided in the era of Cold War American exceptionalism—and toward race and culture. For journalists and academics, from the Depression's end to the sixties' dawning, class passing persisted even as it ebbed. Ultimately, its practitioners turned their method toward crossing a different set of boundaries.

War: Muscle, Sweat, and Rejuvenation

Because the wartime influx of female workers into previously inaccessible industrial jobs was a subject of great social concern, it provoked the era's most notable examples of undercover investigation. Lucy Greenbaum, a journalist, got "the feminine score" on war work by riveting fighter-plane panels in a Curtiss-Wright factory in Buffalo, New York, while Augusta Clawson, a vocational-education teacher, worked as a welder in a Portland, Oregon, shipyard where she also secretly investigated women workers' training and job conditions for the U.S. Office of Education. Elizabeth Hawes, a left-wing fashion designer, closed her business in order to grind gears in a Ridgewood, New Jersey, aircraft plant where she hoped to meet the "common woman," but she proved to be too well known to maintain her cover. Hawes wrote a book chronicling her experiences, as did several other women workers who did not operate clandestinely but who did want to tell their stories. These texts constituted examples of what Michael Denning has called the "laboring of American culture," being rife with images of honorable and dignified physical labor; of eroding gender, ethnic, and racial barriers; and of patriotic self-denial in service to reform at home and to antifascism abroad.[2] Like her earliest undercover predecessors, Lucy Greenbaum was initially shaken by the harshly lit factory's steady glare as she approached it through the early-morning darkness, but she soon found that "life pulsed" amid the "mechanized bedlam" inside.[3] When Greenbaum and her contemporaries ventured across the class line, they carried forward themes emphasized by many of their counterparts from the last years of the Depression; in wartime labor, they found resources for the reinvigoration and reconstitution of personal, class, gender, and national identities.

Although most of these writers thought of war work as temporary, many registered what felt like permanent changes in their personal and class identities. After a few days' work and some initial missteps, Greenbaum styled herself "an old hand" at riveting and a proud contributor to the war effort. Similarly, Clawson was happy to be a "cog" in the war machine and was loath to leave what had become her real life—her job and coworkers—even for a few days' respite to present a report on her investigation.[4] Embracing the Spartan simplicity that had long been a way of life for her proletarian sisters, she learned to relish the raw cabbage shared by a friend at lunchtime. When she dressed up for dinner, Clawson felt herself to be "masquerading as a lady," but she felt herself again when "back in [a welder's] leathers." Alan McCone found that having slipped the "shackle" of white-collar work, he aspired to a new symbol of class success: not being elected to a board of directors, but rising to boilermaker, second class.[5] Elizabeth Hawes concluded that every citizen should work for six months in a factory to learn the virtues of cooperation and collective organization; such sojourners might also be expected to recognize, as Hawes and Clawson did, both the pleasures of machines and the value of labor unions.[6]

Less positively, changing class identities also rendered down-and-outers susceptible to the sting of class snobbery. Clawson suffered the disapproving stares of her own hotel's desk staff, who failed to recognize her when she appeared in the lobby clad in welder's leathers. And when Elizabeth Hawes found herself in factory garb on a bus loaded with New Jersey women's clubbers on an excursion, she bridled at the ladies' disdainful glances and audible complaints that, with erstwhile domestic workers prospering on factory wages, they might have to do their laundry themselves. Repressing the urge to punch a passenger, the disguised dress designer settled for hating them "in the name of every worker of the U.S.A."[7] Such stories of reframed class identities, whether positive or negative, were no doubt deliberately constructed to contribute to wartime discourses of self-sacrifice and patriotism. But as in all undercover texts, the experiences described had their own existential reality and cannot be entirely discounted.

Transformations of gender identity enacted through wartime class shifting could also be striking. Alan McCone, a former college football player gone flabby after ten years of sales work and "soft living" in the suburbs, had been devastated by the sudden loss of his job during the Depression. Concealing his middle-class identity at first, McCone felt "as nervous as a debutante at her coming-out party" when he approached the factory gate wearing properly faded clothing borrowed from a mechanic acquaintance. By the story's end, he had vanquished such feminine anxieties by rebuilding his body, mastering new manual skills, and conquering his former fear of heights. Enjoying the "yeasty masculine humor" of the factory and relishing his newfound membership in the workplace "fraternity" of "right guys" and "hard men," McCone also found his domestic life transformed. The onetime mechanical illiterate abandoned weekend golfing for the proletarian pleasures of rebuilding his car's engine and playing with his children: He had learned at work that even hard men had "a soft spot in their hearts" for the young ones.[8] Reconstituted as a manly husband, McCone reported that his wife bragged of his newfound mechanical prowess to her middle-class friends and that they both enjoyed the challenges of meeting a straitened family budget. McCone's *American Magazine* article sported an imposing three-quarter-page photograph of the grinning author, clad in work clothes and resting an enormous open-end wrench on his shoulder, his begrimed face bathed in light; an adjacent quotation said "I feel more like sticking out my chest and strutting than I ever have in my life." As always, the strenuous life proved an antidote to the degenerative, feminizing tug of excessive modern comforts.[9]

Women who worked undercover during the war years produced texts that interwove narratives of gender transformation and national service with countervailing subtexts of gender-role continuity and minimal long-term social change. For Augusta Clawson and Lucy Greenbaum, it was a given that women of all classes should take up factory work to alleviate wartime labor shortages, and cultural assumptions about gender and work could hardly help but be changed. However, the depth and permanency of such changes remained at best an open question. What seemed most likely to last was the investigators' common recognition that they liked working with tools and machines, contrary to stereotypes of female haplessness in industrial environments. Hawes entered the factory planning to flesh out her feminist critique of the conditions of women's employment, but she found to her surprise that the work genuinely interested her. Similarly, Greenbaum noted that once her coworkers conquered their fear of tools, they became adept and comfortable amid the "labyrinth of machines." All of the women's labor narratives were heavily larded with descriptions of machinery and of industrial processes, carrying forward the undercover discourse's tradition of introducing middle-class readers to alien worlds. In her wartime pamphlet *Mothers in Overalls*, the labor journalist Eva Lapin avowed that the war had demolished the "carefully-nurtured tradition" that women lacked mechanical aptitude.[10]

In line with their newfound comfort with industrial work, female investigators registered a developing bodily strength and confidence. After six days of welder's training and bone-deep exhaustion in the early going, Clawson reported delightedly, *"I'm getting tough!"* She quickly discovered that her muscles needed further developing for the actual work—"Too many of us women are soft"—as did her nerves, which had to be steady for work on high and precarious perches. By the end of two months in the shipyard, her muscles had developed so fully that she no longer suffered from a sore back at day's end. Proud of her sex, she scoffed at talk of women's "pettiness."

Clawson felt herself a "formidable character," as "armed with [her] chipping hammer" she strode through the predawn streets to work. A woman alone in such circumstances before the war, she reflected, would have provoked "holy horror."[11]

Yet such amazonian images were somewhat undercut by the muted but persistent stream of suggestions that the world had not so entirely changed. A reader disturbed by the thought of women wielding rivet guns might have been relieved to learn that, as one of Greenbaum's coworkers put it, their labors were not so different from " 'messing around a kitchen.'" A power drill, after all, was little more than a heavier electric eggbeater. Clawson also engaged in this tendency to domesticate the industrial workplace: "Please don't think we aren't good housekeepers," she pled on behalf of women welders; however muscled and self-confident they might become, they still scrupulously swept the floors and cleaned their benches "as if they were kitchen tables."[12] And for all of her urging that American women flock to the factories, Clawson closed her book with the cautionary note that women with children under age fourteen should think twice before donning a welder's leathers. Where the socialist feminist Hawes argued for expanded child-care facilities and other forms of support for working women, Clawson urged mothers to consider supporting the war effort through less-demanding volunteer activities. Similarly, Greenbaum suggested that neither gender nor class relations were liable to be permanently upset by the influx of women into war work. Most of her coworkers, she reported, continued to cherish "the average woman's American dream" of a "vine-covered cottage enclosing [a] white kitchen." Most of those who hoped to retain their jobs after the war came from working-class backgrounds that had formerly consigned them to lower-paid and less-secure occupations.[13] Whatever personal changes that investigators such as Clawson or Greenbaum felt, they did not tend to see their experiences as emblematic of an imminent transformation of women's roles. Still, Clawson did look forward to proudly telling a future granddaughter about the ships that she had once helped to build; but she doubted that such a granddaughter—in a brighter future, liable to be an admiral herself— would be overly impressed.[14]

If factory labor wrought changes in personal, class, and gender identities, what undercover workers and their aboveground colleagues most often highlighted was the way that war, following closely upon the Depression, seemed to be reconfiguring American national identity writ large. Lucy Greenbaum went looking for the "feminine score," but she also found a newly cross-class, panethnic, transregional image of democracy. Greenbaum toiled under the direction of a handsome and efficient Irish foreman, next to migrants from the Vermont mountains, the Dakota wheatlands, and the cotton fields of Alabama; she also recognized around her the "hardened, reality-lined faces" of Buffalo's own prewar proletarians. In her Oregon shipyard, Clawson befriended former fruit pickers, farmers, and salesmen from Texas, Colorado, and Missouri. McCone counted among his fellow workers a minister, a stockbroker, and a former gangster, as well as longtime veterans of the boilermakers' fraternity. During the Depression, such a hybrid workforce might have been seen as a sign of the times' severity, as the desperate unemployed moved anywhere and accepted any kind of job. But now it was refigured as an index of the patriotic pulling-together by all classes and groups to meet the national emergency. Nell Giles, a *Boston Globe* reporter, listed twelve different ethnic groups in her Lynn, Massachusetts, General Electric plant, concluding that she had "met America": a complex amalgam that "makes democracy a tough baby, impossible to beat."[15]

Yet if these diverse peoples were "all of them 'just plain American,'" as Giles styled them, then for most cross-class observers, to be "American" also meant to be white—a condition that remained unspoken and unmarked. From the evidence of these writers, the process chronicled by historians in which an ethnically diverse, European-descended working class gradually came to be understood as "white" was hardly complete by World War II. Josephine Miklos, a Ph.D.-educated immigrant and erstwhile commercial designer who retained her Austrian accent after a dozen years in the United States, noted that her Irish, Polish, and Lithuanian coworkers in a New England munitions plant—some of them second- and third-generation residents—were still, in the eyes of their "Yankee" neighbors, marked by the stigmata of "racial" differences. The "famous melting pot" had failed them, and only Yankees, she observed, were recognized as "Americans."[16] But if the whitening of Euro-Americans remained a work in progress, the greater divide between white and black went largely unmentioned. Augusta Clawson celebrated the "cross-section of the average American" that was forging a "real democracy" in her Oregon shipyard. But nowhere in her text or in the accompanying illustrations was an African American face to be seen, even though the Portland yards were racially integrated, and black welders, if not common, were certainly to be found.[17] On the country's other coast, Greenbaum's account was equally lacking in evidence that black workers belonged in the expanding idea of Americanness. And in Nell Giles's factory, New England African Americans were said to constitute "a big problem ahead." When a local black minister, identified less respectfully as a "Negro preacher," pressed General Electric to hire more black women, Giles describes him as "ma[king] a big fuss" about the issue, while her coworkers' first concern is that such new hires might expect to use "our toilets." Giles then asserts that surely any qualified worker would be hired, irrespective of race. Yet even the book's typeface betrays a persistent, invidious assertion of difference: When Giles refers to "Negroes" or to the "Negro preacher," the capital "N" is set in a smaller typeface that stands only as tall as a lowercase "n", in contrast to references to "Lithuanians" or "Italians." Perhaps this was Giles's decision, or perhaps an editor at Harper & Brothers decided to split the difference between an original lowercase usage by Giles and the capitalized "N" for which African Americans had long made a point of arguing.[18]

When it came to forging a democratized, cross-class, multiethnic definition of the "'just plain American'" that Clawson, Greenbaum, and Giles celebrated, "Negroes" were often defined out of the picture and across the line. Elizabeth Hawes, writing from a leftist, antiracist perspective, noted that the United States Employment Service used a single category—invidious by implication—for "Women, Negroes, and National Minority Groups." For Hawes, one task of the wartime mobilization must be to make all members of that misshapen category into true "American citizens." And investigators with antiracist aspirations did sometimes find reasons for hope. When Josephine Miklos left New England to work in a New York City shipyard, she discovered that the microcosm of "American unity" who rode her morning bus included not only people of all ethnic and class origins, but black faces as well as white ones. Miklos thus felt herself to be engaged not only in the war effort but also in a project to build a "new world" based on "big ideas" of expanding freedom.[19] Similarly, Hawes clearly recognized that cross-class encounters in wartime industrial workplaces bore some potential to remake American ideas about class, gender and race. But as she further recognized, both from her work in the aircraft plant and later for the United Auto Workers Union, the task was large and far from finished. Wartime investigators had pursued older questions about class while raising newer ones about gender, race, and national identity. As the United States entered the postwar era, social scientists who hoped to grasp the shifting nature of work, class, and poverty under new conditions would bring to bear new theoretical and methodological perspectives as they set out to explore a changing peacetime milieu.

Social Science: Objectivity and the Ethics of Deception

In 1941 and 1942, E. Wight Bakke's two-volume study of the New Haven unemployed drew a flood of glowing reviews in key social-science journals. While the study relied on a range of social-science methods, Bakke's use of the undercover technique was frequently singled out for praise: For one reviewer, Bakke had succeeded brilliantly where his predecessor Whiting Williams had achieved merely "the perversion of a good idea." The books were seen as prefiguring not only a genuine "science of human relations," but also "a unified social science." But if this reception seemed to augur a bright future for undercover investigations, the impact of Bakke's books in stimulating further such studies would prove limited.[20] Class passing would occupy an increasingly precarious position in the postwar repertoire of social-scientific research techniques. A rising ethos of scientific objectivity, a growing articulation of ethical concerns about deceptive research practices, and Cold War–inflected skepticism about class as an analytical category and about poverty as an existential fact would all combine to render such investigations less common.

The postwar career of the veteran down-and-outer and interwar radical Charles Rumford Walker proved emblematic of the turn away from class masquerade and from the critical politics that had sometimes accompanied it, toward a narrower emphasis on objectivist studies of work processes and industrial relations. When Walker returned during the 1946 steel strike to Aliquippa, Pennsylvania—the site of his 1919 undercover stint as a furnace worker—he was not dressed in hard-used clothing garnered from a secondhand store but was a respectably clad affiliate of Yale University's Institute of Human Relations and director of the Yale Technology Project, which orchestrated studies of technology's impact on work and industrial relations. In sharp contrast to his earlier experiences with union-busting bosses, brutal company police, and "maximum rabble rousing" by the barely organized workers, Walker now found a modestly prosperous, labor-friendly town where both management and the civic-minded CIO union played by well-established rules. Peaceful picketing and civil relations reigned, as the union practiced "maximum organization with a minimum of agitation" to protect the new order. In short, the conditions that had once compelled the young Walker to "enlist in steel" and explore the fierce conflicts of an emerging industrial era had apparently reached a state of relatively comfortable equilibrium. What wrinkles remained to be smoothed could be identified and addressed through the methods of objective social science and industrial relations, which Walker would deploy in the numerous workplace studies that he would author or oversee through the Yale Project over the next two decades. His 1946 article about Aliquippa, published by the social-reformist *Survey Graphic* magazine—perhaps a departing nod to his politically engaged younger years—marked the last time that Walker would refer in print to the undercover experiences that had first made him a successful writer and a radical. It seemed that the future lay down a different path.[21]

Walker's path would be a common one as class and poverty lost traction, both as intellectual categories and as public issues, in postwar America. The historian David Kennedy writes that at the end of the 1930s, almost one half of white families and almost 90 percent of black families had been poor, and one worker in seven was unemployed. Yet in a 1940 poll, the robust insistence by Americans of every condition and occupation that they were "middle class" underscored the failure of leftists and social critics, even amid Depression conditions, to establish that poverty and class division were natural and enduring products of a capitalist system. However common had been Depression-era depictions of dispossession and misery, by the late thirties, accounts of downward mobility in popular and academic discourse had with increasing frequency mutated into triumphalist tales of physical, spiritual, and national regeneration. The war then effectively ended unemployment, and twenty million new jobs were created over the next twenty-five years. What was called the middle class—measured as families with annual incomes between $3,000 and $10,000, irrespective of their effective social power—more than doubled during the postwar years, and by 1960 the category embraced nearly two-thirds of all Americans.[22]

In such an environment, many observers concluded that poverty and the working class were no longer salient categories for analyzing American society. Postwar intellectual and popular discourses evinced a distinct downplaying of these concepts, and there was an emerging sense that the term "middle class" was roughly, if not quite literally, coterminous with "American." Thus Charles Walker, who spent the rest of his career studying assembly-line workers in increasingly automated factories, was typical in his 1940 assertion that—Karl Marx to the contrary—the middle class was expanding, as the working class proportionally shrank. Sharing Walker's conviction, postwar social critics focused increasingly on various formulations of middle-class malaise—life in the lonely crowd or among the organization men—while even those writers who remained attuned to the persistence of poverty, as did the economist John Kenneth Galbraith, found it hard to mobilize reformist moral passions around an issue that resisted rising to visibility. Where were the poor, the exploited, the transient? Jack Kerouac, formerly an amateur hobo, announced in a 1960 *Holiday* article that the true American road knight had largely vanished, run out of town by prosperity and the police. As for alienated labor, most of the "men at work" profiled during the 1940s by the writer Richard Thruelsen in a chatty series for the *Saturday Evening Post* seemed cheerfully upward-bound. Characteristic was the textile operative who had rebuffed the Harvard Business School's offer of admission in order to learn his business from the bottom up. By the article's end, he had ascended from the mill floor to upper management—precisely the path that the down-and-outers Charles Walker and Whiting Williams had once set out to follow.[23] The constrictions of class and the threat of poverty ranged from rare to nonexistent in such narratives.

Class was similarly sidelined in the realm of grand theory, where the émigré philosopher Hannah Arendt's influential formulation of "totalitarianism" relegated class to history's dustbin by foregrounding the anxious and alienated individual as the totalitarian state's main target and constituent. In a postwar and post-Holocaust context, as the historian George Cotkin has argued, class was seen by Arendt and likeminded thinkers as a troubling and divisive category, and it was largely displaced by a universal "human condition" as the proper framework for understanding modernity's discontents. Leading industrial sociologists adopted such language, eschewing class and emphasizing the study of "human relations" within the limited "social system" of the factory.[24] And amid sharpening Cold War tensions, to write or speak of class divisions was to use a language associated with discredited Depression radicals and with the postwar international enemy. If class did exist, it was somewhere else. Social scientists often contrasted a rigidly class-defined Soviet Union with a U.S. society allegedly characterized by mobility and pluralism. By 1959—when one-third to one-fifth of Americans lived in poverty and another fifth verged upon it—the sociologist Robert Nisbet declared that in the West generally, and especially in the United States, "the conception of class" had become "largely obsolete."[25]

Social scientists who had recently been preoccupied by unemployment and poverty were drawn increasingly after World War II into what the historian Olivier Zunz has styled the "matrix of inquiry": a network of universities, corporations, institutes, and foundations that produced knowledge of economic and sometimes military utility, and that expanded dramatically during the booming postwar years. One project of social scientists and market researchers within that matrix was to redefine class in America to minimize issues of power and position in the productive system and to reframe individuals as members of a segmented but ever-expanding middle class who measured themselves according to status achieved through consumerism.[26] Investigators such as Whiting Williams, who had consulted for corporations and lectured at Ivy League universities in addition to writing for popular and business publications, had long operated on the margins of this matrix as it evolved over the twentieth century. Charles Walker was drawn fully into it as he grew disillusioned with the radical left in the late thirties, and he took a series of jobs at Yale during the forties, culminating with the directorship of the Technology Project. In the process, Walker distanced himself both politically and methodologically from his undercover past, adopting a depersonalized narrative voice and a language of worker-management cooperation that almost precisely echoed that of the conservative Williams. Postwar shop-floor studies proceeded within a framework of ideas about labor-management relations set by the long-developing "human relations approach," which largely triumphed among management thinkers in the forties.[27] To the extent that undercover investigation remained part of the postwar social scientist's toolkit, it was deployed less frequently as a clandestine method to expose unpleasant realities and to express political commitment, and more often in collaboration with management to improve work processes and enhance the bottom line. Increasingly over these decades, race and culture would displace class as key categories for the social sciences, while the use of undercover methods would be sharply constricted by methodological criticisms and ethical objections.

After Bakke, the most fully realized use of the undercover method during the 1940s and 1950s was by the sociologist Donald Roy, who produced a University of Chicago dissertation and, as a member of the Duke University faculty, several influential scholarly articles based on the technique. If anyone were capable of legitimizing undercover studies in the postwar era, it would have been Roy. He brought unique qualifications and an usually sympathetic perspective to the task. Having gone down-and-out in a Seattle Hooverville for his 1935 master's thesis, Roy was no stranger to the method. Disinclined to see his neighbors as alien others, he had emphasized their essential Americanness, and he depicted them as having largely escaped the debilitating effects of urban shelters that were emphasized by other Depression down-and-outers. Rather, his fellow squatters were "ragged epitomes of rugged individualism" who were creating stable communities by pioneering "many small frontiers" on the fringes of cities across a land where the original frontier had closed. Roy continued to work and wander, and by 1944, he had held some twenty low-level jobs in nineteen different industries as he meandered toward an academic life.[28] He came to rest at the University of Chicago, where his Ph.D. studies were directed by the sociologist Everett Hughes, a key figure in the "second Chicago school," who shared that group's affinity for the empirical and their skepticism toward both quantification and high theory. The wartime and postwar economic booms reintroduced opportunities for undercover factory studies of the sort pioneered by 1920s investigators such as Williams, Walker, and Stanley Mathewson, but which had largely ceased during the Depression. But when Roy hired on as a drill operator in the machine shop at Chicago's Geer Company—a steel processing plant where he worked for eleven months in 1944–1945—he was supporting both a family and his graduate studies, and he simply needed the work. It was only after the first month that he decided to make the workplace the subject of his dissertation research.[29]

Far more than factory down-and-outers of the 1920s, most of whom had been journalists, Roy adopted the scholarly concepts and tools of modern, professional social science to analyze the conditions of work, the nature of workers, and especially the common practice of restricting output—or "soldiering"—under a piecework system. As the sociologists Sutherland and Locke or Theodore Caplow had done for their flophouse and hobo studies in the thirties, Roy embedded his subjective data (anecdotes and selections from his work diary) in a conventional social-scientific framework, building an extensive ethnographic description, replete with charts and footnotes, of the factory's social relations and work culture. Roy incorporated the increasingly central concept of culture into his analysis, understanding his subjects as constituting "a distinct sub-culture."[30] But unlike many Depression-era students of road and shelter life, he did not see this broadly functionalist factory culture as fostering group degeneration. Careful to position himself positively toward the scientific ideal—like all down-and-outers, he was after the " 'cold facts' "[31]—he nonetheless identified unambiguously with his fellow workers, not with management. Unlike Williams or the early Walker, Roy's primary interest was in understanding workers' practices, not in helping management to better gain workers' loyalty. Thus, to Roy, Frederick Taylor's assertion that scientific rate-setting was "democratic," rather than arbitrary and coercive, was not only objectively mistaken but "phony"—as his coworkers knew from bitter experience.[32] At once more professional and more partisan than his predecessors, Roy represented a new merging of the old progressive emphases on science and sympathy.

Roy argued at length for the undercover method's validity, citing recent professional literature on industrial investigation and on participant observation—the term that he used to describe his method—but leaving unmentioned the earlier, less-scientific exemplars from within and beyond sociology who had often been cited by his Depression-era forebears.[33] Roy cast the dissertation as an "exploratory" study of the question "Why do factory machine operatives restrict their output?" He acknowledged that while his method could not produce ironclad scientific conclusions, it did advance a process of inquiry whose results could ultimately be subjected to an "experimental test." However slow and personally taxing the method, Roy insisted that it produced better results than the " 'quick returns' " won from conventional surveys and undisguised observation; the latter, he noted pointedly, were destined mainly for equally quick "interment in social science journals."

Roy was always capable of such slyly insubordinate gestures, but he also paid constant obeisance to the ideal of science. Conceding that his approach precluded the option of varying a single factor while holding others steady, he still asserted that its outcome would prove less "scrubby" than the results of mere "passive attentiveness to an ordered flow of preconceptions unmuddied by reality." Roy relied here on John Dewey's authority to uphold the traditional down-and-outer's pragmatic epistemology of experience as the gateway to raw reality—and also to successful publishing in those same drab professional journals.[34]

Roy was a self-described "sociological 'naturalist.'" Like Josiah Flynt on the trail of tramp specimens, he portrayed himself as an entomologist sallying forth with butterfly net in hand, stalking "restrictus vulgaris in its native haunts." But while Flynt could represent tramps as degenerating, alien others, Roy neither sentimentalized his fellow workers—they could be dishonest, arrogant, and self-seeking—nor condescended to or demonized them. Roy's long history as a laborer meant that although this job was new to him, working men were not. That he claimed to live "literally 'inside the worker's skin'" therefore seemed less forced and artificial than such self-positioning had appeared for most of his forebears. If his data were not conventionally objective, he had a talent for making them seem reliable: The undercover investigator understood " 'where the shoe pinches, because it pinches him.'"[35] Deception, then, was crucial and could even be seen as more scientific than conventional methods. Roy criticized Elton Mayo's model of combining interviews with shop-floor observation, arguing that the undercover approach precluded the distortions typically produced by an experimenter's overt presence. Workers distrusted social scientists who invaded their turf and would not always behave honestly in their presence, but the undercover sociologist who kept his mouth shut about "science"—a word that might brand him a company spy—could probably pass as just another seeker of work. The method also posed unique challenges to the outsider's identity, and Roy recognized the risk that undercover investigators might go native, lapsing into "periods of insouciant citizenship with the groups that they study." But Roy comically contrasted himself with an anthropologist lounging among his subjects on a tropical isle, threatened mainly by "palm wine hangovers"; he reminded the reader that, for the undercover sociologist, "participant observation on the production line is a euphemism for 'work.'" Failing to do the job meant abandoning both project and paycheck.[36]

Roy studied other industrial workplaces, using both undercover and overt methods, for five more years after completing his work at the Geer Company in 1945. When he submitted his dissertation in 1952, Roy burnished his scientific credentials by recording that none of the data he had gathered since his time at Geer would invalidate the results of his research there.[37] And what did that research show about the traditional down-and-outer's quarry, "the worker's mind"? Like previous down-and-outers, Roy concluded that workers' decisions about whether or not to restrict output by adhering to an informal production quota were rational and often (but not always) materially driven. Elton Mayo had been right that workers were not exclusively the self-seeking "economic man" of classical economic theory, but he had been wrong to suggest that they were afflicted by mental dullness or psychopathologies that prevented them from understanding their own interests and adjusting to their circumstances.[38] Advancing the counterdiscourse first articulated by Whiting Williams against Mayo's perspective in the 1920s, Roy argued (with a hint of perverse pleasure) that the word "primitive" described not workers' mentalities, but the inefficient and contradictory procedures that management imposed on labor. It was hardly surprising, then, that factory organization was drawing the attention of anthropologists interested in charting what Roy called a management-induced "cultural drag" in industrial relations, as opposed to a "cultural lag" that supposedly held back both management and labor from adjusting to modern technology.[39] Roy understood his workmates' repeated refrain that "this company stinks!" as he expressed a seething frustration and anger toward policies that he felt unfairly penalized him and that motivated him to work less hard, even at his own expense.[40] But Roy also discovered that workers found noneconomic reasons to work harder, rather than to slack off: sometimes as part of a solitary game or a group ritual to keep themselves occupied and stimulated; sometimes for the sheer pleasure of working fast and rhythmically; sometimes to get production out in spite of management's obstructive rules; and sometimes "just for 'the hell of it.' "[41] They did soldier to avoid rate cutting, to resist the authority of time-study men who sought to engineer their every move, or to reject an imposed ethic of wage-maximizing competitive individualism that did not comport with the hard-won recognition that their " 'station' in life ha[d] become fixed." Thus, it was workers, Roy found, who were truly rational; it was workers who demonstrated "intellectual operations in continuous reciprocal interplay with concrete experience" and who were therefore "the real holders of 'logics of efficiency.'"[42]

Against the industrial relations establishment's inclination to write off workers as nonrational, incapable beings, Roy proposed an explicitly Deweyan version of industrial democracy in which "effective communication" meant not that management directives would be mindlessly obeyed, but that workers' voices would be heeded and their experiences valued in the planning of production. Contesting both Frederick Taylor's call for an "authoritarian social structure" in the factory and Elton Mayo's prescription for top-down administration of therapeutic "medicine" to dissatisfied or unruly workers, Roy argued that production and cooperation could be maximized by the "permeating of decision making down through the lower echelons of the factory hierarchy."[43] This was also to depart significantly from Whiting Williams's model of improved worker-management communication mediated by personnel relations experts, which highlighted American-style opportunity for individual mobility through fixed hierarchies, rather than what Williams saw as a "European" emphasis on security through collective organization. Roy's undercover experiences convinced him that a genuinely "cooperative organization" of workers and managers would not only promote more efficient production, but it would also unify workers' fragmented and frustrating experiences into "wider systems of meaning within a total work life that makes sense."[44] To Donald Roy, a well-traveled worker and academic intellectual, such an outcome did not seem far-fetched.

The articles that Roy published based on his dissertation and related research were well received and influential, but they did not stimulate a new wave of undercover factory investigations. This may have been because Roy swam against the tide in two ways: His ideas did not harmonize well with developments in labor politics, and his approach diverged from scholarly trends within sociology. Regarding the politics of labor relations, Roy recommended increased workers' power on the shop floor and enhanced participation in decision making just at the historical moment when the postwar labor movement was shifting away from such demands in return for greater financial rewards and predictability of employment.[45] And in the realm of professional sociology—which was probably of greater significance to aspiring younger academics whom Roy might have influenced—many practitioners began to march under the banner of scientific objectivity and were increasingly skeptical both of critical perspectives on capitalist organization and of subjective data's utility for scholarship.[46]

On criticizing capitalism, Roy was only partly out of alignment with professional norms. He was not a Marxist and believed that labor and management could ultimately share common goals.[47] And while he did give voice to his fellow workers' frustrations about their limited life prospects, he almost never used the word "class" or advanced any larger theoretical perspective that relied on that concept. He focused mainly on work relations within the factory, and he seldom referred to conditions in the city beyond its gates.[48] Among the workers, Roy saw little evidence of class consciousness. Some cherished petit-bourgeois dreams of owning liquor stores or tire shops. Most were united negatively—against management, and against those perceived as "company men"—far more than positively. While some acknowledged that the United Steel Workers union had improved conditions, most perceived the union mainly as a hand in their wallet at each pay period's end.[49] If Roy's stance was pro-worker, it was hardly a radical one, and it did not prevent him from publishing his work or obtaining a good academic position in the McCarthyite 1950s.

Perhaps more important in limiting Roy's influence were general trends in his field. Research published in American sociological journals between 1945 and 1960 relied increasingly on quantitative techniques. Sophisticated surveys, new forms of interviewing, and "structured observation" supplanted the "personal documents" and social workers' records used by the original Chicago scholars.[50] If the "second Chicago school" did offer a qualitative alternative to the diverging postwar trends toward quantitative analysis and grand theory, it did so within narrowing methodological boundaries that increasingly ceded ground to the scientific ideal. It was Roy's ideas about group organization and workers' ways of dealing with monotony that garnered him attention, not his method for gathering the data. Thus in his much-cited article "Banana Time," based on his undercover sojourn in a Chicago garment factory, Roy did colorfully describe his engagement in time-killing jokes and ritual horseplay; but he then shifted into the acceptably distanced language of science to break down one instance of group grumpiness into seven discrete stages, embedding that analysis in a broader list of ten theoretical considerations extracted from his experiences.[51] If the earlier material engaged and amused his readers, it was the latter component of the article that marked Roy as a serious professional social scientist. The openness within sociology toward participant observers who truly lived their part and deceived their peers was closing down.

This narrowing range of operations may be charted in the postwar literature on participant observation and on sociological method more generally. Roy's first publication based on his Geer experiences—a 1946 piece on output restriction, coauthored with two other Chicago graduate students—cited as authoritative a then-forthcoming article on "Methods for the Study of Human Relations in Industry" by Chicago professors Burleigh B. Gardner and William F. Whyte. Both were leading figures in the university's Committee on Human Relations in Industry, which had supported the three authors' dissertation research through a project directed by Whyte.[52] Fresh from his undercover adventures, Roy may well have been surprised to read the final version of that article, which indicated the field's declining receptivity to covert investigations. This might have been particularly unexpected because

Gardner, in a 1942 review, had praised E. Wight Bakke's work as "brilliant" and had recommended close attention to "its methods of study"—which had included undercover sojourns among the New Haven unemployed. Four years later, while Gardner and Whyte conceded that undercover methods had sometimes gotten good results, they now argued that the undercover observer could gain only a limited perspective on a factory's complex social system. The authors insisted that to grasp the bigger picture, industrial investigators must operate openly: with management's permission, and with workers' and—where one existed—the union's knowledge.[53] Such openness may also have seemed important because the authors worried that management did not respect sociologists or regard sociology as "a *real* social science" that might serve their interests. This anxiety, in addition to contemporary suspicions of class analysis, may explain why the article never referred to "class" or "the working class," and it framed sociologists' task as deploying their "skill in human relations" to foster "cooperative relationships" between workers and management while maintaining positive relations with both. Thus the human relations approach, for which industrial down-and-outers of the 1920s had helped to lay the foundations, came fully to the fore in postwar social science, even as the undercover method was being marginalized.[54]

The delegitimizing of undercover investigation was effected partly by defining it out of participant observation, where it had found temporary sanctuary. Roy called his method participant observation, as Bakke had also done. But although Roy referred to "the simple procedures of" the technique as if its meaning were unambiguous, this was decreasingly the case. Roy and his 1946 coauthors cited the authority of the anthropologist Florence R. Kluckhohn's important 1940 article on the subject, yet Kluckhohn explicitly rejected the undercover method.[55] As the term "participant observation" came into more common use during the 1940s, its meaning was drawn more tightly in ways that excluded deceptive practices. Roy argued for the necessity of deception, but William F. Whyte's *Street Corner Society: The Social Structure of an Italian Slum* (1943), perhaps the most influential participant-observer study of the forties, contained no undercover element. Gardner and Whyte's 1946 article explicitly rejected the method, although as one of Roy's mentors, Whyte certainly knew about Roy's practice.[56] By 1950, an article by Eugene V. Schneider entitled "Limitations on Observation in Industrial Sociology" simply proceeded from the assumption that management must always know of and support investigators' activities—with the unfortunate outcome, from Schneider's perspective, that management pressures usually set limits on investigators' questions and interpretations. But deception was not an alternative. Schneider had little faith in the clandestine investigator's "dubious ability" to interpret workers' unmediated words and behavior. Furthermore, deception could pose a positive danger to workers' interests. Schneider criticized Stanley Mathewson's 1931 undercover study of output restriction for having betrayed information to management about workers' restrictive practices, resulting in the cutting of piece rates.[57]

Collectively, this literature suggests a progressive delegitimization of covert factory studies. Participant observation, as it had come to be understood, would be sanctioned by management and supplemented by conventional questionnaires or interviews. This was the approach of investigators supervised by William F. Whyte—a target of Schneider's criticism that management generally effected "a certain channelling of [investigators'] interests"—in his studies of restaurant and hotel work.[58] Whyte's *Men at Work* (1961), a casebook for sociology students that drew on research since the 1940s, illustrated the status of participant observation by the fifties' end. Far from seeking material for a lurid exposé of restaurant conditions that might echo the work of earlier Chicagoan Frances Donovan, Whyte operated within the postwar matrix of inquiry that united academic with business interests. When Whyte placed a participant observer in the Tremont Hotel coffee shop, she functioned as a provider of notes and insights but was granted no independent narrative voice. Whyte planned and oversaw the operation in full collaboration with management, in order to solve management-defined problems with labor turnover and other matters.[59]

Although the undercover approach was thus under fire within industrial relations studies, and with its published fruits largely limited to Roy's articles, it was not fully discredited in sociologists' methodological writings of the 1950s. By 1960, Howard S. Becker and Blanche Geer wrote that there was still "little agreement" on precisely what constituted participant observation, but they cited as the best overview at the time a 1958 article by Raymond L. Gold, which did acknowledge a practice that Gold called "complete" (concealed) participation as a possible investigative strategy. Other 1950s writers on methodology also mentioned the complete participation variant, but they regularly asserted their own allegiance to overt methods.[60] That they saw no need to justify dismissing the undercover approach suggests its low estate among many sociologists. Gold did not deny the method's legitimacy, but he did underscore the strains it imposed. He believed that practitioners must commonly succumb to fears of self-revelation that would cripple their role-playing ability, or that they would simply go native and lapse into ineffectiveness. Similarly, Henry W. Riecken, one of the co-authors of a 1956 undercover study of a quasi-religious doomsday cult, detailed the many strains felt by the investigators, and he conceded their failure to participate effectively without to some extent affecting the group's dynamics.[61] Gold's and Riecken's caveats thus lengthened the list of hazards that had already been drawn up for undercover studies of industrial settings, and they generalized it to all fields of sociological inquiry.

While these authors' concerns were mainly practical ones, the legitimacy of undercover investigation in sociology was further undermined by broader debates on the ethics of social investigation that emerged during the 1950s and reasserted themselves periodically over the next four decades. The discipline was agitated by the 1958 publication of *Small Town in Mass Society* by Arthur Vidich and Joseph Bensman, an aboveground study of an upstate New York village the authors called "Springdale." Although the townspeople knew they were being surveyed and studied and that Vidich—who lived in the town during the research—was connected to the work, many nonetheless felt shocked and betrayed by the book, which laid bare the community's power relations and portrayed many recognizable figures in unflattering terms. The monograph's publication led to a heated scholarly exchange in the journal *Human Organization*, which was based at the study's sponsoring institution—Cornell University—and edited by a disapproving William F. Whyte. It also culminated in the authors' being hanged in effigy by their irate subjects, which proved at least that these professional sociologists had reached a broader readership than they may have expected.[62]

Following the Vidich affair and another team's controversial infiltration of an Alcoholics Anonymous group, the 1960s would see sociologists issuing increasingly sharp denunciations of deceptive research practices.[63] An influential 1960 survey of fieldwork practices by Buford Junker contributed to this atmosphere of growing methodological self-consciousness and self-criticism. As a product of the second Chicago school, Junker shared its project of legitimizing qualitative studies by partly recasting them to better comport with the reigning scientific ideal. Under the supervision of Everett Hughes and with Raymond Gold's assistance, Junker served as project director of the University of Chicago's Social Sciences Field Training Project in 1951–1952.[64] Interviews with current students and other data gathered by the project showed that undercover studies were still being carried out by Chicago undergraduates, and their experiences contributed to Junker's doubts about the practice's utility and ethical status.

Junker largely adopted Raymond Gold's practical critique of the complete participant model, but he went further by discussing ethical concerns and "problems of identity and self-conception" raised by the method. He addressed these issues far more straightforwardly than had Donald Roy (whom he did not cite), worrying that the investigator who went undercover

risked serious problems with both scientific detachment and personal entanglement: "If he escapes the problems of a spy, he takes on those of a traitor." [65] An advanced student identified as William Schuler, when interviewed
for Junker's study, described the destabilizing effects on his identity when he
went undercover. Schuler struggled with the problem of feigning religious
conversion to gain entry to a sect. He feared that he might be seen in character by fellow students at public events, and he worried about the ethics of
reporting on a group that had generously embraced and confided in him.
Feeling himself first a spy and then a traitor, Schuler found it "difficult to
separate the two roles of scientist and individual." [66] Another undercover
student felt forced to derisively dismiss a fellow welder's suggestion that she
follow the coworker's example and take sociology courses at the university;
having "scandalized" her friend by speaking ill of university study ("What
good would it do me, really?"), she felt sick at having so betrayed "this young
member of the brotherhood of sociologists." The same idealistic student, in
a spirit of loyal friendship, revealed her identity to her fellow workers on
leaving a warehouse job, only to find herself abruptly and painfully alienated
from her former friends. Forced to recognize that "research is meaningless
to them," she now had to abandon her hope "of being an intellectual sharing
the life of these people." [67] From such examples Junker sketched a poignant
picture of the difficulties faced by undercover investigators. He concluded
that sociology had entered a new period of methodological and ethical self-
consciousness since the 1930s, which may help to explain why Kai Erikson
would observe in 1967 that "disguised observation"—which he attacked as
practically and ethically indefensible—was also by then "one of the rarest
research techniques" used by sociologists. [68]

However rare it became, the method did not entirely disappear during
the early 1960s, and it will prove instructive to consider the limited realm
in which it did survive. The topics of class and poverty did not command
great attention in postwar sociology, but a few undercover investigations
were conducted in what had once been called "hobohemia" and was now
dubbed "skid row." [69] Perhaps it is unsurprising that studies of the extremely
marginalized should have escaped the ethical scrutiny aimed at deceptions
perpetrated in better neighborhoods. As Arthur Vidich and Joseph Bensman perceptively pointed out when defending their *Small Town* study, con-
troversies over invaded privacy and unkind portrayals of research subjects
tended to break out only when the people studied were relatively privileged
and able to voice their objections in the public realm. They noted that the
sociological tradition—implicitly, the undercover tradition—of studying
slum dwellers, beggars, industrial workers, taxi dancers, and hoboes had

seldom led to the sort of public outcry and professional soul-searching that their book had provoked. Had they confined their attention to the village's impoverished "shack people," they speculated, they would have raised no hackles among the comfortable.[70] Bearing out this prediction, postwar investigators who lived undercover on skid rows in California, Chicago, and Minnesota neither raised nor gave rise to ethical questions. Lacking management or union authorities with whom to negotiate, they simply moved in to the neighborhoods under study and assumed their roles. Representing their subjects respectfully and sometimes affectionately, they presented their research method dispassionately and simply argued that it got results that could not have been otherwise obtained.[71]

It was especially Minnesota's Samuel Wallace who sought to build on the older undercover tradition, while also departing from it in significant ways. In 1958, Wallace and eight other graduate students lived undercover in Minneapolis's Gateway district while working on a municipally funded study under the supervision of the former tramp investigator Theodore Caplow.[72] They thus continued the 1930s Minnesota tradition that had included Edwin Sutherland, Thomas Minehan, and the younger Caplow. Wallace drew the material for his *Skid Row as a Way of Life* (1965) from the undercover evidence collected for this study. In a gesture to the past, the book was studded with citations to Josiah Flynt, Carleton Parker, George Orwell, Edwin Sutherland and Harvey Locke, Jesse Dees, and Nels Anderson. But Wallace also observed the tightening conventions of social science: There was no first-person narrator, and the author had frequent recourse to the passive voice and to constructions such as "The most casual observer is struck by . . ."[73] The undercover evidence consisted mainly of indented quotes from his own and others' "participant observation journals," marking the continued decline of the down-and-outer's distinct narrative voice.

Other contemporary undercover sociologists followed similar strategies. In an article about drinking rituals on various California skid rows, James Rooney offered distanced descriptions of social processes and did not construct a first-person persona. Ronald VanderKooi used a brief complete-participant stint on Chicago's skid row mainly to reconnoiter and provide a "validity check" on the formal interviews that constituted his principal sources. Departing most fully from undercover conventions was Keith Lovald, one of Samuel Wallace's fellow graduate students, who wrote a dissertation based on the Minneapolis study. While he drew heavily for background and context on the undercover tradition dating back to the Progressive Era, Lovald claimed that his own experience of Gateway life was limited to occasions of "just walking around."[74] He quoted earlier undercover writers on factual matters such as where sheltermen read or sat, but he also criticized their lack of statistical precision and excessive reliance on mere "observations."[75] He was clearly concerned with establishing his own scientific credentials and may therefore have preferred to portray himself as an overt observer. Lovald thus affirmed the value of the undercover tradition while quietly consigning it to the past.

Wallace's *Skid Row as a Way of Life* combined the novel with the familiar not only in form but in content: As in Caplow's "Transiency as a Cultural Pattern," Wallace's key category was not class, but culture. Using terms derived from the older undercover tradition that would soon characterize the culture of poverty and underclass literatures, Wallace argued that skid row was a self-contained subculture, "a deviant and isolated way of life." Such a subculture could be accurately studied only by an "insider"—a figure such as Nels Anderson, Thomas Minehan, or James Rooney—in contrast with various "outsider" sociologists who had failed, in his view, to corner their quarry. On the question of why men came to skid row and stayed there, Wallace registered the increasing postwar dominance of culturalist arguments.[76] He rejected economic explanations rooted in the 1930s as well as newly popular theories of "abnormality" and "undersocialization," none of which he felt grasped the cultural dynamic by which individuals were socialized into the deviant skid-row world. Thus he defined the skid-rower not by structural position or observable characteristics, but by his participation in this distinctive and separate "way of life." Positive intentions notwithstanding, Wallace underscored the inevitable otherness of the extremely poor. The skid-rower drew attention—especially from the legal authorities—"not for what he has done, but for what he is." Wallace insisted upon a pluralist understanding of cultures that positioned him as a social critic and friend to the outcast: "Must the very process of socialization lead straight to 'suburbia'—to wife, kids, the office gang, and PTA? I, for one, must protest." That skid-rowers did not conform to mainstream norms did not mean that they had no norms or values at all, and to acknowledge this was a prerequisite to understanding their culture.[77] Yet this effort to save the poor from the perdition of normlessness cast them instead into a prisonhouse of culture that resonated with older down-and-outers' constructions of the poor as primitive savages. Still, this culture was neither static nor permanent. Like down-and-outer Ronald VanderKooi, who noted "the ethnologist's statement that 'this culture may not be around much longer,'" Wallace believed that skid row was disappearing because of changing work patterns, growing affluence, and urban renewal. Like the erstwhile vanishing hobo and his mythic ancestor, the vanishing Indian, the uncivilized poor were also assumed to be rapidly diminishing in number; they must be studied from the inside, and immediately.[78]

Buford Junker's declaration that postwar sociologists had become increasingly self-critical about method and ethics thus seemed less apt when applied to practitioners of skid-row studies. More fully socialized into disciplinary norms than many of their predecessors, skid-row sociologists embraced the language of science, eschewing first-person narration and obvious reliance on individual experience. Most also did evince a clear sympathy for their subjects. Yet somehow, the study of a vulnerable population who lacked institutional means to ward off intruders did not seem to require the ethical strictures that were rapidly becoming the norm for observations set in more privileged precincts. This would remain true even in the 1970s, when sociologists studying Philadelphia's skid-row denizens (who had somehow failed to vanish) criticized Samuel Wallace's insistence that only those with an insider status could produce successful research. Yet they did not categorically reject evidence obtained by Wallace's method, and they demurred solely on the familiar practical ground that better results could be otherwise obtained; they made no reference to the ethics of exploiting their subjects or invading their privacy.[79] In this view of proper sociological practice, a modicum of undercover evidence might be folded discreetly into a conventionally designed study, as long as it neither called attention to itself rhetorically nor sought to shoulder too much evidentiary weight. Thus in the largest sense, Kai Erikson's 1967 assertion that deceptive studies were wrong but rare was ultimately borne out.

Conclusion

Although there were few wartime down-and-outers, they had been sometimes astute in their observations about gender, race, and national identity. During the postwar decades, social scientists tended increasingly to denigrate the undercover approach, with its focus on class, its unscientific methods, and its questionable ethics. Yet if the idea of passing across the class line seemed to be losing traction in the forties and fifties, the revelatory possibilities of clandestine border crossing began to pique the interest of new kinds of social explorers and commentators, with new and timely concerns, during those same years. These writers would produce a final flurry of undercover texts that would bring to the method a new level of public recognition, while leaving behind most of the earlier class passers' traditional subject matter. In fiction, film, and journalism, matters of religion and race would now be inspected, often to sensational effect, through the undercover lens.

5

Crossing New Lines

From Gentleman's Agreement to Black Like Me

As concerns about class lost legitimacy, both in the social sciences and in American social thought generally, and as the United States approached the era of accelerating civil rights activism, a number of texts explored new kinds of boundary crossing. Two such texts will be of central import in this chapter. First, Laura Z. Hobson's best-selling novel *Gentleman's Agreement* and the movie based on it (both 1947), in which the WASP protagonist and former class passer masquerades as a Jew, served in this transitional period as a mediating text through its interweaving narratives of class, ethnicity, religion, and race, and through its sometimes-awkward attempts to insist that whatever Jews were, they assuredly were not a "race." Second, the novelist John Howard Griffin's memoir *Black Like Me*, the account of a white explorer's venture across the race line into the heart of American darkness, brought the discourse of identity shifting that emerged in the 1940s and 1950s to a culmination in 1961. Griffin's tale also quickly found its way onto celluloid in 1964. In Griffin's downplaying of class as a useful category, and in his rejection of all forms of otherness on universalist grounds, we witness the historical culmination and transformation of the undercover project and its discourses.[1]

"I'll Be Jewish": Evading Difference in *Gentleman's Agreement*

During the postwar decades, it was often novelists, journalists, and other adventurers who pushed forward the down-and-out method and found imaginative new ways to bring its results into the public forum. They did so in a period of great interest in the malleability of individual and social identities, and one during which race—the unresolved "American dilemma"— increasingly gained ascendancy over class as the defining social contradiction in U.S. society. In a context of much wartime and postwar discussion about democracy, pluralism, and the place of minorities in a putatively universalistic "culture of the whole," various inquisitive Americans explored alternative identities and their links to the larger national community.[2] Narratives about passing would be a common means for raising and responding to questions about the place in that community of groups that had traditionally been marginalized—especially Jews and African Americans.

Hobson's novel *Gentleman's Agreement*, in which a gentile journalist passes as a Jew to investigate anti-Semitism, appeared in 1947 amid a flurry of such explorations of group and national identity. Earlier that year, shortly before the filmed version of *Gentleman's Agreement* was released, the movie *Crossfire* debuted. Also a picture critical of anti-Semitism, this noir thriller about the murder of a Jew was adapted from Richard Brooks's 1945 novel *The Brick Foxhole*, in which the murder victim is actually not a Jew but a homosexual man. Thus *Crossfire* enacted a sort of passing in its transition from book to movie.[3] Also in 1947, *Reader's Digest* published the journalist William White's much-discussed story "Lost Boundaries," the fact-based account of a young New Hampshire man who thought himself white but who discovered at age sixteen that his family was passing, forcing him to entirely reconstruct his identity. White's story was quickly expanded into a 1948 book and was then produced as a Hollywood movie in 1949. Elsewhere on the cultural front, 1947 also saw the publication of Sinclair Lewis's best-selling *Kingsblood Royal*, featuring yet another "white" protagonist who is dismayed to discover his black ancestry, as well as the debut of the hit Broadway musical *Finian's Rainbow*, in which a racist Southern senator modeled partly on Mississippi's John Rankin—whom Hobson also targeted in *Gentleman's Agreement* for his overt anti-Semitism—is unexpectedly turned black and must live with the consequences. In 1948, the reporter Ray Sprigle published a sensational series of stories in the *Pittsburgh Post-Gazette* called "I Was a Negro in the

South for 30 Days," in which Sprigle both followed the example of the *Gentleman's Agreement* journalist Phil Green ("I Was Jewish for Eight Weeks") and anticipated the race-crossing odyssey of John Howard Griffin in *Black Like Me* (1961). Sprigle reworked his articles into a book in 1949, the same year that the producer Darryl F. Zanuck and the director Elia Kazan—the team who had filmed *Gentleman's Agreement*—made the passing picture *Pinky*, about a light-skinned African American woman who passes for white.[4]

This expansive attention to the blurred border between white and African American identities signaled the developing transition in social thought toward a focus on the black/white binary that would largely displace class concerns. In undercover discourse, this transition would be most fully enacted through Griffin's book. *Gentleman's Agreement* helped to pave the way for that transition by engaging the question of whether or not Jews were "different" and whether they were a "race." By using Phil's down-and-out experiment to establish that they were neither, the book and movie gathered Jews into the circle of whiteness, of "the Caucasian race" (196). The Americanizing and whitening of Jews had been in process for some time by 1947. Ira Katznelson argues that during the interwar years, Jews had often been classified as a minority race, but that thanks largely to World War II—"a great engine of group incorporation and integration" for Jews—they were more typically seen by the 1940s as "white ethnics." Still, *Lost Boundaries*, in which light-skinned blacks were sometimes thought to be Jews, showed that the categories of race and whiteness remained fluid.[5] Hobson's tale thus participated in a broader, developing discussion. In these closing years of a decade characterized by the historian William Graebner as riddled with "doubt" and "anxiety," uncertainties about personal and group identity were rife, and identity itself—or what Hobson's Phil Green called "identification" (106–107)—proved a ripe subject for interrogation.[6]

As novelists had done since Margaret Sherwood in the 1890s, Laura Z. Hobson used the undercover device to move her main character into unknown territory, and to think on the page about contemporary societal issues. But while Sherwood's concern had been the widening chasm of class, Hobson's book unfolded in the murky zone where religion, ethnicity, and race converged in the postwar popular consciousness. Like the writer Budd Schulberg, who reviewed *Gentleman's Agreement* for the *New Republic*, she worried that the hard-won European struggle against racialized anti-Semitism might yet be lost in the United States. Hobson was the proud daughter of Russian-Jewish immigrant socialist intellectuals; she also was an agnostic who could not read Yiddish but who insisted upon the middle initial "Z" (for Zametkin) "because it held [her] identity intact" in the shadow of the

Anglo-Saxon "Hobson"—a name acquired from a short-lived marriage. *Gentleman's Agreement* was the shot Hobson fired in the "covert war" that she, like Schulberg, believed was raging in postwar America (228). If the shock troops on the other side of that war were the rabid, public anti-Semites—the Gerald L. K. Smiths and the John Rankins—it was their elite but quiet collaborators who constituted "the rear echelons, the home front" (192).[7]

It was to the rear echelons that Hobson addressed herself, and with great success. More than a book and a movie, *Gentleman's Agreement* was an event of 1947. First serialized in *Cosmopolitan*—whose cover proclaimed it "The Novel All America Will Discuss"—it was kept atop the best-seller list for almost six months by positive reviews and eager buyers.[8] The movie rights were sold while the book was still in galleys, and Twentieth Century Fox's Darryl F. Zanuck—who combined idealistic anti-Semitism with an acute commercial instinct—ensured that the picture got the full Oscar treatment. It garnered strong reviews and eight Academy Award nominations, eventually winning Best Picture, Director, and Supporting Actress. In the movies, as the historian Neal Gabler has written, and also among the book-buying public, anti-anti-Semitism had become "highly respectable."[9]

Gentleman's Agreement is a story of undercover investigation that bears similarities to the earlier tradition but also departs significantly from it. The book is not about crossing the line into Jewishness, encountering the other, or exploring a world of difference. It is not about Jews at all. The few Jews who do appear are either fully assimilated, like Phil's friend Dave Goldman, or passing as gentiles, like Phil's secretary, Miss Wales. Rather, the book is about anti-Semites and their sometimes-unwitting allies among gentiles of the middle and upper classes. To conceive and tell this story, Laura Z. Hobson herself had to pass. A Jewish writer trying to imagine how a gentile might learn about anti-Semitism, she had to enter and to represent—by way of her non-Jewish protagonist—the world of genteel anti-Semitism. Hobson knew perfectly well what anti-Semitic slurs and insults felt like. What she did not precisely know was how a gentile investigator would experience them. So she hit upon the undercover device, which, appropriately enough, reminded W. E. B. Du Bois, when he reviewed the novel, of John Steinbeck's dalliance with the method in the 1930s.[10] Hobson may well have had Steinbeck in mind when she made Phil Green the veteran of two Depression-era undercover projects. Phil passed first as an Okie laboring in the California fruit orchards, then as a Pennsylvania miner, and he had written successful magazine series on each adventure. Besides the possible Steinbeck connection, Hobson had another tangential link to the undercover tradition: She was acquainted with Elizabeth Hawes, who had tried to hide her identity while working in a wartime aircraft factory. Like Hawes, Hobson's female protagonist, Katherine Lacey, is a Vassar graduate who has worked in a New Jersey aircraft plant. Kathy is no down-and-outer, but as will be explained below, her class identity is complicated.[11]

Phil's personal history provokes his decision that to study anti-Semitism in a novel way, he must pass as a Jew. In certain respects, he does fit the down-and-outer's profile. A solidly middle-class writer employed by *Smith's* magazine—a liberal weekly that crosses the *New Republic* with *Time*[12]—Phil is also a transient, newly arrived in New York City, and a writer impatient with conventional exposés built on "the same old drool of statistics and protest" (1, 6–7). Stumped for a fresh angle, Phil suddenly recalls that as an Okie, he had found the truths he sought "in his own guts" (62–63). The answer lands upon him like a blow: "It's the only way. I'll *be* Jewish. . . . I can just say it. I can live it myself" (63). But while his editor, John Minify, calls the idea "a hell of a stunt" (72)—evoking the "stunt girls" of earlier exposé journalism—this will be different. Phil frames his research narrowly in cultural and class terms, recognizing that he cannot penetrate the otherness of a "poor, ignorant Jewish peddler behind a pushcart"—or, at the other extreme, that of a wealthy Jewish businessman. So he will simply be himself, changing only his religious identification from lapsed Episcopalian to Jew. That is, he will be like his friend Dave Goldman. Basically unreligious, raised neither rich nor poor, Phil is already like Dave "in every essential" (52). There need be no rituals of divestment or studying up on relevant slang. There is no clear line to cross. Phil wears the same suit, lives in the same apartment, and goes routinely to the new office where he has not previously been known as a gentile. He simply announces his Jewishness during the flow of conversation at a business lunch, and he tells himself, "It's done; I'm in" (80).

Reviewers were divided on the likely efficacy of the undercover device. The *New Yorker* thought the concept "provocative" but poorly executed, while the *Nation's* Joan Griffiths found it "contrived" and unlikely to get Phil to the deeper levels of the issue; she thought this masquerade was less well-suited to its task than Phil's earlier, economically defined undercover expeditions had been. But more common were the positive judgments. Budd Schulberg's *New Republic* review saw the technique as a badge of Phil's "professional thoroughness," while Charles Poore wrote in the *New York Times* that Phil's masquerade enabled him "to see and feel and know" for his readers—that is, to achieve what had always been down-and-outers' principal goals. Reviewers of the film were also mainly convinced that the method was plausible and illuminating. An exception was *Saturday Review's* J. M. Brown, who saw Phil's passing as a mere "stunt," and who echoed earlier critics of the undercover tradition by complaining that the true experiences and feelings of Jews were not discernible to mere "tourists." On the other hand, Elliot Cohen praised the undercover strategy in *Commentary*, noting that what had seemed "creaky" in the novel effectively drove the drama onscreen. Echoing the language of Progressive Era reviewers, Cohen praised the film for carrying the viewer "into the lower depths of high-minded America." Reviews in *Commonweal*, *Life*, and the *New Republic* all concurred that Phil Green's undercover adventures could enable him to fully enter the affective world of a Jew beset by anti-Semites. If the down-and-out method was losing credibility in the formal social sciences, it was apparently gaining adherents among the general public and its tribunes. *Survey Graphic's* James Reid Parker praised the book for discussing anti-Semitism with an analytical sharpness that a sociology professor should envy. Indeed, some educators put the story's device to practical use. Inspired by the movie, the sociologist Arthur Katona assigned his Michigan State College students to pass as Jews or light-skinned blacks while seeking jobs or rental rooms in town. From such "role playing for keeps" exercises, he believed that they "really" learned "what it means to be a Negro or a Jew in a prejudice-ridden society."[13]

Once identified as Jewish, Phil Green duly collects his share of anti-Semitic affronts, both overt and subtle. His editor praises the resultant stories for their fluid integration of facts with personal narrative, suggesting that Phil has achieved the classic down-and-outer's objective. Yet Phil pays a price. The novel is considerably darker in tone than most nonfictional undercover studies. Grounded in unstated Freudian assumptions, it explores in detail the psychological trauma of "identification" as Phil suddenly immerses himself in a set of jarring experiences that real Jews have necessarily learned to cope with throughout their lifetimes. The daily series of petty indignities constitutes for him "a delicate assault on the proud stuff of a man's identity" (97).[14] His personal pain forces him ever further into the despised other's subject position, where he sometimes forgets that "it's just an act" (106). But unlike earlier down-and-outers who struggled with an attraction-repulsion relationship to working-class culture, Phil's fury stems from his sense of entitlement denied. He is accustomed to the privileges accorded a white male gentile; when thwarted, he broods, fumes, and sometimes barely restrains himself from violent assaults on enforcers of the unwritten "gentleman's agreements" that bar Jews from elite clubs, inns, and suburbs. As Phil's natural sensitivity is magnified by his undercover experiences, his fiancée, Kathy Lacey—the niece of his boss, John Minify—believes he is becoming "neurotic" and worries that his torment is driving her toward the same condition (89).

The story thus interweaves the complexities of Phil's life undercover with a developing love story in which Kathy—who is in on the secret—betrays her own unacknowledged anti-Semitic impulses and her reluctance to challenge such feelings in her family and peers. Undercover narratives have always been partly about the investigator's identity, and here the stakes are raised by the introduction of romance. Phil's undercover life both defines their relationship and nearly wrecks it, as each member of the couple must forge an identity vis-à-vis the other. Kathy's initial response to Phil's plan to "*be* Jewish" is "But you're not, Phil, are you?"—followed by much equivocation about how it would not matter, but capped by the insistent query, "Well, *are* you, Phil?" (83). Although it is Kathy who has proposed to her uncle that he run a series on anti-Semitism, she can brook no ambiguity about her beloved's identity. But Phil's commitment to the project constantly thwarts her ability to solidify a conception of just who he really is, and also to maintain a sure sense of her own liberal, anti-Semitic bona fides.

Just who Kathy is also perplexes Phil, and here it becomes evident that *Gentleman's Agreement* has not entirely left behind the problematic of class that defined the earlier undercover tradition. Although the book's overt subject is anti-Semitism, Phil is depicted from the first as riddled with class anxieties, which structure his approach to the project and his relations with the much wealthier Kathy. His identity as a solidly middle-class man has been reinforced by his previous undercover experiences of passing as an uprooted Okie and a coal miner. In both cases, he did go home again after the stories were filed, and he does not depart from his established class identity in becoming a Jew. Instead, his anxieties are now directed upward. When invited into John Minify's elite social realm, where the rich dwell in what Phil calls " 'fingerbowl houses'" redolent of "alien values and importances" (12), he becomes anxious and defensive. At a high-toned dinner party given by Minify, he sturdily insists upon being called "Phil," with its regular-guy ring, over his " 'ritzier'" pseudonym "Schuyler Green." These are not his people, and he feels "tight" and "watchful" among them (13). It is here that he meets Kathy, whose "too-well-bred tone" he immediately resents. Yet he cannot size her up. If her clothes and manner seem "too, in quotes, upper class," her words—"real and good"—evoke other, less elevated social origins (18).

Like Phil, Kathy proves to be a creature of fragmented identity. As he correctly observes to her, "Parts of you don't seem to go with other parts" (22). Kathy is in fact from lower-middle-class origins. The daughter of a failed provincial lawyer, she was once resentful and defensively snobbish in her thwarted aspirations. She has now acquired material comforts and a glossy, broad-minded liberalism, thanks to the aunt and uncle who sent her to Vassar and absorbed her into their New York crowd. Being amicably divorced from a wealthy banker has also made her the owner of property in suburban Darien, Connecticut, where an unwritten gentleman's agreement precludes incursions by prosperous Jews. In the conflicts that follow, Phil tries to appeal to Kathy's core of "inner sweetness" (201)—her aura of being in but not of the country-club set. In their worst moments, he concludes that she has become one of the "nice people" who are not consciously anti-Semitic but who remain, through silence and inaction, the "unknowing helpers and connivers" of the "low-class morons" who burn crosses and beat up Jews (192). By origin, Kathy is not so far removed from the morons. As Phil describes her anonymously in one of his articles, she has achieved the American dream of upward mobility into "the 'smart set' in her community," and "she won't jeopardize that adored status" by violating the community's ground rules. Limited to "little clucking sounds of disapproval," she remains inert: "Her own success story paralyzes her" (228–229). Kathy's dilemma is that she must decide how to integrate the class dimensions of her past and present. But Phil's absorption into his masquerade frightens her. Identity is not to be toyed with: "You were what you were, for the one life you had" (195). She is glad, she confesses to herself, to have been born a white Protestant and then elevated into privilege. Phil, in turn, will wonder throughout the book whether their problems are rooted in her affinity for what a friend calls "'upper-classes stuff'" (220).

With Phil's identity made suddenly ambiguous to Kathy, and hers a conundrum to him from the start, both must literally decide who they are under the pressures induced by Phil's passing; further, they must do so in a way that both resolves the plot's romantic entanglements and strikes a blow for Hobson's vision of gradual progress toward a universalist postwar American democracy. Both leading characters must change, but the onus is especially on Kathy. The down-and-outer never fully returns from his voyage, and Phil does come to identify with the middle-class Jew in an anti-Semitic white-collar world. He will always feel himself "partly Jewish" in that world (164), and his experiences there stiffen his resolve not to live in the house that Kathy owns in restricted Darien—a position that she equates with foolishly trying to "make the whole world over" (187). Kathy changes more fundamentally and, in doing so, allows Phil to achieve the down-and-outer's goal of moving his audience by the force of his words. It is not talking with Phil but reading his undercover articles that forces Kathy to resolve her inner conflicts and confront her Darien neighbors. She defies the gentleman's agreement by renting her Darien house to Dave Goldman, Phil's Jewish friend. Appropriately for a postwar American woman, Kathy defies her neighbors in a defense of domesticity: Dave can now accept a new job in New York and reunite his California-based family in suburban Connecticut. Kathy's action also resolves her conflict with Phil, who is last seen jabbing at Kathy's doorbell on the book's final page. Kathy thus modifies her values to align with Phil's, enacting his investigation's conclusions about the need to confront genteel anti-Semitism, and thereby winning back his affection. Phil's assumption of an undercover role has forced both characters to become integrated individuals; it also enables them as a couple to embody the liberal universalist ideals that Hobson embraced.

It is that universalism, with its intrinsic denial of difference, that finally sets *Gentleman's Agreement* apart from the older undercover tradition. Like many liberals, Hobson believed that the cause of democracy could best be advanced by an Enlightenment-descended insistence that people of all racial and ethnic groups shared fundamentally similar characteristics and capacities, and that, as humans, they also shared certain fundamental rights. It was such thinking, as David Hollinger has shown, that animated a multitude of 1940s artifacts, ranging from the Kinsey reports on sexuality in "the" human male and female to Eleanor Roosevelt's championing of the United Nations Declaration on Human Rights. In the universalist view, historically contingent traits that had arisen to distinguish various groups from one another should be tolerated and even celebrated in a spirit of cultural pluralism, but they should also, somewhat paradoxically, be expected to fade and disappear with time, progress, and modernization.[15]

For Hobson, the agnostic Jew who could not read Yiddish, this meant a distinct change in the framing of undercover discourse. Earlier down-and-outers, exploring the world of the poor and the working class, had expected to find difference; when they did, they had often explained it in essentialist and undemocratic terms. In Hobson's thinking, persistent difference could only be undemocratic and must be denied, not explained. As Phil muses at one point, "the inheritance of acquired characteristics"—the old Lamarckian faith that had underwritten much undercover discourse on class differences—has been recognized as "a myth" (119). But at least in Phil's white-collar world, difference must not simply be historical and transient—it must be entirely superficial. "Take it easy," Phil admonishes Miss Wales, who is disoriented and upset upon learning of his masquerade. "I'm the same guy I was yesterday" (232). He believes that he has "learned about being Jewish" and, more important, that he has "learned a good deal about being anybody" (233). Phil is only able to pass as a Jew because class trumps religion in Hobson's world. Thus a genre that had always emphasized the exploration of difference is here put to the service of celebrating sameness.

Jewishness entails few markers of discernible difference in the world of the comfortable classes where *Gentleman's Agreement* is set. It is more than once asserted that Jews are not a race, and the names of Franz Boas, Ruth Benedict, and Margaret Mead are invoked as evidence (34, 196). Phil's ability to pass provides further proof. "Looking Jewish" is a vague and contingent quality that distinguishes neither Dave Goldman nor Phil. Jews are not a distinct cultural or national group, and they are not even adherents to a particular religion, in the sense that none of the book's characters appear to be observant. Phil can pass by calling himself a Jew because the middle-class Jew is not the other, except when he is targeted for irrational persecution by bigoted gentiles. The historian Richard King writes that universalists typically focused on the perpetrators of injustice, not on their victims. Thus, *Gentleman's Agreement* sees anti-Semitism as a "nonsectarian" and "mostly a Christian problem" (268); Jews exist only as beleaguered objects. Not surprisingly, cosmopolitan Jewish critics of the book and movie objected to this effacement of Jewish religious and cultural distinctiveness in the name of universalism. Diana Trilling observed in *Commentary* that Hobson, like most conventional middle-class liberals, not only ignored "valid differences" between Jews and gentiles but that she even seemed to believe that U.S. society harbored "no other differences" at all. For Trilling, a cultural-pluralist perspective that recognized "the saving human differences" would have improved the novel both aesthetically and as a representation of American life.[16]

In Hobson's undercover tale, the test of American democracy becomes not whether the class divide can be bridged, but whether Jews can be integrated into the anonymous melting pot of the middle class—the class to which, as Elliot Cohen wrote in his review of the movie, all Americans belonged "at least by identification."[17] Phil reaffirmed his class identity first by having passed as a worker among the poor, and now by having passed as a Jew among the middle and upper orders. He is a member of the white-collar working mass, as is Dave Goldman, who will end by "integrating" the WASP bastion of Darien. The book concludes that in democratic America, Jews should be able to function freely in the economic and social worlds for which they qualify by income and culture. Miss Wales should not have to pass as a Christian to work in a Manhattan office building, and Dave should be able to live in a posh suburb; both should be able to live out their class locations, unhindered by their religious or ethnic backgrounds. The down-and-outer's job in *Gentleman's Agreement* is to show how anti-Semitism is dysfunctional for a country trying to achieve that limited level of integration as the "white" middle class expands.

The book's expunging of difference moves Jews into that vaguely inclusive middle class with other now-white immigrant groups, and it clears the stage for drawing the key postwar social boundary—the color line that divides black from white—with clarity and force. Down-and-out narratives had the capacity to blur lines of social division, and *Gentleman's Agreement* does so within the terms of its limited objectives. But when Phil and Kathy agree that modern science divides humankind only into Caucasian, Mongoloid, and Negroid races (196), leaving no room for a Jewish "race," they implicitly reaffirm the reality of racial difference and draw Jews into the circle of whiteness. Defining that circle's perimeter is not a simple matter, as evidenced by a testy exchange between Phil and Miss Wales. When the latter expresses her distaste for the loud and over-rouged "kikey ones" whose presence in the office she fears might threaten her status, Phil reproves her. But he is forced to recognize that, in her mind, the two of them, bearing no external markers of Jewishness, are " 'white' Jews" (154–155). They can pass and are fully assimilable in the world of middle-class whiteness. This does suggest that there are others—poorer, louder, more Jewish-looking—who cannot be drawn into that circle. But lower-class Jews barely exist in *Gentleman's Agreement*, and Hobson leaves the issue unresolved.

On the other hand, the color line does get at least passing mention. As a universalist, Hobson saw anti-Semitism as connected to all forms of bigotry, and her characters regard combating it as a preliminary battle that must precede the more difficult but necessary struggle for black equality. The latter is cast not only as a matter of simple justice—of "getting decent with thirteen million Negroes"—but also of defeating communism, which, for all of its faults, does champion racial equality (184).[18] Readers of the *Cosmopolitan* serialization who were offended by Hobson's racial egalitarianism responded on the letters page in ironically inverted universalist terms, casting her as an all-purpose "Jew-lover, nigger-lover, Commie-pinko-liberal." Hobson remained consistent in her commitments, writing later that if she were to recast *Gentleman's Agreement* for the 1980s, the main character would be "black or Puerto Rican or gay or Mexican-American." Yet paradoxically, to deny that Jews were a race was also to deepen the divide between "whites"—now including Jews—on the one hand, and African Americans on the other.[19] In a country where class was thought to be of declining significance and other forms of difference were effaced or evaded on universalist grounds, one realm of difference proved harder to deny. Neither did it seem so easily penetrable through the traditional mechanism of undercover investigation. That realm lay across the color line.

The Greatest Divide: Science and Experience in *Black Like Me*

Since the 1890s, middle-class investigators had changed their clothes and plunged into the dark city; in 1959, a moderately successful white novelist blackened his skin with chemicals, a sun lamp, and dye, and then rode a New Orleans streetcar into the dark South. In doing so, John Howard Griffin brought to a culmination the process by which former class passers such as the fictitious Phil Green and the real Ray Sprigle had shifted their attention to religion and race—with the latter now defined almost exclusively by the line of color that divided black from white America. For Griffin, what Gunnar Myrdal had termed "the American dilemma" was now American society's central problematic. It was, as he and some of his black interlocutors called it, simply "the problem."[20] And in postwar public and academic minds, the problem was coming to overshadow and subsume the issue of class. Poverty, with its assumed pathologies, increasingly became synonymous—however inaccurately—with blackness. As one reviewer of *Black Like Me* put it, Griffin had addressed "our number one social problem."[21]

Like all previous down-and-outers, Griffin hoped to reshape public discourse by relying on the power of words to convey individual experience. More than any of his predecessors, he succeeded. His story—recounted first in a 1960 series of articles for the black-oriented magazine *Sepia*, then in his 1961 book *Black Like Me* and in its 1964 Hollywood version, and later recurred to in various writings and speeches—seized the public imagination and catapulted the monastically inclined writer into a largely unwonted public role during the climactic years of civil rights and Black Power agitation.[22] During those years, the postwar liberal universalism that had motivated and framed both *Gentleman's Agreement* and *Black Like Me* came under increasing scrutiny, resulting in—among many other social and cultural changes—the effective end of the classic era of undercover investigation. Griffin's book pointed ahead to further experiments with identity, and to a continued cultural fascination with authentic experience, that would endure through the century's close. But a heightened consciousness about the complexity of American identity, and a growing sensitivity to the perils of trying to speak for the other, reduced—though they did not eliminate—the appeal and the legitimacy of experiments in passing downward through the hierarchy of social power. Most later adventurers would neither seek nor find quite the same world of difference that had both enticed and repelled earlier generations of undercover explorers when they had set out to investigate poverty, work, and class in America.

While Griffin's book presented itself as *sui generis*, it did culminate, if it did not precisely grow out of, a tradition of American texts concerned with racial passing—the greater part of which, running from the nineteenth through the mid-twentieth century, addressed the phenomenon of African Americans passing as white. Yet the line could also be crossed in the other direction, especially as the domain of color had once been considerably larger.[23] From the beginnings of the undercover tradition in the Progressive Era, when numerous immigrant groups were not yet regarded as white, the class line was often racialized. Thus in 1907, the white down-and-outer Alexander Irvine counted himself among the "bronzed proletarians"—nonwhite Southern and Eastern Europeans with whom he worked in the Alabama woods—and did not feel far removed from the African American workers, with whom he also associated freely. Similarly in the 1920s, as racialized nativism reached its peak, Whiting Williams and Charles Rumford Walker effectively crossed both racial and class lines when they identified with their Italian, Mexican, and "Hunky" fellow workers. Such thinking was eroded in formal intellectual circles during the later interwar years. By 1940, Mary Gilson—once a Progressive Era down-and-outer, now an industrial economist at the University of Chicago—observed that college classes were widely disseminating the Boasian refutation of dogmas about class and racial hierarchies. Gilson expected that middle-class Americans would soon cease to regard workers as "different in native mental capacity from other groups."[24] But if ideas about class and race were changing by the time of *Gentleman's Agreement*, Jews had been so recently whitened that Laura Z. Hobson still had to assert forcefully that they were not a (nonwhite) race, while Phil Green, her protagonist, does recognize that some Jews are in practice more white—more assimilated, more capable of passing—than others.

If whiteness was conventionally assumed to be the racial norm into which darker people would seek to pass—Griffin was said by one reviewer to have "crossed the color line in reverse"[25]—there also existed a parallel if thinner tradition of narratives about passing from white to black. Albion Tourgée, whose protagonist in the novel *Murvale Eastman* had been a traditional class passer, often urged white Americans to imagine themselves awakening with black skin; among those to whom he suggested this thought experiment were the justices of the U.S. Supreme Court, in his antisegregation brief for the landmark case of *Plessy v. Ferguson* (1896). Texts that fleshed out this idea included *Dr. Huguet* (1891), by the apocalyptic novelist and populist politician Ignatius Donnelly; the Broadway musical *Finian's Rainbow* (1947); the novel *Black Is a Man* (1954), by the poet and Trotskyist intellectual Harry Roskolenko; as well as—after Griffin's rise to prominence—the movie

Watermelon Man (1970), by the African American director Melvin Van Peebles.[26] These tales have in common a white racist protagonist whose skin turns black following some form of divine visitation. After a series of traumatic encounters and adventures, each character renounces his earlier racism and learns what Dr. Huguet observes after being knocked out and jailed by a policeman: "It had been taught me that the mind is the man; but now I perceived that the body is the man" (100).

It was this assertion—that in the American South, the bodily feature of skin color mattered more than class, education, morality, and all else—that John Howard Griffin set out to test. Griffin's project was anticipated by conventional investigative journalists who had explored Southern race relations earlier in the twentieth century, producing works such as Ray Stannard Baker's landmark *Following the Color Line* (1908) and John Spivak's *Georgia Nigger* (1932), a documentary novel with photographs based on Spivak's investigations of Georgia prison conditions. And Griffin's sociological sensibility—he initially thought of his project as mainly of interest to sociologists—echoed that of Robert Park, the leading figure of the early Chicago school and collaborator with Booker T. Washington. Park claimed that during his seven years of studying Southern black life, he "became, for all intents and purposes, for the time, a Negro." But Griffin's truest precursor—though a man of whom Griffin apparently never heard—was the Pittsburgh journalist Ray Sprigle, who in 1948 dramatically fused the traditions of undercover investigation and racial crossing.[27]

Ray Sprigle was something of a distinguished eccentric in the *Pittsburgh Post-Gazette* city room, sporting a ten-gallon sombrero and puffing on a corncob pipe. He was already a well-known journalist by 1948, having won the Pulitzer Prize for his 1937 exposé of Supreme Court Justice Hugo Black's Ku Klux Klan connections, and he had conducted several undercover investigations in and around Pittsburgh, for which he had posed as a black-market meat cutter, a mental-hospital attendant, and—as Hobson's Phil Green had done—a Pennsylvania coal miner.[28] Like other former class passers, in the postwar years Sprigle turned his attention to race. Relying on a dark Florida suntan and a shaven head to give him the appearance of a light-skinned African American, and enlisting the aid of his friend Walter White, Executive Secretary of the NAACP, Sprigle found a black man who was willing to accompany and guide him, and who also connected him with the black businessmen and professionals who facilitated his month-long, four-thousand-mile journey through the South—a trip that he later described as "four endless, fear-filled weeks." Sprigle was an anti–New Deal Republican who claimed to be no reformer, and he insisted that he was only searching for a good story. But he did not hesitate to describe Southern race relations as a "bloodstained tragedy" and acknowledged that his was no impartial survey: He went looking for "evil" in the deep South—Mississippi, Georgia, and Alabama—and he found it in abundance.[29] The resultant twenty-one-part newspaper series ran in fourteen Northern papers. Sprigle was featured in *Time* magazine and on television, besieged by requests for speeches, and inundated by furious letters. From numerous offers to publish his material as a book, he chose Simon and Schuster—the publisher of *Gentleman's Agreement*.[30]

There were further connections between Sprigle, Laura Z. Hobson, and the broader undercover tradition. Supplying the foreword to Sprigle's book was Margaret Halsey, a white writer on race issues who worked at the publishing house; she was also the former sister-in-law of Hobson's editor, Richard L. Simon. Halsey noted that in the wake of *Gentleman's Agreement*, it was "only a question of time" before an enterprising writer would cross the race line in search of firsthand knowledge about Jim Crow. Her logic underscored the fact that although Jews were no longer considered a race, they were still commonly framed in racial terms and seen as somewhat comparable to African Americans. It also demonstrated how race matters were supplanting older questions of class in the public arena. Halsey characterized Sprigle's work as reading like "sociological Jules Verne," evoking past undercover forays into worlds of difference.[31] She praised the book in terms that echoed earlier reviews of undercover literature: The author had provided a worthy supplement to objectivist academic tomes such as Gunnar Myrdal's *An American Dilemma*; he had brought life and vividness to the facts and had infused his material with the unique resonances of personal experience.[32] The connection to *Gentleman's Agreement* seemed obvious and was also noted by *Time*. But Sprigle's adventure was further linked by the *Christian Century* to the very origins of undercover investigation: The reviewer Winfred Garrison compared Sprigle's ability to know how it felt to be black with Walter Wyckoff's efforts to penetrate the mysteries of hobo life. Although skeptical, Garrison still offered the praise that had commonly been accorded earlier down-and-outers when he lauded Sprigle's apparent scientific detachment, his "honest and competent" reporting of what he saw. Garrison observed that Sprigle left it to others to provide solutions—as had many a previous sociological Jules Verne.[33]

Sprigle's book echoed certain features of the earlier undercover tradition, while it also incorporated distinctive elements that anticipated Griffin's *Black Like Me*. His novel rituals of divestment included fruitless efforts to darken his skin with dyes before resorting to the sun's rays, and abandoning the status of "white and free" by entering the Jim Crow car in Washington,

DC, to travel southward.[34] Sprigle announced himself to the reader not as a transracial performer, but as a transformed man: He "was a Negro in the Deep South," who had learned "as well as any white man may" about being black below the border that "us black folk" called "the Smith and Wesson Line." Like many predecessors who feared going native, he did not believe that he would emerge unchanged. Early in the book Sprigle worried, as he felt himself shifting psychologically toward a black perspective, that he would be unable to turn his mind " 'white' again." At the end of his journey, even after crossing back into the North as a white man again, he balked at entering an enticing high-toned restaurant, and he instead sought out a cheap lunch counter that catered to the lower sort. Sprigle ended the book in character, presenting a list of changes that "as a Negro" he had come to think reasonable: "Quit killing us wantonly . . . let us exercise the franchise. . . . Give our children . . . a decent education."[35]

Yet these uses of the first and second person seem largely to have been journalistic affectations, deployed principally at the book's beginning and end to focus the reader's attention. Through most of the narrative, Sprigle made little use of the down-and-outer's self-reflexive narrative voice, and he mainly presented himself as observer and listener: a Northern Negro, largely ignorant of Southern ways, who described what he saw and heard. Unlike most class passers, he did not specify how or when he took notes. But he presented lengthy conversations, presumably reconstructed from memory, in which black informants told stories about the dynamics of sharecropping (which Sprigle styled "grand larceny on a grand scale"),[36] about trying and failing to vote, and about more than one murder. In a tone of understated outrage, punctuated by occasional eruptions of overt sarcasm, he offered his mainly Northern readers a wealth of information about black rural life. And what it meant to live a black life was his principal concern. Unlike Griffin, Sprigle did not seek interactions with whites in order to gauge their perceptions of his supposed blackness. Unlike Griffin's narrative, most of Sprigle's book was less about its author than about the conditions that he observed and the stories he was told.

Some of those stories were certainly calculated to shock. Sprigle was told about Maceo Snipes, a black veteran who defied whites' warnings against trying to vote, was shot three times in the belly and took three days to die. But Sprigle was also effective, as Griffin would later be, in depicting the petty daily complexities of living Jim Crow: for example, having to scramble down a roadside embankment to urinate in the weeds after failing to find an accommodating restroom. Sprigle had been sternly lectured by Southern black friends on the rules of survival—always say "sir" to a white man, never fight back if attacked, do not be "familiar" with white women—and he managed to keep a safely low profile, which was reflected by his restrained narrative presence in the text.[37] It was mainly when Sprigle felt himself to be in physical danger that his black narrative identity came to the fore. Well aware that Southern blacks had long lived under the threat of disciplining violence—"in the shadow of Judge Lynch"—Sprigle spent many an anxious nighttime hour driving Southern highways, hoping to find lodging in the home of a black family. He was tormented by fears of an attack or of an accident that would leave him bleeding to death in a Jim Crow taxi as its driver searched fruitlessly for a Jim Crow hospital. Acknowledging that he only felt safe when sheltered by "my people," Sprigle mainly claimed to be "feeling black" when he felt most beleaguered.[38]

This narrative strategy proved effective with magazine reviewers, who had long praised the more rhetorically restrained undercover texts for their educative potential. Sprigle's measured if relentless recounting of racism's gnawing daily indignities and periodic bloody enormities moved many critics to recommend the book, whether or not they believed that its author had truly grasped what it felt like to be black. Despite various reservations, periodicals ranging from *Christian Century* and *Commentary* to the *Nation* and the *New Yorker* urged audiences to read *In the Land of Jim Crow*, while *Library Journal* encouraged all libraries to purchase it as a clear explication of the subject of race for nonacademic readers. "Many of us have 'passed' for white," wrote Walter White in *Saturday Review*; now he encouraged readers to follow Ray Sprigle across the race line in the other direction.[39]

In the scholarly realm, on the other hand, the limited response reflected tightening restrictions on what counted as evidence for the social sciences. The book was mainly ignored by journals other than those that focused on African American issues. The philosopher Alain Locke argued in *Phylon* that Sprigle's accurate and realistic picture would provide salutary "shock enlightenment" to (presumably white) readers. And in the *Journal of Negro Education*, the sociologist Joseph S. Roucek praised Sprigle's "masterly" account of how it felt to occupy a subordinate status—while also criticizing his method as unscientific and unable to meet professional anthropologists' standards for investigating "esoteric" cultures.[40] Despite the newspaper series' success and notoriety, the generally positive reviews garnered by the book, and a campaign by the *Post-Gazette* to win Sprigle a second Pulitzer, the book sold poorly.[41] This failure to attain full-blown national acclaim may explain why Sprigle, who died in 1957, was largely forgotten by the time Griffin's *Black Like Me* was published in 1961.

In light of its connections to *Gentleman's Agreement*, Sprigle's book may be located in a similar context of postwar social thought. Although the significance of class was supposed to be declining in the United States and class was not the ostensible subject of either work, it still mattered for both texts in unstated ways. Just as Laura Z. Hobson's book insisted that middle-class Jewish cultural and economic attainments should trump ethnoreligious origins and allow for the integration of business offices, resorts, and sub-urbs, so did Ray Sprigle's antisegregationist argument highlight the injustice of barring "intelligent, cultured Negroes" from the rights of full citizenship. Sprigle spent the greater part of his time with such Negroes—profession-als, businessmen, community leaders—and observed that they would never accept Jim Crow, no matter how well appointed its separate train cars might be.[42] Sprigle did not lack concern for the poor, but they were not the principal focus of his journey. Among the very few markers for Southern racial prog-ress that he noted was the case of a prosperous black Georgia farmer who wanted to vote and who pressed his case through contacts with the governor, a black civic organization, and a United States Attorney. When he was duly registered and allowed to vote, whites grudgingly accepted the change—but on the condition, as everyone understood, that none of his poor, sharecrop-per neighbors would try such a stunt.[43] Only an individual's class advance-ment could mitigate the effects of race in the Jim Crow South, and such advancement might be acknowledged only by privileged whites whose status did not hinge solely on their skin color. More strongly than Hobson would have done, Sprigle underscored the class-defined limits of the Georgia farm-er's success; yet compared to her novel, the framing of his book was almost equally narrow.

Where Sprigle most resembled Hobson, and also looked ahead to Grif-fin's perspective on the race issue, was in advancing a liberal-universalist theory of difference that set the three writers apart from earlier generations of down-and-outers. All three would frame that theory, not by invoking historical-cultural arguments or grand abstractions about human nature, but by locating it in the dynamics of family, and especially in a sentimental objectification of the child. Thus in *Gentleman's Agreement*, Phil Green furi-ously rejects Kathy when she threatens to corrupt his son, Tom, by "reassur-ing" the boy that, contrary to his playmates' taunts, he is not Jewish. Even such a backhanded assertion that differences might exist and might matter is not to be tolerated in Phil's rigidly universalist worldview, wherein dif-ference may only be understood hierarchically. In a quieter but analogous scene in *Jim Crow*, Ray Sprigle found that babysitting his black host family's visiting grandchild—who, like Phil's son, bore the ubiquitously American name "Tom"—plunged him into similarly universalist reflections. Watching over the sleeping Tommy, Sprigle mused that "except for his brown skin, this youngster is no different from the thousands of white kids" he had known. Tommy did not yet comprehend that he was black, and that he therefore was consigned to a separate existence. Meanwhile, Sprigle's own daughter, sleeping back in Pennsylvania, would never face the irrational barriers that Tommy would confront. Echoing Kathy's guilt-ridden admission in *Gentleman's Agreement* that she was glad to be white and Protestant, and glad not to suffer the results of being otherwise—" 'God, it would be awful'"—Sprigle admitted to himself, as he looked down on the sleeping Tommy, that he was selfishly "glad that my young one is white—in this free America."[44] In both books, the argument against bigotry ultimately turned on the juxtaposition of a guilty adult with an innocent child, the latter a universal being irrespective of skin color, its future predetermined by irrational forces that might yet be vanquished by reason and knowledge, by the fruits of experience— perhaps by the fruits of investigations like Phil Green's and Ray Sprigle's. In *Black Like Me*, a similar evocation of domestic universalism, again offered by a privileged black/white man who loomed over the scene like a household angel, would provide the linchpin for Griffin's argument against racism.

If Griffin's was not the first experiment in white-to-black passing, it proved by far the most influential one. In 1959—three years after the Montgomery Bus Boycott's conclusion, and just before sit-ins and freedom rides erupted across the South—Griffin lived as a black man for six weeks in Louisiana, Mississippi, Alabama, and Georgia. In *Black Like Me* he produced a best-selling study of the American dilemma that was also a universalist manifesto. Race relations in the South furnished the details, but "the real story" was "the universal one of men who destroy the souls and bodies of other men." Griffin insisted that he might equally have been a German Jew, a Mexican American, "or a member of any 'inferior' group." Such narratives would differ in their particulars, but "the story would be the same."[45]

The book appeared in 1961 to laudatory reviews, and it was pronounced by the *Spectator*'s Raleigh Trevelyan to be not only a "searing document" but emphatically not a "stunt," as the black reviewers Louis Lomax and Haywood Burns also both noted. Lomax observed in *Saturday Review* that this story came from the heart of a man who had known "the pain of being different," having endured ten years of blindness induced by a war wound.[46] The *San Francisco Chronicle* praised the book's "authenticity"—long a touchstone for down-and-outers—at a historical moment when, as Archibald MacLeish had complained in 1960, American liberals had increasingly become institution-building "spectators" who seldom inserted themselves "into the common life." Griffin did just that, in a way that garnered greater attention than any previous undercover investigator had commanded, and that contributed to the cult of authentic experience, which would especially galvanize young people during the next two decades.[47]

Why did he do it? Between 1961 and 1977, Griffin offered a series of explanations for his decision to go undercover as a black man. Readers of *Black Like Me* encountered an anguished Christian moralist with a personal obsession—an urgency about the race issue comparable to what earlier down-and-outers had felt about the explosive potential of class divisions. "For years the idea had haunted me," the book began. By the bottom of the first page, the narrator had concluded that passing was "the only way" to comprehend the sting of racial discrimination. In the beginning, then, John Howard Griffin presented himself as a man who simply saw what had to be done, and he did it. But in an epilogue to the 1977 edition, he offered a somewhat different version of his motives. That epilogue was written in the wake of the civil rights and Black Power upheavals, which—as Griffin readily acknowledged—had made increasingly problematical the idea of a white man speaking on behalf of blacks. Griffin now asserted that "black men" had told him that he could only grasp their reality if he were "to wake up some morning in a black man's skin," just as Ignatius Donnelly's astonished protagonist had done. A year later, in the last published reconsideration of his undercover experiences, Griffin further explained that he had initially been enlisted by a sociologist from the University of Texas to conduct a survey-research study; the plan had been to gather evidence from black and white Southerners about alleged suicidal tendencies among blacks. Most black respondents had refused to fill out the form, many writing back that they would not be understood, with a few suggesting that in order to grasp their situation, the investigator would need to wake up black.[48] In Griffin's final telling, then, here had been the book's initial impetus.

Griffin's framing of his purpose for passing had thus changed dramatically. In his original construction of the story, Griffin had presented himself as a liberal moralist horrified by racism and willing to put himself at risk in order to speak for the racial other, whose own words would never be heeded by whites. He was praised for this by African American reviewers. Louis Lomax agreed that white readers who had proven themselves immune to the eloquence of Richard Wright or James Baldwin might be moved by Griffin's tale. Similarly, Haywood Burns acknowledged that although "countless Negroes" had made similar observations, white society might pay attention to a white man telling this story.[49] In the very different context of the mid-1970s, Griffin presented his experiment as having been suggested—even authorized—by thoughtful African Americans who distrusted the standard procedures of social science. Griffin now cast himself as a white man who listened to black voices and heeded their advice, learning from them that a scientific method embedded in racist assumptions, whatever its pretensions to universalistic objectivity, would not produce truth.[50] In both contexts, the author's framing seemed calculated to purge the text of any sensationalism or hint of morbid white fascination with blackness. But in his later revisiting of the book's genesis, Griffin was able to make his motives and sensibility change with the times.[51]

What exactly did Griffin expect to learn from his undercover adventure? He darkened his skin, Griffin later wrote, to "test if we were really involved in racism in this land," a claim that he said whites routinely denied.[52] While the willful naïveté of such a question seems patent, especially coming from a man who claimed already to have studied race issues for twenty years, it probably reflected Griffin's belief that he must state clearly what was already obvious to all blacks and many whites. The "we" is also crucial: Postwar universalists typically focused their attention on the oppressor, not the oppressed. Just as *Gentleman's Agreement* was really about discriminatory gentiles and not Jews, so *Black Like Me* was especially about racist whites—not excepting Griffin himself, as he acknowledged—and not primarily about African Americans. The book was an indictment of white racism, as imaginatively experienced and represented by a black/white man; it was not a systematic exploration of black culture or an attempt to portray it ethnologically, in the manner of earlier class passers. Griffin found no neo-Lamarckian, degenerating underclass. Where Ray Sprigle turned his eyes outward to the land of Jim Crow and sought to survey its landscape, Griffin conducted an inward enterprise that emphasized individual encounters between his black self and those across the color line. Because this was his method, many of the book's most dramatic scenes depicted his interactions with whites who denied him elementary rights, interrogated him about black sexuality, or threatened him. But like Hobson, Griffin found that persistent, systemic injustice rested less on the outrageous acts of the "overt bigot" than on the quiescence of respectable whites "whose faces radiated decency"—those like the drugstore clerk who politely directed him to walk seventeen blocks for a drink of water while ignoring the tap at her elbow.[53] It was this sort of evidence that Griffin surely expected to find, and he found it in abundance. The book rebuked not only Southern white collaborators with Jim Crow, but complacent white readers everywhere.

Griffin hoped to learn about race but not particularly about class, which he claimed to hold constant in his experiment. He did not share earlier down-and-outers' emphasis on labor, except as a phenomenon secondary to racial discrimination. The time he spent working at a shoeshine stand functioned mainly as a ritual of descent, through which Griffin learned less about work than about being a Negro. He described repeated efforts to obtain other jobs based on his middle-class skills as a typist and photographer; in every case, his "gracious smile" earned him only a "gracious rebuff." When he sought factory work, a foreman forthrightly told him that his and other plants were systematically removing African American workers from better jobs, intending to drive most blacks out of the state except for those few who were needed to do the hardest and dirtiest tasks. Griffin wrote many years later that he did do "menial" jobs such as unloading trucks and carrying luggage in train stations, and he subsisted mainly on beans as he tried to live on his wages.[54] But these experiences did not appear in *Black Like Me*. To have explored the worlds of black labor would have diluted Griffin's focus on interactions with whites, and this would have drawn him more deeply into the sort of ethnological exploration that he had chosen not to undertake. He certainly acknowledged the centrality of the Jim Crow labor market to black life. Indeed, the Marxist Paul Peters's description of his time spent sweating among black New Orleans dockworkers echoed faintly through Griffin's rueful meditations by the Mobile docks. Griffin recounted how he had once walked these streets as a younger white man, and how he had then believed that the gracious white gentry and their black "beasts of burden" made up a single natural order. However, he now recognized that the black men laboring on the dock occupied the only space their white neighbors and employers would afford them. Griffin drew the universalist lesson: The world looked different to a black man, "not because he is Negro, but because he is suppressed."[55] He did not hesitate to draw this conclusion but did not care to investigate work on its own terms. Work—or the lack of it—served mainly to illustrate the results of racism. For Griffin, class was epiphenomenal.

Griffin shared Hobson's universalism, although he later came to respect the Black Power movement's particularistic assertions of pride and independence. But at the time of *Black Like Me*, he seemingly possessed no neutral language to describe difference, which for him could only denote "the intrinsic other": "Intrinsic difference always implies some degree of inferiority."[56] This distinguished him from the classic down-and-outer, who usually foregrounded difference and addressed it through a consciousness that mixed romantic attraction with dread. Other distinctions also followed from Griffin's universalism. Aside from shaving his head, his rituals of divestment focused entirely on the processes by which he darkened his skin, and not on clothing, language, or physical bearing. He intended to change nothing about himself beyond his pigmentation, retaining his class identity and enacting a scientific experiment in which a single variable—color—would be tested. Uninterested in exploring any distinctive African American culture, Griffin did not initially expect to pass among blacks, who he assumed would immediately recognize him as a white man, and to whom he intended to explain himself honestly.[57]

Griffin later claimed that he always revealed his whiteness to black families with whom he stayed, because of the danger to which he was exposing them; but he insisted that most did not believe him or that they thought him "delusional." He also concluded that in believing he could not pass, he was "thinking white," assuming that all blacks had stereotypical Negroid features and ignoring the history of racial mixing in the South. Griffin saw this immediately once he "became" black, although he had never noticed it as a white man: Among blacks there was "every kind of bone structure," pigmentation, and eye color. He further realized that any concern that he could not "talk black" was unfounded, as he encountered the broad range of speech patterns and dialects to be found among African Americans. Ray Sprigle, with only a suntan to darken his skin, had reached similar conclusions about the diversity of attributes among those defined as black. Ultimately, their universalism drove both men to see race—in the parlance of a later era—as a social construction.[58]

In *Black Like Me* and in later writings, Griffin would often refer to "being" black; but he did so because he believed that skin color had no intrinsic meaning and that it served only as a marker and focus for whites' stereotypical assumptions.[59] Just a few hours in disguise provided ample evidence to demonstrate for his readers what he certainly already knew: how meaning-laden skin color actually was for whites. To become "wholly a Negro," as he described himself upon the first shocking view of his black-skinned visage in a mirror, was to become so only in the eyes of the white onlooker. From that moment, he "became two men," both observer and observed, with both always present and each uneasily regarding the other. The "Griffin that was" had become invisible—unlike most class passers, Griffin was confident that blackness had rendered him unrecognizable—but what mattered for his experiment were the white world's reactions to his visible black self. Griffin went undercover to dramatize the universalist tenet that difference was illusory and to prove thereby that peoples and their rights must be understood uniformly.[60]

John Griffin culminated and transcended the history of undercover investigation, embodying its longtime tension between scientific objectivity and sympathetic identification, but he raised the stakes by crossing what had seemed the least-permeable border in American life. Like Alvan Sanborn and Margaret Sherwood, he brought to his work the sensibility of a socially concerned novelist, along with an awareness of formal social-scientific knowledge. Like most of his undercover predecessors, he chafed at the latter's limitations; like some, he made that tension part of his narrative. Positioning himself toward the imagined reader, Griffin claimed that his decision to frame the work as a personal odyssey, rather than as a social-scientific study, had come only after his emergence from undercover. In his preface, Griffin explained rather vaguely that *Black Like Me* had begun as a "scientific research study" of Southern race relations, but when he had later tried to organize his materials, the superiority of immediate experience over objective data had asserted itself. For reasons both intellectual and existential, then, he had opted to foreground the "crudity and rawness" of his own story.[61]

Like most undercover studies, *Black Like Me* straddled the line between science and sympathy. Griffin noted his concern that harsh experiences were eroding his professed spirit of "scientific detachment,"[62] and he occasionally cited conventional scholarship as if to right the balance between raw subjectivity and scientism. Thus, to bolster his case that African American and white families embraced similar moral values, ideals, and goals—a case grounded in his brief sojourn with a rural black family—he invoked a current monograph on black families in New Orleans. The scientific ideal always hovered in the book's background: Reviewers praised Griffin, as they had Sprigle, for his spare and "unmelodramatic" prose and lack of "crusading" tone.[63] But connections between Griffin's sort of work and mainstream social science were thinning. In 1959 the young sociologist Keith Lovald, having drawn upon evidence from the older undercover tradition to contextualize his study of Minneapolis's Gateway district, went on to reject the method as unscientific; in 1960 the sociologist Buford Junker—while recognizing a role for personal documents in scholarship—questioned the legitimacy of undercover methods, and he sought to push the discipline closer to an objectivist ideal. Nonacademic reviewers praised Griffin for rejecting this "current style" of "arid" statistical analysis in order to convey more visceral realities.[64] But academia would not give Griffin's experiment the sort of attention that it had once accorded Walter Wyckoff or Frances Donovan.

Still, Griffin relied heavily upon social-scientific authority and data, even if he ultimately judged them insufficient for his purpose. Since the 1920s, the concept of culture had played an ever-greater role in undercover discourse, sometimes with quite negative implications for representations of the worker and the poor. Departing from that mode, Griffin showed no inclination to depict blacks as encapsulated by a debilitating, inferior culture. He was fully aware that anthropologists had punctured the "master delusion" that peoples marked by difference were simply "undeveloped versions of our-selves." But while he used the Boasian tradition to criticize white racism, he did so mainly to insist upon the imperative of universal inclusiveness, not to highlight the integrity of other cultures. Citing Lionel Trilling, Griffin argued that "culture is a prison."[65] For Griffin, as for previous down-and-outers, the key to unlocking that prison was experience: He must take what even lib-eral white Southerners would regard as a "somewhat repulsive step down." As a middle-class intellectual who descended among the others, Griffin was horrified when the sight of his black face in a mirror churned up deeply ingrained racist sentiments. But in the narrative that followed—a chapter in John Griffin's spiritual autobiography, projected onto the landscape of the American South—he claimed to require just five days' experience to con-clude that otherness was an illusion, that all humans belonged to a single family.[66] He would find his clinching evidence not in the public world of Jim Crow, where interracial encounters were warped by pervasive white racism, but in the domestic realm of black familial life, where the particularities of struggle and persistence vindicated universalist values.

To make his case, Griffin dealt forthrightly with the issue of otherness in a way that no previous down-and-outer had done. In the narrative that emerges piecemeal from Griffin's various writings, he presented his life as a protracted struggle to escape the strictures of self/other thinking. He attempted to dis-solve the very categories that had underlain all previous undercover inves-tigations of poverty, class, and difference. Griffin's corpus of writings thus constituted a kind of universalist bildungsroman. He cast his life story as one of progress toward the realization "that the *Other* is not other at all, that the *Other* is me": from his origins as a middle-class Texas youth who had been taught to see both blacks and poor whites as marked by innate difference; to his confrontation with Nazi anti-Semitism as a member of the underground in occupied France; to his wartime service in the Solomon Islands, when he was forced to recognize his own inferiority as a helpless outsider who was regularly guided through the jungle by a five-year-old child; to his postwar struggles with blindness, and his seemingly miraculous re-emergence into the world of sight. From all of this he concluded, "superficial" differences notwithstanding, that "all men are united."[67] This lesson was one not only of race but of class, and it applied equally to African Americans and to those he had once been taught to call "white trash."[68] At the turning point in his bildungsroman, Griffin resolved to use his God-given second sight to work for racial justice by crossing the color line and dissolving all difference into unity. After the ringing affirmation of liberal universalism marked by the success of *Black Like Me*, and by the rise of the social movement that lifted the book to even greater prominence, clandestine ventures across American social boundaries into worlds of difference would never look quite the same.

In many of its key scenes, the book that Griffin produced was less a direct exploration of black society than a series of conversations about race relations. The initial mirror scene, much discussed by scholars, affirmed Griffin's feelings of otherness and divided identity, as did subsequent confrontations with his black self in other mirrors.[69] Experiences with racist whites angered him, but he avoided plunging fully into the black world of bars, blues, and jazz, which simultaneously depressed him and affronted his refined sensibility.[70] The book therefore lacked those primitivist celebrations of the other's vitality, which had often marked earlier accounts of undercover investigation and which Griffin would have found merely racist. Much of his narrative consisted of agonized self-examination, or of conversations—either with thoughtful blacks, or with whites who revealed their racism in overt or subtle ways. When he did generalize about black life, Griffin drew less on ethnographic exploration or primitivist stereotypes than on his conversations with African Americans, as when he discussed "the problem" with members of black New Orleans's "educated and affluent" leadership class over coffee at the YMCA. Class did matter, it seemed: In this elevated company, Griffin's "feeling of disorientation diminished"—only to be violently revived shortly thereafter by another glimpse of himself in a mirror.[71]

The conversations continued but the narrative gained momentum as Griffin left New Orleans to ride buses and hitchhike into Mississippi and Alabama. In a sequence of increasingly infuriating hitchhiking episodes, he was subjected to interrogations about black sexual practices and was even invited to expose himself to satisfy one driver's curiosity. Griffin sturdily insisted throughout these discussions that any apparent differences between the races were environmental in origin: "We are all born blank," he declared, in good universalist fashion. The civilizing power of domesticity was also confirmed by a rare positive encounter with a white man, whose decency Griffin attributed to the man's overflowing love for his child. But a subsequent ride called such hopes into question, as the driver—both a father and a grandfather, and an "amiable, decent American" with the demeanor of a respected "civic leader"—gradually revealed himself to be a vicious and violent racist, a proud rapist of black women, who ended by grimly advising Griffin that in Alabama, black men who stepped out of line quickly went *completely off the record*."[72]

This horrific ride and its dispiriting sequel—an unpleasant interaction with the rude and distrustful operators of a rural café—set the stage for the book's central redemptive scene. If the mind-broadening nature of domestic bonds had just been proven illusory in one case, they were about to be dramatically reaffirmed in another, as Griffin left the road for one of his few extended ventures into black social experience. Offered a ride and a night's lodging by a black sawmill worker, he was carried from the highway's utter darkness into a realm of soft kerosene lamplight and giggling children. When Harriet Beecher Stowe wrote *Uncle Tom's Cabin*, she relied heavily on readers' predictable outrage at slavery's violation of domestic ideals; in much the same way, Griffin used images of black domesticity to delegitimize modern racism. As he later described it, in watching parents and children deal with mundane concerns that ranged from paying the bills to who would do the dishes, "I was seeing that in families everything is the same for all people."[73]

Black Like Me's warmly domestic interlude, set in a two-room shanty occupied by two parents and six children, was sentimental but not entirely evasive. Griffin did not understate the painful aspects of this barren backwoods haven, from the sawmill worker's explanation of the exploitative conditions of his labor, to the dinner of boiled beans augmented by Griffin's gifts of bread and candy, to the nightmare about a racist white assault that awakened him shouting. But the scene served principally to assert Griffin's main message and to dramatize his own full conversion to its terms. Just as Ray Sprigle had contemplated the divergent futures of the sleeping black Tommy and his distant white daughter, Griffin pondered the "cruel contrasts" between the celebration of his daughter's fifth birthday, occurring in Texas that same evening, and the present meager "party." The universalist imperative of justice for all was again grounded in an idealization of the domestic. Griffin's utter alienation from his own whiteness and submersion in the "isolating effects" of his "Negro-ness" were momentarily muted, as he encountered this family "not as a white man and not as a Negro, but as a human parent" who could only decry the unjust constriction of any child's future.[74]

Reviewers emphasized the power of this scene, and Griffin frequently returned to it in his later writings, insisting that it was only by entering the domestic circle of this and other black families that he came to know "emotionally" what he had already known "intellectually": "that the *Other* was not other at all; that within the context of home and family life," all humans faced the same issues and problems; and that "all men are united" at last.[75] Further developing this theme, he would later reframe his "deepest motive" for going undercover as an attempt to save his own children from growing up in an environment poisoned by racism. Griffin's last book-length reconsideration of his undercover experiences, the 1977 volume *A Time to Be Human*, featured numerous full-page photographs of sturdy black parents posing with adorable children. The book resembled an African American chapter from

The Family of Man, the photographer Edward Steichen's classic 1955 paean to liberal universalism.[76]

In the structure of *Black Like Me*, the sawmill family episode served Griffin not only as a rejoinder to the hitchhiking scene's denial of domesticity's softening benefits; it also allowed the undercover author to use his unique rhetorical tools to evoke an emotional response, strategically deploy social-scientific data, and assert his own beneficent power. Writing first, like Ray Sprigle, in heartstring-tugging terms of the children—his own and his hosts', with "their large eyes, guileless, not yet aware" of their probable fate—Griffin then shifts smoothly into observing that "recent scientific studies" belied racist myths about African American intelligence and sexuality. That statement might have lacked force, had Griffin not positioned himself to insist that only an undercover narrator's voice carried the authority to make such academic evidence socially effectual. For Griffin, objective knowledge was a start. But only direct experience with African Americans' domestic lives could convincingly ground universalist egalitarian assertions; racist denigrations of blacks "simply prove untrue when one lives among them."[77] This assertion of knowledge and authority was a step not taken by most previous down-and-outers, who had studied work and poverty in their public settings, or in the transient sites of domesticity that were improvised by hoboes or by homeless families on the road. And when Griffin spoke for others, it was not to consign them to a separate, self-contained culture, but to assimilate them to an imagined, universal family of man. This was both an abstract and an intimate enterprise. It was only by entering the familial circle that Griffin could sustain his grandest truth claims. While there, he also realized the therapeutic potential that his predecessors had so often found in the undercover method's hardening rigors and humanizing contacts. As he would later recall, Griffin now felt that he had been "healed" of his own lifelong racism.[78] To achieve his goals, he had constructed for himself a degree of narrative authority that was unprecedented in the genre. He had wielded that authority over both subjects and readers. And with his discursive resolution of difference into unity—into a sentimentalized realm of universal domesticity—Griffin had imaginatively reconciled sympathy with science.

The sawmill family scene proved the climax of Griffin's tale of universalist affirmation and personal redemption. When he left the next morning, the theme of youth's promise was renewed as Griffin got his first ride from a pair of white boys: "Like many of their generation," they proved "kinder than the older ones."[79] Griffin's concerns about his own otherness also visibly abated. Purged of those deep-lying racial sentiments that had surfaced in the original mirror scene and occasionally thereafter, Griffin proved decreasingly concerned by the sight of his own blackness in his next two encounters with his reflection. His sense of otherness having been attenuated and normalized, he was ready to make his way to Montgomery. There he found the atmosphere, charged by Martin Luther King's "determined spirit of passive resistance," a bracing change.[80]

If Laura Z. Hobson's modest model for social reform had mainly entailed changing the minds of "nice people" and elite suburbanites, Griffin's was more ambitious, beginning within the circle of domesticity but extending to the sphere of public struggle that King's Montgomery Bus Boycott had already exemplified. Griffin's later writings would show respect for more militant forms of black activism and expression, but in 1961 he could serve as the voice of universalist reason and harmony. He could be the black/white man who embraced King's integrationist project, before the assumptions that underlay both men's efforts would be challenged later in the decade. That changes did lie ahead was already evident by 1964 in the harder-edged movie version of *Black Like Me*. Near the film's end, a militant young black protester called Thomas Newton—invented for the movie by the leftist screenwriters Gerda Lerner and Carl Lerner—furiously attacks the Griffin character for having failed as a white man to raise his voice for civil rights and for having assumed a role that he can easily shed at will.[81] It was but a short step from Newton's insistence that blacks would get their rights "by our own strength" to Stokely Carmichael's 1966 call for "Black Power," which made it clear that African Americans now expected to speak for themselves. Although Griffin would always have his admirers and occasional acolytes, the moment when a white liberal might perform the racial other and then speak on his behalf had largely ended.[82]

But while that moment endured, *Black Like Me* seized the public's attention. This remarkably self-reflexive book chronicled not only its author's spiritual autobiography, but also its own production and initial reception. In the final pages, Griffin described his return to Texas and to whiteness, his writing of the *Sepia* articles, and the resultant sensation: television interviews, magazine coverage, threatening phone calls, a hanging-in-effigy in his hometown. Reviews of the book often mentioned this notoriety, which effectively set the stage for *Black Like Me*'s success.[83] Reviewers were overwhelmingly positive, although, typically for the undercover tradition, some doubted that Griffin's method could truly have taught him what it felt like to be black.[84] But black and white reviewers agreed that white readers could learn much from Griffin about daily life across the color line. And the black scholar-activist Louis Lomax, who found the book "moving and troubling" and "generally excellent," thought that Griffin had come closer to grasping the black experience than any white man before him. Similarly, a brief review in the NAACP organ *Crisis* approved of Griffin's reliance on experience over abstract empathy, although it found the book's quality "very uneven."[85]

The *New York Herald Tribune* complained that Griffin had done "a disservice" to black writers who regularly made similar points, but Lomax affirmed Griffin's own sense that his book would likely gain sympathetic white attention, while Haywood Burns added ruefully that black critiques of Jim Crow might command a broader hearing now that they had "been given certification by a white man." In a thoughtful review that linked Griffin's project to the undercover tradition, *Commonweal's* Bruce Cooke observed that as with George Orwell's *Down and Out in Paris and London,* readers' reactions must be tempered by the knowledge that the author could walk away from his assumed identity. But while Cooke oddly echoed Kathy of *Gentleman's Agreement* in thinking it "almost perverse to tamper with one's identity in this way," he concluded that Griffin's harrowing experiences and subsequent persecution at the hands of his Texas neighbors had earned him the right to be taken seriously. In the end, Cooke urged his audience to read "this strange, pain-filled book."[86]

The enthusiastic popular reception for *Black Like Me* was not paralleled in the academic world, suggesting how much had changed since the era of Josiah Flynt and Cornelia Stratton Parker. An amateur investigator such as Griffin might buttress his arguments with occasional citations to social-scientific literature, but the traffic seldom ran in the other direction. Scholarly journals were disinclined to review books by amateurs, and most ignored *Black Like Me.* As with Sprigle's book, the scholarly response was mainly limited to journals that were specifically devoted to race issues. Thus *Race and Class* reviewed the book positively, while *Phylon* judged that it offered the "urgent human dimension" that most scholarly studies omitted. An exception was the *British Journal of Sociology,* which briefly addressed Griffin's book in a review that assessed five recent studies of U.S. race relations. Peter I. Rose argued that this avowedly unscientific work should be read by practitioners of participant observation and that sociologists generally should not dismiss it as mere "unconfirmed reportage," because its main points were confirmed by the suitably scientific and empirical studies also under review. In line with Rose's advice, some sociologists did see the book's value in supplementing their scientific work, and they cited it occasionally in footnotes. According to his biographer, Griffin received letters from sociologists who regarded him as a serious participant in professional discussions about race.[87] And as had been true for the *Gentleman's Agreement* movie, educators praised the book for its classroom utility. The publication of *Black Like Me* coincided with the expanding use of paperback books in high school and college English courses, and the widespread assignment of Griffin's book was often noted in education journals.[88] But the limited response from social science scholars showed how marginalized down-and-outers had become in professional discourse. Nonobjectivist studies such as Griffin's would mainly be noticed in the popular media; the undercover method was no longer taken seriously as a scholarly tool.

As Griffin was transformed from a novelist of modest attainments into a well-known civil rights activist—he gave some 1,100 lectures in the ensuing years[89]—his book and its method reverberated through subsequent race-relations discourse. Grace Halsell, a white journalist, with Griffin's knowledge and support, explored the South of the late 1960s as a black/white woman for her book *Soul Sister* (1969). For Halsell, this would be the first in a series of ethnic masquerades. Later white-to-black narratives would range from a Lois Lane comic book story entitled "I Am Curious (Black!)" (1970) to Joshua Solomon's Pulitzer-nominated "Skin Deep" (1994), a product of Solomon's college internship at the *Washington Post*. In yet another twist in the history of undercover investigation, Lawrence Otis Graham, a black New York City attorney and writer, reversed Griffin's rules, retaining his race while descending in class to bus tables at a high-toned Connecticut country club and to fight off roaches in a Harlem rooming house.[90] While all of these efforts offered distinctive contributions to the discourse, none could have replicated the impact of Griffin's foundational work. That moment had passed.

Both within and beyond academia, not only its method but its message would soon render *Black Like Me* an emblem for a quickly bygone era. By rejecting racist particularism, Griffin joined Laura Z. Hobson in vaguely embracing the great undifferentiated family of man. Diana Trilling's criticism that *Gentleman's Agreement*, in its eagerness to discredit anti-Semitism, had failed to recognize the legitimacy of any form of Jewish distinctiveness or difference, would have been equally applicable to Griffin's work. Ironically, Griffin had cited Trilling's husband Lionel to the effect that the "prison of culture" must be unlocked.[91] Yet surely Trilling had not meant that Americans could simply throw open the prison gates and merge into a sea of sameness. Like Hobson, Griffin had simply sidestepped any attempt to grapple with American pluralism in his headlong rush toward the universalist goal. For both writers, undercover investigations that were meant to deflate undemocratic assertions of otherness ended in a form of universalism that denied all difference.

While this could seem laudable in 1961, it would no longer do after 1966, as Americans were increasingly confronted by the reality of their society's heterogeneous character and by the need to make democratic sense of it. Even within the narrower frame of Griffin's 1961 book, his domestic-universalist generalizations could seem vapid and sentimental when counterposed to the hard specifics of racist discrimination, hostility, and violence that punctuated his narrative and gave it genuine force. Further, Griffin's initial assertion that this book could have been about any subordinated or despised group framed racism as a psychological reflex—an irrational one, as Hobson had framed anti-Semitism—more than as a societal force linked to specific historical and economic conditions (although his futile efforts to find work rendered him acutely aware of the latter). The coming emphasis on Black Power would foreground culture, economics, and politics—factors that were at best secondary in Griffin's account. Black Power would be about pride and solidarity, community control, and independent political and economic initiatives.[92] As Griffin came to understand, this was to move far beyond the limitations of what was, paradoxically, his rather narrow universalist vision. Both *Gentleman's Agreement* and *Black Like Me* used the undercover device to advance postwar liberal universalist thought toward its climactic expressions in such moments as Martin Luther King, Jr.'s 1963 "I Have a Dream" speech and the Civil Rights Act of 1964. But unlike postwar liberals, racists never abandoned their belief in difference. It would take the Black Power movement, along with other movements grounded in the affirmation of discrete identities, to assert the salience of difference from an antiracist, antihierarchical perspective. As Griffin recognized in his later writings, this shift would render his sort of experiment obsolete.

But Griffin's book—still in print and selling briskly—remained the post-1960s cultural emblem and touchstone for identity experiments of all descriptions. In the year 2000 a distinguished African American historian invoked *Gentleman's Agreement*, *Black Like Me*, and *Soul Sister* to suggest that every white American could learn something by living black for two months.[93] Also notable was the ubiquity of the "Like Me" construction, as in the title "Male Like Me": a *New York Times* review of Norah Vincent's *Self-Made Man* (2005), a white-lesbian-to-white-male impersonation narrative. The *Times* respectfully compared Vincent's book to Griffin's memoir while underscoring—in familiar legitimizing language—that neither was a "stunt." Yet Vincent's book also suggested the distance traveled since the heyday of class passing and its culmination in Griffin's project. As the reviewer David Kamp pointed out, far from portraying a descent into alien worlds of difference, Vincent's book was mainly a thoughtful and empathetic re-examination of various sites of ordinary masculine experience—a bowling league, door-to-door selling—that readers probably thought they already knew. But

Vincent's conclusions were anything but universalist: Women and men, she argued, "*are* that different in agenda, in expression, in outlook, in nature." Vincent seemed convinced that there was no such "mystical unifying creature" as a human being; there were men, and there were women. In a postmodern era of identity explorations, assertions of equality were not to be made on universalist grounds.[94]

Conclusion

If *Gentleman's Agreement* is now only dimly remembered, *Black Like Me* left a lasting imprint. During and after the 1960s, it contributed to a broad and swelling egalitarian assault on denigrations of variously defined others. But that assault largely dispensed with Griffin's underlying perspective. Both the structure and the content of his life's narrative—the bildungsroman that traced his development from believer in otherness to committed universalist—forever immured the author in the historical moment of his book's appearance. Despite his later affirmations that post-universalist tendencies such as Black Power were entirely legitimate in their motivations, he also consistently reasserted an ardent belief in the universalist creed. Thus in the brief 1979 essay "Beyond Otherness," written in the last year of his life, Griffin revisited both the initial *Black Like Me* mirror scene and the countervailing scenes of black domesticity; again he concluded that "in families everything is the same for all people."[95]

Racial and class passing had sometimes overlapped since the Progressive Era, when "race" had been a more capacious category. This became less true as the circle of whiteness expanded through the century and as a more narrowly defined conception of race surpassed class as the defining category in American social thought and public discourse. Griffin's experiment thus marked the climax of a long history. His example pointed forward less to efforts at replication, such as Halsell's and Solomon's, than to a broader understanding of identities that might be constructed and borders that might be crossed. Werner Sollors has argued that the age of racial passing as a key American literary and cultural problematic ran from the nineteenth through the first half of the twentieth century, until the civil rights and Black Power movements undermined its main assumptions.[96] The era of class passing—which mainly relied on comparable assumptions about fixed social hierarchies and indelible differences—ran roughly the same chronological course. From the 1960s forward, American social explorers tended to see difference less invidiously and would cobble identities from multiple sources while seeking out new borders to cross. Yet expanding the circle of whiteness had not abolished the idea of race. If the significance of class was thought to have declined, class could still be melded with race in academic and popular social thought during the twentieth century's last decades, when a few determined investigators would again cross over into the provinces of poverty.

PART IV

Conclusion

6

Finding the Line in Postmodern America, 1960–2010

In 1967 Whiting Williams published his final book, *America's Mainspring and the Great Society: A Pick-and-Shovel Outlook*. Largely a restatement of his long-familiar ideas about the forging of identity through work and the dangers of a welfare state, the book's only fresh undercover material hearkened back to Williams's experiences in the early 1930s. There were few reviews, and the critical response was dismissive. *Choice* did not recommend the book for college libraries, seeing Williams as a relic and criticizing the index for displaying "social science jargon" that Williams had not used in the text. It was telling that this index had been prepared by a professor, a "real" social scientist whose imprimatur may have been intended to give the book more scholarly heft in an intellectual environment increasingly hostile to uncredentialed amateurs.[1] As a pioneer of undercover investigation, Williams had once successfully straddled the academic and popular publishing worlds. But such a stretch was less plausible by the later 1960s. Down-and-outers did not disappear after the 1960s, but they would operate in dramatically changed contexts.

Borders, Identities, Contexts

The great age of covert industrial investigation was largely over, especially for those who coveted recognition and success on the tenure track. A range of adventurers continued to ply the undercover technique, but less commonly to enter the worlds of hard work and poverty. Laura Z. Hobson proved unintentionally prescient when she depicted the characters in *Gentleman's Agreement* joking at the book's end about the protagonist Phil Green's next likely assignment: "I was a woman for eight weeks?" By the early twenty-first century, cross-gender masquerades would prove to be no joke. In the wake of Black Power and the related social movements it spawned, the "roots" fascinations of the 1970s, and the emergence in the 1980s of multiculturalism, the United States saw vigorous and proliferating assertions of identities that were grounded variously in race, ethnicity, gender, sexuality, and religion. In this setting, the idea that one might cross some definitive social border to explore a singular unknown class no longer seemed self-evidently true. There were many borders to cross in post-sixties America, and many possible meanings might be attached to such crossings.[2]

Undercover investigation had always been a self-reflexive endeavor, and the nature of selfhood was also coming to be understood in new ways. The earliest, proto-modernist down-and-outers had inaugurated their search for authenticity by challenging the Victorian conviction that outward performances of selfhood must be firmly anchored to a fixed inner self. Across the twentieth century, generations of modernist social explorers used class passing not only to better grasp the nature of their society, but also to test the increasing tension between self and performance, between social origin and the potential for personal reinvention. As the 1950s ended, the sociologist Erving Goffman's influential study *The Presentation of Self in Everyday Life* (1959) posited that the modern self normally expressed itself through situationally appropriate "presentations." But from the 1960s through the 1980s, the modernist assumptions underlying Goffman's work were challenged. In 1988, the postmodernist theorist Judith Butler argued against Goffman that there was no essential or authentic inner self—only performance, through which selves were constructed. Late-century Americans had entered an age of hybridized identities and multiple performances, in which females might pass for males, gays for straights, whites for blacks, prosperous blacks for poor ones, thin women for fat ones, adults for high schoolers—and, still, middle-class journalists and social scientists passed for hoboes, meatpackers, waitresses, domestic workers, and impoverished street people.[3]

John Howard Griffin's 1961 experiment had foregrounded racial masquerade as a fruitful form of social exploration, but poverty was also due for one of its periodic rediscoveries. While the 1962 publication of Michael Harrington's *The Other America* conventionally serves as a sign for resurgent awareness about the tenacity of poverty, such resurgences were destined to recur through the rest of the century as the economy lurched up and down across the decades. In that environment, undercover discourse was reshaped by multiple factors. With the massive economic restructuring sometimes called "deindustrialization," a shrinking industrial labor force offered fewer options for undercover penetration. Growth in service work, on the other hand, created new opportunities. Rather than seeking work in a factory or field, the journalist Barbara Ehrenreich labored in a restaurant, for a housecleaning service, and as a retail clerk; Alex Frankel, a business writer, worked for Starbuck's, Home Depot, the United Parcel Service, and the Gap; and the sociologist Amy Flowers went undercover in the phone sex industry. A few found work in industrial settings during these years of job insecurity, plant closures, and globalizing production. The anthropologist María Patricia Fernández-Kelly explored garment labor in a Mexican maquiladora just across the U.S. border; a sociologist, Tom Juravich, worked in a small New England wire mill that subcontracted to corporate customers; and perhaps most poignantly, the journalist Solange De Santis, who worked undercover in an Ontario General Motors plant as it prepared to shut down, found herself chronicling the end of an era. For her fellow workers, this job would soon be neither a source of security nor a dreaded lifelong grind. Ehrenreich encountered a similarly grim picture for the professional middle class when she sought employment in corporate management.[4] The landscape of work had changed dramatically.

The intellectual contexts for undercover investigations were also shifting. From the 1890s through the 1930s, down-and-outers had melded contemporary views on class with current ideas about evolution, culture, and race in order to picture the poor for middle-class readers: sometimes as vital, uninhibited, and vibrantly alive; sometimes as primitive, uncivilized, and devolving; and in both cases, as a breed apart from their middle-class selves. By the 1940s, a shift away from such essentialist formulations had become evident in works such as E. Wight Bakke's late-Depression unemployment studies, and then in the postwar industrial scholarship of Donald Roy. But the unstable blend of Boasian cultural relativism and liberal universalism that shaped the thinking of Laura Hobson and John Griffin, which dominated much postwar reformist thought, eroded in the decades after *Black Like Me*. Difference came roaring back, often as a source of pride and as a basis for group mobilization. But degraded images of otherness also reemerged as debates arose among scholars and in the popular media about a self-replicating "culture of poverty," and then about the emergence of a similarly isolated and hereditary "underclass." Users of both categories tended to focus on the African American poor and to emphasize behavioral traits over economic condition or constraint, with culture serving as a transmitting vehicle that could seem vaguely biological and powerfully deterministic.[5]

Two paths now opened before clandestine investigators. A few absorbed and used the new terminology. In 1995, the filmmaker and author Peter Davis wrote about his brief but frightening journey through the "American hell" of the urban, mainly black underclass. Davis feared that the very existence of such an isolated and pathological culture showed that American poverty was becoming hereditary. A language of "us" against the "others" permeated this agonized white liberal's effort to deal with having been mugged by a black man, an event that he described at the book's beginning. Struggling to acknowledge his subjects' full humanity, Davis also observed soberly that "they are our enemies, and they know it even if we don't." Like many undercover predecessors, Davis brooded on social apocalypse. For him, the underclass was a ticking bomb that might soon explode.[6]

Yet most recent down-and-outers took a different path, resisting the newest efforts to meld class and poverty with culture and race. Many reflected a post-sixties egalitarian receptivity to difference that derived from connections to the civil rights, New Left, and feminist movements. Wary of the culture of poverty and underclass ideas, they forged their own paths toward dealing with difference. The older universalism was now typically infused by a new appreciation for pluralism and difference. Ted Conover, a journalist who went undercover as a hobo, echoed Griffin's universalism in harboring the "subversive idea that a human is a human" and insisting that the hobo was "one of us"; but he also pointedly portrayed Mexican migrant workers as the contemporary bearers of a mythic American hobo tradition that had traditionally been figured as white and Euro-American. Also in line with this post-sixties sensibility, most down-and-outers of this era grew more circumspect about speaking on behalf of their subjects. Barbara Ehrenreich did see herself as "speaking for them," but she was quick to point out that she did so only from a distance—a notable reticence, considering Ehrenreich's working-class origins and leftist political sympathies. While individual down-and-outers had always been equivocal on this issue, Ehrenreich represented a decisive change from Bessie and Marie Van Vorst's 1903 declaration that they would serve as the workers' "mouthpiece." Such imperial self-assurance was now a thing of the past.[7]

Down-and-outers thus worked in recognizable but shifting social and intellectual contexts. Journalists continued to rediscover poverty and to plunge into hard, poorly paid work. So did a diminishing number of social scientists, who found the undercover technique increasingly hedged about with methodological and ethical restrictions. Those who believed that the poor were largely undeserving, should not be coddled, or belonged to an underclass tended toward the rightward side of the political spectrum, while those on the left—the great majority of down-and-outers—generally rejected such thinking.[8] As their Progressive Era forebears had done, twenty-first-century investigators assessed the prospects of what they still called the "American dream." While the subtitle of Ehrenreich's *Bait and Switch* referred to the *(Futile) Pursuit* of that grail, in Adam Shepard's *Scratch Beginnings* (2008) a newly minted college graduate launched his undercover *Search for the American Dream* explicitly to disprove Ehrenreich's argument and to affirm the dream's viability.[9] As these clashing titles suggest, undercover narratives continued to connect with contemporary social thought and with public discourses on work and poverty, and to participate in ongoing American reconsiderations of culture and class.

Undercover America in the Sixties and Afterward

In the decades after *Black Like Me*, why were new generations of writers drawn to the undercover method? Some cited their predecessors in the tradition. In the 1980s, Ted Conover and María Patricia Fernández-Kelly were inspired to cross the class line partly by Griffin's racial masquerade, while the anthropologist Steve Striffler would in turn credit Fernández-Kelly and the contemporary undercover journalists Tony Horwitz and Charlie LeDuff as models for his 2005 study of a chicken-processing plant. But for the most part, this was a disconnected tradition in which few down-and-outers showed any awareness of their past. The economist John R. Coleman invoked George Orwell but no American class passers in his *Blue Collar Journal* (1974). The sociologist Tom Juravich shrewdly analyzed the negative outcomes of Taylorism and the "human relations approach" to factory management, stressing the lost opportunity to tap workers' informal knowledge of production processes, with no reference to insights gleaned by Whiting Williams and Charles Rumford Walker six decades earlier. In their 1985 search for the "new underclass," Dale Maharidge, a journalist, and Michael Williamson, a photographer, hoboed to Cleveland and to San Antonio— onetime homes of Williams and of Maury Maverick—but mentioned neither. The business journalist Alex Frankel seemed to think his 2007 study of the "human element" in modern work—his inquiry into workers' minds, and into the ways workers sought meaning in labor—was entirely original; Frankel apparently had no idea how closely he echoed Williams. Barbara Ehrenreich seemed to invoke the classic undercover tradition at the beginning of her much-admired book *Nickel and Dimed* (2001), when she recounted having suggested to her editor that someone should explore modern low-wage labor by doing "the old-fashioned kind of journalism—you know, go out there and try it for themselves." But while Ehrenreich was generally aware of the early muckrakers, and possibly some of the undercover investigators, she referred to none by name, and she acknowledged that she had not actually read the muckrakers' work.[10] Recent down-and-outers were not usually motivated by the desire to participate in a living tradition.

What did motivate them? Some used undercover work to advance through graduate school by returning to or recalling trades practiced earlier in life—truck driving, beer bottling, taxi dancing[11]—while others were driven by idealism, a conviction that class mattered, and a desire to grasp workers' experiences. John Coleman, the president of Haverford College and an economist of national reputation, was shocked and perplexed by a famous incident in 1970 when New York City construction workers violently attacked antiwar demonstrators. Unable to identify fully with either side, he felt that he must learn firsthand about "the world of work," and so he plunged into eight weeks of itinerant manual labor. Coleman thus hoped to position himself as an interclass mediator, in the tradition of many earlier down-and-outers. Further to the left was a Johns Hopkins political scientist, Richard Pfeffer, who sounded a familiar class passers' complaint: His college and postgraduate educations had failed to address class and work, so he had to educate himself by driving a forklift in a Baltimore factory. Pfeffer's sensitivity to class and hunger for experience were typical of investigators who were shaped by the New Left. A similar impulse drove some sixties radicals to embrace downward mobility, connect with the poor, and achieve new levels of personal authenticity by joining Students for a Democratic Society's Economic Research and Action Project (ERAP). By contrast, the journalist Solange De Santis disavowed any radical political agenda in her decision to take up factory work. But the impact of the feminist movement could be sensed in her determination to experience the world of hard physical labor, a realm traditionally restricted to men, and one quite different from the comfortable world of business journalism in which she had long successfully functioned.[12]

Finally, some social explorers went down and out for the old, familiar reason that taking to the highway or hopping a freight train felt better than staying put. This was typically the mind-set of young men steeped in the literary works of romantic vagabondage by Jack London, Woody Guthrie, John Steinbeck, and Jack Kerouac; some had even read Josiah Flynt. Shaped by countercultural critiques of war, conformity, and consumerism, and thirsting for authentic experience among modernity's cast-off noble savages, they tried hoboing.[13] Most played the role only part-time, trying to blend in when they could, but revealing their identities when they needed information or help from the professionals. After the photojournalist Michael Mathers failed in his attempts to deploy "spy" gear in a Minneapolis hobo jungle—his hidden tape recorder repeatedly jammed—he learned to start by establishing at least a semblance of friendship, before openly explaining his project and asking permission to take pictures.[14] Like Mathers, most hobo explorers wrote journalistic accounts, although Douglas Harper's *Good Company* (1982) was based on the sociology dissertation he completed under Everett Hughes, who had also been Donald Roy's advisor.[15] In the end, most found that vagabondage was hard, hazardous, and not so romantic. Maharidge and Harper both observed that by the century's turn, homelessness was no longer a bohemian alternative lifestyle, but a fixed and frightening feature of the American landscape. The journalist Steven Kotler learned the hard way that freight hopping—which almost cost him an arm—was essentially a more mobile, more dangerous version of urban homelessness. And some amateur hoboes still felt the threat of going native. By the time Ted Conover, an Amherst anthropology student, reached Everett, Washington, he had become all too adept at living the "horrible" hobo life. His identity wavered; he grew increasingly uncertain about "where they ended and I began." Conover had set out to become a tramp much as John Howard Griffin had become a Negro, but Conover found that he "had come way too close." Afraid of losing himself entirely, he followed the example of bookish down-and-outers since Walter Wyckoff and sought refuge in the comforts of a public library. Remarkably, a sympathetic young library worker proved also to be an enthusiastic sociology major who had just completed a three-day sojourn on Portland's skid row: " 'It was *so* interesting!' "[16] No doubt it was, but Conover recognized that he needed to get off of the hobo road before it became his permanent home.

Journalists or sociologists, hoboes or working stiffs, down-and-outers had always hoped to achieve a combination of personal and professional goals through their somewhat peculiar endeavor. Richard Pfeffer put it most starkly: He needed to test himself in the alien factory environment, and he also needed a book for tenure. No doubt Solange De Santis spoke for many when she expressed the hope that manual labor, beyond providing her with new material, might free her from the limits of a comfortably middle-class upbringing and a white-collar career in which she felt "trapped." Needing more than a change of scene, she wanted to be "transformed" by her venture into the "strange land" of factory life. But if De Santis carried forward the modernist quest for authenticity, these investigations were never solely about the investigator. In De Santis's doomed auto plant, the lives of the workers were also being transformed, and in a terrible way; she hoped to do something socially useful by telling their stories. The old Progressive Era conviction that truth telling, when it unites scientific scrutiny with sympathetic identification, can change the world still coursed powerfully through the veins of these late-century explorers—even if disappointment with the written word's political limitations too often followed. Maharidge and Williamson chronicled their 1985 hobo odyssey into the world of the "new underclass" in the hope that informed Americans would not tolerate "what was going on"; in a new epilogue to the even grimmer 1995 edition of *Journey to Nowhere*, Maharidge acknowledged disconsolately that "now everyone knows what's going on."[17]

How did the method change in recent decades? Disguised journalists still took to the streets as poor people and to the workplaces as employees, although the jobs they found were sometimes novel—as when Gloria Steinem did a stint as a Playboy bunny to reveal conditions in that sector of the burgeoning service economy.[18] The media, through which investigations reached the public, had also changed. In 1992, ABC News initiated a controversial covert investigation by planting two producers as workers in Food Lion grocery stores in North and South Carolina. Following the network's televised revelations about unsanitary practices in the stores' meat departments, Food Lion sued ABC—not for libel but for the fraudulent placement of investigators in the workplace. Food Lion's initial 1997 court victory was reversed by a Federal Appeals Court in 1999, which ruled that journalists' First Amendment rights trumped Food Lion's privacy claims. During this confrontation over the undercover method's legitimacy, ABC invoked Nellie Bly, Upton Sinclair, and the "great tradition" of American undercover journalism. A Food Lion attorney retorted that he was "not aware of any great tradition of going undercover." But in this case, the underappreciated great tradition triumphed.[19]

In formal scholarship, on the other hand, uses of the undercover method dwindled in number and contracted in scope. Social scientists, influenced by disciplinary norms of objectivism, seldom fully immersed themselves in the working life. Keeping their professional distance, few attempted to construct the sort of vivid first-person identity that had been common as recently as Donald Roy's work. Typical was one investigator who wrote of himself as "the senior author" or "the new man," except when incorporating first-person excerpts from his field notes. The latter, which included infor-mal and sometimes profane language, were duly distanced from the schol-arly text by appearing as indented block quotes in a smaller font.[20] Some undercover social scientists told selected coworkers what they were up to, and in the resultant publications, some isolated their undercover personal accounts to a single chapter within monographs that otherwise followed mainstream scholarly conventions of data presentation and narrative voice.[21] Textbooks and methodological works, continuing a trend that dated to the 1950s, legitimized mainstream participant observation partly by distancing it from deceptive methods.[22] Slum and street studies were conventionally done aboveground, and authors sometimes made a point of disavowing any attempt to pass.[23] Industrial investigations also extended trends that dated to the 1950s, as the accepted model now mandated getting management's permission and functioning openly in the workplace. Again, authors often made a point of their overt status, as if to distance themselves from earlier undercover factory studies that were no longer endorsed by their profession or allowed by management.[24] Richard Pfeffer's case dramatized the poten-tial danger of not playing by the new rules, as Pfeffer proved right to worry that his Johns Hopkins colleagues in political science might not consider his method "professional." They denied him tenure for a book that was deemed insufficiently scholarly—perhaps for its overtly Marxist argument, as well as for its unorthodox methodology. While all of the factors that contributed to his fate cannot be known, for Richard Pfeffer, going undercover may have been a firable offense.[25]

It was ultimately an extension of the 1950s ethical debates about decep-tion that essentially ended undercover investigations in sociology and anthropology by the late 1990s. Some scholars had defended deception on the ground that their revelations might lead to improved conditions for their subjects or that they might contribute to a broader social transfor-mation.[26] But from the 1970s onward, rising controversy swirled around a series of studies. Not all were technically undercover, and most did not focus on labor or poverty, but all raised troubling issues about investigators who assumed false identities or gathered information from unsuspecting subjects. Those subjects ranged from seekers of gay male sex and devotees of doomsday religious cults to rural fisher folk and urban police officers. Eminent sociologists such as Kai Erikson and Herbert Gans, affronted by undercover tactics and other deceptive methods, insisted that deception was not only practically ineffectual but also simply wrong. After a series of sometimes heated exchanges in journal articles and at professional meetings, in 1997 the American Sociological Association (ASA) issued a revised code of ethics that required investigators to obtain informed consent from subjects and that proscribed deceptive practices under most circumstances. When the American Anthropological Association similarly revised its code in 1998, it did so with advisory input from members of the ASA Committee on Ethics.[27] Although the long-term effects of such codes are not easily assessed, it does seem clear that by the late 1990s, after a century of relatively steady production in the social sciences, professional concerns about method and ethics had largely put an end to undercover studies of work and poverty. Debates continued over scientism, objectivity, and nonprofessionals' contributions to knowledge,[28] but down-and-outers and their texts would no longer figure in those arguments.

Conclusion: Progress and Poverty in Postmodern America

What news have recent travelers brought back from their forays into De Santis's "strange land" across the class line? Much of what they found will not seem new to readers who have come this far. After likening themselves to scientists and describing their rituals of divestment, they learned the frustrations of searching for work and services. They learned how to hustle for dishwashing jobs, and how to dodge the police. They learned that no job was truly "unskilled," and that acquiring skills was seldom "a snap." After working too hard at first, they learned to soldier. Working multiple jobs in a low-wage economy, they experienced a new version of the "long turn" that Whiting Williams and Charles Walker had so bitterly criticized. They saw that their fellow workers were not stupid and could be shrewd judges of workplace power relations, that they usually wanted to work well and took pride in their labor, and that they often felt that management got in the way of their efforts. In the workplace, investigators found most other workers to be generous with help and advice. In the streets and shelters, they found that destitute people often shared what they had: a cigarette butt, a shoelace, food. In most of these accounts, the poor did not acquire the sinister aura sometimes imparted to them by Walter Wyckoff or by Sutherland and Locke's investigators. But neither were they sentimentalized. Workers, like most people, could be sloppy, petty, and vengeful. Street people and hoboes could be dangerous; one had to know the rules. Like their predecessors, recent down-and-outers took refuge in books and high culture, fretted about going native, and reminded themselves that however hard the life was, it was not real— and that it was genuinely, brutally hard for the meat cutters, construction workers, garment sewers, and homeless vagrants for whom this *was* life.[29] So they walked away, as down-and-outers have always done: They were able to tell their stories because they were not what they seemed and because their lives—usually from the beginning—had been so different from those of their subjects.

None of this was entirely new. Yet Barbara Ehrenreich's *Nickel and Dimed*, to consider the best-known undercover text of its time, was still received as if it brought fresh dispatches from across the class line. In part, Ehrenreich essentially updated an old story through her explorations of low-wage work. But by doing this in the age of Clintonian "welfare reform," she sharply challenged those resilient American convictions that had been so powerfully revitalized since Ronald Reagan's presidency: that ours is not a class society, that the meanest among us face no structural barriers to mobility, that anyone with twenty-five dollars and sufficient gumption can make it out of poverty—as Ehrenreich's college-educated, middle-class critic Adam Shepard believed. So she did bring fresh news, as her work addressed the distinctive political-economic and cultural conditions that dominated the end of the American twentieth century.

But perhaps what most distinguished Ehrenreich and her contemporaries from earlier generations was their post-civil rights, post-New Left resistance to casting the poor as alien others, despite the ubiquity of culture-of-poverty and underclass language by the century's end. Such resistance had not always been typical of down-and-outers. From the Gilded Age to the twenty-first century, encountering difference was a characteristic experience of modernity and postmodernity.[30] To go down and out was to seek difference. To conflate difference with a degraded otherness that induced fear, disgust, and a determination to build even higher social barriers was always one potential outcome of such journeys—but it is not, as I hope to have shown, the inevitable outcome.[31] However common were such negative representations in the early days of undercover investigation, the practice was always responsive to new contexts, and sometimes to democratizing impulses. Progressive Era efforts to reveal the unknown class while reinforcing middle-class identities through depictions of otherness were partly reshaped in the 1920s by discourses of labor militancy and industrial democracy, if also by those of industrial psychology and personnel management; in the 1930s by Depression suffering and critiques of unchained capitalism, if also by variable deployments of the culture concept; in wartime by imperatives of national solidarity, if also by racial exclusionism; and in later decades by liberal-universalist and egalitarian-pluralist frameworks that increasingly distinguished between difference and alien otherness. The tradition was never a static one, and most of its products were distinctly more democratic by the century's closing decades.

Still, in a diverse and hierarchically divided society, the domestication of difference and the normalization of otherness were never fully achievable—not in the streets and factories, and not on the printed page. In every undercover account, however sympathetically it may have been framed, the reader senses the unassimilable strangeness, the ineradicable feelings of difference, that shaped the writer's experiences and attempts to represent them. This resonant, vaguely magnetic strangeness gave these counternarratives to the American dream their purchase on readers' imaginations. Down-and-outers told discomforting stories that Americans both did and did not want to hear. Those stories were sometimes fraught with the tellers' own fears of the varieties of difference they had encountered, and they also brought unsettling reminders about the permeability of the line they had crossed. But reality, as the writers were equipped to understand it, remained their touchstone. They tried to represent what they thought to be real and authentic. They hoped to make their compatriots see and reflect on the persistent presence of an unknown class.

In recognizing that they lived in a world of difference, undercover investigators also had to decide what the origins and nature of difference really were. In their texts, the explanatory balance between structure and culture, between economy and essence, was always a tense and fraught one. The signals that readers received were usually mixed. By the late twentieth century, the sharpness, and even the positioning, of the lines that writers drew between "us" and "them" had changed significantly. Those lines remain in flux. And as long as ours remains a divided society, social investigators will continue to explore uncharted realms and to search out unknown classes. What light they will cast on their subjects, and to what effect, will depend on the intellectual tools available to them and on the larger contexts in which they work. We will continue to construct meanings for difference, which will remain a condition of our existence in national and global orders that become ever more fluid and diverse. The long-lived conundrum of progress and poverty that perplexed and motivated the first down-and-outers may yet be resolved, if Americans should determine to undertake far-reaching economic and social transformations. In a society so transformed, there would be no unknown class in the old sense. We would still live in a world of difference. But that would be a good place to live.

NOTES

INTRODUCTION

1. Mrs. John Van Vorst and Marie Van Vorst, *The Woman Who Toils: Being the Experiences of Two Gentlewomen as Factory Girls* (New York: Doubleday, Page, 1903), 3–5, 168; George Orwell, *Down and Out in Paris and London* (London, 1933; New York: Harcourt, Brace Jovanovich, 1961).

2. Frances Donovan, *The Woman Who Waits* (Boston: Gorham Press, 1920), 11–12. By referring here to Jacob Riis's classic study, I mean to suggest the distinction between my subjects, with their commitment to masquerade and their far greater degree of immersion in the world of workers and the poor, and the broader discursive tradition of looking at the poor and the marginalized of which Riis's book is the best-known example. See Jacob Riis, *How the Other Half Lives: Studies among the Tenements of New York*, ed. and introd. David Leviatin (New York, 1890; reprint, Boston: Bedford Books, 1996). Studies of the broader tradition include Robert M. Dowling, *Slumming in New York: From the Waterfront to Mythic Harlem* (Urbana: University of Illinois Press, 2007), and Chad Heap, *Slumming: Sexual and Racial Encounters in American Nightlife, 1885–1940* (Chicago: University of Chicago Press, 2009).

3. Following the economist Michael Zweig, I understand "class" to signify where one stands in a dynamic structure of power relations, not as a condition reducible to income, wealth, or life conditions (which do vary with class). Poverty, according to Zweig, is a condition that often characterizes the lives of working-class people who contend with low-wage work, irregular employment, and protracted unemployment. Understood in this way, class bears obvious connections to gender and race. See Michael Zweig, "Six Points on Class," in *More Unequal: Aspects of Class in the United States*, ed. Michael D. Yates (New York: Monthly Review Press, 2007), 173–176. On the American resistance to class analysis, see Reeve Vanneman and Lynn Weber, *The American Perception of Class* (Philadelphia: Temple University Press, 1987). For a penetrating analysis of how class was denied in the Van Vorsts' era, see Shelton Stromquist, *Reinventing "The People": The Progressive Movement, the Class Problem, and the Origins of Modern Liberalism* (Urbana: University of Illinois Press, 2006).

4. John Howard Griffin, *Black Like Me* (New York, 1961; New York: Penguin, 1996).

5. Charles Loring Brace, *The Dangerous Classes of New York and Twenty Years' Work among Them*, 3rd ed. (New York, 1872; reprint, Montclair, NJ: Smith, Patterson, 1967); Ken Auletta, *The Underclass* (New York: Random House, 1982). This genealogy is discussed in Herbert Gans, *The War against the Poor* (New York: Basic Books, 1995), 11–57, and in

Michael B. Katz, *Improving Poor People: The Welfare State, the "Underclass," and Urban Schools as History* (Princeton: Princeton University Press, 1995), 9–35.

6. Michael Katz alludes to such a conflation in "The Urban 'Underclass' as a Metaphor of Social Transformation," in *The "Underclass" Debate: Views from History* (Princeton: Princeton University Press, 1993), 11. The classic account of the Boasian paradigm shift is George W. Stocking, *Race, Culture, and Evolution: Essays in the History of Anthropology* (New York: Free Press, 1968). Richard H. King explores the sometimes-mixed legacy of the culture concept's triumph in *Race, Culture, and the Intellectuals, 1940–1970* (Washington, DC: Woodrow Wilson Center Press, 2004).

7. Stocking discusses the persistence of Lamarckism in *Race, Culture, and Evolution*, 234–269; see also Peter Bowler, *The Eclipse of Darwinism: Anti-Darwinian Evolution Theories in the Decades around 1900* (Baltimore: Johns Hopkins University Press, 1983), 98–106.

8. For the controversy surrounding the term "underclass," see Bil E. Lawson, ed., *The Underclass Question* (Philadelphia: Temple University Press, 1992), and Katz, "Underclass" Debate.

9. Donovan, *Woman Who Waits*, 11–12. If, as Donovan claimed, she searched the libraries and solicited the Bureau of Labor for precedents, surely she would have found Amy Tanner's and Maud Younger's accounts of undercover waitressing; the very title of her book could have been modeled on the Van Vorsts' *Woman Who Toils*. See Amy E. Tanner, "Glimpses at the Mind of a Waitress," *American Journal of Sociology* 13 (July 1907): 48–55, and Maud Younger, "The Diary of an Amateur Waitress," *McClure's Magazine* 28 (March and April 1907): 543–552, 665–677.

10. Solange De Santis, *Life on the Line: One Woman's Tale of Work, Sweat and Survival* (New York: Doubleday, 1999), 251.

11. Relevant works include Laura Hapke, *Tales of the Working Girl: Wage-Earning Women in American Literature, 1890–1925* (New York: Twayne, 1992), 45–67; Frank Tobias Higbie, "Crossing Class Boundaries: Tramp Ethnographers and Narratives of Class in Progressive Era America," *Social Science History* 21 (Winter 1997): 559–592; Mark Pittenger, "A World of Difference: Constructing the 'Underclass' in Progressive America," *American Quarterly* 49 (March 1997): 26–65; Eric Schocket, "Undercover Explorations of the 'Other Half,' or the Writer as Class Transvestite," *Representations* 64 (Fall 1998): 109–133; Cathryn Halverson, "The Fascination of the Working Girl: Dorothy Richardson's *The Long Day*," *American Studies* 40 (Spring 1999): 95–115; Jean Marie Lutes, "Into the Madhouse with Nellie Bly: Girl Stunt Reporting in Late Nineteenth-Century America," *American Quarterly* 54 (June 2002): 217–253; Patrick J. Chura, " 'Vital Contact': Eugene O'Neill and the Working Class," *Twentieth-Century Literature* 49 (Winter 2003): 520–546.

12. Peter Hitchcock, "Slumming," in *Passing: Identity and Interpretation in Sexuality, Race, and Religion*, ed. Maria Carla Sanchez and Linda Schlossberg (New York: NYU Press,

2001), 180–183; Mark Collins, "Look at Low-Wage Workers Not Quite on the Money," *Boulder Daily Camera Friday Magazine* (September 26, 2003): 20; Barbara Ehrenreich, *Nickel and Dimed: On (Not) Getting By in America* (New York: Metropolitan, 2001).

13. Hitchcock, "Slumming," 182.

14. Hitchcock addresses position and identification in "Slumming," 168–172. I emphasized middle-class identity and reinscribing the class line in "A World of Difference." For other examples, see David Leviatin, "Framing the Poor: The Irresistability of How the Other Half Lives," introduction to Riis, *How the Other Half Lives*, 28–31; Chura, " 'Vital Contact,' " 534; and Lutes, "Into the Madhouse," 221, 228. Alon Rachamimov makes a cogent case against the assumption that transgression necessarily reaffirms hierarchy in "The Disruptive Comforts of Drag: (Trans)Gender Performances among Prisoners of War in Russia, 1914–1920," *American Historical Review* 111 (April 2006): 375–377, 382. For useful interdisciplinary reflections on these issues, see Judith Roof and Robin Wiegman, eds., *Who Can Speak? Authority and Critical Identity* (Urbana: University of Illinois Press, 1995), especially Linda Martin Alcoff, "The Problem of Speaking for Others," 97–119, and Andrew Lakritz, "Identification and Difference: Structures of Privilege in Cultural Criticism," 3–29.

CHAPTER 1

1. Following recent historians of progressivism, I understand the Progressive Era as beginning in the 1890s and ending at or shortly after World War I. See, for example, Maureen A. Flanagan, *America Reformed: Progressives and Progressivisms, 1890s–1920s* (New York: Oxford University Press, 2007). For a more elongated view of progressivism, see Elisabeth Israels Perry, "Men Are from the Gilded Age, Women Are from the Progressive Era," *Journal of the Gilded Age and Progressive Era* 1 (January 2002): 25–48. Scholarship touching on Progressive Era undercover investigation includes Patrick J. Chura, " 'Vital Contact': Eugene O'Neill and the Working Class," *Twentieth-Century Literature* 49 (Winter 2003): 520–546; Cathryn Halverson, "The Fascination of the Working Girl: Dorothy Richardson's *The Long Day*," *American Studies* 40 (Spring 1999): 95–115; Laura Hapke, *Tales of the Working Girl: Wage-Earning Women in American Literature, 1890–1925* (New York: Twayne, 1992), 45–67; Frank Tobias Higbie, *Indispensable Outcasts: Hobo Workers and Community in the American Midwest, 1880–1930* (Urbana: University of Illinois Press, 2003); Jean Marie Lutes, "Into the Madhouse with Nellie Bly: Girl Stunt Reporting in Late Nineteenth-Century America," *American Quarterly* 54 (June 2002): 217–253; Kathryn J. Oberdeck, *The Evangelist and the Impresario: Religion, Entertainment, and Cultural Politics in America, 1884–1914* (Baltimore: Johns Hopkins University Press, 1999); Mark Pittenger, "A World of Difference: Constructing the 'Underclass' in Progressive America," *American Quarterly* 49 (March 1997): 26–65; Jonathan Prude, "Experiments in Reality: Wyckoff's *Workers*," in

What Democracy Looks Like: A New Critical Realism for a Post-Seattle World, ed. Amy Schrager Lang and Cecelia Tichi (New Brunswick: Rutgers University Press, 2006), 144–160; Eric Schocket, "Undercover Explorations of the 'Other Half,' or the Writer as Class Transvestite," *Representations* 64 (Fall 1998): 109–133; Mary Suzanne Schriber and Abbey Zink, "Elizabeth L. Banks and Her Campaigns of Curiosity," introduction to Elizabeth Banks, *Campaigns of Curiosity: Journalistic Adventures of an American Girl in Late Victorian London* (London, 1894; reprint, Madison: University of Wisconsin Press, 2003), vii–xliv; Gregory R. Woirol, *In the Floating Army: F. C. Mills on Itinerant Life in California, 1914* (Urbana: University of Illinois Press, 1992).

2. Jack London, *The People of the Abyss* (New York: Macmillan, 1903).

3. Michael Denning, *The Cultural Front: The Laboring of American Culture in the Twentieth Century* (London: Verso, 1996), 28–29. On this generation, see also Christine Stansell, *American Moderns: Bohemian New York and the Creation of a New Century* (New York: Henry Holt, 2000). "Modernism" is here construed as a culture distinct from Victorianism in the manner of Daniel Joseph Singal, "Towards a Definition of American Modernism," *American Quarterly* 39 (Spring 1987): 7–26. See also Daniel Walker Howe, "Victorianism as a Culture," *American Quarterly* 27 (December 1975): 507–532; Warren Susman, " 'Personality' and the Making of Twentieth-Century Culture," in his *Culture as History: The Transformation of American Society in the Twentieth Century* (New York: Pantheon, 1984), 271–285; and T. J. Jackson Lears, *No Place of Grace: Antimodernism and the Transformation of American Culture, 1880–1920* (Chicago: University of Chicago Press, 1983), 36–38. Concerns about going native are expressed in Frances Donovan, *The Woman Who Waits* (Boston: Gorham Press, 1920), 10; Josiah Flynt, *My Life* (New York: The Outing Publishing Company,1908), 11; and Anonymous, *Four Years in the Underbrush: Adventures of a Working Woman in New York* (New York: Charles Scribner's Sons, 1921).

4. Dana recounts that he had first thought to pass as a common seaman but was immediately found out. But the scholar Thomas Philbrick notes that in later years, when traveling on business, Dana sometimes donned sailor's garb in order to explore such rough urban terrain as New York City's notorious Five Points. See Richard Henry Dana, Jr., *Two Years before the Mast*, ed. and introd. Thomas Philbrick (1840; New York: Penguin, 1981), 40–41; Thomas Philbrick, introduction to Dana, *Two Years*, 15. On women who served as Civil War soldiers in male disguise, see Elizabeth D. Leonard, *All the Daring of the Soldier: Women of the Civil War Armies* (New York: Norton, 1999), and DeAnne Blanton and Lauren Cook, *They Fought Like Demons: Women Soldiers in the American Civil War* (Baton Rouge: Louisiana State University Press, 2002).

5. Mark Twain, *The Prince and the Pauper* (Boston: James R. Osgood, 1882); *A Connecticut Yankee in King Arthur's Court* (New York: Charles L. Webster, 1889).

6. Peter Keating, introduction to Keating, ed., *Into Unknown England 1866–1913: Selections from the Social Explorers* (Manchester, UK: Manchester University Press, 1976), 16–27. Studies of British undercover investigators include Mark Freeman, " 'Journeys into Poverty Kingdom': Complete Participation and the British Vagrant, 1866–1914," *History Workshop Journal* 52 (Autumn 2001): 99–121; Seth Koven, *Slumming: Sexual and Social Politics in Victorian London* (Princeton: Princeton University Press, 2004); Lucy Delap, "Campaigns of Curiosity: Class Crossing and Role Reversal in British Domestic Service, 1890–1950," *Left History* 12 (Fall/Winter 2007): 33–63; and Judith R. Walkowitz, *City of Dreadful Delight: Narratives of Sexual Danger in Late-Victorian London* (Chicago: University of Chicago Press, 1992), 36–38. For British perceptions of the poor and studies of poverty generally, see also Deborah Epstein Nord, "The Social Explorer as Anthropologist: Victorian Travellers among the Urban Poor," in *Visions of the Modern City*, ed. William Sharpe and Leonard Wallock (Baltimore: Johns Hopkins University Press, 1987), 122–134; Gareth Stedman Jones, *Outcast London: A Study of the Relationship between Classes in Victorian Society* (Oxford, UK: Clarendon Press, 1971); Gertrude Himmelfarb, *The Idea of Poverty: England in the Early Industrial Age* (New York: Knopf, 1984); and Himmelfarb, *Poverty and Compassion: The Moral Imagination of the Late Victorians* (New York: Vintage, 1991).

7. Frau Dr. Minna Wettstein-Adelt, *3 ½ Monate Fabrik Arbeiterin* (Berlin: J. Leiser, 1893); Paul Göhre, *Three Months in a Workshop: A Practical Study*, trans. A. B. Carr, prefatory note by Richard T. Ely (Leipzig, 1891; New York: Charles Scribner's Sons, 1895). Henry W. Farnum, a reviewer, compared the American tramp investigator Walter Wyckoff's undercover study with Göhre's and Wettstein-Adelt's books: see *Yale Review* 8 (May 1899): 107. Göhre's book was positively reviewed in the following: *Nation* 53 (November 19, 1891): 397–398; *International Journal of Ethics* 2 (April 1892): 393–395, by G. von Gizycki; *Westminster Review* 143 (February 1895): 217–218; *Dial* 18 (March 16, 1895): 178–179, by Charles R. Henderson (graduate professor of the investigators Annie Marion MacLean, Frances Kellor, and Edwin H. Sutherland); *International Journal of Ethics* 5 (April 1895): 407, by J. S. MacKenzie; *Annals of the American Academy of Political and Social Science* 6 (July 1895): 136–137, by William Harbutt Dawson. For more on Göhre, consult Richard J. Whiting, "Historical Research in Human Relations," *Academy of Management Journal* 7 (March 1964): 45–53.

8. Göhre, *Three Months*, x; Ely, prefatory note to Göhre, *Three Months*, vii–viii. Göhre went on to a successful career in German Social-Democratic politics. According to Whiting's "Historical Research" (52), Göhre's investigative example was also followed in France. Oddly, Göhre appeared to disagree with Ely that all industrial societies naturally followed the same evolutionary progression (see Göhre, *Three Months*, ix). I discuss Ely's evolutionism in *American Socialists and Evolutionary Thought, 1870–1920* (Madison: University of Wisconsin Press, 1993), 32–34, 36–42.

9. Annie Marion MacLean, "The Sweat-Shop in Summer," *American Journal of Sociology* 9 (November 1903): 289; Richard T. Ely, *Ground under Our Feet: An Autobiography* (New York: Macmillan, 1938), 188.

10. John Kasson, *Rudeness and Civility: Manners in Nineteenth-Century Urban America* (New York: Hill and Wang, 1990), 110–111. Stephenson's adventures are described in "Tramps and Work-Houses," *Harper's Weekly* 22 (February 4, 1878): 106. The tradition of police infiltrating tramp mobilizations continued with Kelly's Army. See, for example, "Police Man Poses as Hobo," Oakland *Tribune* (March 6, 1914): 3. On middle-class fears of revolutionary upheaval, see Robert V. Bruce, *1877: Year of Violence* (Indianapolis: Bobbs-Merrill, 1959).

11. Albion Winegar Tourgée, *Murvale Eastman: Christian Socialist* (New York: Fords, Howard, and Hulbert, 1890), 206.

12. The term is from Kasson, *Rudeness and Civility*, 78.

13. Stuart Blumin, "Explaining the New Metropolis: Perception, Depiction and Analysis in Mid-Nineteenth Century New York City," *Journal of Urban History* 11 (November 1984): 18–19, 28; Paul S. Boyer, *Urban Masses and Moral Order in America, 1820–1920* (Cambridge: Harvard University Press, 1978), 127–129. The title of Helen Campbell's book suggests the binary consciousness common to portrayals of the city: *Darkness and Daylight: Lights and Shadows of New York Life. A Woman's Narrative* (Hartford, CT, 1891; reprint, Detroit: Singing Tree Press, 1969). Social investigators on both sides of the Atlantic increasingly recognized that such binary perceptions were inaccurate: see Walkowitz, *City of Dreadful Delight*, 31–32, and Stuart Blumin, *Emergence of the Middle Class: Social Experience in the American City, 1760–1900* (Cambridge: Cambridge University Press, 1989), 287.

14. Kasson, *Rudeness and Civility*, 77–80; Alan Trachtenberg, *The Incorporation of America: Culture and Society in the Gilded Age* (New York: Hill & Wang, 1982), 125–127; Charles Loring Brace, *The Dangerous Classes of New York and Twenty Years' Work among Them* (New York, 1872; reprint, Montclair, NJ: Smith, Patterson, 1967); Jacob Riis, *How the Other Half Lives: Studies among the Tenements of New York*, ed. and introd. David Leviatin (New York, 1890; reprint, Boston: Bedford Books, 1996).

15. Joshua Brown, *Beyond the Lines: Pictorial Reporting, Everyday Life, and the Crisis of Gilded-Age America* (Berkeley: University of California Press, 2003), 144–149; Kasson, *Rudeness and Civility*, 25; Blumin, *Emergence of the Middle Class*, 258. On the perennial difficulty of clearly defining the "middle class," see Burton Bledstein, ed., *The Middling Sorts: Explorations in the History of the American Middle Class* (New York: Routledge, 2001).

16. Reverend Frank Charles Laubach, "Why There Are Tramps: A Study Based upon an Examination of One Hundred Men" (Ph.D. diss., Columbia University, 1916), 5. On the Gilded Age background to this fear of the unruly poor, see Eugene Leach, "The Literature of Riot Duty: Managing Class Conflict in the Streets, 1877–1927," *Radical History*

Review 56 (Spring 1993): 23–50, and Leach, "Chaining the Tiger: The Mob Stigma and the Working Class, 1863–1894," *Labor History* 35 (Spring 1994): 187–215. Leach examines the intellectual underpinnings of such fears in "Mastering the Crowd: Collective Behavior and Mass Society in American Social Thought, 1917–1939," *American Studies* 27 (Spring 1986): 99–114.

17. This assiduous pursuit of data was most famously exemplified by *Hull-House Maps and Papers* (New York: T. Y. Crowell, 1895). See also Robert A. Woods, ed., *The City Wilderness: A Settlement Study* (Boston: Houghton Mifflin, 1898). For an influential urban research protocol, see Robert E. Park, "The City: Suggestions for the Investigation of Human Behavior in the City Environment," *American Journal of Sociology* 20 (March 1915): 577–612. Frederick C. Mills summed up contemporary theories of poverty and unemployment in his Columbia University dissertation, *Contemporary Theories of Unemployment and of Unemployment Relief* (New York, 1917; reprint, New York: AMS Press, 1968).

18. An example of the therapeutic mode based on Progressive Era experiences was Frank A. Crampton, *Deep Enough: A Working Stiff in the Western Mine Camps* (Denver: A. Swallow, 1956). Among the involuntary experimenters with downward mobility, the many examples include Theodore Dreiser, *An Amateur Laborer*, ed. and introd. Richard W. Dowell (Philadelphia: University of Pennsylvania Press, 1983), and Mariner J. Kent, "The Making of a Tramp," *Independent* 55 (March 19, 1903): 667–670. By the historian Cecil Fairfield Lavell, see "Man Who Lost Himself: An Enforced Experiment in Labor," *Atlantic Monthly* 120 (November 1917): 589–598; "From the Diary of a Laborer," *Atlantic Monthly* 123 (May 1919): 644–654; and "Letters of a Down-and-Out," *Atlantic Monthly* 111 (February and March 1913): 190–197, 368–377. Regarding purposeful deception, I do not address, for example, Dorothy Richardson's *The Long Day: The Story of a New York Working Girl as Told by Herself* (New York: Century Company, 1905) because her book presents itself as the product of an anonymous worker, never naming Richardson as a middle-class person venturing into a different world to study it; this omitted a crucial feature of the down-and-out writer's establishment of identity, authority, and power.

19. Brooke Kroeger, *Nellie Bly: Daredevil, Reporter, Feminist* (New York: Times Books/ Random House, 1994), 85–89, 101–105, 206–207; Penelope Harper, " 'She Waited in Bloomers': Women Reporters Go Undercover in New York City, 1887–1910," paper presented at the meeting of the Organization of American Historians, Washington, DC, March 1995; Lutes, "Into the Madhouse," 239–240. For women writers' critical commentary on the stunt genre, see Elizabeth L. Banks, "American 'Yellow Journalism,' " *Living Age* 218 (September 3, 1898): 644, 648, and Haryot Holt Cahoon, "Women in Gutter Journalism," *Arena* 17 (March 1897): 568, 574. Later investigators sometimes worried that their work might be dismissed as "stunts": see Mary Barnett Gilson, *What's Past Is Prologue* (New York: Harper & Brothers, 1940), 34.

20. Banks's popularity in Britain was affirmed in Marion Leslie, "An American Girl in London: An Interview with Miss Elizabeth Banks," *The Young Woman* 3 (November 1894): 58–62. New Yorkers' awareness of Banks was assumed in a local magazine's review in *The Critic* 23 (April 27, 1895): 304. Banks reported in her autobiography that her work was reprinted in New York City newspapers and that she was met at the dock by reporters and hailed as a "heroine" upon returning to the United States. But she complained that *Campaigns of Curiosity* did not sell well in America and that it had not been properly copyrighted. See Elizabeth L. Banks, *The Autobiography of a "Newspaper Girl"* (New York: Dodd, Mead, 1902), 93–94, 143, 196–199. Besides the London edition, published by Cassell in 1894, F. T. Neely of Chicago published a U.S. edition that same year. But I found no reviews other than the *Critic*'s, in sharp contrast to other undercover books.

21. Wyckoff published a series of articles in *Scribner's* in 1897–1898, beginning with "The Workers: An Experiment in Reality," *Scribner's* 22 (August 1897): 196–206. This material formed part of the two-volume book that followed: *The Workers: An Experiment in Reality*, vol. 1: *The East* (New York: Charles Scribner's Sons, 1897); and *The Workers: An Experiment in Reality*, vol. 2: *The West* (New York: Charles Scribner's Sons, 1898). A later book, much of which also appeared first in *Scribner's*, drew on the same experiences: *A Day with a Tramp and Other Days* (New York: Charles Scribner's Sons, 1906). Flynt's articles appeared in the *Century*, the *Forum*, *Harper's Weekly*, *Everybody's Magazine*, and the *Atlantic Monthly*, among others. They began with "The American Tramp," *Contemporary Review* 60 (August 1891): 253–261. From those experiences came Flynt's *Tramping with Tramps* (New York: The Century Company, 1899).

22. Stephen Crane, "An Experiment in Misery," in *Stephen Crane: Stories and Tales*, ed. Robert Wooster Stallman (New York: Vintage, 1955), 27–38. Crane's story appeared first in the *New York Press* (April 22, 1894); it was republished in the British edition of his collection *The Open Boat and Other Stories* (London: Heinemann, 1898). Further citations to "Experiment in Misery" refer to the version in Stallman's collection. Stallman restored brief introductory and concluding sections that appeared in the newspaper version, but Crane dropped them when he republished the story in *The Open Boat*. In the fugitive introduction, the story's protagonist watches a tramp and discusses with a companion the idea of going down-and-out, thus alerting the reader to the nature of the experiment.

23. Alvan Francis Sanborn, "Anatomy of a Tenement Street," *Forum* 18 (January 1895): 554–572; "A Study of Beggars and Their Lodgings," *Forum* 19 (April 1895): 200–213; *Moody's Lodging House and Other Tenement Sketches* (Boston: Copeland and Day, 1895); *Meg McIntyre's Raffle and Other Stories* (Boston: Copeland and Day, 1896).

24. C. W. Noble, "The Border Land of Trampdom," *Popular Science Monthly* 50 (December 1896): 252–258.

25. Annie Marion MacLean, "Two Weeks in Department Stores," *American Journal of Sociology* 4 (May 1899): 721–741; Margaret Sherwood, *Henry Worthington, Idealist*

(New York: Macmillan, 1899). One other important text of the times that suggests the popularity of the undercover method was Charles M. Sheldon's immensely popular social-gospel tract *In His Steps*, in which a dying tramp serves as the imparter of unpleasant truths to complacent churchgoers. Sheldon's book, although not a down-and-out narrative, was partly built on the author's 1891 undercover experiences in the slums of Topeka, Kansas. See Sheldon, *In His Steps: "What Would Jesus Do?"* (New York: George Munroe's Sons, 1896), and Paul S. Boyer, *"In His Steps*: A Reappraisal," *American Quarterly* 23 (Spring 1971): 60–78.

26. Flynt, "American Tramp," 254; "Life among German Tramps," *Century* 46 (October 1893): 803. Flynt's education is discussed in "Willard, Josiah Flint [*sic*]," *Dictionary of American Biography* 21, Supplement 1 (New York: Charles Scribner's Sons, 1944), 706, and in Louis Filler, *The Muckrakers: Crusaders for American Liberalism* (Chicago: Henry Regnery, 1968), 70.

27. Crane, "Experiment in Misery," 27–28; Alan Trachtenberg, "Experiments in Another Country: Stephen Crane's City Sketches," in *American Realism: New Essays*, ed. Eric J. Sundquist (Baltimore: Johns Hopkins University Press, 1982), 144, 149.

28. Marie Van Vorst, *Amanda of the Mill* (Indianapolis: Bobbs-Merrill, 1904).

29. On Crane's method and its larger contexts, see Michael Robertson, *Stephen Crane, Journalism, and the Making of Modern American Literature* (New York: Columbia University Press, 1997), 95–106; and Keith Gandal, *The Virtues of the Vicious: Jacob Riis, Stephen Crane, and the Spectacle of the Slum* (New York: Oxford University Press, 1997). O. Henry, "The Higher Pragmatism," in *Forty-One Stories*, ed. Burton Raffel (New York: Signet Classics, 1984), 134.

30. Christopher Benfey, *The Double Life of Stephen Crane* (New York: Knopf, 1992), 147–148. A clear connection between the two men is not, however, easily established. The series of *Scribner's* articles that became Wyckoff's book did not begin appearing until 1897, although he did begin working on them sometime after commencing a social-science graduate fellowship at Princeton in 1894—the same year that Crane published his "Experiment in Misery." The two men were linked through Crane's roommate and illustrator, Corwin Knapp Linson, who eventually illustrated one of Wyckoff's articles. Stanley Wertheim and Paul Sorrentino clarify the Linson connection in *The Crane Log: A Documentary Life of Stephen Crane, 1871–1900* (New York: G. K. Hall, 1994), 97–101. See also "Wyckoff, Walter Augustus," *Dictionary of American Biography* 20 (New York: Charles Scribner's Sons, 1936), 574–575.

31. The principal exceptions were Annie Marion MacLean, Edwin A. Brown, and Whiting Williams, who went undercover well into their forties and fifties. MacLean was born in approximately 1870, and she would have been at least in her early forties by the time her last undercover study was published in 1923, although the text suggests that the research may have been done a few years earlier. Edwin Brown was fifty-two and retired from business when he started his cross-country lodging-house tour in

1909. And Whiting Williams, born in 1878, was already forty-one at the time of his first down-and-out excursion in 1919, and he descended again as late as 1932, when he was fifty-four. Mary Jo Deegan, "Annie Marion MacLean," in *Women in Sociology: A Bio-Bibliographical Sourcebook*, ed. Mary Jo Deegan (New York: Greenwood Press), 280; Edwin A. Brown, *Broke: The Man without the Dime* (Chicago: Browne and Howell Company, 1913), xi; Daniel A. Wren, *White Collar Hobo: The Travels of Whiting Williams* (Ames: Iowa State University Press, 1987).

32. Chura, " 'Vital Contact'"; Stansell, *American Moderns*, 60–62.

33. Jane Addams, "The Subjective Necessity for Social Settlements," in her *Twenty Years at Hull House* (New York: Signet Classics, 1960), 98; Sherwood, *Henry Worthington*, 9, 73.

34. Ruth Crocker, *Social Work and Social Order: The Settlement Movement in Two Industrial Cities, 1889–1930* (Urbana: University of Illinois Press, 1992), 224–225; Glenda Elizabeth Gilmore, ed., *Who Were the Progressives?* (Boston: Bedford/St. Martin's, 2002). For the longer intellectual history of this tension, see Morton White, *Science and Sentiment in America: Philosophical Thought from Jonathan Edwards to John Dewey* (New York: Oxford University Press, 1972).

35. Linda Gordon, "Social Insurance and Public Assistance: The Influence of Gender in Welfare Thought in the United States, 1890–1935," *American Historical Review* 97 (February 1992): 33; "A Year's Best Books," *Outlook* 60 (December 3, 1898): 817–818; Phyllis Blanchard, review of *The Woman Who Waits*, by Francis Donovan, *American Journal of Sociology* 26 (March 1921): 640.

36. Wyckoff, *The Workers*, 1:viii; Sanborn, "Study of Beggars," 200; Margaret Chase and Stuart Chase, *A Honeymoon Experiment* (Boston: Houghton Mifflin, 1916), front matter. For an example of the difficulty of establishing scientific credibility in a down-and-out study, see Frances Kellor, *Out of Work: A Study of Employment Agencies, Their Treatment of the Unemployed and Their Influence upon Home and Business* (New York: G. P. Putnam's Sons, 1904), v–vii, 2–5.

37. Cornelia Stratton Parker, "The Human Element in the Machine Process," *Annals of the American Academy of Political and Social Science* 90 (July 1920): 86–88. Presumably the passage quoted (p. 87) was a lightly veiled reference to Parker's recently deceased husband, Carleton Parker, a well-known professor of labor economics.

38. Whiting Williams, *What's on the Worker's Mind: By One Who Put on Overalls to Find Out* (New York: Charles Scribner's Sons, 1920), 3–4. Down-and-out accounts appeared or were reviewed widely in academic, reform, opinion, and popular magazines such as the *American Journal of Sociology*, the *Survey*, the *Nation*, and *Scribner's*, as well as in a range of newspapers, including the *New York Times*.

39. Theodore Waters, "Six Weeks in Beggardom," Part I, *Everybody's Magazine* 11 (December 1904): 789; Inez A. Godman, "Ten Weeks in a Kitchen," *Independent* 53 (October 17, 1901): 2459; Anonymous, *Four Years in the Underbrush*, 3; Fannie Hurst, *Anatomy of Me* (Garden City, NY, 1958; reprint, New York: Arno Press, 1980), 1, 4, 8.

40. Chase and Chase, *Honeymoon Experiment*, 88; Rheta Child Dorr, *A Woman of Fifty* (New York: Funk and Wagnalls, 1924), 164; Lillian Pettengill, *Toilers of the Home: The Record of a College Woman's Experience as a Domestic Servant* (New York: Doubleday, Page, 1903), viii; Cornelia Stratton Parker, *Wanderer's Circle* (Boston: Houghton Mifflin, 1934), 89–90.

41. Charles Rumford Walker, *Steel: The Diary of a Furnace Worker* (Boston: Atlantic Monthly Press, 1922), vii; Cornelia Stratton Parker, *Working with the Working Woman* (New York: Harper and Brothers, 1922), ix; Williams, *What's on the Worker's Mind*. Investigators' emphases on psychology and the "worker's mind" became more prominent in the 1920s, and they will be further addressed in chapter 2.

42. Charlotte Perkins Gilman, *What Diantha Did* (London: T. Fisher Unwin, 1912), previously serialized in Gilman's magazine *The Forerunner* in 1910; Gilman, review of *Out of Work*, by Frances Kellor, *The Critic* 46 (March 1905): 280.

43. MacLean, "Sweat-Shop in Summer," 289–290. On the courting of hardship, see also Mrs. John Van Vorst and Marie Van Vorst, *The Woman Who Toils: Being the Experiences of Two Gentlewomen as Factory Girls* (New York: Doubleday, Page, 1903), 4; Chase and Chase, *Honeymoon Experiment*, 82–83; Walker, *Steel*, v–vi; Flynt, "American Tramp," 375; MacLean, "Two Weeks in Department Stores," 721–722.

44. "Tramps and Work-Houses," 106; Josiah Flynt, "The Tramp's Politics," *Harper's Weekly* 43 (November 4, 1899): 1124. Two works of undercover fiction that bespoke their authors' uneasy blend of fear and idealism, but that resolved those tensions with images of class reconciliation, were Tourgée, *Murvale Eastman*, and Enoch Johnson, *A Captain of Industry* (Boston: C. M. Clark, 1908).

45. Pettengill, *Toilers of the Home*, viii; Banks, *Autobiography*, 88, 95; Dorr, *Woman of Fifty*, 160; C. S. Parker, *Wanderer's Circle*, 251.

46. A central text of this phenomenon was Theodore Roosevelt, "The Strenuous Life," in his *The Strenuous Life* (New York: Century Company, 1902), 1–21. On Rooseveltian strenuosity, see Gail Bederman, *Manliness and Civilization: A Cultural History of Gender and Race in the United States, 1880–1917* (Chicago: University of Chicago Press, 1995), 184–196, and see, generally, Lears, *No Place of Grace*, and Miles Orvell, *The Real Thing: Imitation and Authenticity in American Culture, 1880–1940* (Chapel Hill: University of North Carolina Press, 1989). The impulse toward masculine strenuosity could also be expressed in more conservative college students by strikebreaking: see Stephen H. Norwood, *Strikebreaking and Intimidation* (Chapel Hill: University of North Carolina Press, 2002), 15–33.

47. Brace, *Dangerous Classes*, 339–340.

48. James's version of strenuosity is evident in "On a Certain Blindness in Human Beings," in his *Essays on Faith and Morals*, ed. Ralph Barton Perry (New York: Meridian Books, 1962), 279–280; his use of Wyckoff appears in "What Makes a Life Significant?" in *Essays on Faith and Morals*, 299–301. On "experience" in fin-de-siècle philosophy,

see George Cotkin, *Reluctant Modernism: American Thought and Culture, 1880–1900* (New York: Twayne, 1992), 33–35, and Robert Westbrook, *John Dewey and American Democracy* (Ithaca, NY: Cornell University Press, 1991), 68, 77, 321–327. On some of the problems inherent to grounding authority in experience, see James Clifford, *The Predicament of Culture: Twentieth-Century Ethnography, Literature and Art* (Cambridge: Harvard University Press, 1988), 35–37, and Joan W. Scott, "The Evidence of Experience," *Critical Inquiry* 17 (Summer 1991): 773–797.

49. James, "On a Certain Blindness," 259, 284. Down-and-outers who cited the influence of Dewey or of James included Benjamin Clarke Marsh, *Lobbyist for the People* (Washington, DC: Public Affairs Press, 1953), 5–6; Frederick C. Mills quoted in Woirol, *In the Floating Army*, 15; and Whiting Williams, *Mainsprings of Men* (New York: Charles Scribner's Sons, 1925), 212n, 270, 297n, 300. Many were also educated at the University of Chicago, where the influence of Dewey and James on Robert Park and W. I. Thomas is well documented: see Martin Bulmer, *The Chicago School of Sociology; Institutionalization, Diversity, and the Rise of Sociological Research* (Chicago: University of Chicago Press, 1984).

50. Alexander Irvine, *From the Bottom Up* (New York: Doubleday, Page, 1910). For more on Irvine, see Oberdeck, *Evangelist and the Impresario*; Marianne Doezema, *George Bellows and Urban America* (New Haven: Yale University Press, 1992), 123–137; Arnaldo Testi, "The Gender of Reform Politics: Theodore Roosevelt and the Culture of Masculinity," *Journal of American History* 81 (March 1995): 1527–1529; Stuart Pratt Sherman, "The Autobiography of Josiah Flynt," review of *My Life*, by Josiah Flynt, *Nation* 88 (February 25, 1909): 188. On the broader context of intellectuals' strenuous pursuit of "reality," see Christopher P. Wilson, *The Labor of Words: Literary Professionalism in the Progressive Era* (Athens: University of Georgia Press, 1985), 113–114, and David Shi, *Facing Facts: Realism in American Thought and Culture, 1850–1920* (New York: Oxford University Press, 1995).

51. Paul Ernest Anderson, "Tramping with Yeggs," *Atlantic Monthly* 136 (December 1925): 747; Cecil Fairfield Lavell, "From the Diary of a Laborer," 654; Fern Babcock, "Higher Education: A College Student Studies Labor Problems at First Hand," *Survey* 57 (December 15, 1926): 384; Chase and Chase, *Honeymoon Experiment*, 50.

52. Wyckoff, *The Workers*, 1:40; Sanborn, *Moody's Lodging House*, 4; Annie Marion MacLean, *Wage-Earning Women* (New York: Macmillan, 1910), 103; Mills quoted in Woirol, *In the Floating Army*, 128.

53. George Cotkin, *William James, Public Philosopher* (Urbana: University of Illinois Press, 1994), 109.

54. "Wyckoff," *Dictionary of American Biography*, 574; Wyckoff, *The Workers*, 1:5, 2:40. On strenuous masculinity, see John Kasson, *Houdini, Tarzan, and the Perfect Man* (New York: Hill & Wang, 2001). While this model of maleness was not the only one available at the century's turn, it was the one to which many down-and-outers seemed

most drawn. For a model for historicizing masculine identity that maintains but modifies the emphasis on virility and strenuosity, see Clyde Griffen, "Reconstructing Masculinity from the Evangelical Revival to the Waning of Progressivism: A Speculative Synthesis," in *Meanings for Manhood: Constructions of Masculinity in Victorian America*, ed. Mark C. Carnes and Clyde Griffen (Chicago: University of Chicago Press, 1990), 183–204.

55. On maleness and the discourse of authenticity, see T. J. Jackson Lears, "Sherwood Anderson: Looking for the White Spot," in *The Power of Culture*, ed. Richard Wightman Fox and T. J. Jackson Lears (Chicago: University of Chicago Press, 1993), 13–15. Questions of identity and reform intertwine in C. S. Parker, *Wanderer's Circle*, 89–90, and Babcock, "Higher Education," 384; Donovan, *Woman Who Waits*, 16; Virginia Kemp Fish, "Frances R. Donovan," in Deegan, *Women in Sociology*, 132–133. On Donovan generally, see Heather Paul Kurent, "Frances R. Donovan and the Chicago School of Sociology: A Case Study in Marginality" (Ph.D. diss., University of Maryland, 1982). On gender, sociology, and social work, see Rosalind Rosenberg, *Beyond Separate Spheres: Intellectual Roots of Modern Feminism* (New Haven: Yale University Press, 1982), 28–53; Dorothy Ross, *The Origins of American Social Science* (Cambridge: Cambridge University Press, 1991), 158; Ellen Fitzpatrick, *Endless Crusade: Women Social Scientists and Progressive Reform* (New York: Oxford University Press, 1990), 71–91.

56. James T. Patterson, *America's Struggle against Poverty 1900–1985* (Cambridge: Harvard University Press, 1986), 22–23; Orvell, *The Real Thing*, 132–133; Crane, "Experiment in Misery," 32.

57. On the persistence of Lamarckism, see George W. Stocking, *Race, Culture, and Evolution: Essays in the History of Anthropology* (New York: Free Press, 1968), 234–269, and Peter Bowler, *The Eclipse of Darwinism: Anti-Darwinian Evolution Theories in the Decades around 1900* (Baltimore: Johns Hopkins University Press, 1983), 98–106. Stocking (*Race, Culture, and Evolution*, 253, 267) shows that Lamarckism, although waning in the social sciences after about 1900, still implicitly underpinned much social-scientific argumentation during the Progressive Era. Bowler, *Eclipse of Darwinism*, 139–140, shows that natural scientists had largely rejected Lamarckism by the 1920s. Robert C. Bannister argues that while attributing to Lamarck a belief in "willful" adaptation was probably a misreading, it was nonetheless a widespread and a popular one: see Bannister's *Social Darwinism: Science and Myth in Anglo-American Social Thought* (Philadelphia: Temple University Press, 1979), 22.

58. On the "vicious circle" or "cycle" of poverty, see Patterson, *America's Struggle against Poverty*, 22; Campbell, *Darkness and Daylight*, 99.

59. Brown, *Broke*, xii; Chase and Chase, *Honeymoon Experiment*, 83; Stuart Chase, "Portrait of a Radical," *Century* 108 (July 1924): 295–296.

60. Pettengill, *Toilers of the Home*, vii; Jessie Davis, pseud., "My Vacation in a Woolen Mill," *Survey* 40 (August 10, 1918): 538; Chase and Chase, *Honeymoon Experiment*, 8.

61. Kellor, *Out of Work: Employment Agencies*, 2–5; Elizabeth Banks, review of *Out of Work*, by Frances Kellor, *New York Times*, December 10, 1904, Supplement: 845. The reviewer Mary K. Ford expressed similar support for Kellor's method in *Current Literature* 38 (March 1905): 237–238.

62. Martha S. Bensley, "Experiences of a Nursery Governess," *Everybody's Magazine* 12–13 (January-August 1905): 25–31, 204–210, 319–324, 469–474, 629–634, 749–754, 51–55, 180–184; Charlotte Teller and Martha S. Bensley, *The Sociological Maid* (1906; Washington, DC: Library of Congress Photoduplication Service, 1976); Martha Bensley Bruére and Robert W. Bruére, *Increasing Home Efficiency* (New York: Macmillan, 1912), 71.

63. MacLean, "Two Weeks in Department Stores," 721; Brown, *Broke*, 3; Van Vorst and Van Vorst, *Woman Who Toils*, 5, 168 (in the two separately authored sections of their book, both Van Vorsts used the term "mouthpiece"). Not all down-and-outers were quite this naïve, or at least they were not consistently so. Some did note that they could not fully enter into the worker's psychology, either because they had economic resources upon which to fall back (for example, Brown, *Broke*, 6), or because the poor were too fundamentally "different" (Wyckoff, *The Workers*, 2:148). Wyckoff's references to "vital knowledge" and "book-learned lore" appear in *The Workers*, 1:vii, 3.

64. Van Vorst and Van Vorst, *Woman Who Toils*, 173; Emily Fogg Mead, review of *The Woman Who Toils*, by Mrs. John and Marie Van Vorst, *Annals of the American Academy of Political and Social Science* 22 (July 1903): 239.

65. Examples of sensitivity to language and efforts to change it include Waters, "Six Weeks," I:790; Pettengill, *Toilers of the Home*, 5; and Williams, *What's on the Worker's Mind*, 7.

66. Dorr, *Woman of Fifty*, 162; Pettengill, *Toilers of the Home*, 7; MacLean, "Sweat-Shop in Summer," 294; Williams, *What's on the Worker's Mind*, 4; Willard D. Straight, "As a Tramp Would See It: The Story of a Little Journey through Northern New York," *The Era* 33 (1900–1901): 27.

67. Rheta Child Dorr was "Louise Clark" and Cornelia Stratton Parker was "Connie Park." The quote is from Dorr, *Woman of Fifty*, 162.

68. C. S. Parker, *Working with the Working Woman*, 4. Annie Marion MacLean also found gum chewing to be an emblematic working-class practice (MacLean, *Wage-Earning Women*, 102). Kathy Peiss notes that the more respectable, uplift-oriented working-women's clubs campaigned against both slang and gum chewing: see Peiss, *Cheap Amusements: Working Women and Leisure in Turn-of-the-Century New York* (Philadelphia: Temple University Press, 1986), 174.

69. Johnson, *Captain of Industry*, 42–43; Van Vorst and Van Vorst, *Woman Who Toils*, 174; Theodore Waters, "Six Weeks in Beggardom," Part II, *Everybody's Magazine* 12 (January 1905): 70; London, *Abyss*, 12–13, 8, 140–144; Jack London, *Martin Eden* (New York: Macmillan, 1908).

70. Josiah Flynt, "Two Tramps in England," *Century* 50 (June 1895): 290; Chase and Chase, *Honeymoon Experiment*, 12–14.

71. Sherwood, *Henry Worthington*, 281.

72. Wyckoff, *The Workers*, 1:3; Sanborn, *Moody's Lodging House*, 1; Crane, "Experiment in Misery," 27.

73. Sanborn, *Moody's Lodging House*, 2–3.

74. Walker, *Steel*, 16; Donovan, *Woman Who Waits*, 20; Pettengill, *Toilers of the Home*, 4; Kellor, *Out of Work: Employment Agencies*, 11. Pettengill's book was subtitled *The Record of a College Woman's Experience as a Domestic Servant.*

75. Alexander Irvine, *The Magyar: A Story of the Social Revolution* (Girard, KS: Socialist Publishing Company, 1911), 52; Straight, "As a Tramp Would See It," 27–28; Chase and Chase, *Honeymoon Experiment*, 16. Irvine's *The Magyar* was a novel based on his undercover experiences.

76. Chase and Chase, *Honeymoon Experiment*, 17; Wyckoff, *The Workers*, 1:124; Donovan, *Woman Who Waits*, 173; see also Williams, *What's on the Worker's Mind*, 69. Jack London, "What Life Means to Me," *Cosmopolitan Magazine* (March 1906): 527; Joan Hedrick, *Solitary Comrade: Jack London and His Work* (Chapel Hill: University of North Carolina Press, 1982), chapter 8.

77. Wyckoff, *The Workers*, 1:61, 66–67. One scholarly reviewer scored Wyckoff for falsely identifying with workers when he was always free to return to his privileged life (a fact of which Wyckoff was acutely aware): A. M. Day, review of *The Workers*, by Walter A. Wyckoff, *Political Science Quarterly* 14 (December 1899): 700; Wyckoff, *The Workers*, 2:82–83. Rheta Child Dorr pondered the same issue in *Woman of Fifty*, 164. Amy E. Tanner, "Glimpses at the Mind of a Waitress," *American Journal of Sociology* 13 (July 1907): 50–51. On the post–World War II "culture of poverty" discourse, see O'Connor, *Poverty Knowledge*, 99–124.

78. Mills quoted in Woirol, *In the Floating Army*, 86; Josiah Flynt, "How Men Become Tramps," *Century* 50 (October 1895): 944–945; Flynt, *Tramping*, 54; Flynt, *My Life*, 11. On the addictive qualities of tramping, see also A-No. 1 [pseud. Leon Ray Livingston], *The Curse of Tramp Life*, 4th ed. (Cambridge Springs, PA: The A-No. 1 Publishing Company, 1912), 2. "Wanderlust" is discussed in Orlando Lewis, *Vagrancy in the United States*, paper presented at the National Conference of Charities and Commons, Minneapolis, June 14, 1907 (New York: Printed at private expense, 1907), 3; Peter A. Speek, "The Psychology of Floating Workers," *Annals of the American Academy of Political and Social Science* 69 (January 1917): 72–78; Charles B. Davenport, *The Feebly Inhibited* (Washington, DC: Carnegie Institute, 1915), 7, 9–12; J. Harold Williams, "Hereditary Nomadism and Delinquency," *Journal of Delinquency* 1 (September 1916): 209–230; and Nels Anderson, *The Hobo: The Sociology of the Homeless Man* (Chicago, 1923; reprint, introd. Nels Anderson, Chicago: University of Chicago Press, 1961), xvii, 82.

79. Waters, "Six Weeks," 2:70–71, 76–77. The tale of the fruit-stand owner is also recounted in S. H. B., "Street Begging in New York," *Charities* 4 (January 1900): 3, and a parallel story appears in Sanborn, *Moody's Lodging House*, 66. In a similar vein, Elizabeth Banks recounted common London legends of secretly rich crossing sweepers who kept broughams and country houses on their earnings (see *Campaigns of Curiosity*, 130). And in Arthur Conan Doyle's "The Man with the Twisted Lip" (1891), Sherlock Holmes unmasks a former investigative journalist and actor who once impersonated a beggar for a story, then took up full-time begging as an easy source of abundant income: see *The Complete Sherlock Holmes* (Garden City, NY: Doubleday, 1960), 229–244.

80. Wyckoff, *The Workers*, 1:5, 11, 23, 50; Van Vorst and Van Vorst, *Woman Who Toils*, 22; Anonymous, *Four Years in the Underbrush*, 6.

81. Mills quoted in Woirol, *In the Floating Army*, 45, 43, 47, 61; Wyckoff, *The Workers*, 1:140–143.

82. Anonymous, *Four Years in the Underbrush*, 256, 259. For demands that tramps and beggars be punished, see Flynt, "The American Tramp," 259–261, and Waters, "Six Weeks," 2:76.

83. London, *Abyss*, 15. Keating notes that such near misses were common among British investigators in *Into Unknown England*, 17–18.

84. For example, see Maud Younger, "The Diary of an Amateur Waitress," *McClure's Magazine* 28 (April 1907): 666–667.

85. Van Vorst and Van Vorst, *Woman Who Toils*, 158; Anonymous, *Four Years in the Underbrush*, 3.

86. Wyckoff, *The Workers*, 2:148; Dorr, *Woman of Fifty*, 164.

87. C. S. Parker, *Wanderer's Circle*, 256.

88. Sanborn, *Moody's Lodging House*, 3; Wyckoff, *The Workers*, 2:84; Pettengill, *Toilers of the Home*, 359. Jack London meditated on the mutability of class identity and on related evolutionary considerations in his short story "South of the Slot," in which a down-and-out sociologist crosses over and permanently joins the working class: see *The Strength of the Strong* (New York: Leslie-Judge, 1914), 34–70. This story is also discussed in my *American Socialists and Evolutionary Thought, 1870–1920* (Madison: University of Wisconsin Press, 1993), 208–211.

89. Walker, *Steel*, 144; Wyckoff, *The Workers*, 2:77, 251–252; C. S. Parker, *Working with the Working Woman*, 12.

90. Göhre, *Three Months*, 41, 46; Banks, *Campaigns of Curiosity*, 95; Sanborn, *Moody's Lodging House*, 90; Pettengill, *Toilers of the Home*, 372–373; Waters, "Six Weeks," 74–75; Davis, "My Vacation," 541; Anonymous, *Four Years in the Underbrush*, 84–85.

91. For example, Davis, "My Vacation," 540, sharply contradicted the negative views of workers in Speek, "Psychology of the Floating Workers," 74, 76–78, and in George R. Stetson, "Industrial Classes as Factors in Racial Development," *Arena* 41 (February 1909): 77–89.

92. Donovan, *Woman Who Waits*, 45, 55–56; Hurst, *Anatomy of Me*, 179–180.

93. Josiah Flynt, "A Colony of the Unemployed," *Atlantic Monthly* 78 (December 1896): 800; Flynt, "What Tramps Read," *The Critic* 36 (June 1900): 564–567; Sanborn, *Moody's Lodging House*, 88–89, 93.

94. Chase and Chase, *Honeymoon Experiment*, 23, 158; MacLean, *Wage-Earning Women*, 115; Sanborn, *Moody's Lodging House*, 160, 135.

95. Mrs. John Van Vorst, "The Woman of the People," *Harper's Monthly Magazine* 106 (May 1903): 871–885. Articles by the Van Vorsts that later became part of *The Woman Who Toils* first appeared in *Everybody's Magazine* 7 (September-December 1902): 211–225, 361–377, 413–425, 540–552, and *Everybody's Magazine* 8 (January 1903): 3–17. Mary Manners, "The Unemployed Rich—A Day in the Life of a New York Lady of Fashion," *Everybody's Magazine* 7 (September 1902): 282–287. Stephen Crane had also reversed course for "An Experiment in Luxury" (1894), in *Stephen Crane: Prose and Poetry* (New York: Library of America, 1984), 549–557.

96. The following all appeared in *Harper's Monthly Magazine* 106 (May 1903): Justus Miles Foreman, "The King O' Dreams," 837–845; Waldemar Bogoras, "A Strange People of the North," 846–851; Octave Thanet, "The Brothers," 853–862; Arthur Symons, "Constantinople," 863–870 (Symons was a friend of Josiah Flynt's and wrote the introduction to Flynt's autobiography: see Flynt, *My Life* [New York: Outing Publishing Company, 1908], xi–xxi); and G. W. Ritchie, "Photographing the Nebulae with Reflecting Telescopes," 886–895. Van Vorst, "Woman of the People," 871.

97. Walter Rauschenbusch, *Christianity and the Social Crisis* (New York: Macmillan, 1907), 251–252. Micaela di Leonardo notes that British reformers also Africanized their impoverished compatriots: see *Exotics at Home: Anthropologies, Others, American Modernity* (Chicago: University of Chicago Press, 1998), 134. Owen Kildare, *My Old Bailiwick: Sketches from the Parish of "My Mamie Rose"* (New York: Fleming H. Revell, 1906), 86.

98. Benjamin Clarke Marsh, *Lobbyist for the People: A Record of Fifty Years* (Washington, DC: Public Affairs Press, 1953), 11, 13. Marsh was a graduate student of the economist Simon Patten at the University of Pennsylvania when he went undercover as a beggar in 1903–1904: see *Lobbyist*, 5–6.

99. Ely, prefatory note to Göhre, *Three Months*, viii; Grace Isabel Colbron, review of *The Woman Who Toils*, by Mrs. John Van Vorst and Marie Van Vorst, *Bookman* 17 (April 1903): 187–188; Alfred Hodder, "The Clan and the Boss," review of *People of the Abyss*, by Jack London, *Critic* 44 (March 1904): 217; review of *Tramping with Tramps*, by Josiah Flynt, *Nation* 69 (October 26, 1899): 321.

100. Marianna Torgovnick, *Gone Primitive: Savage Intellects, Modern Lives* (Chicago: University of Chicago Press, 1990), 18; Van Vorst and Van Vorst, *Woman Who Toils*, 27, 75; Donovan, *Woman Who Waits*, 224.

101. London, *Abyss*, 3; James Clifford, *The Predicament of Culture: Twentieth-Century Ethnography, Literature, and Art* (Cambridge: Harvard University Press, 1988), 13–14.

102. Pettengill, *Toilers of the Home*, vi. Deborah Epstein Nord has pointed out that British social investigators of the middle and late nineteenth century commonly used a similar "anthropological" language of Dark Continents and strange, perhaps subhuman life forms or separate races to describe the British poor. Nord argues that such language should not be taken literally, that the ethnological pose provided a way for scientifically oriented reformers to write about the distinctive qualities of the poor from a stance of dispassion and objectivity that was foreclosed within other current languages of derision, uplift, or moralism. But in the American context discussed here, I believe that the language of exoticism and otherness should be taken seriously. Certainly these investigators wished to appear scientifically objective and empiricist. But the majority of down-and-out texts, along with the vast bulk of related writings about poverty that formed their broader context (see, for example, the discussion of Robert Hunter's *Poverty* below), so regularly and pervasively used the language of separate race or species, of devolution and degeneration both within and between generations, with suitable references to current scientific ideas and thinkers, that I think it cannot be dismissed as a useful pose for a new breed of reformer. This language did not simply adorn these texts; it lay at the very heart of their arguments, even as it sharpened their emotional thrust. See Deborah Epstein Nord, "The Social Explorer as Anthropologist: Victorian Travellers among the Urban Poor," in *Visions of the Modern City*, ed. William Sharpe and Leonard Wallock (Baltimore: Johns Hopkins University Press, 1987), 122–134. See also di Leonardo, *Exotics at Home*, 134, for a view more in line with my own.

103. Van Vorst and Van Vorst, *Woman Who Toils*, facing 240, 301. The hereditarian criminal anthropologist Cesare Lombroso argued that particular combinations of atavistic features added up to a "type," and such thinking informed efforts to construct generic criminal physiognomies from composite photographs. See Lombroso, "Criminal Anthropology: Its Origins and Applications," *Forum* 20 (September 1895): 36–37; David Papke, *Framing the Criminal: Crime, Cultural Work, and the Loss of Critical Perspective, 1830–1900* (Hamden, CT: Archon, 1987), 163. On visual constructions of ideal Americanism, see Shawn Michelle Smith, *American Archives: Gender, Race, and Class in Visual Culture* (Princeton: Princeton University Press, 1999). In this context, even though down-and-outers did not always specify any debt to hereditarian formalism and sometimes explicitly disavowed it (as in Flynt, *Tramping*, 8–9, 26), their propensity for picturing what they called "types" still powerfully conveyed the message that these images were to be viewed through Lombrosian lenses. As noted below, Flynt flagrantly contradicted his own attacks on Lombroso.

104. Anonymous, *Four Years in the Underbrush*, 70; Dorr, *Woman of Fifty*, 184.

105. On Irish and Italians, see Anonymous, *Four Years in the Underbrush*, 259, 264; on "stagnant scum," Van Vorst and Van Vorst, *Woman Who Toils*, 12; and on "white" Americans, Frederick C. Mills quoted in Woirol, *In the Floating Army*, 52. Most helpful on the tangled matter of how immigrants came to be "white" are Matthew Frye

Jacobson, *Whiteness of a Different Color: European Immigrants and the Alchemy of Race* (Cambridge: Harvard University Press, 1998), and David R. Roediger, *Working toward Whiteness: America's Immigrants Become White* (New York: Basic Books, 2005).

106. On the conceptual confluence of race and class, see Richard Slotkin, *The Fatal Environment* (Middletown, CT: Wesleyan University Press, 1985), 74–76, 301–324, 480–489. George W. Stocking, Jr., discusses the melding of race and nationality in *Race, Culture, and Evolution*, 245, and in *Victorian Anthropology* (New York: Free Press, 1987), 235–236. And see generally Gary Gerstle, *American Crucible: Race and Nation in the Twentieth Century* (Princeton: Princeton University Press, 2001), and Roediger, *Working toward Whiteness,* especially 57–92.

107. Anonymous, *Four Years in the Underbrush,* 201.

108. Brace, *Dangerous Classes*; Karl Marx and Friedrich Engels, *The Communist Manifesto,* ed. Paul M. Sweezy and Leo Huberman (New York: Modern Reader, 1968), 21.

109. MacLean, "Sweat-Shop in Summer," 308; Van Vorst and Van Vorst, *Woman Who Toils,* 171; see also Josiah Flynt, "The Tramp's Politics," *Harper's Weekly* 43 (November 4, 1899): 1124.

110. Anonymous, *Four Years in the Underbrush,* 3, 201, 202; Van Vorst and Van Vorst, *Woman Who Toils,* 20.

111. Irvine, *From the Bottom Up,* 264; Anonymous, *Four Years in the Underbrush,* 201; Brown, *Broke,* 190; Flynt, *Tramping,* 5.

112. Chase and Chase, *Honeymoon Experiment,* 37.

113. Irvine, *From the Bottom Up,* 266; Van Vorst and Van Vorst, *Woman Who Toils,* 244, 293; Theodore Roosevelt, prefatory letter, in Van Vorst and Van Vorst, *Woman Who Toils,* vii–viii.

114. London, *Abyss,* 14, 168, 229–231; Younger, "Diary," 543–547; Donovan, *Woman Who Waits,* 24–27, 30.

115. Younger, "Diary," 547; Donovan, *Woman Who Waits,* 171.

116. Van Vorst and Van Vorst, *Woman Who Toils,* 159, 242 (emphasis in original).

117. Ibid., 255.

118. Ibid., 242, 255, 260; Chase and Chase, *Honeymoon Experiment,* 98–99.

119. Flynt, *Tramping,* 2–27, 33; Stetson, "Industrial Classes," 185.

120. Wyckoff, *The Workers,* 2:319, 321. See Stocking, "The Critique of Racial Formalism," in his *Race, Culture, and Evolution,* 161–194.

121. Wyckoff, *The Workers,* 2:321, 38–39.

122. Robert Hunter, *Poverty* (New York: Macmillan, 1904), v.

123. Hunter, *Poverty,* 131, 69, 7, 65, 92, 318; R. L. Dugdale, *The Jukes: A Study in Crime, Pauperism, Disease, and Heredity* (New York: G. P. Putnam's Sons, 1877). Hunter also relied on the authority of E. Ray Lankester's *Degeneration: A Chapter in Darwinism* (London: Macmillan, 1880); see Hunter, *Poverty,* 128. A similar if less lurid argument was advanced by the economists W. Jett Lauck and Edgar Sydenstricker in their *Conditions*

of Labor in American Industries: A Summarization of the Results of Recent Investigations (New York: Funk & Wagnalls, 1917), 171.

124. Ross, *Origins*, 387.

125. Stocking details the role of Lamarckism in the process by which "culture" could be substituted for "race" in social-scientific discourse: see *Race, Culture, and Evolution*, 263–266. Walter Benn Michaels further develops the idea that in the United States, although it has been deployed to undercut racial determinism, the culture concept has ironically "turned out to be a way of continuing rather than repudiating racial thought." See Michaels, "Race into Culture: A Critical Genealogy of Cultural Identity," *Critical Inquiry* 18 (Summer 1992): 684.

126. Examples include the biologist Herbert William Conn's *Social Heredity and Social Evolution: The Other Side of Eugenics* (New York: Abingdon Press, 1914), and Walter Robinson Smith, "The Role of Social Heredity in Education," *American Journal of Sociology* 24 (March 1919): 566–580. For the impact on Richard T. Ely of the social psychologist James Mark Baldwin's formulation of social heredity, see Ely, *Studies in the Evolution of Industrial Society* (New York: Macmillan, 1903), 453–458, and Pittenger, *American Socialists and Evolutionary Thought,* 41. Baldwin believed that he was offering an alternative to Lamarckism, but his construct produced many of the same outcomes and operated just as deterministically as a Lamarckian mechanism would have. See Baldwin, *Social and Ethical Interpretations in Mental Development* (New York: Macmillan, 1897), 547, and Robert J. Richards, *Darwin and the Emergence of Evolutionary Theories of Mind and Behavior* (Chicago: University of Chicago Press, 1987), 473–475. According to Richards, the paleontologist and eugenicist Henry Fairfield Osborn believed that Baldwin's concept of "organic selection," which would select useful traits preserved by social heredity, had reconciled Lamarckism with Darwinism (493). This would be another way to explain the progressive deterioration of survivors in a degrading and dangerous environment. The ultimate product would be a hereditary "underclass."

127. Lester Frank Ward, "The Transmission of Culture by the Inheritance of Acquired Characters," *Forum* 11 (May 1891): 312, 318–319.

128. Franz Boas, *The Mind of Primitive Man* (New York: Macmillan, 1911); Gunnar Myrdal, *An American Dilemma: The Negro Problem and American Democracy* (New York: Harper and Row, 1944).

129. On the Boasian paradigm shift, see Stocking, *Race, Culture and Evolution*, and Carl Degler, *In Search of Human Nature: The Decline and Revival of Darwinism in American Social Thought* (New York: Oxford University Press, 1991), especially chapter 3.

130. Francis Donovan began her study of waitresses in 1917 and published *The Woman Who Waits* in 1920, while the anonymous author of *Four Years in the Underbrush* remained undercover from 1916 to 1920, publishing the book in 1921. During the years of U.S. involvement in the war, besides this ongoing research and Sinclair's novel, only two

articles appeared: from Cecil Fairfield Lavell, a Columbia University historian, who described an unplanned, amnesiac detour through the workers' world in "Man Who Lost Himself" and from Jessie Davis, who wrote "Vacation in a Woolen Mill" (1918).

131. Upton Sinclair, *King Coal* (New York: Macmillan, 1917). When Macmillan initially rejected a much larger version of the novel, Sinclair cut it in half, revised the first part into what became *King Coal,* and then rewrote the remainder as a sequel to focus on the 1914 Ludlow Massacre. Macmillan rejected *The Coal War,* which Sinclair declined to rewrite. It was later reconstructed from Sinclair's drafts by the scholar John Graham, who published it with an extensive introduction: Upton Sinclair, *The Coal War: A Sequel to "King Coal,"* ed. and introd. John Graham (Boulder: Colorado Associated University Press, 1976).

132. London, "South of the Slot," 34–70; and see my *American Socialists and Evolutionary Thought,* 208–211.

133. Chase, "Portrait of a Radical," 297.

134. Sue Ainslie Clark and Edith Wyatt, "Women Laundry Workers in New York," *McClure's Magazine* 36 (February 1911): 401–414; Frances Kellor, *Out of Work: A Study of Unemployment* (New York: G. P. Putnam's Sons, 1915). Kellor defended the undercover method in *Out of Work: Employment Agencies,* 2–5. Reviews of the first edition that praised its approach—usually noting its reformist intent—included Charlotte Perkins Gilman in *The Critic* 46 (March 1905): 280; Elizabeth Banks in *New York Times,* December 10, 1904, Supplement: 845; Mary K. Ford in *Current Literature* 38 (March 1905): 237–238; Charles R. Henderson (Kellor's graduate mentor) in *American Journal of Sociology* 10 (January 1905): 558, and also in the *Dial* 38 (March 1, 1905): 156; John Graham Brooks, *International Journal of Ethics* 16 (July 1906): 511–512; Sophonisba P. Breckenridge, *Journal of Political Economy* 13 (March 1905): 297–298; *Review of Reviews* 30 (December 1904): 760. Academic reviewers of the revised version were not necessarily pleased by its bid for objectivist respectability, complaining that the book's main value had been in its "popular form," or alternatively, that its untidy empiricism and lack of embracing argument rendered it unscientific: Theresa S. McMahon in *American Economic Review* 5 (September 1915): 614; William Leiserson in *Political Science Quarterly* 30 (December 1915): 684–685.

135. Mills, *Contemporary Theories of Unemployment,* 120.

136. R. Alan Lawson, *The Failure of Independent Liberalism, 1930–1941* (New York: G. P. Putnam's Sons, 1971), 75–76. On Chase's career, see Robert B. Westbrook, "Tribune of the Technostructure: The Popular Economics of Stuart Chase," *American Quarterly* 32 (Autumn 1980): 387–408.

137. Chase, "Portrait of a Radical," 295–299.

138. Ibid., 301–304.

139. Ibid., 299–304.

CHAPTER 2

1. "They Know Real Toil," *Collier's* 75 (March 28, 1925): 18–19. Beard quoted in Thomas Bender, *A Nation among Nations: America's Place in World History* (New York: Hill and Wang, 2006), 247. Lynn Dumenil addresses the "New Era" in *The Modern Temper: American Culture and Society in the 1920s* (New York: Hill and Wang, 1995), 7; Whiting Williams, *What's on the Worker's Mind: By One Who Put on Overalls to Find Out* (New York: Charles Scribner's Sons, 1920).

2. For such comparative references, see, for example, Roger N. Baldwin, review of *Steel: The Diary of a Furnace Worker*, by Charles Rumford Walker, *The World Tomorrow* 6 (February 1923): 57–58, and review of *Working with the Working Woman*, by Cornelia Stratton Parker, *Literary Review of the New York Evening Post* (March 18, 1922): 512.

3. Don D. Lescohier, *The Labor Market* (New York: Macmillan, 1919), 271–275, 311–324.

4. Ibid., 94, 96, 101.

5. On welfare capitalism, see Stuart D. Brandes, *American Welfare Capitalism, 1880–1940* (Chicago: University of Chicago Press, 1976), and Kim McQuaid, *A Response to Industrialism: Liberal Businessmen and the Evolving Spectrum of Capitalist Reform, 1886–1960* (New York: Garland, 1986). The term "prosperity decade" comes from George Soule, *Prosperity Decade; From War to Depression: 1917–1929* (New York: Rinehart, 1947). Lescohier, *Labor Market*, 96 (emphasis in original). The influence of Simon Patten, who pioneered social thought centering on pleasurable consumption, is evident, if unacknowledged: see Patten's *The New Basis of Civilization* (New York: Macmillan, 1907).

6. Williams, *What's on the Worker's Mind*, 193; Whiting Williams, *Mainsprings of Men* (New York: Charles Scribner's Sons, 1925), 300. See also Williams, "Discussion," *Bulletin of the Taylor Society* 7 (June 1922): 93–94. On Williams's background, see Daniel A. Wren, *White Collar Hobo: The Travels of Whiting Williams* (Ames: University of Iowa Press, 1987), 4–11.

7. For example, see Stanley B. Mathewson, *Restriction of Output among Unorganized Workers*, with chapters by William M. Leiserson, Henry S. Dennison, and Arthur E. Morgan (New York: Viking, 1931). JoAnne Brown addresses the power of scientific language in *The Definition of a Profession: The Authority of Metaphor in the History of Intelligence Testing, 1890–1930* (Princeton: Princeton University Press, 1992), 3–7. On the struggle over objectivity in sociology, see Robert C. Bannister, *Sociology and Scientism: The American Quest for Objectivity, 1880–1940* (Chapel Hill: University of North Carolina Press, 1987).

8. A. J. Todd, review of *The Hobo*, by Nels Anderson, *American Journal of Sociology* 29 (September 1923): 238–239.

9. Anderson called Hobohemia an "isolated cultural area" in *The Hobo: Sociology of the Homeless Man* (Chicago, 1923; reprint, Chicago: University of Chicago Press, 1961),

14. The term "Hobohemia" apparently came from a 1917 article in the *Chicago Daily News* by the reporter Harry M. Beardsley: see Nels Anderson, *The American Hobo: An Autobiography* (Leiden: Brill, 1975), 169. On the complexities of culture and race in Chicago sociology, see Vernon Williams, Jr., *Rethinking Race: Franz Boas and His Contemporaries* (Lexington: University Press of Kentucky, 1996), 96, and Henry Yu, *Thinking Orientals: Migration, Contact, and Exoticism in Modern America* (New York: Oxford University Press, 2001), 47–52.

10. Frederick R. Wedge, *Inside the I.W.W.: A Study of the Behavior of the I.W.W. with Reference to Primary Causes* (Berkeley, CA: F. R. Wedge, 1924). Wedge's self-published book was not reviewed in any national publication that I have found.

11. George L. Moore, "My Adventures as a Bowery Hobo," *World Outlook* 6 (August 1920): 17, 48; Cloudsley Johns, "Exit the Down-and-Outs," *Collier's* 65 (February 14, 1920): 56. On Johns's connection to London, see June 16, 1900, and December 6, 1901, letters from London to Johns, in *Letters from Jack London*, ed. King Hendrix and Irving Shepard (New York: Odyssey Press, 1965), 107, 126. Reviews of *In Darkest London*, by Mrs. Cecil Chesterton, *Saturday Review of Literature* 141 (July 24, 1926): 371, and *New York Times* (July 13, 1926): 26. The down-and-outer Anthony Muto described New York unemployment in "Breakfast, Bedroom, and Bath in Subway," *Literary Digest* 101 (June 8, 1929): 54–56; see also F. L. Kellogg, "New Faces on the Bowery," *Survey* 74 (April 1, 1930): 15–17.

12. For examples, see reviews of *The Main Stem*, by William Edge, *Bookman* 66 (February 1928): 692–694, and *Survey* 59 (November 1, 1927): 171; of *Steel: The Diary of a Furnace Worker*, by Charles Rumford Walker, *Administration* 5 (January 1923): 107–108; of *The Saleslady* by Frances Donovan, *Nation* 129 (October 23, 1929): 470–471; and of *Restriction of Output*, by Stanley B. Mathewson, *Social Science* 7 (April 1932): 202.

13. Charles Rumford Walker, *Bread and Fire* (Boston: Houghton Mifflin, 1927), 120–121; further references appear parenthetically in the text. The reviewers noted were John Farrar, *Bookman* 65 (July 1927): 584, and Burton Rascoe, *Arts & Decoration* 27 (August 1927): 58. Powers Hapgood, *In Non-Union Mines: The Diary of a Coal-Digger* (New York: Bureau of Industrial Research, 1922), 19.

14. Bingham's letter quoted in Char Miller, *Fathers and Sons: The Bingham Family and the American Mission* (Philadelphia: Temple University Press, 1982), 171. For Bingham's top-down reformism in the 1930s, see Alfred M. Bingham, *Man's Estate: Adventures in Economic Discovery* (New York: Norton, 1939), 397–398. Robert Bussel, *From Harvard to the Ranks of Labor: Powers Hapgood and the American Working Class* (University Park: Pennsylvania State University Press, 1999), 24. On Walker's political evolution, see Alan M. Wald, *The New York Intellectuals: The Rise and Decline of the Anti-Stalinist Left from the 1930s to the 1980s* (Chapel Hill: University of North Carolina Press, 1987), 55–56, 151–152; and Mary Lethert Wingerd, "Radical Politics and the Minnesota Labor Movement: Legacies of *American City*," foreword to Charles Rumford Walker,

American City: A Rank and File History of Minneapolis (New York, 1937; reprint, Minneapolis: University of Minnesota Press, 2005), ix–xxxiv.

15. Cornelia Stratton Parker, *Working with the Working Woman* (New York: Harper & Brothers, 1922), vii; Williams, *What's on the Worker's Mind*, v; Charles Rumford Walker, *Steel: The Diary of a Furnace Worker* (Boston: Atlantic Monthly Press, 1922), 3. The social worker and child welfare advocate Lucille Milner was driven by similar concerns about labor's postwar role, and she went undercover in a New York City feathered-ornament shop, an experience she later recalled in her autobiography, *Education of an American Liberal* (New York: Horizon Press, 1954), 92–115. On some intellectuals' hopes for far-reaching postwar "reconstruction," see Lewis Perry, *Intellectual Life in America: A History* (Chicago: University of Chicago Press, 1989), 326–327.

16. Walker, *Steel*, 4, v–vi.

17. Ibid., 3–4; Stuart Chase, "Portrait of a Radical," *Century* 108 (July 1924): 300.

18. "Most Arrested American," *Literary Digest* 86 (July 11, 1925): 50–55; Brown's earlier tramping days were recounted in his *Broke: The Man without the Dime* (Chicago: Browne and Howell, 1913). Annie Marion MacLean, "Four Months in a Model Factory," *Century* 106 (July 1923): 436–444. MacLean's data predated the war, but she believed them relevant to 1920s practices (444). Another undercover article may also have been researched before the twenties: "On Picket Duty," *Forum* 70 (December 1923): 2199–2206. MacLean earned much of her living during the decade from popular journalism and books, so she may have recycled older experiences for these articles. Consumers League of New York, *Behind the Scenes in a Hotel* (New York: Consumers League of New York, 1922), and *Behind the Scenes in Canneries* (New York: Consumers League of New York, 1930); both reprinted in *The Consumers League of New York: Behind the Scenes of Women's Work*, ed. David J. Rothman and Sheila M. Rothman (New York: Garland, 1987). Donovan's first book, *The Woman Who Waits* (Boston: Gorham Press, 1920), was researched in 1917 and published in 1920. *The Saleslady* (Chicago: University of Chicago Press, 1929), with an introduction by Robert Park, appeared in the University of Chicago Sociological Series, whose purpose was to publish "newer developments" in sociology (front matter).

19. Baldwin, age thirty-five when he went undercover in 1919, was older than the others, but he still measured his own and others' experiences against college learning: see his review of Walker, *Steel*, 57–58. Powers Hapgood, "Casual Labor and Mining A1–A2," *New Student* 12 (May 19, 1923): 5; "Students Try Work," *New Student* 12 (May 19, 1923): 5–6. Besides Baldwin's review of *Steel*, the special issue included Powers Hapgood, "From College to the Ranks of Labor," and Alice Kimball, "In the Silk," *The World Tomorrow* 6 (February 1923): 49–50, 50–51. Another article noted the author's earlier down-and-out stint in a steel mill: Herbert Atchinson Jump, "That Plumber of Yours," 35–36.

20. Kimball, "In the Silk," 50; Joseph Freeman, *An American Testament: A Narrative of Rebels and Romantics* (New York: Farrar & Rinehart, 1936), 362–363; Bingham, *Man's Estate*, 23.

21. Bingham, *Man's Estate*, 21–23; Peggy Lamson, *Roger Baldwin: Founder of the ACLU* (Boston: Houghton Mifflin, 1976), 17–18.

22. Bingham, *Man's Estate*, 211; Lamson, *Roger Baldwin*, 118–120; Robert C. Cottrell, *Roger Nash Baldwin and the American Civil Liberties Union* (New York: Columbia University Press, 2000), 109; "Students Try Work," 6; Fern Babcock, "Higher Education: A College Student Studies Labor Problems at First Hand," *Survey* 57 (December 15, 1926): 384.

23. Baldwin, review of *Steel*, 57; "Students Try Work," 5.

24. Thomas F. Healy, "The Hobo Hits the Highroad," *American Mercury* 8 (July 1926): 338; Glen H. Mullin, *Adventures of a Scholar-Tramp* (New York: The Century Company, 1925), 103. Mullin's background is noted by Albert E. Stone, preface to Charles Elmer Fox, *Tales of an American Hobo* (Iowa City: University of Iowa Press, 1989), xix.

25. Hapgood, "Casual Labor," 5; Bussel, *From Harvard*, 21–42; Cottrell, *Roger Baldwin*, 108–109. Lucille Milner, a down-and-outer and later the longtime secretary of the American Civil Liberties Union, was a close friend of Baldwin's and also of Glen Mullin's, whose help with her book she acknowledged; her undercover stint just preceded Baldwin's, so she may have helped to inspire it. See Milner, *Education of an American Liberal*, front matter, and chapters 5 and 6.

26. Consumers League, *Behind the Scenes in Canneries*, 7; Babcock, "Higher Education," 383–384; Bingham quoted in Miller, *Fathers and Sons*, 169.

27. Walker, *Steel*, vii.

28. Babcock, "Higher Education," 384; Kimball, "In the Silk," 51; Hapgood, *In Non-Union Mines*; Walter Spooner, "From Prince Albert to Overalls," *World Outlook* 5 (November 1919): 55; Charles Rumford Walker, "Peace or War in Steel?" *Independent* 114 (May 9, 1925): 530–531, 540; Williams, *What's on the Worker's Mind*, 71.

29. "Most Arrested American," 53; Donovan, *Saleslady*, 79; Hapgood, *In Non-Union Mines*, 3–4; Walker, *Steel*, vi–vii; Williams, *What's on the Worker's Mind*, 173; William Z. Foster, "An Industrial Mrs. Partington," review of *What's on the Worker's Mind*, by Whiting Williams, *Freeman* 2 (January 5, 1921): 404.

30. Nels Anderson, "Summary of a Study of 400 Tramps, Summer 1921," *On Hoboes and Homelessness*, ed. Raffaele Rauty (Chicago: University of Chicago Press, 1998), 80–89.

31. Anderson, introduction to the Phoenix Edition, *The Hobo*, xiii, 40. Anderson wrote in his introduction to the 1961 edition of *The Hobo* that his 1920 trip to Chicago to begin graduate school had been his final freight ride (xi). However, in "400 Tramps," written in 1921 but published posthumously, he reported that he had ridden freights from Salt Lake to Chicago for that 1921 trip (80–81). I take the earlier-written report to be the more reliable. Nels Anderson continued to write until near the end of his life: see "A Stranger at the Gate: Reflections on the Chicago School of Sociology," *Urban*

Life 11 (January 1983): 396–406. And see Raffaele Rauty, "Introduction: Nels Anderson 1889–1986," in *On Hobos and Homelessness*, ed. and introd. Raffaele Rauty (Chicago: University of Chicago Press, 1998), 1–17.

32. Pauline V. Young called Anderson a participant observer in *Scientific Sociological Surveys and Research* (New York: Prentice-Hall, 1951), 203; on the method, see Jennifer Platt, "The Development of the 'Participant Observer' Method in Sociology: Origin, Myth, and History," *Journal of the History of the Behavioral Sciences* 19 (October 1983): 379–393. Anderson, *The Hobo*, xiii; Anderson, *American Hobo*, 16.

33. Anderson, *The Hobo*, v, xiii; Anderson, *American Hobo*, 165–166.

34. Nels Anderson, *Men on the Move* (Chicago: University of Chicago Press, 1940), 1–2; Anderson, *American Hobo*, 170.

35. Josiah Flynt, "The American Tramp," *Contemporary Review* 60 (August 1891): 253; Anderson, *The Hobo*, 94; Anderson, *American Hobo*, 170.

36. Anderson, "400 Tramps," 80–81; Anderson, *American Hobo*, 164, 166; *The Hobo*, xxviii.

37. Anderson, "400 Tramps," 82–89. On page 85, Anderson acknowledges as his model the respected work of Alice Solenberger, *One Thousand Homeless Men* (New York: Charities Publication Committee, 1911). The report is cited in *The Hobo*, 278, and in "The Juvenile and the Tramp," *Journal of Criminal Law, Criminology, and Police Science* 14 (August 1923): 293. Anderson recalls his mentors' support in *The Hobo*, xii–xiii. Park also supported the publication of Frances Donovan's *The Saleslady* in the same series: Robert E. Park, introduction to Donovan, *The Saleslady*, vii–ix.

38. Examples of undercover hoboes include "Amateur Hobo Finds the Road Not So Bad," *Literary Digest* 97 (June 9, 1928): 63–67; Paul Ernest Anderson, "Tramping with Yeggs," *Atlantic* 136 (December 1925): 747–755; Mabelle Hathaway Brooks, "Working in the California Fruit," *Haldeman-Julius Monthly* 4 (June 1926): 97–99; Samuel Milton Elam, "Pick and Shovel Stiff: Sketches," *New Republic* 60 (September 4, 1929): 69–72; Elam, "Lady Hoboes," *New Republic* 61 (January 1, 1930): 164–167. For fictional variants, the latter of which was based on the author's real experiences, see Edgar Wallace, *The Northing Tramp* (New York: A. L. Burt, 1926), and William Edge, *The Main Stem* (New York: Vanguard Press, 1927). Floyd Dell discussed the intellectual context of romantic vagabondage in *Intellectual Vagabondage* (New York, 1926; reprint, Chicago: Ivan R. Dee, 1990), 251–256. An example of the tramp as the figure for Dell's "spiritual vagabondage" and for 1920s anti-babbitry is William Saroyan, "Portrait of a Bum," *Overland Monthly* 86 (December 1928): 421, 424. On hoboes in 1920s culture, see Todd DePastino, *Citizen Hobo: How a Century of Homelessness Shaped America* (Chicago: University of Chicago Press, 2003), chapter 6, and Tim Cresswell, *The Tramp in America* (London: Reaktion, 2001).

39. Harry Kemp, review of *The Hobo*, by Nels Anderson, *New Republic* 35 (August 22, 1923): 364–365. On hobo writers, see Douglas Wixson, *Worker-Writer in America:*

Jack Conroy and the Tradition of Midwestern Literary Radicalism, 1898–1990 (Urbana: University of Illinois Press, 1994), 102.

40. Nels Anderson, "The Trend of Urban Sociology," in *Trends in American Sociology*, ed. George A. Lundberg, Read Bain, and Nels Anderson (New York: Harper and Brothers, 1929), 295–296; "What Mills Do to Men," review of *Bread and Fire*, by Charles Rumford Walker, *Survey* 58 (August 1, 1927): 472; "On the Bum," review of *The Main Stem*, by William Edge, *Survey* 59 (November 1, 1927): 171; *The Hobo*: map on p. 15.

41. Nels Anderson and Eduard C. Lindeman, *Urban Sociology: An Introduction to the Study of Urban Communities* (New York: Knopf, 1928), xxxi–xxxii; Nels Anderson, "The Slum: A Project for Study," *Social Forces* 7 (September 1928): 88; Anderson, "Trend of Urban Sociology," 262. Anderson discusses this period of his career in *American Hobo*, 180.

42. Anderson, "Trend of Urban Sociology," 262. Anderson frequently acknowledged his lack of sociological sophistication and the immaturity of *The Hobo*: see his *Men on the Move*, 1–3, and *American Hobo*, 160–170. That he supported "personal contact" between sociologists and their subjects shows that Anderson did not believe that only genuine hoboes could be reliable observers—"that only a hobo can write about a hobo"—as is asserted by Laura Browder in *Slippery Characters: Ethnic Impersonators and American Identities* (Chapel Hill: University of North Carolina Press, 2000), 182. Anderson wrote along this line only in his pseudonymous, self-described "parody" (*Men on the Move*, 1–2) of romanticized hobo writing, "Dean Stiff's" *The Milk and Honey Route: A Handbook for Hobos* (New York: Vanguard Press, 1931), vi–vii. Critical though Anderson was of his own and others' practice, he did not insist that all outsiders' efforts to write about the poor were futile.

43. Anderson, "The Slum," 88; "Trend of Urban Sociology," 270, 295–296.

44. Nels Anderson, review of *The Saleslady*, by Frances Donovan, *Survey* 63 (November 15, 1929): 230; Anderson, "Work: We Begin to be Serious about It," *New Outlook* 157 (April 1, 1931): 473. As noted above, Annie MacLean relied on popular magazines rather than the *American Journal of Sociology* to publish her down-and-out studies in the twenties. Positive reviews of Donovan's *Saleslady* included *Booklist* 26 (December 1929): 101–102; *Nation* 129 (October 23, 1929): 470–471; and *Spectator* 143 (October 26, 1929): 603. The most negative response was by Howard P. Becker, *Annals of the American Academy of Political and Social Science* 148 (March 1930): 305–306. More mixed were Ruth Shonle Cavan, *American Journal of Sociology* 35 (January 1930): 676, and E. M. P., *Sociology and Social Research* 14 (November-December 1929): 189. On Anderson's career trajectory, see Rauty, introduction to *On Hobos and Homelessness*, 1, 14.

As the professional reviews suggest, the future of undercover research in sociology lay with the strategy of embedding firsthand material in conventional social-scientific narrative and analysis. Debates leading to this strategy began in the 1920s—especially around concepts of participant observation, impersonal confession, and the "anonymous stranger"—but reached fruition in the 1930s, so will be discussed in chapter 3.

45. F. Stuart Chapin, "Editor's Foreword," in Lundberg, *Trends*, ix. Also in Lundberg, see Dorothy P. Gary, "The Developing Study of Culture," 172–220.

46. Anderson, "The Slum," 87–88; Ruth Benedict, *Patterns of Culture* (Boston: Houghton Mifflin, 1934), 51–52; Anderson, *The Hobo*, 14.

47. Anderson, *The Hobo*, 14. On the autonomy of culture and its interpenetration with race, see Herbert Adolphus Miller, *Races, Nations, and Classes: The Psychology of Domination and Freedom* (Philadelphia: J. B. Lippincott, 1924), 140–141; Miller, "Race and Class Parallelism," *Annals of the American Academy of Political and Social Science* 140 (November 1928): 1–5; Charles A. Ellwood, "Social Evolution and Cultural Evolution," *Journal of Applied Sociology* 11 (March-April 1927): 308–314; Niles Carpenter, *Sociology of City Life* (New York: Longmans, Green, 1931), 424. On Chicago sociology's shift from structure to culture, see Alice O'Connor, *Poverty Knowledge: Social Science, Social Policy, and the Poor in Twentieth-Century U.S. History* (Princeton: Princeton University Press, 2001), 18–19, 49–54.

48. Read Bain and Joseph Cohen, "Trends in Applied Sociology," in Lundberg, *Trends,* 387; Read Bain, "Trends in American Sociological Theory," in Lundberg, *Trends*, 96.

49. Persistent hereditarianism is evidenced in E. J. Lidbetter, "Pauperism and Heredity," *Eugenics Review* 14 (March 1922): 152–163, and Henry C. Schumacher, "Personality and Its Development as It Is Affected by Financial Dependency and Relief-Giving," *Family* 9 (July 1928): 140–144. H. E. Elder suggested a eugenic solution in *Social Science* 3 (May-July 1928): 329. Anderson noted his skepticism in "Trend of Urban Sociology," 284. On heredity and race in the Lundberg volume, see Bain, "Trends," 96; John F. Markey, "Trends in Social Psychology," 124; and Gary, "Developing Study of Culture," 192–193.

50. Bain, "Trends," 86. On the rejection of Lamarckism, see Erville B. Woods, "Heredity and Opportunity," *American Journal of Sociology* 26 (July 1920): 3, and Peter Bowler, *The Eclipse of Darwinism: Anti-Darwinian Evolution Theories in the Decades around 1900* (Baltimore: Johns Hopkins University Press, 1983), 139–140. C. S. Parker, *Working with the Working Woman*, 231, 235–236, 240, 245. Parker's use of the term "vicious circle" is interesting in light of its later importance. Alice O'Connor points out that while Gunnar Myrdal did not invent the idea, its prominence in *An American Dilemma* (1944) would make it the liberal thinkers' "reigning metaphor" for understanding poverty's persistence over the next three decades. See *Poverty Knowledge*, 96.

51. Anderson, *Men on the Move*, 1–2.

52. Cornelia Stratton Parker, *Wanderer's Circle* (Boston: Houghton Mifflin, 1934), 93; Arland D. Weeks, *Psychology of Citizenship* (Chicago: A. C. McClurg, 1917), 80; Williams, *What's on the Worker's Mind*, 6, v. For Williams's further proletarian adventures, see his *Full Up and Fed Up: The Worker's Mind in Crowded Britain* (New York: Charles

Scribner's Sons, 1921), and *Horny Hands and Hampered Elbows: The Worker's Mind in Western Europe* (New York: Charles Scribner's Sons, 1922). Williams's life and career are chronicled in Wren, *White Collar Hobo*.

53. Glenn Plumb and William G. Roylance, *Industrial Democracy: A Plan for Its Achievement* (New York: B. W. Huebsch, 1923); Ordway Tead, *Human Nature and Management: The Applications of Psychology to Executive Leadership* (New York: McGraw-Hill, 1929); Ordway Tead and Henry C. Metcalf, *Personnel Administration: Its Principles and Practices* (New York: McGraw-Hill, 1920), 256; Frederick Winslow Taylor, *The Principles of Scientific Management* (New York: Norton, 1911); David Montgomery, *The Fall of the House of Labor: The Workplace, the State, and American Labor Activism, 1865–1925* (Cambridge: Cambridge University Press, 1987), 421; Nelson Lichtenstein and John Harris Howell, eds., *Industrial Democracy in America: The Ambiguous Promise* (New York: Cambridge University Press, 1993); Samuel Haber, *Efficiency and Uplift: Scientific Management in the Progressive Era, 1890–1920* (Chicago: University of Chicago Press, 1964), 160–167; Gillespie, *Manufacturing Knowledge*, 16–36; Jane Lancaster, *Making Time: Lillian Moller Gilbreth, a Life beyond "Cheaper by the Dozen"* (Boston: Northeastern University Press, 2004). In William Graebner's study of what he ironically calls "democratic social engineering," he shows that many older progressives who had earlier focused their efforts around settlement house work and immigrant issues migrated during the 1920s to industrial relations. Down-and-outers and fellow travelers Williams, Mary Gilson, Ordway Tead, and Mary Parker Follett all followed this pattern; Charles Walker's engagement with social activism followed, rather than preceded, his undercover experiences, but he also ended up as a labor relations expert in his later years. Williams, Gilson, and the ex-socialist Henri DuBreuil were all involved with the Taylor Society during the 1920s, when it sought to soften and humanize Taylor's approach. See Graebner, *The Engineering of Consent: Democracy and Authority in Twentieth-Century America* (Madison: University of Wisconsin Press, 1987), 3–5, 75–88.

54. Mathewson, *Restriction of Output*, 158.

55. On the scientific, organizational impulse in progressivism, see Haber, *Efficiency and Uplift*; Brown, *Defining a Profession*; Ellis W. Hawley, *The Great War and the Search for a Modern Order: A History of the American People and Their Institutions, 1917–1933* (New York: St. Martin's Press, 1979).

56. Ordway Tead, "Trends in Industrial Psychology," *Annals of the American Academy of Political and Social Science* 149 (May 1930), Part I: 118–119; Tead, "Guilds for America," *Intercollegiate Socialist* 7 (February-March 1919): 31–33; Williams, *Full Up*, 247–278.

57. See Gillespie, *Manufacturing Knowledge*, 5, 30–32; Matthew Hale, Jr., *Human Science and Social Order: Hugo Munsterberg and the Origins of Applied Psychology* (Philadelphia: Temple University Press, 1980); Loren Baritz, *Servants of Power: A History of the Use of Social Science in American Industry* (Middletown, CT: Wesleyan University Press, 1960), 21–76.

58. Taylor, *Principles*, 59.

59. For example, like Walker (*Steel*, 48–49), Williams showed a critical awareness of classical economics (*What's on the Worker's Mind*, 293–294), but he drew more sympathetically on the contemporary economists Carleton H. Parker (224–226) and Thorstein Veblen (125); the industrial relations scholars Mary Parker Follett (*Mainsprings*, 308) and Ordway Tead (44); the sociologists Herbert Miller (189), W. I. Thomas (147), and Charles R. Henderson (231); and the philosophers William James (*What's on the Worker's Mind*, 244, 270) and John Dewey (*Mainsprings*, 139, 300). Similarly, Cornelia Stratton Parker cited a broad array of influences. Besides drawing upon the views of her husband, the labor economist Carleton Parker, her work was also informed by her studies at the New School with Veblen, Graham Wallas, James Harvey Robinson, and A.A. Goldenweiser: see *Wanderer's Circle*, 50.

60. Gillespie, *Manufacturing Knowledge*, 210–211.

61. Montgomery, *Fall of the House of Labor*, 410–411.

62. Leila Zenderland, *Measuring Minds: Henry Herbert Goddard and the Origins of American Intelligence Testing* (Cambridge: Cambridge University Press, 1998), 281–299, 311–315; Morris Viteles, *Industrial Psychology* (New York: Norton, 1932), 121, 317, 610.

63. Kimball Young, *Mental Differences in Certain Immigrant Groups: Psychological Tests of the South Europeans in Typical California Schools with Bearing on the Educational Policy and on the Problems of Racial Contacts in this Country* (Eugene: University of Oregon Press, 1922); Arthur Hanko, "Reducing Foreign Labor Turnover," *Industrial Management* 61 (May 1921): 367–369; Katherine M. H. Blackford, M.D., and Arthur Newcomb, *The Job, The Man, The Boss*, revised edition (Garden City, NY: Doubleday, Page, 1921); Daniel Nelson, *Managers and Workers: Origins of the Twentieth-Century Factory System in the United States, 1880–1920*, 2nd ed. (Madison: University of Wisconsin Press, 1995), 80–82. On the racialist underpinnings of job selection in early industrial psychology, see Hugo Munsterberg, *Psychology and Industrial Efficiency* (Boston: Houghton Mifflin, 1913), 129–132. Critiques of "scientific" job-assignment based on racial and ethnic criteria appeared in Boyd Fisher, *Mental Causes of Accidents* (Boston: Houghton Mifflin, 1922), 269; Tead, *Human Nature and Management*, 201; and Mary Gilson, *What's Past Is Prologue* (New York: Harper & Brothers, 1940), 64.

64. Whiting Williams actually preceded Mayo and his group as an investigator of the Hawthorne works, where he studied operations and recommended changes to personnel policies from 1922 to 1924. Williams's biographer, Daniel Wren, argues that Western Electric's personnel policies, which they called "human relations" and which were already considered quite progressive at the time of the Mayo studies, were rooted in Williams's earlier recommendations and that Williams's work should be seen as a "prelude to the Hawthorne experiments" (*White Collar Hobo*, 77–84). Williams had used the term "human relations" to refer to employee-management relations as early as 1918 in his *Human Relations in Industry* (Washington, DC: U.S. Department of Labor,

1918). The term dated at least to Progressive Era concerns about the impact of industrialization on workers: see Paul Kellogg, editor's foreword to Elizabeth Beardsley Butler, *Women and the Trades,* Volume I of *The Pittsburgh Survey* (New York, 1909; reprint, New York: Arno Press, 1969), 4. As discussed below, the "human relations approach" would become an umbrella term for personnel policies informed by social-scientific research in the 1930s and after.

65. Elton Mayo, "Civilization: The Perilous Adventure," *Harper's* 149 (October 1924): 590–597; "Psychopathologic Aspects of Industry," *Transactions of the American Neurological Association* 57 (1931): 468–475; *The Human Problems of an Industrial Civilization* (New York: Macmillan, 1933), 168–188; Gillespie, *Manufacturing Knowledge,* 150, 187.

66. Zenderland, *Measuring Minds,* 492n. Williams cited Mayo's "The Irrational Factor in Human Behavior," *Annals of the American Academy of Political and Social Science* 110 (November 1923): 117–130, in *Mainsprings,* 55.

67. Williams, *What's on the Worker's Mind,* 305.

68. Bussel, *From Harvard;* C. S. Parker, *Working with the Working Woman,* 246.

69. Thomas G Spates, *Human Values Where People Work* (New York: Harper & Brothers, 1960), 3–4; Williams, *What's on the Worker's Mind,* 3.

70. Williams, *What's on the Worker's Mind,* 7; Walker, *Steel,* 14.

71. Williams, *What's on the Worker's Mind,* 10, 133, 274, 277; C. S. Parker, *Wanderer's Circle,* 89–90.

72. Donovan, *Woman Who Waits,* 63; Walker, *Steel,* 144; "Walker, Charles Rumford," *National Cyclopedia of American Biography* (Clifton, NJ: James T. White, 1980).

73. Williams, *Horny Hands,* x; Walker, *Steel,* 139; Williams, *Mainsprings,* 239.

74. Williams, *What's on the Worker's Mind,* 244, 125; Walker, *Steel,* vi.

75. Weeks, *Psychology of Citizenship;* Henry Herbert Goddard, *Human Efficiency and Levels of Intelligence* (Princeton: Princeton University Press, 1920); Young, *Mental Differences.*

76. Williams, *What's on the Worker's Mind,* 295; Gilson, *Past Is Prologue,* 24–26.

77. Williams, *What's on the Worker's Mind,* 223–226.

78. Parker was a well-known progressive labor economist until his sudden death in 1918, and he was the husband of the down-and-outer Cornelia Stratton Parker. Carleton Parker's investigators, Frederick C. Mills and Paul Brissenden, both became well-known economists at Columbia University in the 1920s. Brissenden was Ordway Tead's colleague in Columbia's circle of industrial relations experts. He also wrote the first substantial study of the IWW, although the book made no explicit references to Brissenden's time in the union. Carleton H. Parker, *The Casual Laborer and Other Essays* (New York: Harcourt, Brace and Howe, 1920); Gregory R. Woirol, *In the Floating Army: F. C. Mills on Itinerant Life in California, 1914* (Urbana: University of Illinois Press, 1992); Bruce E. Kaufman, *The Origins and Evolution of the Field of Industrial Relations in the United States* (Ithaca, NY: Institute of Labor Relations, 1993), 47–48;

Paul F. Brissenden, *The I.W.W.: A Study of American Syndicalism* (New York: Columbia University Press, 1919). Brissenden's detached style comported with the post-undercover objectivism of his colleague Mills in the latter's *Contemporary Theories of Unemployment and of Unemployment Relief* (New York, 1917; reprint, New York: AMS Press, 1968). Both books were the products of young scholars establishing their professional credentials through publication by an academic press (Columbia); neither mentioned its author's brush with proletarian life.

79. Williams, *What's on the Worker's Mind*, 244; *Mainsprings*, 210–212.

80. Williams, *What's on the Worker's Mind*, 5, 166, 201, 131, 217.

81. Walker, Gilson, and Mathewson were all involved in personnel work; Cornelia Stratton Parker hoped to become so but apparently never succeeded, although she pursued a very active speaking career on related topics (see C. S. Parker, *Wanderer's Circle*, 50). A fellow traveler, Ordway Tead, coauthored the first major text on personnel management: Tead and Metcalf, *Personnel Administration*.

82. Walker, *Steel*, 76–77; Lois G. Sutherland Spear, review of *Steel*, by Charles Rumford Walker, *New Republic* 31 (January 1923): 260.

83. A socialist novel that details work processes is Leroy Scott, *The Walking Delegate* (New York: Doubleday, Page, 1905). For reviewers' assertions about the likely influence of Walker's *Steel*, see the reviews in *Administration* 5 (January 1923): 107–108; *New Republic* (259–260); and *Literary Review of the New York Evening Post* (November 25, 1922): 241. For similar assessments of Williams's *Worker's Mind*, see *American Journal of Sociology* 27 (July 1921): 124–126; *Bookman* 52 (February 1921): 556–557; and *Nation* 111 (November 10, 1920): 533–535.

84. Gillespie, *Manufacturing Knowledge*, 210; Williams, *Mainsprings*; Wren, *White-Collar Hobo*, 73–99; F. L. W. Richardson, Jr., and Charles Rumford Walker, *Human Relations in an Expanding Company* (New Haven: Labor and Management Center, Yale University, 1948); Charles Rumford Walker, "The Problem of the Repetitive Job," *Harvard Business Review* 28 (May 1950): 54–58; Charles Rumford Walker and Robert H. Guest, *The Man on the Assembly Line* (Cambridge: Harvard University Press, 1952); Charles Rumford Walker, Robert H. Guest, and Arthur N. Turner, *The Foreman on the Assembly Line* (Cambridge: Harvard University Press, 1956).

85. Williams, *Human Relations in Industry*; Gillespie, *Manufacturing Knowledge*, 127–151, 196–197; Bruce E. Kaufman, *Managing the Human Factor: The Early Years of Human Resource Management in American Industry* (Ithaca, NY: ILR Press, 2008); Mayo, "Civilization," and "Psychopathologic Aspects."

86. Cornelia Stratton Parker, "The Human Element in the Machine Process," *Annals of the American Academy of Political and Social Science* 90 (July 1920): 83–88.

87. C. S. Parker, *Wanderer's Circle*, 93; Williams, *What's on the Worker's Mind*, 31; *Full Up*, v; C. S. Parker, *Working with the Working Woman*, xvi–xvii.

88. For the critique of Taylor's psychology, see Williams, *What's on the Worker's Mind*, 80, 293; Charles S. Myers, *Mind and Work* (New York: Putnam's, 1921); Henri DuBreuil, *Robots or Men? A French Workman's Experience in American Industry*, trans. Frances and Mason Merrill (New York: Harper & Brothers, 1930), 65–66; Haber, *Efficiency and Uplift*, 164–165. Elton Mayo, "What Every Village Knows," *Survey Graphic* 26 (December 1937): 697.

89. On the movement of some immigrant groups toward whiteness, see Matthew Frye Jacobson, *Whiteness of a Different Color: European Immigrants and the Alchemy of Race* (Cambridge: Harvard University Press, 1998), 91–136, and David R. Roediger, *Working toward Whiteness: How America's Immigrants Became White* (New York: Basic Books, 2005). On the concomitant deepening during the 1920s of a color-based racial divide, see Matthew Pratt Guterl, *The Color of Race in America, 1900–1940* (Cambridge: Harvard University Press, 2001).

90. George S. Stocking, Jr., relates Boas's critique of "racial formalism" to the broader intellectual "revolt against formalism" described by Morton White: see Stocking, *Race, Culture, and Evolution: Essays in the History of Anthropology* (Chicago: University of Chicago Press, 1982), 161–163, and Morton White, *Social Thought in America: The Revolt against Formalism* (Boston: Beacon Press, 1957).

91. Walker, *Steel*, 125; "Hunkies," in early twentieth-century slang, referred loosely to Central and Eastern European immigrants who were usually unskilled and uneducated: see Roediger, *Working toward Whiteness*, 43-45. Williams, *What's on the Worker's Mind*, 19, 78, 250, 16–17, 99, 127. Jane Addams, *Twenty Years at Hull House* (New York: Signet Classics, 1960), 169–185; Randolph Bourne, "Trans-National America," *Atlantic* 118 (July 1916): 86–97; Horace Kallen, "'Americanization' and the Cultural Prospect," in his *Culture and Democracy in the United States: Studies in the Group Psychology of the American People* (New York: Boni & Liveright, 1924), 150–172.

92. On repetitive labor and mental degeneration, see Weeks, *Psychology of Citizenship*, 58–63, and Arthur Pound, "Mills and Minds," *Bulletin of the Taylor Society* 7 (June 1922): 83–91. Calls for reform came from Babcock, "Higher Education," 384, and MacLean, "Model Factory," 439.

93. Kimball, "In the Silk," 50; DuBreuil, *Robots*, 110–111; Williams, "Discussion," 94; Walker, *Steel*, 68, 124.

94. See also Whiting Williams, "What's Machinery Doing to Us?" in *Problems of Civilization*, ed. Baker Brownell (New York: D. Van Nostrand, 1929), 43–64. For an industrial educator's perspective resembling that of Williams, Walker, and Kimball, see Frank Henry Selden, "Have We a Just Standard of Industrial Intelligence?" *American Journal of Sociology* 24 (May 1919): 654–652, and "Industrial Intelligence and the Present World-Crisis," *American Journal of Sociology* 25 (September 1919): 195–201. The 1920s debates over monotony and productivity are summed up in Viteles, *Industrial Psychology*, 512–559.

95. C. S. Parker, *Working with the Working Woman*, 16; Williams, *What's on the Worker's Mind*, 21; Walker, *Steel*, 157.

96. Williams, *What's on the Worker's Mind*, v, 281; Walker, *Steel*, vii.

97. Williams, *What's on the Worker's Mind*, 128.

98. Taylor, *Principles*, 13–15; Whiting Williams, "More Production? Say, Where D'ya Get That Stuff?" *Annals of the American Academy of Political and Social Science* 89 (May 1920): 183–186; Williams, *What's on the Worker's Mind*, 15, 284; Walker, *Steel*, 48–49, 93–94; Mayo, "Psychopathologic Aspects," 475; Mathewson, *Restriction of Output*, 152–153.

99. Williams, *What's on the Worker's Mind*, 312; C. S. Parker, *Working with the Working Woman*, 236.

100. Williams, *What's on the Worker's Mind*, 20; C. Wright Mills, *White Collar: The American Middle Classes* (New York: Oxford University Press, 1951), xii–xiii; Taylor, *Principles*, 38–39; C. S. Parker, *Working with the Working Woman*, 236–237; Williams, *Mainsprings*, 246–248; Tead, "Trends," 110–111, 118.

101. Williams, *What's on the Worker's Mind*, 178, 182–183.

102. Ibid., 140–141, 244.

103. Ibid., 68; Walker, *Steel*, 157; Williams, *Full Up*, v (emphasis in original); Gillespie, *Manufacturing Knowledge*, 210–239; Mills, *White Collar*, xv.

104. Whiting Williams, "That the People May Decide," *Collier's* 68 (July 23, 1921): 7–8; Babcock, "Higher Education," 384; Donovan, *Woman Who Waits*, 92; Kimball, "In the Silk," 51; Gilson, *Past Is Prologue*, x.

105. Munsterberg, *Psychology and Industrial Efficiency*, 3; Hale, *Human Science*, 161; Spates, *Human Values*, 3–4, 53–54; Walker, *Steel*, 127.

106. Williams, *Full Up*, 4.

107. Williams, *What's on the Worker's Mind*, v, 38; *Full Up*, 306; *Mainsprings*, 243–244; Mayo, "Psychopathologic Aspects," 474–475.

108. Sanford Jacoby, *Employing Bureaucracy: Managers, Unions, and the Transformation of Work in American Industry, 1900–1945* (New York: Columbia University Press, 1985), 279–280; C. S. Parker, *Wanderer's Circle*, 95; Walker, *Steel*, 128–129; Whiting Williams, "How'd You Like to Be a Labor Leader?" *Collier's* 71 (February 24, 1923): 6.

109. William James, "On a Certain Blindness in Human Beings" (1899), in his *Essays on Faith and Morals*, ed. Ralph Barton Perry (New York: Meridian Books, 1962), 259–284; quoted in Williams, *Mainsprings*, 210. Donovan, *Woman Who Waits*, 145; Williams, *What's on the Worker's Mind*, 14, 196.

110. Williams, *What's on the Worker's Mind*, 283, 134.

111. Ibid., 224–226; *Mainsprings*, 144–145.

112. C. S. Parker, "Human Element," 86–87; Williams, *What's on the Worker's Mind*, 224–226. Carleton Parker had pioneered the application of instinct theory to the IWW, and would exercise a strong influence over class passers and other students

of industrial relations in the late teens and 1920s, setting some on a path toward a Mayo-like emphasis on workers' irrationality. See C. H. Parker, *The Casual Laborer*, especially "Motives in Economic Life," 125–165, and Ordway Tead, *Instincts in Industry: A Study of Working-Class Psychology* (Boston: Houghton Mifflin, 1918). On Tead's debt to Carleton Parker, see *Instincts*, xiv. Parker's influence may have been somewhat extended by the extraordinary popularity of Cornelia Parker's memoir, *An American Idyll: The Life of Carleton H. Parker* (Boston: Atlantic Monthly Press, 1919): see James D. Hart, *The Popular Book: A History of America's Literary Taste* (New York: Oxford University Press, 1950), 242, 312. Carl Degler chronicles the deterioration of instinct theory over the 1920s and 1930s in his *In Search of Human Nature: The Decline and Revival of Darwinism in American Social Thought* (New York: Oxford University Press, 1991), 162–166.

113. C. S. Parker, *Working with the Working Woman*, 232–235; Williams, *What's on the Worker's Mind*, 86; Williams, "That the People," 8. For management's new emphasis on what a contemporary researcher called "'feelings as instruments of control,'" see Eugene McCarraher, "'An Industrial Marcus Aurelius': Corporate Humanism, Management Theory, and Social Selfhood, 1908–1956," *Journal of the Historical Society* 5 (Winter 2005): 98.

114. Walker, *Steel*, 125; "Copper: A Study in Ingots and Men," *Atlantic* 131 (June 1923): 751–759; "Seven to Six, An Hour Out for Lunch," *Atlantic* 134 (August 1924): 229–237.

115. Williams, *What's on the Worker's Mind*, 277; *Full Up*, v–vi.

116. Jacoby, *Employing Bureaucracy*, 280. The "long turn" debate ended when public and political pressures brought the eight-hour day to U.S. Steel in 1923: see David Brody, *Labor in Crisis: The Steel Strike of 1919* (Philadelphia: J. B. Lippincott, 1965), 177–178. Stressing the class passers' relevance to this debate were reviews of Walker's *Steel* in *New Republic* (260) and in *New York Evening Post* (241); and reviews of Williams's *Worker's Mind* in *American Journal of Sociology* (124–126), *New Republic* 25 (January 26, 1921): 266–267 (by Ordway Tead), and *Nation* (533). Among many examples of critics praising the books' informative value are reviews of C. S. Parker, *Working with the Working Woman*, in *Bookman* 55 (April 1922): 202; of Williams, *What's on the Worker's Mind*, in *Booklist* 17 (December 1920): 96; and of Walker's *Steel* and Williams's *Horny Hands* in *American Journal of Sociology* 30 (March 1925): 615. For investigators' views on tensions between industrial democracy and welfare capitalism, see MacLean, "Model Factory," 444; Williams, *What's on the Worker's Mind*, 263, 312; C. S. Parker, "Human Element," 86.

117. Williams, *Horny Hands*, ix–x, 3; "Discussion," 93; *Mainsprings*, 300.

118. See for example Tead, *Human Nature and Management*, 44, 201; Viteles, *Industrial Psychology*, 191–196; Miller, *Races, Nations, and Classes*, 130–137. See also Gilson, *Past Is Prologue*, 24–25.

119. Ordway Tead, review of *Management and the Worker* by Fritz Roethlisberger and William Dickson, *Advanced Management* 5 (April-June 1940): 93. Tead regularly drew

upon and cited Williams through the 1920s and 1930s: see *Human Nature and Management*, 22, 67, 116; "Trends," 118. Williams's books would be cited appreciatively in management literature for decades: see Spates, *Human Values*, 3–4; Robert Saltonstall, *Human Relations in Administration* (New York: McGraw-Hill, 1959), 56–57. On Williams's impact, see also Morrell Heald, *The Social Responsibilities of Business: Company and Community, 1900–1960* (Cleveland: Press of Case Western Reserve University, 1970), xv, 24–25, 61, 100.

120. Baritz, *Servants of Power*.

121. Williams, *What's on the Worker's Mind*, 255, 302, 233; *Full Up*, 294–295; Tead, review of *Full Up and Fed Up*, by Whiting Williams, *Political Science Quarterly* 37 (June 1922): 345.

122. MacLean, "Model Factory," 444. On the eclipse of honest class antagonism by the rise of the "social self" in American thought, see Jeffrey Sklansky, *The Soul's Economy: Market Society and Selfhood in American Thought, 1820–1920* (Chapel Hill: University of North Carolina Press, 2002).

123. Tead, "Trends," 110; Mayo, "Psychopathologic Aspects," 475.

124. Bingham, *Man's Estate*, 27–28.

125. Paul Peters, "I'm Hunting for a Job," *Harper's* 158 (March 1929): 466.

CHAPTER 3

1. Robert S. Lynd, "When Boys and Girls Turn Box-Car Hoboes," review of *Boy and Girl Tramps of America*, by Thomas Minehan, *New York Herald Tribune Books* (July 8, 1934): 1.

2. *Sullivan's Travels*, directed by Preston Sturges (Paramount, 1941; DVD, New York, NY: Criterion Collection, 2001).

3. Lawrence F. Hanley, "Popular Culture and Crisis: King Kong Meets Edmund Wilson," in *Radical Revisions: Rereading 1930s Culture*, ed. Bill Mullen and Sherry Lee Linkon (Urbana: University of Illinois Press, 1996), 242–263; Edmund Wilson, *The American Jitters: A Year of the Slump* (New York: Scribner's, 1932); Norma Lee Browning, "We Live in the Slums," *Forum* 102 (August 1939): 56–60. For typically angry downward-mobility narratives by anonymous authors, see "In the Ditch: What the Workers in CWA Ditches Think and Talk About," *New Outlook* 163 (February 1934): 34–36, and "I Know What Poverty Is," *American Mercury* 38 (June 1936): 201–206.

4. Excellent studies of the documentary impulse include William Stott, *Documentary Expression and Thirties America* (New York: Oxford University Press, 1973), and David Peeler, *Hope among Us Yet: Social Criticism and Social Solace in Depression America* (Athens: University of Georgia Press, 1987). Although racial passing was the subject of much writing in the interwar years and will be mentioned occasionally in this

chapter, the connections between racial and class passing will be discussed more fully in chapter 5.

5. Terry A. Cooney, *Balancing Acts: American Thought and Culture in the 1930s* (New York: Twayne, 1995), 158.

6. "The People of the USA—A Self-Portrait," *Fortune* 21 (February 1940): 14, 20; Cooney, *Balancing Acts*, 55–56; David M. Kennedy, *Freedom from Fear: The American People in Depression and War, 1929–1945* (New York: Oxford University Press, 1999), 322. On why growing numbers of Americans identified themselves as "middle class," see Olivier Zunz, *Why the American Century?* (Chicago: University of Chicago Press, 1998), chapters 4 and 5. For middle-class anxiety during the Depression, see Loren Baritz, *The Good Life: The Meaning of Success for the American Middle Class* (New York: Knopf, 1989), and Mary C. McComb, *Great Depression and the Middle Class: Experts, Collegiate Youth and Business Ideology, 1929–1941* (New York: Routledge, 2006).

7. Matthew Josephson, "The Other Nation," *New Republic* 75 (May 17, 1933): 14–15.

8. Maury Maverick, *A Maverick American* (New York: Covici, Friede, 1937), 150–153, 164–165; Donald Francis Roy, "Hooverville: A Study of a Community of Homeless Men in Seattle" (master's thesis, University of Washington, 1935), 2, 5, 13; Thomas Minehan, *Boy and Girl Tramps of America* (New York: Farrar & Rinehart, 1934; reprint, Seattle: University of Washington Press, 1976, introd. Donald W. Whisenhunt), xxii, xxiv. For another example, see Samuael Kirson Weinberg, "A Study of Isolation among Chicago Shelter-House Men" (master's thesis, University of Chicago, 1935), 3–4; Herbert McCanlies, in "Transients in California" (Sacramento, CA: Division of Special Surveys and Studies, 1936), 180–181, 183, 263–265. Donald Roy's method was unusual: He conducted interviews and mapped the community under the ruse that he was an ordinary Hooverville denizen who had been hired by a local relief agency to gather information that would facilitate the distribution of relief ("Hooverville," 5, 9–14). Roy's findings are summarized in his "Hooverville—A Community of Homeless Men," *Studies in Sociology* 4 (Winter 1939–Summer 1940): 37–45.

9. Thomas Minehan, "Boys and Girls on the March," *Parents Magazine* 10 (March 1935): 14; Minehan, *Lonesome Road: The Way of Life of a Hobo* (Evanston, IL: Row, Peterson, 1941), 4.

10. Martha Gellhorn, *The Trouble I've Seen* (New York: William Morrow, 1936); Lorena Hickok, *One-Third of a Nation: Lorena Hickok Reports on the Great Depression*, ed. Richard Lowitt and Maurine Beasley (Urbana: University of Illinois Press, 1981); Lauren Gilfillan, "Weary Feet," *Forum* 90 (October 1933): 201–208.

11. Michael Gold, "Go Left, Young Writers!" *New Masses* 4 (January 1929), in *Mike Gold: A Literary Anthology*, ed. Michael Folsom (New York: International Publishers, 1972), 188; Paul Peters, "I'm Hunting for a Job," *Harper's Monthly Magazine* 158 (March 1929): 463–464; Sender Garlin, "Paul Peters—Revolutionary Playwright; An Interview," part

1, *Daily Worker* (May 15, 1934): 5; Malcolm Goldstein, *The Political Stage: American Drama and Theatre of the Great Depression* (New York: Oxford University Press, 1974), 60.

12. Peters, "I'm Hunting," 463, 464.

13. Thomas Patrick Minehan, "A Study of the Attitudes of Transient Men and Boys in St. Paul, Minnesota" (master's thesis, University of Minnesota, 1933), xxiii; Peters, "I'm Hunting," 467; Garlin, "Paul Peters," 5; John Kazarian, "The Starvation Army," part 1, *Nation* 136 (April 12, 1933): 396; part 3 (April 26, 1933): 473.

14. Maverick, *Maverick American*, 153, 155, 164–166; McCanlies, "Transients," 156–158.

15. Eric Hatch, *My Man Godfrey* (Boston: Little, Brown, 1935); *My Man Godfrey*, directed by Gregory La Cava (Universal, 1936; DVD, New York, NY: Criterion Collection, 2002); Edward Newhouse, "Sights and Sounds," *New Masses* 21 (September 29, 1936): 29; Graham Greene, "The Cinema," *Spectator* 157 (October 2, 1936): 543.

16. Minehan, *Boy and Girl Tramps*, chapter 15. Reviewers found this chapter on tribalism especially compelling: see reviews by Ruth Pearson Koshuk, *American Journal of Sociology* 42 (July 1936): 148–149, and J. M. R., *Southwestern Social Science Quarterly* 15 (December 1934): 265. George Outland, an academic who worked with the short-lived Federal Transient Service, expressed the common concern about homosexuality in his influential study *Boy Transiency in America* (Santa Barbara, CA: Santa Barbara State College Press, 1939), 65. Undercover reports on the issue included Minehan, "Study of Attitudes," 119, 128–129, and *Boy and Girl Tramps*, 141–149; Edwin H. Sutherland and Harvey J. Locke, *Twenty Thousand Homeless Men* (Chicago: J. B. Lippincott, 1936), 6–7, 113; McCanlies, "Transients," 172, 189, 225–226; and Roy, "Hooverville: A Study," 11–12, 88. George Orwell reported having been told by a tramp who approached him that homosexuality was similarly " 'general among tramps of long standing' " in Britain: *Down and Out in Paris and London* (London, 1933; New York: Harcourt, Brace Jovanovich, 1961), 147.

17. On the rising incidence of female hoboes, understood as an index of the Depression's seriousness, see "Editorial Paragraphs," *Nation* 137 (August 9, 1933): 143. A sociologist's discussion of the issue for general audiences was Walter Reckless, "Why Women Become Hoboes," *American Mercury* 31 (February 1934): 175–180. Undercover perspectives came from Thomas Minehan, "Girls of the Road," *Independent Woman* 13 (October 1934): 316–317, 335; Minehan, *Boy and Girl Tramps*, 39, 133, 139, 169, 177; McCanlies, "Transients," 73, 219; Maverick, *Maverick American*, 164; Kazarian, "Starvation Army," 398–399. Two other relevant articles whose authors' undercover statuses were ambiguous were Samuel Milton Elam, "Lady Hoboes," *New Republic* 61 (January 1, 1930): 164–169, and Edward L. Flannery, "Ladies of the Road," *Literary Digest* 114 (August 13, 1932): 33. *Wild Boys of the Road*, directed by William A. Wellman (Warner Brothers, 1933; DVD, in *Forbidden Hollywood Collection, Volume Three*, Burbank, CA: Warner Home Video, 2009); Ben Reitman, *Sister of the Road: The Autobiography of*

Box-Car Bertha (New York: Gold Label Books, 1937); Roger A. Bruns, *The Damndest Radical: The Life and World of Ben Reitman* (Urbana: University of Illinois Press, 1987), 262–263; Todd DePastino, *Citizen Hobo: How a Century of Homelessness Shaped America* (Chicago: University of Chicago Press, 2003), 286n.

18. "Speaking of Pictures . . . This Is a Primer for Hobo 'Gaycats,' " *Life* 3 (October 4, 1937): 14–17. A "gaycat"—a novice hobo—was especially vulnerable to accidents, as the public was periodically reminded. In *Wild Boys of the Road*, a main character is maimed when his foot gets caught in a railyard track and is severed by a train.

19. Minehan, *Boy and Girl Tramps*, 176. Minehan also wrote that "no white boy admitted" to having sex with a black girl (138). If this was true, it may have been partly because there were few black girls on the road. He offered no breakdown by race in his tables, but he made no other mention in the text of black females. In all, Minehan obtained first-person data on 1,377 boys and only 88 girls (253). Roy, "Hooverville: A Study," 42, 92; McCanlies, "Transients," 144; Maverick, *Maverick American*, 156, 165–166; Theodore Caplow, "Transiency as a Cultural Pattern," *American Sociological Review* 5 (October 1940): 737.

20. Sutherland and Locke, *Twenty Thousand Homeless Men*, 56. Weinberg, "Study of Isolation," also found some ethnic and racial hostility, although less so against African Americans, who were typically segregated to a separate shelter (47). Weinberg was a graduate student who worked undercover in Sutherland and Locke's study.

21. Kazarian, "Starvation Army," 473; Minehan, "Study of Attitudes," 87; Minehan, *Boy and Girl Tramps*, 163–164, 170; Edward Newhouse, *You Can't Sleep Here* (New York: Macaulay, 1934), 220–221; Melvin J. Vincent, "Social Fiction Notes," review of *I Went to Pit College*, by Lauren Gilfillan, *Sociology and Social Research* 18 (May-June 1934): 497. Further references to the novels will appear parenthetically in the text.

22. Roy, "Hooverville: A Study," 93; Charles Rumford Walker, "Relief and Revolution," *Forum* 88 (September 1932): 152–158; Robert W. Beasley, "Care of Unattached, Destitute Men in Chicago with Special Reference to the Depression" (master's thesis, University of Chicago, 1933), 74; Sutherland and Locke, *Twenty Thousand Homeless Men*, 116, 13–14; McCanlies, "Transients," 153, 231, 227–228.

23. Paul Peters, "Cotton Mill," *American Mercury* 17 (May 1929): 3–4, 5, 9.

24. Whiting Williams, "The Hopeful American Worker," *Saturday Evening Post* 205 (June 17, 1933): 8; "What's on the Worker's Mind," *Industrial Relations* 3 (August 1932): 2; "The Worker's Mind Today," *Personnel Journal* 9 (February 1931): 403 (emphasis in original). On Williams's loyalty to Hooverian individualism, see "The Worker's Mind Today," 402–403, and "But You Can't Let People Starve," *Survey* 67 (February 1, 1932): 459–460. Williams's correspondence with Hoover is discussed in Daniel A. Wren, *White Collar Hobo: The Travels of Whiting Williams* (Ames: Iowa State University Press, 1987), 116.

25. Minehan, "Boys and Girls on the March," 72; Maverick, *Maverick American*, 151–152, 166, 167–176, 9, 11, chapters 29 and 30, 360, 238.

26. Minehan, "Study of Attitudes," 23, 196–197; Anderson cited in Minehan, *Boy and Girl Tramps*, 196; in Sutherland and Locke, *Twenty Thousand Homeless Men*, 11, 190; in Jesse Walter Dees, Jr., *Flophouse*, 2nd edition (Francestown, NH, 1940; Francestown, NH: Marshall Jones, 1948), viii; in Caplow, "Transiency," 732.

27. Sutherland and Locke, *Twenty Thousand Homeless Men*, 38; Jesse Walter Dees, Jr., "The Effect of Modern Relief Policies on Shelters for Homeless Men in Chicago, December, 1938" (master's thesis, Northwestern University, 1942), 1–2; Dees, *Flophouse*, vii–viii. The bulk of *Flophouse* was based on the undercover research that Dees began when an undergraduate in 1935, and he continued for his master's thesis research in 1938. The 1948 version differed from its 1940 predecessor only by including three pages (143–145) that sketchily addressed changes from 1939 to 1948. Caplow, "Transiency," 732, 733, 735, 731. In addition to studying at Chicago, Sutherland—like Minehan and Caplow—also had a Minnesota connection, having taught there (from 1926 to 1929) before joining the Chicago faculty in 1930. Sutherland left Chicago for Indiana University in 1935, and he became president of the American Sociological Society in 1939. On Sutherland, see Gilbert Geis and Colin Goff, introduction to Edwin H. Sutherland, *White Collar Crime: The Uncut Version* (New Haven: Yale University Press, 1983), xxii–xxvii. Other graduate theses based on undercover research included Daniel S. Russell, "The Roadhouse: A Study of Commercialized Amusements in the Environs of Chicago" (master's thesis, University of Chicago, 1931); Paul G. Cressey, *The Taxi-Dance Hall* (Chicago, 1932; reprint, New York: AMS Press, 1971); and Weinberg, "Study of Isolation." Sutherland and Locke described their team of undercover graduate students in *Twenty Thousand Homeless Men*, 5–7.

28. On method in social science during this period, see Robert C. Bannister, *Sociology and Scientism: The American Quest for Objectivity, 1880–1940* (Chapel Hill: University of North Carolina Press, 1987), and Mark C. Smith, *Social Science in the Crucible: The American Debate over Objectivity and Purpose, 1918–1941* (Durham: Duke University Press, 1994), 5–8, 47–48. On the Chicago School and subjective data, see Martin Bulmer, *The Chicago School of Sociology: Institutionalization, Diversity, and the Rise of Sociological Research* (Chicago: University of Chicago Press, 1984), 93, 101, and Rolf Lindner, *The Reportage of Urban Culture: Robert Park and the Chicago School* (Frankfurt am Main, Germany, 1990; trans. Adrian Morris, New York: Cambridge University Press, 1996), 82. Viven M. Palmer, *Field Studies in Sociology: A Student's Manual* (Chicago: University of Chicago Press, 1928), 8–9, 172, 10–11; Robert E. Park, "The City as Social Laboratory," in *Chicago: An Experiment in Social Science Research*, ed. T. V. Smith and Leonard D. White (Chicago: University of Chicago Press, 1929), 1–19; Ernest W. Burgess, "Basic Social Data," in Smith and White, *Chicago*, 47–66. Palmer did cite Cressey and Russell—Chicago contemporaries involved in undercover investigations— but not their predecessors, in her acknowledgments (ix). Robert E. Park, introduction to Frances R. Donovan, *The Saleslady* (Chicago: University of Chicago Press, 1929),

vii–ix. And in an essay that reviewed studies of institutions, including department stores, Burgess mentioned his student Paul Cressey's work (then still in manuscript), but not Donovan's or Annie MacLean's publications on restaurants and department stores: Burgess, "Studies of Institutions," in Smith and White, *Chicago*, 169n.

29. Reviewers of E. Wight Bakke's partly undercover studies of the New Haven unemployed did not distinguish between the participant-observer approach he had employed in his earlier work in Great Britain and the undercover method used in the New Haven research. See reviews of Bakke's *The Unemployed Worker* and *Citizens without Work* (both New Haven: Yale University Press, 1940) by Colston E. Warne, *Annals of the American Academy of Political and Social Science* 217 (September 1941): 196, and by C. W. Guillebaud, *Economic Journal* 52 (March 1942): 104–105. Bakke himself called his undercover graduate students "participant observers" in *Unemployed Worker*, 376. Dees was also referred to as a participant observer in reviews of the later edition of *Flophouse*: see reviews by Herman H. Long in *Phylon* 10 (fourth quarter 1949): 427–428, and by Edward Galway, *Survey* 85 (March 1949): 181.

30. Eduard C. Lindeman, *Social Discovery* (New York: Republic, 1924), 179–180, 191–193; Jennifer Platt, "The Development of the 'Participant Observation' Method in Sociology: Origins, Myth, and History," *Journal of the History of the Behavioral Sciences* 19 (October 1983): 379–393.

31. Bannister, *Sociology and Scientism*, 10, 204–205; Bain received the Ph.D. from the University of Michigan in 1926 (266n). Read Bain, "The Impersonal Confession and Social Research," *Journal of Applied Sociology* 9 (May-June 1925): 356–361; Minehan, "Study of Attitudes," 52–53; Cressey, *Taxi-Dance Hall*, xvii-xviii; Paul Goalby Cressey, "A Comparison of the Roles of the 'Sociological Stranger' and the 'Anonymous Stranger' in Field Research" (previously unpublished, 1927), *Urban Life* 12 (April 1984): 103–109, 111–112, 113, 118.

32. Cressey, *Taxi-Dance Hall*, xviii, 3–14.

33. Minehan, *Boy and Girl Tramps*, xxii–xxviii, 247–248. Minehan's master's thesis, which addressed the undercover method and its possible shortcomings (46–64), showed a high degree of methodological self-consciousness. Minehan surreptitiously recorded conversations from memory as soon as possible after they occurred. He clearly then edited that material for smoothness and clarity; his informants did not stammer or grope for words on the printed page.

34. Positive popular reviews included Ferguson, "The World Below"; Herschel Brickell, "Books on Our Table," *New York Post* (June 23, 1934): 7; *New York Times Book Review* (July 1, 1934): 10; Wallace M. Goldsmith, "Charity Begins Abroad," *Saturday Review of Literature* 11 (August 11, 1934): 43; John J. Honigmann, "Devil-May-Care," *Commonweal* 21 (November 23, 1934): 127–128; Lynd, "Boys and Girls," 1; and N. M. Grier, "Youth without Work," *Christian Century* 51 (September 5, 1934): 1117. Reviewers for scholarly journals who rated the book highly included Ella Winter in *Pacific Affairs* 7 (December

1934): 473–474; Leroy Allen in *Social Science* 10 (January 1935): 85; J. M. R. in *Southwestern Social Science Quarterly* 15 (December 1934): 265; and James S. Plant in *Mental Hygiene* 19 (January 1935): 122–123. The critical comments quoted (from what were otherwise positive reviews) came from Ruth Pearson Koshuk in *American Journal of Sociology* 42 (July 1936): 149, and M. H. N. in *Sociology and Social Research* 20 (March-April 1936): 391. Anderson reviewed the book twice: in *Survey* 71 (January 1935): 26–27, and in *Journal of Criminal Law and Criminology* 25 (November 1934): 659. Anderson complained that he was still chained to *The Hobo* in the *Survey* review (26).

35. Bulmer, *Chicago School*, 92; Cressey, *Taxi-Dance Hall*, 31. Uses by sociologists of the culture concept included Nels Anderson, "The Slum: A Project for Study," *Social Forces* 7 (September 1928): 87–88; Dean Stiff [pseud. Nels Anderson], *The Milk and Honey Route* (New York: Vanguard Press, 1931), 2; Sutherland and Locke, *Twenty Thousand Homeless Men*, 162; Minehan, *Boy and Girl Tramps*, especially chapter 15; Caplow, "Transiency." Beyond down-and-outers, the idea that hoboes shared a distinctive culture was widely held: see George Milburn, *The Hobo's Hornbook* (New York: Ives Washburn, 1930); Harlan Gilmore, *The Beggar* (Chapel Hill: University of North Carolina Press, 1940), 95–96.

36. On 1930s sociologists' substitution of cultural for racial inferiority even as the field shifted focus from older racialist thinking to cultural analysis, see James B. McKee, *Sociology and the Race Problem: The Failure of a Perspective* (Urbana: University of Illinois Press, 1993), 96–97. The entanglement of the culture concept with older hierarchical perspectives based in evolutionary thought may be an example of how the modes of thinking that Fred H. Matthews called "processual" and "structural" sometimes tensely coexisted in single individuals and research programs. See Matthews, "Social Scientists and the Culture Concept, 1930–1950: The Conflict between Processual and Structural Approaches," *Sociological Theory* 7 (Spring 1989): especially 87–89.

37. A good example of murkiness regarding environment and heredity was Charles A. Ellwood, "Social Evolution and Cultural Evolution," *Journal of Applied Sociology* 11 (March-April 1927): 308–314. Frank H. Hankins of Smith College, and in 1938 the president of the American Sociological Association, offered a sympathetic overview of recent research on the "interaction of the biological and the social" in "Research in Social Biology," *Sociology and Social Research* 17 (July-August 1933): 514–518. For a historical perspective on the behavioral dimensions of the term "underclass," see Michael B. Katz, "The Urban 'Underclass' as a Metaphor of Social Transformation," in *The "Underclass" Debate*, ed. Michael B. Katz (Princeton: Princeton University Press, 1993), 3–23. Sutherland's commitment to the culture concept may be charted in "The Biological and Sociological Processes," in *The Urban Community: Selected Papers from the Proceedings of the American Sociological Society*, ed. E. W. Burgess (Chicago: University of Chicago Press, 1926), 70–78; "Mental Deficiency and Crime," in *Social Attitudes*, ed. Kimball Young (New York: Henry Holt, 1931), 522–529; and "Social Process in Behavior

Problems," *Publications of the American Sociological Society* 26 (August 1932): especially 60–61. Sutherland and Locke emphasized the importance of economic conditions (for example, 178–185) as against heredity, but they also noted the difficulty of weighting one factor more heavily than the other (24, 48–49).

38. Sutherland and Locke, *Twenty Thousand Homeless Men*, 22–24. Sutherland continued to emphasize culture in his later work. In a review of Nels Anderson's *Men on the Move* (Chicago: University of Chicago Press, 1940), he criticized Anderson for failing to grasp the distinctive culture of late 1930s transients, because he had not lived with them as he had done for *The Hobo*. See *American Journal of Sociology* 47 (September 1941): 237–238. On Sutherland's cultural theory of criminality, see *The Sutherland Papers*, ed. Albert Cohen, Alfred Lindesmith, and Karl Schuessler (Bloomington: Indiana University Press, 1956), 2–20.

39. The quasi-Lamarckian quote about "disuse" comes from a study that was frequently cited during the 1930s: John N. Webb, *The Migratory-Casual Worker* (Washington, DC, 1937; reprint Cambridge, MA: Da Capo Press, 1971), 93. See also Kingsley Davis, *Youth in the Depression* (Chicago: University of Chicago Press, 1935), 5–6; Minehan, "Boys and Girls on the March," 70; and "Girls of the Road," 335.

40. Minehan, "Girls of the Road," 335; Minehan, *Boy and Girl Tramps*, 120–121, 210, 219; Minehan, *Lonesome Road*, 64; Nels Anderson, "Are the Unemployed a Caste?" *Survey Graphic* 24 (July 1935): 346.

41. Sutherland and Locke, *Twenty Thousand Homeless Men*, v; Dees, *Flophouse*, viii.

42. Dees, *Flophouse*, 12 (emphasis added). For a comparable expression of revulsion at eating habits, see Sutherland and Locke, *Twenty Thousand Homeless Men*, 4. Both food and the way it was eaten always shocked undercover investigators, and describing the horrors of the first meal in a mission, flophouse, or shelter was a set piece in these texts. Eating not only displayed modes of public deportment and types of food that were alien to the investigators' middle-class sensibilities, but it also suggested other bodily activities such as toilet habits and sex, at which the writers usually only hinted. The movie *Sullivan's Travels* offered a cinematic version of this set-piece scene.

43. Dees, *Flophouse*, 131.

44. Praise for the book's treatment of shelterization was expressed in the following reviews: Howard Rowland, *American Journal of Sociology* 43 (November 1937): 512; Nels Anderson, *American Sociological Review* 2 (February 1937): 144; Anonymous, *Sociology and Social Research* 21 (January-February 1937): 290–291; MacEnnis Moore, "Light without Leading," *Survey* 72 (October 1936): 319. The term was said to have been coined by Chicago shelter case workers (144). Ideas about shelterization and quoted passages are from 92–93, 162, 148, 66–68, 156; the process was fully detailed in chapter 7.

45. Sutherland and Locke, *Twenty Thousand Homeless Men*, 14–15, 161; Dees, *Flophouse*, 58–59, 133–134.

46. Dees, *Flophouse*, viii, 126, 131–134, 139.

47. Ibid., 45.

48. Shelterization was used until at least the middle 1960s: see Samuel E. Wallace, *Skid Row as a Way of Life* (Totowa, NY: Bedminster Press, 1965), 168. It then apparently reemerged with the 1990s homelessness crisis: Anthony Marcus, *Where Have All the Homeless Gone? The Making and Unmaking of a Crisis* (New York: Bergahn Books, 2006), 76. The term's origins seem not to be well understood by sociologists (77–78n). Marcus criticized the concept partly in response to a controversial article by Jeffrey Grunberg and Paula F. Eagle, "Shelterization: How the Homeless Adapt to Shelter Living," *Hospital and Community Psychiatry* 41 (May 1990): 521–525. Further, Ione Y. DeOllos, in *On Becoming Homeless: The Shelterization Process for Homeless Families* (Lanham, MD: University Press of America, 1997), cited Sutherland and Locke several times and devoted a chapter to shelterization (123–141). For a later example, see Russell Schutt, "Shelterization in Theory and Practice," *Anthropology of Work Review* 24 (Spring/Summer 2003): 4–13. On the genealogy of poverty language from "dangerous class" to underclass, see Herbert Gans, *The War against the Poor* (New York: Basic Books, 1995), and Alice O'Connor, *Poverty Knowledge* (Princeton: Princeton University Press, 2001). Marcus argues that "the issue [of shelterization, including the term] reappears with each period of mass usage of emergency temporary shelter" (78).

49. Sutherland and Locke, *Twenty Thousand Homeless Men*, 52–53.

50. Dees, *Flophouse*, ix, 142–143; Sutherland and Locke, *Twenty Thousand Homeless Men*, 204.

51. Sutherland and Locke, *Twenty Thousand Homeless Men*, 5; Dees, *Flophouse*, 130.

52. John Reed club quoted in Barbara Foley, *Radical Representations: Politics and Form in U.S. Proletarian Fiction, 1929–1941* (Durham: Duke University Press, 1993), 94. Still indispensable on the interwar literary left are Daniel Aaron, *Writers on the Left* (New York: Oxford University Press, 1961), and Walter B. Rideout, *The Radical Novel in the United States 1900–1954: Some Interrelations of Literature and Society* (Cambridge, MA, 1956; reprint, New York: Hill & Wang, 1966). See also Michael Denning, *The Cultural Front: The Laboring of American Culture in the Twentieth Century* (London: Verso, 1996).

53. Jack Conroy, *The Disinherited* (New York: Covici, Friede, 1933); Robert Cantwell, *The Land of Plenty* (New York: Farrar & Rinehart, 1934); Albert Halper, *The Foundry* (New York: Viking, 1934). Nelson Algren, preface (1965) to *Somebody in Boots* (New York, 1935; reprint, New York: Thunder's Mouth Press, 1987), 6–7. On Algren in this period, see H. E. F. Donohoe, *Conversations with Nelson Algren* (New York: Hill & Wang, 1964), 21–61, and Bettina Drew, *Nelson Algren: A Life on the Wild Side* (New York: G. P. Putnam's Sons, 1989), 13–74. Tom Kromer, *Waiting for Nothing* (New York: Knopf, 1935). On Kromer, see the afterword in *Waiting for Nothing and Other Writings*, ed. Arthur D. Casciato and James L. W. West III (Athens: University of Georgia Press, 1986), 263–270.

54. John Steinbeck, *Their Blood Is Strong* (San Francisco: Simon J. Lubin Society of California, 1938); *The Grapes of Wrath* (New York: Viking Press, 1939); Jackson J. Benson, *The True Adventures of John Steinbeck, Writer* (New York: Viking, 1984), 332–346, 359–363; Edward Newhouse, *You Can't Sleep Here* (New York: Macaulay, 1934); "Autobiographical Sketch," *Wilson Library Bulletin* 11 (May 1937): 588; *This Is Your Day* (New York: L. Furman, 1937); *The Hollow of the Wave* (New York: W. Sloane, 1949); Billy Ben Smith, *The Literary Career of Proletarian Novelist and New Yorker Short Story Writer Edward Newhouse* (Lewiston, NY: Edwin Mellen Press, 2001), 15–29; Lauren Gilfillan, *I Went to Pit College* (New York: Literary Guild, 1934); Gilfillan, "Weary Feet," 201–208. On Gilfillan, see Alan M. Wald, *Trinity of Passion: The Literary Left and the Antifascist Crusade* (Chapel Hill: University of North Carolina Press, 2007), 154–166, and Paula Rabinowitz, *Labor and Desire: Women's Revolutionary Fiction in Depression America* (Chapel Hill: University of North Carolina Press, 1991), 150–157.

55. Paul Peters and George Sklar, *Stevedore: A Play in Three Acts* (New York: Covici, Friede, 1934).

56. Daniel Aaron identifies "Paul Peters" as the pseudonym of Harbor Allen in *Writers on the Left*, 166–167. Peters was identified as a University of Wisconsin graduate and *New Masses* writer in Goldstein, *Political Stage*, 60, 428n. Peters described his travels in Garlin, "Paul Peters," 5. Other left-wing cultural work by Peters included his involvement with the book *Proletarian Literature in the United States: An Anthology*, ed. Granville Hicks, Joseph North, Michael Gold, Paul Peters, Isidor Schneider, and Alan Calmer; introd. Joseph Freeman (New York: International Publishers, 1935). Peters's ill-fated attempt to translate and adapt Bertolt Brecht's *The Mother* for a Theatre Union production is discussed in Laura Bradley, *Brecht and Political Theatre: The Mother on Stage* (Oxford, UK: Clarendon Press, 2006), 142–155. For more on the Theatre Union and on Peters, see Mark Weisstuch, "The Theatre Union, 1933–1937: A History" (Ph.D. diss., City University of New York, 1982).

57. Peters, "I'm Hunting," 462, 464. On Whitman's importance to the left, see Aaron, *Writers on the Left*, 402n.

58. Peters, "I'm Hunting," 468. Featured in both the article and the play were Blacksnake Johnson, Joe Crum, Mose Venable, and Angrum. From "Dockwallopers" to *Stevedore*, Fag Williams, Tom Veal, and Yallah Celestine became Rag Williams, Jim Veal, and Bobo Valentine. In numerous cases, lines that appeared in the play were lifted verbatim or nearly so from the article. See, for example, Yallah's observation that "a good nigger is just a scared nigger": "Dockwallopers," *American Mercury* 20 (July 1930): 320, and *Stevedore*, 30–31.

59. Peters, "Dockwallopers," 320. Brooks Atkinson, "Drama of the Race Riot in 'Stevedore,' Put On by the Theatre Union," *New York Times* (April 19, 1934): 33; F. F., "Drama," *Saturday Review of Literature* 10 (July 7, 1934): 797; Anonymous, *Survey Graphic* 28 (August 1934): 396. The theater historian Malcolm Goldstein has more recently praised

the language for its realism, contrasting it with the "spuriously noble" dialogue typically produced by middle-class writers for working-class characters: *Political Stage*, 67.

60. Peters, "Dockwallopers," 320, 321.

61. Ibid., 321, 325–326.

62. John Howard Lawson, "Towards a Revolutionary Theatre: The Artist Must Take Sides," *New Theatre* 1 (June 1934): 6. On the left-wing theater scene, see Jay Williams, *Stage Left* (New York: Charles Scribner's Sons, 1974), and Goldstein, *Political Stage*. On the Communist Party and the race issue, see Mark Naison, *Communists in Harlem during the Depression* (New York: Grove Press, 1984), and Robin Kelley, *Hammer and Hoe: Alabama Communists during the Great Depression* (Chapel Hill: University of North Carolina Press, 1990). Anne Fletcher sets *Stevedore* in the context of other radical antiracist plays of the 1930s in "Fighting One 'Ism' with Another: The Communist Party Fights Racism in the South: Scottsboro Dramatizations and *Stevedore*," *Theatre Symposium* 11 (2003): 50–62.

63. Sender Garlin, "Paul Peters—Revolutionary Playwright; An Interview," part 2, *Daily Worker* (May 16, 1934): 5; Garlin, "Paul Peters," part 1:5; Paul Peters, *8 Who Lie in the Death House* (New York: National Committee for the Defense of Political Prisoners, 1933), 5.

64. Garlin, "Paul Peters," part 1:5; Williams, *Stage Left*, 109–110, 114; John Houseman, *Run-Through: A Memoir* (New York: Simon & Schuster, 1972), 257; Peters and Sklar, *Stevedore*, front matter. Charles Rumford Walker praised *Stevedore* as one of the thirties' best productions in "Theatre on the Left," *Nation* 148 (June 24, 1939): 730–731.

65. Garlin, "Paul Peters," part 2:5; Williams, *Stage Left*, 114–117; J. K. H., "'Stevedore,'" *New York Times* (October 2, 1934): 18; Joseph Wood Krutch, "Drama on the Barricades," *Nation* 138 (May 2, 1934): 515; Michael Gold, "Stevedore," *New Masses* 11 (May 1934): 28; Jim Haskins and N. R. Mitgang, *Mr. Bojangles: The Biography of Bill Robinson* (New York: William Morrow, 1988), 220–221. Malcolm Goldstein writes that, according to his interview with George Sklar, Robinson's leap was planned in advance to show Robinson's approval of the Theatre Union's antiracist practices: *Political Stage*, 66. The Seattle event is described in Nancy Wick, "Playing with History," http://www.washington.edu/alumni/columns/dec95/stevedore.html (accessed May 28, 2008). A revival of *Stevedore* was mounted by the director Valerie Curtis-Newton at the University of Washington in 1996.

66. Denning, *Cultural Front*, 366.

67. Goldstein, *Political Stage*, 69; "Paul Robeson Stirs Audience in London," *New York Times* (May 7, 1935): 26; Williams, *Stage Left*, 120, 46; Naison, *Communists in Harlem*, 151–152; Garlin, "Paul Peters," part 2:5.

68. Atkinson, "Drama of the Race Riot," 33; Anonymous, *Survey Graphic*, 396; Gold, "Stevedore," 28–29; Eugene Gordon, "From *Uncle Tom's Cabin* to *Stevedore*," *New Theatre*

2 (July 1935): 21–23; Brooks Atkinson, "Rioting on the Waterfront," *New York Times* (April 29, 1934): xi.

69. Gold, "Stevedore," 92.

70. On language and culture, see, for example, Ellwood, "Social Evolution and Cultural Evolution," 312. Rogers quoted in Naison, *Communists in Harlem*, 152.

71. Stark Young, review of *Stevedore*, by Paul Peters and George Sklar, *New Republic* 78 (May 9, 1934): 367; F. F., "Drama," 797; Atkinson, "Drama of the Race Riot," 33; Anonymous, *Survey Graphic*, 396; Atkinson, "Rioting on the Waterfront," xi.

72. Atkinson, "Rioting on the Waterfront," xi; Granville Hicks, *The Great Tradition: An Interpretation of American Literature since the Civil War*, revised edition (New York, 1935; reprint, New York: Biblo and Tannen, 1967), 322; Gordon, "From *Uncle Tom's Cabin*," 23.

73. Peters, "Dockwallopers," 320; F. F., "Drama," 797.

74. Recent works by African American authors included Nella Larsen, *Passing* (New York: Knopf, 1929), and George S. Schuyler, *Black No More* (New York: Macaulay, 1931). Thinking across the race line from the other direction, Ignatius Donnelly's *Doctor Huguet* (Chicago, 1891; reprint, New York: Arno Press, 1969) was a little-read novel about a Southern white aristocrat who unexpectedly turned black. These issues will be explored more fully in chapter 5.

75. The Coen Brothers' movie of this title does quote occasionally from *Sullivan's Travels*: *O Brother, Where Art Thou?* directed by Joel Cohen (Touchstone Pictures, 2000; DVD, Burbank, CA: Touchstone Home Video, 2001). The Sturges scholars Brian Henderson and Jay Rozgonyi have both asserted that "Sinclair" refers to Sinclair Lewis, perhaps because Lewis's satirical bent seems similar to Sturges's. But Lewis's work had far less connection than Upton Sinclair's to the social-realist tradition supposedly represented by *O Brother*. See Brian Henderson, ed. and introd., *Five Screenplays by Preston Sturges* (Berkeley: University of California Press, 1985), 533; Jay Rozgonyi, *Preston Sturges's Vision of America* (Jefferson, NC: McFarland, 1995), 91.

76. Sutherland and Locke, *Twenty Thousand Homeless Men*, 92–93; Minehan, *Boy and Girl Tramps*, 18; *I Am a Fugitive from a Chain Gang*, directed by Mervyn LeRoy (Warner Brothers, 1932; DVD, Burbank, CA: Warner Home Video, 2005); Kathleen Moran and Michael Rogin, "'What's the Matter with Capra?': *Sullivan's Travels* and the Popular Front," *Representations* 71 (Summer 2000): 121.

77. Jean-Jacques DuPuich, "*Les Voyages de Sullivan*" (1973), in *Preston Sturges: A Guide to References and Resources*, ed. Ray Cywinski (Boston: G. K. Hall, 1984), 103. Other reviews that emphasized *Sullivan's* mixture of comic with serious themes included Louise Levitas, "Veronica Lake Hides Light under Bushel of Hobo Grime in Latest Sturges Film," *PM* (January 18, 1942): 46–47, and "Sullivan's Travels," *Variety* (December 10, 1941): 8.

78. Preston Sturges, *Preston Sturges by Preston Sturges*, adapted and edited by Sandy Sturges (New York: Simon and Schuster, 1990), 295. On Sturges's commitment to authorial control, see Diane Jacobs, *Christmas in July: The Life and Art of Preston Sturges* (Berkeley: University of California Press, 1992), 243–244.

79. Contemporary reviews that advanced the face-value interpretation included Philip T. Harting, "Woe Is Me, Woe Is You, Woe Is," *Commonweal* 35 (February 13, 1942): 419; "Movie of the Week: *Sullivan's Travels*," *Life* 12 (January 26, 1942): 51–54; "Movies," *Newsweek* 19 (February 9, 1942): 64. More recent writers who respond to the movie in this vein include Christian Zimmer, "La Leçon de Sullivan" (1974), in Cywinski, *Preston Sturges*, 105, and David Thomson, "America in the Dark: Hollywood and the Gift of Unreality" (1977), in Cywinski, *Preston Sturges*, 108. Eric Schocket calls the movie "politically evasive" in his "Undercover Explorations of the 'Other Half,' or the Writer as Class Transvestite," *Representations* 64 (Fall 1998): 113.

80. Morris Dickstein, "The Dream of Mobility in 1930s Culture," in Mullen and Linkon, *Radical Revisions*, 226, 233–237, quoted 237.

81. Fannie Hurst, *Imitation of Life* (New York: P. F. Collier, 1933); *Imitation of Life*, directed by John M. Stahl (Universal Pictures, 1934; DVD, Universal City, CA: Universal Studios, 2003); James Curtis, *Between Flops: A Biography of Preston Sturges* (New York: Harcourt Brace Jovanovich, 1982), 94, 100; Donald Spoto, *Madcap: The Life of Preston Sturges* (Boston: Little, Brown, 1990), 119.

82. *The Great McGinty*, directed by Preston Sturges (Paramount, 1940; DVD, Universal City, CA: Universal Studios, 2006). A sampling of 1930s films whose themes are variously echoed in *Sullivan's Travels* would include *I Am a Fugitive from a Chain Gang* (1932), *Hallelujah I'm a Bum* (1933), *A Man's Castle* (1933), *Wild Boys of the Road* (1933), *It Happened One Night* (1933), *Modern Times* (1936), *My Man Godfrey* (1936), *The Amazing Adventure* (1936), *Holiday* (1938), *Maid's Night Out* (1938), *The Grapes of Wrath* (1940), *Meet John Doe* (1941), and *Reaching for the Sun* (1941).

83. Jacobs, *Christmas in July*, 248. Jacobs offers no documentation for this anecdote in what is otherwise a deeply researched and well-documented study, and I have been unable to substantiate it in any other source. Moran and Rogin also tell this story ("What's the Matter with Capra?" 117) but do not cite any authority for it. Sturges was friends with both men, and Wyler and Huston did work together on at least two movies of the early 1930s—*The Storm* (1930) and *A House Divided* (1931)—neither of which concerned poverty. Jacobs's statement that Huston and Wyler "planned to make a film about wild kids on the road" implies that they may have been researching *Wild Boys of the Road*, released by Warner Brothers in 1933. That picture, however, was directed not by William Wyler, but by William Wellman. I have proceeded on the assumption that although some of the details may be incorrect, the story is accurate.

84. Sturges, *Preston Sturges*, 295.

85. Minehan, *Boy and Girl Tramps*, 248, xxii, xxv, xxvii; Caplow, "Transiency," 731.

86. Although *The Lady Eve* listed Sturges as the writer and director, Monckton Hoffe was credited for the original story: Henderson, introduction to *Sullivan's Travels*, in *Five Screenplays*, 518.

87. Sturges, *Preston Sturges*, 35, 294–295.

88. See, for example, the review of *People of the Abyss*, by Jack London, *The Bookman* 18 (1903): 647–648; review of *The Saleslady*, by Frances R. Donovan, *Annals of the American Academy of Political and Social Science* 148 (March 1930): 305–306.

89. An instance of the first is Lillian Pettengill, *Toilers of the Home: The Record of a College Woman's Experience as a Domestic Servant* (New York: Doubleday, Page, 1903), vi; and of the second, Walter Wyckoff, *The Workers: An Experiment in Reality*, vol. 2: *The West* (New York: Charles Scribner's Sons, 1898), 82–84.

90. Sturges, *Sullivan's Travels*, in *Five Screenplays*, 614.

91. Ibid., 616.

92. "Movie of the Week," 54. Powell and Blondell starred in *Gold Diggers of 1933* and *Gold Diggers of 1937*. On jockers and punks, see Josiah Flynt, "Homosexuality among Tramps," appendix to Havelock Ellis, *Studies in the Psychology of Sex*, 3rd edition (Philadelphia, 1901; revised and expanded, Philadelphia: F. A. Davis, 1919), vol. 2, 359–367; Minehan, *Boy and Girl Tramps*, 141–143.

93. For critics' appreciation of this scene, see "The New Pictures," *Time* 39 (February 9, 1942): 36, and "Sullivan's Travels" (*Variety*), 8.

94. Sturges, *Sullivan's Travels*, 679.

95. Ibid., 683.

96. Although this information is spelled out in the script, it is inaudible (to this listener) amid the cacophony of the movie scene. Sturges, *Sullivan's Travels*, 680.

97. See, for example, Bosley Crowther, *New York Times* (January 29, 1942): 25, and C. M. Cluny, "*Les Voyages de Sullivan*. Un Divertissment Nonconfortable" (1973), in Cywinski, *Preston Sturges*, 102–103.

98. On perceptions that Depression-era poverty was not structural, see James T. Patterson, *America's Struggle against Poverty 1900–1985* (Cambridge: Harvard University Press, 1986), 75, and Kennedy, *Freedom from Fear*, 322. Stuart Chase, "The Twilight of Communism in the USA," *Reader's Digest* 39 (September 1941): 25–28.

99. Bakke, *Citizens without Work*, 85–86, 105, 301–306.

100. Caplow, "Transiency," 732–734, 735, 737–739.

CHAPTER 4

1. Alan McCone, "Good-bye, White Collar," *American Magazine* 134 (November 1942): 40–41, 99–100; also in *Readers Digest* 41 (December 1942): 23–26. Not an investigator, McCone initially concealed his class identity out of fear that the other workers would harass him; he was soon unmasked.

2. Lucy Greenbaum, "I Worked on the Assembly Line," *New York Times Magazine* (March 28, 1943): 18; Augusta H. Clawson, *Shipyard Diary of a Woman Welder* (New York: Penguin, 1944); Elizabeth Hawes, *Why Women Cry: or, Wenches with Wrenches* (New York: Reynall & Hitchcock, 1943), xvii–xviii, 58, 112–113. Books by female workers who did not operate undercover but whose experiences provide context included Nell Giles, *Punch In, Susie! A Woman's War Factory Diary* (New York: Harper and Brothers, 1942); Constance Bowman and Clara Marie Allen, *Slacks and Calluses: Our Summer in a Bomber Factory* (New York, 1944; Washington, DC: Smithsonian Institution Press, 1999, introd. Sandra M. Gilbert); and Josephine Miklos, *I Took a War Job* (New York: Simon & Schuster, 1943). On the "laboring" of culture, see Michael Denning, *The Cultural Front: The Laboring of American Culture in the Twentieth Century* (London: Verso, 1996). On women workers in World War II, see Susan H. Hartmann, *The Home Front and Beyond: American Women in the 1940s* (Boston: Twayne, 1982).

3. Greenbaum, "I Worked," 19.

4. Clawson, *Diary*, 3, 150–152.

5. Ibid., 149, 42; McCone, "Good-bye," 100. For similar accounts of the lure of permanent working-class life, see Miklos, *I Took a War Job*, 220, and Giles, *Punch In*, 141, 152.

6. Hawes, *Wenches*, 152, 68, 76–78, 115–123. Hawes joined and later worked for the United Auto Workers, while Clawson joined the International Brotherhood of Boilermakers, Iron Ship Builders, Welders, and Helpers of America.

7. Clawson, *Diary*, 41–52; Hawes, *Wenches*, 29–30.

8. McCone, "Good-bye," 40–41, 100.

9. Ibid., 41. For similar accounts of manly self-reconstruction through physical labor—though without McCone's temporary undercover component—see also Clair M. Cook, "Deus in Machina: Value of a Year of Industrial Work for the Minister or Prospective Minister," *Christian Century* 60 (October 13, 1943): 1164–1165, and Clifford Roberts, "Now I Work in a Factory," *Reader's Digest* 36 (June 1940): 89–91.

10. Hawes, *Wenches*, 68; Greenbaum, "I Worked," 37; Eva Lapin, *Mothers in Overalls* (New York: Workers Library, 1943), 6.

11. Clawson, *Diary*, 29, 157, 43.

12. Greenbaum, "I Worked," 37; Clawson, *Diary*, 31.

13. Hawes, *Wenches*, 55–57, 63, 150–155; Clawson, *Diary*, 180; Greenbaum, "I Worked," 38.

14. Clawson, *Diary*, 41.

15. Greenbaum, "I Worked," 18; Clawson, *Diary*, 157; McCone, "Good-bye," 100; Giles, *Punch In*, 140.

16. Miklos, *I Took a War Job*, 79. On the forging of whiteness from the waning of ethnic distinctions formerly understood as racial, see David R. Roediger, *Working toward Whiteness: How America's Immigrants Became White* (New York: Basic Books, 2005); Matthew Frye Jacobson, *Whiteness of a Different Color: European Immigrants and the Alchemy of Race* (Cambridge: Harvard University Press, 1998); Gary Gerstle,

Working-Class Americanism: The Politics of Labor in a Textile City, 1914–1960 (Princeton: Princeton University Press, 2002). Miklos's experiences may be illuminated by Gary Gerstle's argument that while Americans of European immigrant background were moving toward full inclusion in American society by the 1940s, World War II invigorated traditions of both inclusive civic nationalism and exclusionary racial nationalism. See Gerstle, *American Crucible: Race and Nation in the Twentieth Century* (Princeton: Princeton University Press, 2001), 187–237.

17. Clawson, *Diary*, 157. Portland's black population swelled from 1,931 in 1940 to 22,000 in 1945; in 1944, over 7,700 African Americans worked in the three Portland-area shipyards. Black men and women did not easily gain access to or advance within skilled jobs in the shipyards, but they were far from absent. See Quintard Taylor, *In Search of the Racial Frontier: African Americans in the American West, 1528–1990* (New York: Norton, 1998), 254–255; Amy Kesselman, *Fleeting Opportunities: Women Shipyard Workers in Portland and Vancouver during World War II and Reconversion* (Albany: SUNY Press, 1990), 41–42; Chauncey Del French with Jessie French, *Waging War on the Home Front: An Illustrated Memoir of World War II*, ed. Lois Mack and Ted Van Arsdol (Corvallis: Oregon State University Press, 2004), 11–13.

18. Giles, *Punch In*, 139–140. On the debate over capitalization, see Sterling Stuckey, *Slave Culture: Nationalist Theory and the Foundations of Black America* (New York: Oxford University Press, 1987), 240, 394n; *The Correspondence of W. E. B. Du Bois*, ed. Herbert Aptheker (Amherst: University of Massachusetts Press, 1973), 1:171–172. Nell Giles did refer positively to the presence of Chinese workers in the factory; perhaps in her view they had been granted a wartime exemption from their non-"white" status. Karen J. Leong observed that, after Pearl Harbor, Chinese Americans became part of the federal government's "Americans all" ideology, as represented by the repeal of the Chinese Exclusion Act and military support for China against Japan: see Leong, *The China Mystique: Pearl S. Buck, Anna May Wong, Mayling Soong, and the Transformation of American Orientalism* (Berkeley: University of California Press, 2005), 97.

19. Hawes, *Wenches*, 50; Miklos, *I Took a War Job*, 220–221.

20. Passages quoted from reviews of E. Wight Bakke, *The Unemployed Worker* and *Citizens without Work* (New Haven: Yale University Press, 1940), appeared in William S. Hopkins, "Labor and Labor Organizations," *American Economic Review* 31 (June 1941): 412, 413, and Martin Cohn, "Studies in Unemployment," *Canadian Forum* 21 (April 1941): 26. Other reviews that praised the undercover method included Mirra Komarovsky, *American Sociological Review* 6 (August 1941): 593–596; Burleigh B. Gardner, *American Journal of Sociology* 47 (March 1942): 777–778; Colston E. Warne, *Annals of the American Academy of Political and Social Science* 217 (September 1941): 196–197; and C. W. Guillebaud, *Economic Journal* 52 (March 1942): 104–107. On Bakke's limited influence, see Reeve Vanneman and Lynn Weber Cannon, *The American Perception of Class* (Philadelphia: Temple University Press, 1987), 284–285; the authors' concern is not

method, but subsequent social scientists' failure to heed Bakke's conclusions, and their consequent tendency to form inaccurate assumptions about the connections between class psychology and social outcomes.

21. Charles Rumford Walker, "Steel: A Retrospect," *Survey Graphic* 35 (April 1946): 126–127; *Steel: The Diary of a Furnace Worker* (Boston: Atlantic Monthly Press, 1922), 4. On Walker's post-World War II work, see "Walker, Charles Rumford," *National Cyclopedia of American Biography* (Clifton, NJ: James T. White, 1980).

22. David M. Kennedy, *Freedom from Fear: The American People in Depression and War, 1929–1945* (New York: Oxford University Press, 1999), 857. On Americans' tendency to identify themselves as "middle class," see "The People of the USA—A Self-Portrait," *Fortune* 21 (February 1940): 14, 20. The narrowness of income-based definitions of class is addressed by Michael Zweig, "Six Points on Class," in *More Unequal: Aspects of Class in the United States*, ed. Michael D. Yates (New York: Monthly Review Press, 2007), 173–182. Late 1930s downward-mobility narratives with happy endings included Norma Lee Browning, "We Live in the Slums," *Forum* 102 (August 1939): 56–60; Clifford Roberts, "Now I Work in a Factory," *Reader's Digest* 36 (June 1940): 89, 91; and Pastor Ignotus, "Experiment in Polite Poverty," *Christian Century* 55 (July 20, 1938): 893–895.

23. Charles Rumford Walker, "Snapshot of a White-Collar Worker," *Atlantic* 165 (April 8, 1940): 557; David Riesman, with Reuel Denney and Nathan Glazer, *The Lonely Crowd: A Study of the Changing American Character* (New Haven: Yale University Press, 1950); William H. Whyte, *The Organization Man* (New York: Simon and Schuster, 1956); Jack Kerouac, "The Vanishing American Hobo," *Holiday* 27 (March 1960): 60–61, 112–113; Richard Thruelsen, *Men at Work* (New York: Harper and Row, 1950), 151–166.

24. George Cotkin, *Existential America* (Baltimore: Johns Hopkins University Press, 2003), 135–136; Burleigh S. Gardner and William Whyte, "Methods for the Study of Human Relations in Industry," *American Sociological Review* 11 (August 1946): 511.

25. James T. Patterson, *America's Struggle against Poverty, 1900–1985* (Cambridge: Harvard University Press, 1986), 85; Frank Stricker, *How America Lost the War on Poverty—and How to Win It* (Chapel Hill: University of North Carolina Press, 2007), 12–13.

26. Olivier Zunz, *Why the American Century?* (Chicago: University of Chicago Press, 1998), 4, 94–111; see also John S. Gilkeson, Jr., "American Social Scientists and the Domestication of 'Class,' 1929–1955," *Journal of the History of the Behavioral Sciences* 31 (October 1995): 331–346.

27. For Walker's postwar views on labor-management cooperation, see "Produce, or Else!" *Saturday Evening Post* 219 (August 24, 1946): 51–52. For articles that reflected his Depression-era radicalism, see " 'Red' Blood in Kentucky: Why 100% Americans Turn Communist," *Forum* 87 (January 1932): 18–23, and "Relief and Revolution," *Forum* 88 (September 1932): 152–158. Walker's deradicalization is recounted in Alan M. Wald, *The New York Intellectuals: The Rise and Decline of the Anti-Stalinist Left from the 1930s to*

the 1980s (Chapel Hill: University of North Carolina Press, 1987), 151–152. On postwar personnel management and the "human relations approach," see Elizabeth Fones-Wolf, *Selling Free Enterprise: The Business Assault on Labor and Liberalism, 1945–1960* (Urbana: University of Illinois Press, 1994), 73–96.

28. Donald Francis Roy, "Hooverville: A Study of a Community of Homeless Men in Seattle" (master's thesis, University of Washington, 1935), 75–76, 95–97; "Restriction of Output by Machine Operators in a Piecework Machine Shop: A Preliminary Analysis" (Ph.D. diss., University of Chicago, 1952), 36. Roy also summed up the results of his master's research in "Hooverville—A Community of Homeless Men," *Studies in Sociology* 4, 1–2 (Winter 1939–Summer 1940): 37–45.

29. Donald Roy, review of *Manufacturing Consent* by Michael Burawoy, *Berkeley Journal of Sociology* 24–25 (1980): 329; Roy, "Restriction of Output," 36, 87. Roy (1909–1980) was in his mid-thirties when he started at Geer. On Hughes and the second Chicago school, see Joseph R. Gusfield, preface to Gary Alan Fine, ed., *A Second Chicago School? The Development of a Postwar American Sociology* (Chicago: University of Chicago Press, 1995), x–xi. For more on Roy, see Michael Burawoy, "Donald Roy: Sociologist and Working Stiff," *Contemporary Sociology* 30 (September 2001): 453–458; Howard S. Becker, "Introductory Note to Donald Roy's Article on Conflict and Cooperation in the Factory," *Qualitative Sociology* 29 (March 2006): 55–57.

30. Donald Roy, "Banana Time: Job Satisfaction and Informal Interaction," *Human Organization* 18 (Winter 1959): 167.

31. Roy was quoting the sociologist Pauline Young in this passage from "Restriction of Output," 39.

32. Ibid., 28–30, 97.

33. Ibid., 3–4, 36–49. Roy cited the following recent scholars on participant observation: Pauline Young, in 'Restriction of Output," 39; Burleigh Gardner and William F. Whyte, and also Florence Kluckhohn, in Orvis Collins, Melville Dalton, and Donald Roy, "Restriction of Output and Social Cleavage in Industry," *Applied Anthropology* 5 (Summer 1946): 14. While Roy did cite one of Charles Rumford Walker's publications from Walker's later, Yale-affiliated period (see "Banana Time," 161), he did not mention Walker's *Steel*.

34. Roy, "Restriction of Output," 2–4. Just as earlier down-and-outers had often cited William James and John Dewey, Roy showed the strong imprint of Dewey's influence, citing him frequently on the unity of experience, feeling, and knowledge: see "Restriction of Output," 3, 527–529; "Efficiency and the Fix: Informal Intergroup Relations in a Piecework Machine Shop," *American Journal of Sociology* 60 (November 1954): 266; "Banana Time," 166. Howard Becker praised Roy's "adept" use of Dewey, and he noted Dewey's impact on all Chicago sociologists in his "introductory note" to Roy's posthumously published "Cooperation and Conflict in the Factory: Some Observations and Questions Regarding Conceptualization of Intergroup

Relations within Bureaucratic Social Structures," *Qualitative Sociology* 29 (March 2006): " 57.

35. Roy, "Restriction of Output," 4, 44.

36. Ibid., 47, 49.

37. Ibid., 36.

38. Ibid., 499–518, 18, 97–98.

39. Donald Roy, "Quota Restriction and Goldbricking in a Machine Shop," *American Journal of Sociology* 57 (March 1952): 442.

40. Roy, "Restriction of Output," 196.

41. Ibid., 505, 509, 32; "Cooperation and Conflict," 63; see also "Quota Restriction" and "Banana Time."

42. Roy, "Restriction of Output," 97–98; Collins, Dalton, and Roy, "Restriction of Output," 13–14; Roy, "Efficiency and the Fix," 266.

43. Roy, "Restriction of Output," 17, 33.

44. Whiting Williams, "What Workers Worry About," *Nation's Business* 33 (August 1945): 39–40; Roy, "Efficiency and the Fix," 266; "Work Satisfaction and Social Reward in Quota Achievement," *American Sociological Review* 18 (October 1953): 514.

45. What *Fortune* magazine called the 1950 "Treaty of Detroit" between the United Auto Workers and General Motors, which has been seen as a marker for this shift in postwar labor relations, was concluded shortly before Roy defended his dissertation: see Nelson Lichtenstein, *State of the Union: A Century of American Labor* (Princeton: Princeton University Press, 2002), 122–125.

46. David Paul Haney, *The Americanization of Social Science: Intellectuals and Public Responsibility in the Postwar United States* (Philadelphia: Temple University Press, 2008); Jennifer Platt, *A History of Sociological Research Methods in America: 1920–1960* (New York: Cambridge University Press, 1996), 292.

47. Roy, "Restriction of Output," 2; "Efficiency and the Fix," 266.

48. A rare exception occurred when Roy connected the misery he saw while walking through a black neighborhood to the extreme wealth enjoyed by the executives of his company. However, he later backed off from this connection and it did not lead to any broader social critique: Roy, "Restriction of Output," 341–342. The radical sociologist Michael Burawoy, who coincidentally did his 1974–1975 field research in the same shop where Roy had once worked, would later criticize what he regarded as Roy's limited analysis in his *Manufacturing Consent: Changes in the Labor Process under Monopoly Capitalism* (Chicago: University of Chicago Press, 1979), 34–35.

49. Roy, "Restriction of Output," 490–491, 442, 438–439, 434.

50. Platt, *History of Methods*, 272. On the declining status of personal documents, see Robert Angell, "A Critical Review of the Development of the Personal Document Method in Sociology, 1920–1940," in *The Use of Personal Documents in History, Anthropology*

and Sociology, ed. Louis Gottschalk, Clyde Kluckhohn, and Robert Angell (New York: Social Sciences Research Council, 1945), especially 231.

51. Roy, "Banana Time," 166–168. For more on the second Chicago school, see the following in Fine, *Second Chicago School?*: Gary Alan Fine, introduction, 1–16, and Paul Colomy and J. David Brown, "Elaboration, Revision, Polemic, and Progress in the Second Chicago School," 17–81. In the vast 1950s literature on sociological method and participant observation, I have found no one who cited Donald Roy—although his dissertation (pp. 42–49) and his articles made a strong case for the efficacy of his concealed method.

52. Collins, Dalton, and Roy, "Restriction of Output," 1. On the Committee on Human Relations in Industry, see Jennifer Platt, "Research Methods and the Second Chicago School," in Fine, *Second Chicago School?*, 86.

53. Gardner, review of Bakke, 778; Gardner and Whyte, "Methods," 506–507.

54. Gardner and Whyte, "Methods," 506, 508. Whyte acknowledged that his approach to human relations had grown directly from Mayo's Western Electric research: Whyte, *Human Relations in the Restaurant Industry* (New York: McGraw-Hill, 1948), 373–374. The historians John S. Gilkeson, Jr., and Olivier Zunz identify Committee chair W. Lloyd Warner as a key figure in the redefining and sidelining of class (previously understood especially through work relations), and the elevation of status and consumption as postwar social-science categories; Zunz also points to Gardner as having similar significance. See Gilkeson, "Domestication," 337–342; Zunz, *Why the American Century*, 99–104.

55. Roy, "Restriction of Output," 3–4. Jennifer Platt has shown that there was a long history of ambiguity about the meaning of "participant observation": "The Development of the 'Participant Observer' Method in Sociology: Origin, Myth, and History," *Journal of the History of the Behavioral Sciences* 19 (October 1983): 379–393. Florence R. Kluckhohn, "The Participant Observer Technique in Small Communities," *American Journal of Sociology* 46 (November 1940): 336–337, 343; Collins, Dalton, and Roy, "Restriction of Output," 1. It appears from the article's text that, of the three coauthors, only Roy worked undercover.

56. William Foote Whyte, *Street Corner Society: The Social Structure of an Italian Slum* (Chicago, 1943; 4th edition, Chicago: University of Chicago Press, 1993). In addition to overseeing the project that funded Roy's dissertation research, Whyte enlisted Roy, along with other collaborators, for his book *Money and Motivation: An Analysis of Incentives in Industry* (New York: Harper & Brothers, 1955). In an introductory "Note of Appreciation," Roy and his fellow contributors praised Whyte for having pushed them to explore "the world of reality"—the down-and-outer's stock in trade (p. xii).

57. Eugene V. Schneider, "Limitations on Observation in Industrial Sociology," *Social Forces* 28 (March 1950): 282–283. The rate-cutting incident is detailed in Stanley B. Mathewson, *Restriction of Output among Unorganized Workers*, with chapters by William M. Leiserson, Henry S. Dennison, and Arthur E. Morgan (New York: Viking,

1931), 46. Mathewson's own account is ambiguous; it is impossible to know whether the investigator who spoke to a department head had obtained his information while undercover or through conventional interviewing, as both methods were used (pp. 7–8). But it does seem unlikely that the worker would have revealed such information had he known to whom he was talking.

58. Schneider, "Limitations on Observation," 183n. On Whyte's methods, see *Human Relations in the Restaurant Industry*, 359–361; *Men at Work* (Homewood, IL: Dorsey Press, 1961), 511–517; *Participant Observer: An Autobiography* (Ithaca, NY: ILR Press, 1994), 313–318. In a variant of this approach, the sociologist Ely Chinoy was known to be an investigator by union officials and by his fellow workers, but not by management, when he briefly worked in 1946 at a Lansing, Michigan, General Motors plant for his study *The Automobile Workers and the American Dream* (Garden City, NY: Doubleday, 1955). Chinoy also later interviewed company officials (see pp. 26–27).

59. Whyte, *Men at Work*, 511–513; this research was done in 1945. Whyte used a similar approach for *Human Relations in the Restaurant Industry* (1948). He called a later version of this method "participant action research": *Participant Observer*, 313–318.

60. Howard S. Becker and Blanche Geer, "Participant Observation: The Analysis of Qualitative Field Data," in *Human Organization Research: Field Relations and Techniques*, ed. Richard C. Adams and Jack J. Preiss (Homewood, IL: Dorsey Press, 1960), 268n; Raymond L. Gold, "Roles in Sociological Field Observations," *Social Forces* 36 (March 1958): 217, 219–220. Other proponents of overt participation included Morris S. Schwartz and Charlotte Green Schwartz, "Problems in Participant Observation," *American Journal of Sociology* 60 (January 1955): 344, 346, and Arthur J. Vidich and Joseph Bensman, *Small Town in Mass Society* (Princeton: Princeton University Press, 1958), 355–360. The term "complete participant" was still occasionally used later in the century: see Charles Vaught and Daniel L. Smith, "Incorporation and Mechanical Solidarity in an Underground Coal Mine" (1980), in *The Cultural Study of Work*, ed. Douglas Harper and Helene Lawson (Lanham, MD: Rowman & Littlefield, 2003), 96–115. The investigator's degree of anonymity was ambiguous in this case, as he was occasionally addressed as "professor" by his fellow miners (pp. 107, 109).

61. Gold, "Roles," 219–220; Henry W. Riecken, "The Unidentified Interviewer," *American Journal of Sociology* 62 (September 1956): 210–212; Leon Festinger, Henry W. Riecken, and Stanley Schachter, *When Prophecy Fails* (Minneapolis: University of Minnesota Press, 1956), 237–252.

62. Vidich and Bensman, *Small Town*, xiv–xv; Charlotte Allen, "Spies Like Us: When Sociologists Deceive Their Subjects," *Lingua Franca* 7 (November 1997): 34–35. Documents from the post-publication controversy were reproduced as chapter 14 of the revised edition of *Small Town in Mass Society* (Princeton University Press, 1968). Those documents show that deception was not the sole issue in this controversy, but clearly many townspeople felt that they had somehow been "taken" by Vidich, who had not

only lived but had taught Sunday school in their midst. Ironically, in light of the ensuing dispute, the real "Springdale" was the town of Candor. A novel that drew on the Festinger and Vidich studies and their aftermaths was Alison Lurie's *Imaginary Friends* (London: Heinemann, 1967): see especially 1–10. Lurie was the daughter of a sociologist, and her first husband was a Cornell faculty member beginning in 1961; she later also joined the Cornell faculty.

63. See, for example, Julius A. Roth, "Comments on 'Secret Observation,'" *Social Problems* 9 (Winter 1962): 283–284; Kai Erikson, "A Comment on Disguised Observation in Sociology," *Social Problems* 14 (Spring 1967): 366–373.

64. Buford H. Junker, *Field Work: An Introduction to the Social Sciences* (Chicago: University of Chicago Press, 1960); Colomy and Brown, "Elaboration, Revision, Polemic," 28. Other products of Chicago training included Howard S. Becker, Blanche Geer, Raymond Gold, Morris S. Schwartz, and Arthur Vidich. Thus the legitimization project discussed here had something of an intrafamilial character. Everett C. Hughes, "Introduction: The Place of Field Work in Social Science," in Junker, *Field Work*, vii.

65. Ibid., 105, 35–39.

66. Junker implied that he used pseudonyms (p. 106) but did not say so directly; ibid., 122–124.

67. Ibid., 125.

68. Ibid., 163; Erikson, "Comment," 366.

69. Although "skid row" was an older term, it took precedence in the postwar era; see, for example, Keith Arthur Lovald, "From Hobohemia to Skid Row: The Changing Community of the Homeless Man" (Ph.D. diss., University of Minnesota, 1960).

70. Vidich and Bensman, *Small Town*, 407–408. Whyte's *Street Corner Society* was eventually challenged on ethical grounds, but only in the 1990s when such ethical self-consciousness had become rife in the profession: see Whyte, xi–xiii and 357–371.

71. James F. Rooney, "Group Processes among Skid Row Winos," *Quarterly Journal of Studies on Alcohol* 22 (September 1961): 447–448; Ronald C. VanderKooi, *Skid Row and Its Men: An Exploration of Social Structure, Behaviors and Attitudes* (East Lansing: Institute for Community Development and Services, Michigan State University, 1963), 8–9; Samuel E. Wallace, *Skid Row as a Way of Life* (Totowa, NY: Bedminster Press, 1965), 158–160.

72. Theodore Caplow, Keith A. Lovald, and Samuel E. Wallace, *A General Report on the Problem of Relocating the Population of the Lower Loop Redevelopment Area* (Minneapolis: Minneapolis Housing and Redevelopment Authority, 1958).

73. Wallace, *Skid Row*, 31.

74. VanderKooi did, however, include a long and colorful footnote describing his night in a cheap hotel, during which he claimed to have outlasted Nels Anderson's best effort to get his money's worth, but which ended abruptly in a close confrontation with a cockroach: *Skid Row and Its Men*, 8–9. Lovald, "From Hobohemia to Skid Row," 473.

75. Lovald, "From Hobohemia to Skid Row," 469.

76. Theodore Caplow, "Transiency as a Cultural Pattern," *American Sociological Review* 5 (October 1940): 731–739; Wallace, *Skid Row*, 151–152, 159–160, 134, 141. On the rise to prominence of culturalist arguments, see, for example, Howard Brick, "Talcott Parsons's 'Shift Away from Economics,' 1937–1946," *Journal of American History* 87 (September 2000): 490–514.

77. Wallace, *Skid Row*, 134, 129–135, 139–144, 148–149.

78. VanderKooi, *Skid Row and Its Men*, 28; Wallace, *Skid Row*, 170–171, 202.

79. Leonard U. Blumberg, Thomas E. Shipley, Jr., and Irving W. Shandler, *Skid Row and Its Alternatives: Research and Recommendations from Philadelphia* (Philadelphia: Temple University Press, 1973), 243–245, 252.

CHAPTER 5

1. Laura Z. Hobson, *Gentleman's Agreement* (New York: Simon & Schuster, 1947); further references will appear parenthetically in the text. *Gentleman's Agreement*, directed by Elia Kazan (20th Century Fox, 1947; DVD, Beverly Hills, CA: 20th Century Fox Studio Classics, 2003). John Howard Griffin, *Black Like Me* (New York, 1961; New York: Penguin, 1996); *Black Like Me*, directed by Carl Lerner (Hilltop, 1964; DVD, United Home, 2002).

2. On the rising conviction in the 1940s that race trumped class as the key U.S. social issue, see Gunnar Myrdal, *An American Dilemma: The Negro Problem and Modern Democracy* (New York: Harper & Brothers, 1944); Walter A. Jackson, *Gunnar Myrdal and America's Conscience : Social Engineering and Racial Liberalism, 1938–1987* (Chapel Hill: University of North Carolina Press, 1990); Gary Gerstle and Steve Fraser, introduction to *The Rise and Fall of the New Deal Order, 1930–1980* (Princeton: Princeton University Press, 1989), xv–xvi, xix; Alan Brinkley, *The End of Reform: New Deal Liberalism in Recession and War* (New York: Knopf, 1995), 164–170; Ira Katznelson, *When Affirmative Action Was White* (New York: Norton, 2005). On the idea of a "culture of the whole" and its assimilationist ambitions, see William S. Graebner, *The Age of Doubt: American Thought and Culture in the 1940s* (Boston: Twayne, 1991), 69–100. And on postwar liberal universalism generally, see Richard King, *Race, Culture, and the Intellectuals, 1940–1960* (Baltimore: Johns Hopkins University Press, 2004), 2–12; David A. Hollinger, *Postethnic America: Beyond Multiculturalism* (New York: Basic Books, 1995), 51–56.

3. *Crossfire*, directed by Edward Dmytryk (RKO, 1947; DVD, Atlanta, GA: Turner Home Entertainment, 2005); Richard Brooks, *The Brick Foxhole* (New York: Harper & Brothers, 1945). Yet another layer of identity confusion would have been added had the production head, Dore Schary, succumbed to the American Jewish Committee's bizarre suggestion that he change the first-gay-then-Jewish victim to an African

American, supposedly to avoid inflaming anti-Semitic viewers: see Neal Gabler, *An Empire of Their Own: How the Jews Invented Hollywood* (New York: Crown, 1988), 299; for the full story of the book-to-movie adaptation, see Jennifer Langdon, *Caught in the Crossfire: Adrian Scott and the Politics of Americanism in 1940s Hollywood* (New York: Columbia University Press, 2008), chapter 5.

4. William Lindsay White, "Lost Boundaries," *Reader's Digest* 51 (December 1947): 135–154; White, *Lost Boundaries* (New York: Harcourt, Brace & World, 1948); *Lost Boundaries*, directed by Alfred L. Werker (Louis de Rochemont Associates, 1949; DVD, Burbank, CA: Warner Home Video, 2009); Sinclair Lewis, *Kingsblood Royal* (New York: Grosset & Dunlap, 1947). *Finian's Rainbow*, with lyrics by the left-liberal songwriter E. Y. "Yip" Harburg, opened on Broadway in January 1947 and ran for 725 performances: Internet Broadway Database, http://www.ibdb.com/production.php?id=1507 (accessed January 11, 2010). A film version, directed by Francis Ford Coppola, was released by Warner Bros.-Seven Arts in 1968 (DVD, Burbank, CA: Warner Home Video, 2005). Ray Sprigle's series "I Was a Negro in the South for 30 Days" began on August 9, 1948, and ran in the *Pittsburgh Post-Gazette* for twenty-one days; it is available at http://www.post-gazette.com/sprigle/default.asp (accessed June 23, 2011); Sprigle, *In the Land of Jim Crow* (New York: Simon & Schuster, 1949). "Sprigle" is pronounced like "wiggle," according to "Meat Makes News," *Time* 45 (April 30, 1945): 61. *Pinky*, directed by Elia Kazan (20th Century Fox, 1949; DVD, Beverly Hills, CA: 20th Century Fox Home Entertainment, 2005).

5. Katznelson, *When Affirmative Action Was White*, 103; see also Karen Brodkin, *How Jews Became White Folks and What That Says about Race in America* (New Brunswick: Rutgers University Press, 1998). White, "Lost Boundaries," 139, 141.

6. Graebner, *Age of Doubt*, 105–106. For a history of the concept of "identity," see Philip Gleason, "Identifying Identity: A Semantic History," *Journal of American History* 69 (March 1983): 910–931. On *Gentleman's Agreement*, *Pinky*, and *Lost Boundaries* as passing films, see Michael Rogin, *Blackface, White Noise: Jewish Immigrants in the Hollywood Melting Pot* (Berkeley: University of California Press, 1996), 220–228.

7. Budd Schulberg, "Kid-Glove Cruelty," *New Republic* 116 (March 17, 1947): 36; Laura Z. Hobson, *Laura Z.: A Life* (New York: Arbor House, 1983), 7–10. Hobson wrote a two-volume autobiography: both volumes were entitled *Laura Z.*, but they were not numbered and the second volume added a subtitle: *Years of Fulfillment* (New York: D. I. Fine, 1986). For convenience, I will refer to them as *Laura Z.* 1 and 2. In *Gentleman's Agreement*, the protagonist refers angrily to a true incident in which the notoriously racist and anti-Semitic Mississippi Congressman John Rankin referred to the journalist Walter Winchell as a "little Kike" (52–53).

8. Hobson, *Laura Z.* 1, 379, 393, 399–400. Charles Poore, in a *New York Times* review, confirmed *Cosmopolitan's* prediction, writing that *Gentleman's Agreement* was indeed "one of the most-discussed novels of the year." Rex Stout of the *New York Herald*

Tribune judged it both a first-rate story and an "overwhelming" work of propaganda. Few reviewers took the book seriously as literature, but most found that it read reasonably well and made an important point. Typical in its condescending praise was the *Survey Graphic*'s assessment that thanks to the novel's ladies-magazine prose and plot, multitudes of readers who would never open the *Nation* or *New Republic* would eagerly devour Hobson's book "as they sit under the dryer." See Charles Poore, "Books of the Times," *New York Times* (February 27, 1947): 19; Rex Stout, "A Jew for Two Months—What He Learned," *New York Herald Tribune*, (March 9, 1947): 5; James Reid Parker, *Survey Graphic* 36 (May 1947): 312–313. Similar in tone and substance were the following reviews: *Catholic World* 165 (June 1947): 285–286; Anne Whitmore, *Library Journal* 72 (February 15, 1947): 320; Joan Griffiths, "A Limited Device," *Nation* 164 (May 3, 1947): 521; Schulberg, "Kid-Glove Cruelty," 36; W. E. B. Du Bois, "Schuyler Green's Metamorphosis," *New York Times* (March 2, 1947): 5, 36; Struthers Burt, *Saturday Review of Literature* 30 (March 12, 1947): 14. Unambiguously negative were an anonymous review in the *New Yorker* 23 (March 1, 1947): 94, 97, which pronounced the book "glib" and "slick," and Diana Trilling, "Americans without Distinction," *Commentary* 3 (March 1947): 290–292, in which Trilling found Hobson's book—its worthy goals notwithstanding—a predictably dull "thesis novel" that unfortunately exemplified most contemporary liberal thought and culture. Trilling then denounced the latter—in a grand rhetorical flight that landed rather distant from its point of origin—as "totalitarian" for their policing of the national mind.

9. Hobson, *Laura Z.* 1, 396; *Laura Z.* 2, 43. Zanuck's Oscar ambitions were noted in "New Picture: Gentleman's Agreement," *Time* 50 (November 17, 1947): 105, and "Movie of the Week: *Gentleman's Agreement*," *Life* 23 (December 1, 1947): 95. Generally positive reviews included Elliot E. Cohen, "Mr. Zanuck's 'Gentleman's Agreement': Reflections on Hollywood's Second Film about Anti-Semitism," *Commentary* 5 (January 1948): 51–56; Philip Hartung, "Not for Escapists," *Commonweal* 47 (November 21, 1947): 144–145; R. L. H, "Movies: Gentleman's Agreement," *New Republic* 117 (November 17, 1947): 38; "Experiment in Prejudice," *Newsweek* 30 (November 17, 1947): 97–98; Hermione Rich Isaacs, "The Films in Review," *Theatre Arts* 32 (January 1948): 32–33. The reviews in *Newsweek*, *Theatre Arts*, and *Time* all pronounced the film a better, more economical vehicle for its message than the book had been. Predictably acerbic in its dismissal of the picture was the *New Yorker* 23 (November 15, 1947): 117–118, by John McCarten; equally unimpressed was D. Mosdell of the *Canadian Forum* 28 (May 1948): 39–40, who judged the movie a "preposterous fable" that undermined its own message. Gabler, *An Empire of Their Own*, 349–350.

10. Hobson, *Laura Z.* 1, 332–333; Du Bois, "Schuyler Green's Metamorphosis," 5.

11. Hobson, *Laura Z.* 1, 233; *Laura Z.* 2, 21.

12. Hobson worked as a promotional writer at *Time* for five years. See *Laura Z.* 1, 366; *Laura Z.* 2, 16–17.

13. See the book reviews cited above from the *New Yorker* (94, 97), *Nation, New Republic, New York Times,* and *Survey Graphic* (312). For film reviews, see J. M. Brown, "If You Prick Us," *Saturday Review of Literature* 30 (December 6, 1947): 70–71; Cohen, "Mr. Zanuck's," 51–52; the *Commonweal, Life,* and *New Republic* reviews cited above. Arthur Katona, "Social Drama in Education," *Educational Forum* 13 (May 1949): 464–466.

14. On Freud's concept of "identification" and the emergence of "identity" in 1930s and 1940s psychology and sociology, see Gleason, "Identity," 915–918. Hobson refers in her memoirs to Freud and to the analyst she was seeing at the time of the book's publication: *Laura Z.* 2, 26–27.

15. Hollinger, *Postethnic America,* 52–55; King, *Race, Culture, and the Intellectuals,* 2–3; Philip Gleason, "Minorities (Almost) All: The Minority Concept in American Social Thought," *American Quarterly* 43 (September 1991): 400.

16. King, *Race, Culture and the Intellectuals,* 6; Trilling, "Americans without Distinction," 290–292. Similar reservations about the filmed version were expressed by Elliot Cohen, "Mr. Zanuck's," 56, and by Hermione Rich Isaacs, "Films in Review," 33.

17. Cohen, "Mr. Zanuck's," 54.

18. On the entanglement of civil rights issues with Cold War imperatives, see Mary L. Dudziak, *Cold War Civil Rights: Race and the Image of American Democracy* (Princeton: Princeton University Press, 2000).

19. Hobson, *Laura Z.* 1, 393; *Laura Z.* 2, 313. The film, probably in deference to white Southern sensibilities that might limit ticket sales, does not draw these connections except in the "kikey ones" scene, when Phil tells Miss Wales that he finds terms such as "kike" and "nigger" equally reprehensible. For fuller readings of the book's connections to questions of Jewish racialization and whiteness, see Matthew Frye Jacobson, *Whiteness of a Different Color: European Immigrants and the Alchemy of Race* (Cambridge: Harvard University Press, 1998), 125–131, and Judith E. Smith, *Visions of Belonging: Family Stories, Popular Culture, and Postwar Democracy, 1940–1960* (New York: Columbia University Press, 2004), 156–165.

20. Griffin, *Black Like Me,* 35–36.

21. Review of *Black Like Me,* by John Howard Griffin, *Library Journal* 87 (May 1962): 2038. On the emergence of the black/white binary, see King, *Race, Culture, and the Intellectuals,* 7, and Hollinger, *Postethnic America,* 97–98. The broader shift in social thought away from class and toward race and other social and cultural issues is addressed in Howard Brick, "Talcott Parsons's 'Shift Away from Economics,' 1937–1946," *Journal of American History* 87 (September 2000): 490–514. Daryl Michael Scott discusses the tension between pathologists and structuralists and the racialization of class among social scientists in *Contempt and Pity: Social Policy and the Image of the Damaged Black Psyche* (Chapel Hill: University of North Carolina Press, 1997), 141–144. Jacqueline Jones argues that class remained the greatest divide in the United States in *The Dispossessed: America's Underclasses from the Civil War to the Present* (New York: Basic

Books, 1992). Michael Harrington would soon present a less-racialized portrait of the postwar poor in *The Other America* (New York: Macmillan, 1962).

22. Beyond the original book and film, Griffin revisited his experiences in published works including "Epilogue: What's Happened Since *Black Like Me*" (1976), in *Black Like Me* (1961; New York: Penguin, 1996), 161–188; "The Intrinsic Other" (1966), in *The John Howard Griffin Reader*, ed. Bradford Daniel (Boston: Houghton Mifflin, 1968), 464–467; *A Time to Be Human* (New York: Macmillan, 1977); and "Beyond Otherness" (1979), in *Black Like Me*, Definitive Griffin Estate Edition (San Antonio, TX: Wings Press, 2006), 211–212.

23. The history of racial passing is summed up in Werner Sollors, *Neither Black nor White Yet Both: Thematic Explorations of Interracial Literature* (New York: Oxford University Press, 1997), 247–284. For perspectives on the politics of passing, see Elaine K. Ginsberg, "Introduction: The Politics of Passing," in Ginsberg, ed., *Passing and the Fictions of Identity* (Durham: Duke University Press, 1996), 1–18, and Gayle Wald, *Crossing the Line: Racial Passing in Twentieth-Century U.S. Literature and Culture* (Durham: Duke University Press, 2000), viii–ix. Several examples of white-to-black passing are noted by Sollors, *Neither Black*, 493–495n, and Baz Dreisinger, *Near Black: White-to-Black Passing in American Culture* (Amherst: University of Massachusetts Press, 2008). The Gilded Age geologist Clarence King's secret life as a black Pullman porter and husband to a black woman is detailed in Martha A. Sandweiss, *Passing Strange: A Gilded Age Tale of Love and Deception across the Color Line* (New York: Penguin, 2009).

24. Alexander Irvine, "My Life in Peonage," Part I: "The Situation as I Found It," *Appleton's Magazine* 9 (June 1907): 643; Mary Barnett Gilson, *What's Past Is Prologue* (New York: Harper and Brothers, 1940), 24–25. The triumph of the Boasian culture concept over earlier racialist social thought is summed up in John S. Gilkeson, "Culture and the Americans: The Diffusion of the Anthropological Concept of Culture in the United States, 1887–1939," *Canon* 2 (Spring 1995): 9–23.

25. Review of *Black Like Me*, by John Howard Griffin, *Bulletin from Virginia Kirkus Service* 29 (August 1961): 718.

26. Leslie Singer Lomas, "The Fool's Paradox: Race, Religion, and Radicalism in the Writings of Albion Winegar Tourgée" (Ph.D. diss., University of Colorado, 2010), 231–232, 456–458; on *Plessy*, 374. Ignatius Donnelly, *Dr. Huguet* (Chicago, 1891; reprint New York: Arno Press, 1969); further references will appear parenthetically in the text. Donnelly's apocalyptic writings most famously included *Caesar's Column* (Chicago: F. J. Schulte, 1890). Harry Roskolenko, *Black Is a Man* (New York: Padell, 1954); on Roskolenko, see Alan M. Wald, *The New York Intellectuals: The Rise and Decline of the Anti-Stalinist Left from the 1930s to the 1980s* (Chapel Hill: University of North Carolina Press, 1987), 180–181. Related themes were explored, if superficially, in the later films *Soul Man*, directed by Steve Miner (Balcor Film Investors, 1986; DVD, Beverly Hills,

CA: Anchor Bay Entertainment, 2002), and *Identity Crisis*, directed by Melvin Van Peebles (Block & Chip Productions, 1989; DVD, Santa Monica, CA: Xenon, 2006).

27. Ray Stannard Baker, *Following the Color Line: An Account of Negro Citizenship in the American Democracy* (New York: Doubleday, Page, 1908); John L. Spivak, *Georgia Nigger* (New York: Brewer, Warren, and Putnam, 1932). Robert Bonazzi, afterword (1996) to John Howard Griffin, *Black Like Me* (1961; New York: Penguin, 1996), 189; Robert E. Park, "Life History," in Fred J. Baker, "The Life Histories of W. I. Thomas and Robert E. Park," *American Journal of Sociology* 79 (September 1973): 258. Bonazzi states that Griffin was unaware of Sprigle in Bonazzi's afterword (2006) to John Howard Griffin, *Black Like Me*, Definitive Griffin Estate Edition (San Antonio, TX: Wings Press, 2006), 235–236. This seems likely, because Griffin was blind from 1947 to 1957, and Sprigle died in 1957, three years before Griffin's *Sepia* articles gave him national notoriety. Sprigle makes clear in his book (5) that his main connection to the civil rights movement was Walter White, Executive Secretary of the NAACP, who died in 1955.

28. "Meat Makes News," 61; Sprigle, *Jim Crow*, back matter.

29. On former class passers' turn toward race, see Gilson, *What's Past Is Prologue*, xi; Lucille Milner, "Jim Crow in the Army," *New Republic* 110 (March 13, 1944): 339–342; Jesse Walter Dees, Jr., and James S. Hadley, *Jim Crow* (Ann Arbor, MI, 1951; reprint Westport, CT: Negro University Press, 1970). Called only "my companion" to protect him, Sprigle's guide has been identified as John Wesley Dobbs, a black Masonic official, civil rights activist, and Atlanta political figure: on Dobbs, and on Sprigle generally, see Bill Steigerwald, "Sprigle's Secret Journey," http://www.post-gazette.com/sprigle/Sprigleintroduction.asp (accessed August 12, 2009). Sprigle, *Jim Crow*, 1, 5, 7–9, 18.

30. "The Press: Brother Crawford," *Time* 52 (August 16, 1948): 49; "Jim Crow's 'Other Side,'" *Time* 52 (September 6, 1948): 49; Steigerwald, "Sprigle's Secret Journey"; Edwin F. Brennan, "Sprigle Series Stirs Letters, Lectures, Book," *Editor and Publisher* 81 (October 2, 1948): 26.

31. Dinitia Smith, "Margaret Halsey, 86, a Writer Who Lampooned the English," *New York Times* (February 7, 1997): D18; Margaret Halsey, foreword to Ray Sprigle, *In the Land of Jim Crow* (New York: Simon and Schuster, 1949), vii.

32. Halsey, foreword, vii–viii. Many reviews of Sprigle's book praised it on this ground: see reviews by Walter R. Harrison, *Rural Sociology* 15 (March 1, 1950): 97–98; Margaret E. Monroe, *Library Journal* 74 (March 1949): 818–819; and "Books Briefly Noted," *New Yorker* 25 (May 28, 1949): 101. Strangely, the sharpest condemnation for lack of objectivity and unfairness to the South, complete with a citation to a social-scientific critique of "personal documents," came from Anatole Broyard in *Commentary* 8 (July 1949): 102. Broyard has since been revealed as having been a black man passing for white. Broyard's long-hidden racial identity is discussed in Henry Louis Gates, Jr., "White Like Me," *New Yorker* 72 (June 17, 1996): 66–81.

33. "Brother Crawford," 49; W. E. G. [Winfred Ernest Garrison], review of *In the Land of Jim Crow*, by Ray Sprigle, *Christian Century* 66 (June 1, 1949): 686.

34. Sprigle, *Jim Crow*, 10.

35. Ibid., 1, 15, 215.

36. Ibid., 36.

37. Ibid., 111.

38. Ibid., 102.

39. See reviews cited above from *Christian Century* (686), *Commentary* (103), *Nation* 169 (July 2, 1949): 19, *New Yorker* (101), *Library Journal* (819). Walter White, "Maggots of Democracy," *Saturday Review of Literature* 32 (June 11, 1949): 16.

40. Alain Locke, "Wisdom de Produndis: Review of the Literature of the Negro, 1949," Part II, "The Social Literature," *Phylon* 11 (1st Quarter 1950): 173; Joseph S. Roucek, "Jim Crow," *Journal of Negro Education* 19 (Winter 1950): 63–64. In the only other scholarly review I found, Walter R. Harrison—like Roucek—noted that Sprigle had uncovered no new empirical data but had offered an account of what it felt like to be black: *Rural Sociology*, 97–98.

41. Steigerwald, "Sprigle's Secret Journey"; Bonazzi, afterword (2006), 235.

42. Sprigle, *Jim Crow*, 11.

43. Ibid., 42.

44. Hobson, *Gentleman's Agreement*, 195; Sprigle, *Jim Crow*, 197. Census records show that "Tom" was an extraordinarily popular name for boys born between 1880 and 1960 in the United States: see "Think Baby Names," http://www.thinkbabynames.com/meaning/1/Tom (accessed April 2, 2010).

45. Griffin, *Black Like Me*, 5.

46. Raleigh Trevelyan, "Tourist Class," *Spectator* 209 (August 31, 1962): 310; Louis E. Lomax, "It's Like This," *Saturday Review of Literature* 44 (December 9, 1961): 54; W. Haywood Burns, review of *Black Like Me*, by John Howard Griffin, *Race & Class* 4, No. 2 (1963): 75. Other positive reviews included *Booklist* 58 (October 1961): 116; *Bulletin from Virginia Kirkus Service* 29 (August 1961): 718; Joseph Duffey, "Masking as Black," *Christian Century* 79 (January 1962): 16; Bruce A. Cook, "What Is It Like to Be a Negro," *Commonweal* 27 (October 1961): 128–129; Milton S. Byam, *Library Journal* 86 (October 1961): 3295; *Library Journal* 87 (May 1962): 2038; *New Yorker* 37 (October 7, 1961): 209; Dan Wakefield, "Traveling Second Class," *New York Times Book Review* (October 22, 1961): 45. Griffin recounted his experiences with blindness in the posthumously published *Scattered Shadows: A Memoir of Blindness and Vision* (New York: Orbis Books, 2004): see especially 113–121.

47. The *Chronicle* quote, long used to promote the book, appears most recently on the back of the 2003 Penguin paperback edition of *Black Like Me*; Archibald MacLeish, "Jane Addams and the Future," *Social Service Review* 35 (March 1961): 5. On the importance of the search for "authenticity" among postwar youth, see Doug Rossinow, *The*

Politics of Authenticity: Liberalism, Christianity, and the New Left in America (1998), 2–8, 18–20. One who obtained Griffin's blessing to follow his example was the journalist Grace Halsell, who blackened her skin to investigate black female identity for her book *Soul Sister* (New York: World Publishing, 1969).

48. Griffin, *Black Like Me*, 7; Griffin, "Epilogue" (1976), 161; Griffin, *Time to Be Human*, 19–22. On speaking for blacks, see *Time to Be Human*, 3, and Bonazzi, afterword (2006), 228–230. Griffin mentions a report on the "suicide tendency among Southern Negroes" on the book's first page (7), but he does not identify himself as its author and presents it as the final factor that provoked him to act on the idea that had so long haunted him.

49. Lomax, "It's Like This," 53–54; Burns review, 75. An anonymous reviewer for the *Negro Digest* expressed doubts that Griffin could really have understood black experiences but still endorsed the book as valuable for white readers, and also for complacent blacks: see Robert Bonazzi, *Man in the Mirror: John Howard Griffin and the Story of "Black Like Me"* (Maryknoll, NY: Orbis Books, 1997), 177. Recent scholars who have taken Griffin to task for speaking for the other include Eric Lott, "White Like Me: Racial Cross-Dressing and the Construction of American Whiteness," in *Cultures of United States Imperialism*, ed. Amy Kaplan and Donald Pease (Durham: Duke University Press, 1993), 474–495, and Gayle Wald, "'A Most Disagreeable Mirror': Reflections on White Identity in *Black Like Me*," in *Passing and the Fictions of Identity*, ed. Elaine K. Ginsberg (Durham: Duke University Press, 1996), 151–177. I believe that we must take seriously these contemporary African American responses if we are to assess the historical significance of Griffin's enterprise.

50. Griffin, *Time to Be Human*, 21.

51. The story was reframed yet again in 1989 by the journalist Ernest Sharpe, who claimed that it was Adelle Martin, a black *Sepia* editor, who suggested the passing idea. The article lacks citations, but Sharpe apparently relied on an unpublished Griffin autobiography. In *Black Like Me* Griffin mentioned discussing the project with Martin, but he presented her as initially skeptical. See Ernest Sharpe, Jr., "The Man Who Changed His Skin," *American Heritage* 40 (February 1989): 51; Griffin, *Black Like Me*, 9.

52. Griffin, *Time to Be Human*, 24–25; *Black Like Me*, 161.

53. Griffin, *Time to Be Human*, 53–55; *Black Like Me*, 99.

54. Griffin, *Black Like Me*, 42, 46, 100; *Time to Be Human*, 36–39.

55. Griffin, *Black Like Me*, 101.

56. Ibid., 184–188; Bonazzi, afterword (2006), 228; Griffin, "Intrinsic Other," 464.

57. Griffin, *Black Like Me*, 10; *Time to Be Human*, 26–27.

58. Griffin, *Time to Be Human*, 30, 54–55; Sprigle, *Jim Crow*, 22.

59. Griffin, *Time to Be Human*, 29.

60. For an analysis of Griffin's story that also links it to postwar universalism, while emphasizing its moral dimensions and especially the concept of empathy, see George

Cotkin, *Morality's Muddy Waters: Ethical Quandaries in Modern America* (Philadelphia: University of Pennsylvania Press, 2010), 113–134. For a different reading of the book that emphasizes the construction of white masculinity through racial "cross-dressing," see Lott, "White Like Me." In a related vein, Gayle Wald argues that Griffin relied unwittingly on "an essentialist construction of 'whiteness'" while passing as "a universal, neutral subject, the masterful interpreter" of black experience ("Disagreeable Mirror," 156, 161). As argued above, I do not believe that Griffin sought to be such a "masterful interpreter." I also find that Lott and Wald, like some writers on earlier down-and-outers, see little in the method but the reinscription of whatever line was being crossed. Throughout this book, my perspective has been a somewhat different one.

61. Griffin, *Black Like Me*, 5.

62. Ibid., 115.

63. Ibid., 113–114; John H. Rohrer and Munro S. Edmonson, eds., *The Eighth Generation: Cultures and Personalities of New Orleans Negroes* (New York: Harper & Brothers, 1960). Such reviews included Wakefield, "Traveling Second Class," 45; *Booklist* (116); Duffey, "Masking as Black," 16.

64. Wakefield, "Traveling Second Class," 45; Duffey, "Masking as Black," 16.

65. Griffin, *Black Like Me*, 70; "Intrinsic Other," 464.

66. Griffin, *Black Like Me*, 9. He wrote in "Intrinsic Other," 466, that he reached this conclusion "within five days" of beginning his experiment, which does not jibe with the text of *Black Like Me*. In *Time to Be Human*, 32, he said four to five days but did not specify when they occurred.

67. Griffin, "Intrinsic Other," 466; *Time to Be Human*, 1–25; Bonazzi, afterword (2006), 218–222.

68. Griffin, *Time to Be Human*, 7, 10, 22.

69. Griffin, *Black Like Me*, 37, 68–69. The mirror scene figures in virtually any analysis of Griffin's book, in addition to providing the title for Bonazzi's biography, *Man in the Mirror*.

70. Griffin, *Black Like Me*, 67, 68; Griffin, "Preface to Gabriel Cousin's *L'Opéra Noir*" (1963), in Daniel, *Griffin Reader*, 454.

71. Griffin, *Black Like Me*, 35–37.

72. Ibid., 91–93, 94–95, 101–105 (emphasis in original).

73. Harriet Beecher Stowe, *Uncle Tom's Cabin* (Boston: John P. Jewett, 1852); Griffin, *Time to Be Human*, 32.

74. Griffin, *Black Like Me*, 111, 113.

75. See reviews by Duffey, "Masking as Black," 16, and Leon W. Lindsay, "Individuals and Segregation," *Christian Science Monitor* (October 20, 1961): 12. Griffin, "Intrinsic Other," 466; *Time to Be Human*, 32; "Beyond Otherness," 211.

76. Griffin, *Time to Be Human*, 24; Edward Steichen, *The Family of Man* (New York: Simon and Schuster, 1955).

77. Griffin, *Black Like Me*, 113–114.

78. Griffin, *Time to Be Human*, 32.

79. Griffin, *Black Like Me*, 115–116.

80. Ibid., 116, 118–119.

81. The Lerners were Old Leftists whose strongly pro-civil rights views had been shaped by 1940s Popular Front and Communist Party activism. This background is detailed in Gerda Lerner's memoir *Fireweed: A Political Autobiography* (Philadelphia: Temple University Press, 2002), but that story concludes in the late 1950s, before *Black Like Me* and as Lerner was about to enter academia, where she would forge a career as a path-breaking historian of women. The screenplay, Carl Lerner's direction, and the actor James Whitmore's performance combined to construct an angry, hard-drinking, rock-throwing protagonist who only occasionally recalled the gentle Christian demeanor projected by Griffin in the book. Griffin commented that such behavior would surely have gotten him killed: see Bonazzi, *Man in the Mirror*, 148.

82. In addition to Grace Halsell's undercover sojourn, a later attempt to follow Griffin's example—in which the author lasted only two days—was Joshua Solomon's "Skin Deep: My Own Journey into the Heart of Race-Conscious America," *Washington Post* (October 30, 1994): C-1.

83. *Booklist* review, 116; Lindsay, "Individuals and Segregation," 12.

84. Lindsay, "Individuals and Segregation," 12; Stuart H. Loory, "He Crossed the South's Racial Boundary," *New York Herald Tribune* (October 15, 1961): 13.

85. Duffey, "Masking as Black," 16; Lomax, "It's Like This," 53–54; Burns review, 75; "Books in Brief," *Crisis* 69 (January 1962): 57.

86. Loory, "He Crossed," 13; Burns review, 75; Cook, "What Is It Like," 128–129.

87. Burns review, 75; Robert P. Stuckert and Irwin D. Rinder, "The Negro in the Social Science Literature: 1961," *Phylon* 23 (Summer 1962): 125; Peter I. Rose, "Race Relations in the U.S.A.," *British Journal of Sociology* 16 (June 1965): 161. The book was cited, for example, in Thomas F. Pettigrew, "Continuing Barriers to Desegregated Education in the South," *Sociology of Education* 38 (Winter 1965): 107. Bonazzi, afterword (1996), 189.

88. See Kenneth L. Donelson, "Using Paperbacks: Some Why's and How's," *The English Journal* 53 (March 1964): 191–195; Marjorie R. Empacher and Katherine W. Trickey, "Easy-to-Read Adult Books for Senior High School Students," *The English Journal* 57 (February 1968): 193–195; Richard P. Fulkerson, "Using Full-Length Books in Freshman English," *College Composition and Communication* 24 (May 1973): 218–220.

89. Bonazzi, afterword (2006), 216.

90. After *Soul Sister*, Halsell passed as a Native American for *Bessie Yellowhair* (New York: Morrow, 1973) and as a Mexican immigrant for *The Illegals* (New York: Stein and Day, 1978); she reflected on these experiences in her memoir *In Their Shoes* (Fort Worth: Texas Christian University Press, 1996). Robert Kanigher, Werner Roth, and Vince Colletta, "I Am Curious (Black)!" *Superman's Girlfriend Lois Lane* 106 (November

1970); for more on Solomon, see Kristi Tousignant, "Alumnus Finds Screenwriting Niche," *Diamondback Online* (September 13, 2007), http://www.diamondbackonline.com/2.2795/alumnus-finds-screenwriting-niche-1.284713 (accessed March 22, 2010), and Lawrence Otis Graham, *Member of the Club: Reflections on Life in a Racially Polarized World* (New York: HarperCollins, 1995).

91. Griffin, "Intrinsic Other," 464; "Beyond Otherness," 212.

92. William L. Van Deburg, *New Day in Babylon: The Black Power Movement and American Culture, 1965–1975* (Chicago: University of Chicago Press, 1992).

93. Nell Irvin Painter, "Reparations: Be Black Like Me," letter to the editor, *Nation* 270 (May 22, 2000): 2.

94. David Kamp, "Male Like Me," *New York Times Book Review* (January 22, 2006): 1, 8; Norah Vincent, *Self-Made Man: One Woman's Journey into Manhood and Back Again* (New York: Viking, 2006), 281–282. Griffin took the phrase "black like me" from a Langston Hughes poem, part of which served as the book's epigraph. Vincent's experiences had their harrowing aspects—as evidenced by her next book, an account of time spent in mental institutions that she attributed at least partly to the psychic aftershocks induced by researching *Self-Made Man*. See Vincent, *Voluntary Madness: My Year Lost and Found in the Loony Bin* (New York: Viking, 2008).

95. Griffin, "Beyond Otherness," 211–212.

96. Sollors, *Neither Black*, 283–284.

CHAPTER 6

1. Whiting Williams, *America's Mainspring and the Great Society: A Pick-and-Shovel Outlook* (New York: Frederick Fell, 1967); reviewed in *Choice* 4 (Fall 1968): 1417. I have located only one scholarly review—a one-sentence summary—in *Personnel Journal* 46 (June 1967): 385.

2. Laura Z. Hobson, *Gentleman's Agreement* (New York: Simon & Schuster, 1947), 268; Norah Vincent, *Self-Made Man: One Woman's Journey into Manhood and Back Again* (New York: Viking, 2006). The term "identity" in its contemporary sense only came into general usage in the 1950s and 1960s, and it owed much to the influence of the psychologist Erik Erikson: see Philip Gleason, "Identifying Identity: A Semantic History," *Journal of American History* 69 (March 1983): 910–931. On American identities in the 1970s and after, see David A. Hollinger, *Postethnic America: Beyond Multiculturalism* (New York: Basic Books, 1995), 98–104.

3. Erving Goffman, *The Presentation of Self in Everyday Life* (Garden City, NY: Doubleday, 1959), especially 17–76. Remarkably, Goffman found that impersonating "a hobo or unskilled worker" would not constitute a breach of faith with one's audience, in contrast with passing as someone of more exalted status, such as a priest or physician (59–60). Judith Butler rejected Goffman's view of the self in "Performative Acts and

Gender Constitution: An Essay in Phenomenology and Feminist Theory," *Theatre Journal* 40 (December 1988): 528. For recent stories of passing across various social boundaries, see Brooke Kroeger, *Passing: When People Can't Be Who They Are* (New York: Public Affairs, 2003); Vincent, *Self-Made Man*; Joshua Solomon, "Skin Deep: My Own Journey into the Heart of Race-Conscious America," *Washington Post* (October 30, 1994): C-1; Lawrence Otis Graham, *Member of the Club: Reflections on Life in a Racially Polarized World* (New York: HarperCollins, 1995); "Tyra Banks Experiences Obesity through Fat Suit," http://abcnews.go.com/GMA/BeautySecrets/story?id=1 (accessed January 3, 2006); Cameron Crowe, *Fast Times at Ridgemont High* (New York: Simon & Schuster, 1981); David Owen, *High School* (New York: Viking, 1981); *Never Been Kissed*, directed by Rajah Gosnell (Fox 2000 Pictures, 1999; Beverly Hills, CA: Twentieth Century Fox Home Entertainment, 2003).

4. Michael Harrington, *The Other America: Poverty in the United States* (New York: Macmillan, 1962). On deindustrialization, see Barry Bluestone and Bennett Harrison, *The Deindustrialization of America: Plant Closings, Community Abandonment, and the Dismantling of Basic Industry* (New York: Basic Books, 1982), and Jefferson Cowie and Joseph Heathcott, eds., *Beyond the Ruins: The Meanings of Deindustrialization* (Ithaca, NY: ILR Press, 2003). Barbara Ehrenreich, *Nickel and Dimed: On (Not) Getting By in America* (New York: Metropolitan Books, 2001); Alex Frankel, *Punching In: The Unauthorized Adventures of a Front-Line Employee* (New York: HarperCollins, 2007); Amy Flowers, *The Fantasy Factory: An Insider's View of the Phone Sex Industry* (Philadelphia: University of Pennsylvania Press, 1998); Tom Juravich, *Chaos on the Shop Floor: A Worker's View of Quality, Productivity, and Management* (Philadelphia: Temple University Press, 1985); María Patricia Fernández-Kelly, *For We Are Sold, I and My People: Women and Industry in Mexico's Frontier* (Albany: SUNY Press, 1983); Solange De Santis, *Life on the Line: One Woman's Tale of Work, Sweat and Survival* (New York: Doubleday, 1999); Ehrenreich, *Bait and Switch: The (Futile) Pursuit of the American Dream* (New York: Metropolitan Books, 2005).

5. Oscar Lewis elaborated his views in *Five Families: Mexican Case Studies in the Culture of Poverty* (New York: Basic Books, 1959); *The Children of Sanchez: Autobiography of a Mexican Family* (New York: Random House, 1961); and *La Vida: A Puerto Rican Family in the Culture of Poverty—San Juan and New York* (New York: Random House, 1966). See also Susan M. Rigdon, *The Culture Façade: Art, Science, and Politics in the Work of Oscar Lewis* (Urbana: University of Illinois Press, 1988). On the common tendency to conflate nonwhite (and especially black) skin with poverty and pathology, see Jacqueline Jones, *The Dispossessed: America's Underclasses from the Civil War to the Present* (New York: Basic Books, 1992), especially 269–273. Discussions of the "underclass" were stimulated by Ken Auletta, *The Underclass* (New York: Random House, 1982). From the enormous outpouring of scholarship debating the concept, the following have proven useful for this study:

Jones, *The Dispossessed*; Bil E. Lawson, ed., *The Underclass Question* (Philadelphia: Temple University Press, 1992); Michael B. Katz, ed., *The "Underclass" Debate: Views from History* (Princeton: Princeton University Press, 1993); Stephen Steinberg, "The Underclass: A Case of Color Blindness, Left and Right," in his *Turning Back: The Retreat from Racial Justice in American Thought and Policy* (Boston: Beacon, 1995), 137–155; James T. Patterson, "America's 'Underclasses,' Past and Present," *Proceedings of the American Philosophical Society* 141 (March 1997): 13–29. For emphases on behavior and culture, see Adolph Reed, Jr., "The Underclass as Myth and Symbol: The Poverty of Discourse about Poverty," *Radical America* 24 (January-March 1990): 22, 27, and Michael Katz, "The Urban 'Underclass' as a Metaphor of Social Transformation," in Katz, *"Underclass" Debate*, 4, 12. Tracing the genealogy that runs from older terms such as "undeserving poor" and "feebleminded" through the culture of poverty and the underclass are Herbert Gans, *The War against the Poor* (New York: Basic Books, 1995), 11–57, and Michael B. Katz, *Improving Poor People: The Welfare State, the "Underclass," and Urban Schools as History* (Princeton: Princeton University Press, 1995), 9–35.

6. Peter Davis, *If You Came This Way: A Journey through the Lives of the Underclass* (New York: John Wiley, 1995), 1, 4, 17–24. Davis relied heavily on the ideas of the liberal black sociologist William Julius Wilson, calling him "the eminence grise of underclass theory," and both citing and interviewing him for the book (see 17, 23, 100–102). Wilson later became critical of the underclass idea. For his more recent efforts to balance structural with cultural explanations of poverty, see his *More Than Just Race: Being Black and Poor in the Inner City* (New York: Norton, 2009).

7. Ted Conover, *Coyotes: A Journey through the Secret World of America's Illegal Aliens* (New York: Vintage, 1987), xvii, xix; Conover, *Rolling Nowhere* (New York: Viking, 1984), 274. Political commitments shaped by the social movements of the 1960s and afterward are evident in numerous writers discussed in this chapter, including Douglas Harper, *Good Company* (Chicago, 1982; updated and expanded edition, Boulder, CO: Paradigm, 2006), 2; "Interview with Barbara Ehrenreich," in Cecilia Tichi, *Exposés and Excess: Muckraking in America, 1900/2000* (Philadelphia: University of Pennsylvania Press, 2004), 118–119; Richard Pfeffer, *Working for Capitalism* (New York: Columbia University Press, 1979), 1–6, 9–10; John Calder, introduction to Robert Linhart, *The Assembly Line* (Paris, France, 1978; trans. Margaret Crosland, Amherst: University of Massachusetts Press, 1981), 7–9; Judith Rollins, *Between Women: Domestics and Their Employers* (Philadelphia: Temple University Press, 1985), 5–8, 234–235; and Deborah Fink, *Cutting into the Meatpacking Line: Workers and Change in the Rural Midwest* (Chapel Hill: University of North Carolina Press, 1998), xiii–xiv, 5. On speaking for working people and the poor, see Tichi, "Interview with Barbara Ehrenreich," 122, and Mrs. John Van Vorst and Marie Van Vorst, *The Woman Who Toils: Being the Experiences of Two Gentlewomen as Factory Girls* (New York: Doubleday, Page, 1903), 5, 168.

For academic considerations of this question, see Judith Roof and Robin Wiegman, eds., *Who Can Speak? Authority and Critical Identity* (Urbana: University of Illinois Press, 1995).

8. I have identified only two avowedly conservative down-and-outers from this period: Marvin Olasky (the intellectual architect of President George W. Bush's "compassionate conservatism") and the sociologist Daniel McMurry. See Olasky, *The Tragedy of American Compassion* (Washington, DC: Regnery/Gateway, 1992), 209–210, and McMurry, "Hard Living on Easy Street," *Chronicles* 12 (August 1988): 15–29. On the left, in addition to Ehrenreich, another representative figure is the political scientist Richard M. Pfeffer; see his *Working for Capitalism*.

9. Adam Shepard, *Scratch Beginnings: Me, $25, and the Search for the American Dream* (New York: Collins, 2008).

10. Conover, *Rolling Nowhere*, 215; Fernández-Kelly, *For We Are Sold*, 108; Steve Striffler, *Chicken: The Dangerous Transformation of America's Favorite Food* (New Haven: Yale University Press, 2005), 174; Tony Horwitz, "9 to Nowhere," *Wall Street Journal* (December 1, 1994): A1, 8, 9; Charlie LeDuff, "At a Slaughterhouse, Some Things Never Die," *New York Times* (June 16, 2000): A1, A24–A25. John R. Coleman, *Blue Collar Journal: A College President's Sabbatical* (Philadelphia: J. B. Lippincott, 1974); Coleman was also cited as an inspiration by De Santis in *Life on the Line*, 38–39. Juravich, *Chaos*, 86–91; Dale Maharidge and Michael Williamson, *Journey to Nowhere: The Saga of the New Underclass* (Garden City, NY: Dial Press, 1985); Frankel, *Punching In*, 6–7; Ehrenreich, *Nickel and Dimed*, 1; Tichi, "Interview with Ehrenreich," 122.

11. Lawrence J. Ouellet, *Pedal to the Metal* (Philadelphia: Temple University Press, 1994); Clark Molstad, "Control Strategies Used by Industrial Brewery Workers: Work Avoidance, Impression Management and Solidarity," *Human Organization* 47 (Winter 1988): 354–360; Mary V. Meckel, *A Sociological Analysis of the California Taxi-Dancer: The Hidden Halls* (Lewiston, NY: Edwin Mellen, 1995). Molstad and Meckel used records kept while working, but before their projects had been formalized.

12. Coleman, *Blue Collar Journal*, 169–171. Coleman's book became the basis of a television movie: *The Secret Life of John Chapman*, directed by David Lowell Rich (Jozak Company; Paramount Television, 1976). He also chronicled further undercover adventures, including "Diary of a Homeless Man," *New York* 16 (February 21, 1983): 26–35. Pfeffer, *Working for Capitalism*, 1. On ERAP, see Maurice Isserman, *If I Had a Hammer: The Death of the Old Left and the Birth of the New Left* (Urbana: University of Illinois Press, 1987), 216–217; De Santis, *Life on the Line*, 7–8, 10.

13. Michael Mathers, *Riding the Rails* (Boston: Gambit, 1973), 1; Douglas Harper, *Good Company* (Chicago: University of Chicago Press, 1982), 163–164; Harper, *Good Company*, 2nd edition (2006), 2.

14. Maharidge and Williamson, *Journey to Nowhere*, 8; Harper, *Good Company*, (2006), 126. Only Conover remained fully undercover, at least until late in the book (214);

he was known to be a college student on the road, but not a writer. Similarly, Harper revealed himself and his academic goals to his main informant near the end of *Good Company* (126). Mathers, *Riding the Rails*, 52–56.

15. Harper, *Good Company*, ix.

16. Dale Maharidge and Michael Williamson, *Journey to Nowhere: The Saga of the New Underclass*, 2nd edition (New York: Hyperion, 1995), 191–201; Harper, *Good Company* (2006), 187–191; Steven Kotler, "Damn Track: Hobo Hell," *Maxim* 3 (June 1, 1999): 109–114, http://www.stevenkotler.com/node/63 (accessed August 18, 2010); Conover, *Rolling Nowhere*, 213–215.

17. Pfeffer, *Working for Capitalism*, 6; De Santis, *Life on the Line*, 8–10, 12–13; Maharidge and Williamson, *Journey to Nowhere* (1995), 191.

18. Gloria Steinem, "I Was a Playboy Bunny" (*Show* magazine, 1963) in Steinem, *Outrageous Acts and Everyday Rebellions*, 2nd edition (New York: Henry Holt, 1995), 32–75. A popular television movie version of Steinem's articles was *A Bunny's Tale*, directed by Karen Arthur (ABC Circle Films, 1985; VHS, Burbank, CA: ABC Video, 1992). Explorers of urban poverty included Barnard L. Collier, "Down and Out on the Bowery: How It Feels," *New York* 2 (May 12, 1969): 24–29, and Michael de Yoanna, "Homeless in the Land of Plenty," *Boulder Daily Camera* (December 15–17, 2000): 1, 6–8. Social work and the welfare bureaucracy were investigated by the journalist Edgar May in *The Wasted Americans: Cost of Our Welfare Dilemma* (New York: Harper & Row, 1964) and by Barbara Sabol, a New York City welfare official, whose story was told in Alison Mitchell, "Passing as Welfare Recipient, Agency Head Finds Indignity," *New York Times* (February 5, 1993): A1. Areas of expanding job opportunities were the subjects of Jane H. Lii, "Week in Sweatshop Reveals Grim Conspiracy of the Poor," *New York Times* (March 12, 1995): A-1, and Ted Conover, *Newjack: Guarding Sing Sing* (New York: Random House, 2000).

19. The Food Lion case was summarized on "Morning Edition," National Public Radio, January 23, 1997, and in Felicity Barringer, "Appeals Court Rejects Damages against ABC in Food Lion Case," *New York Times* (October 21, 1999): 1A.

20. Charles Vaught and David L. Smith, "Incorporation and Mechanical Solidarity in an Underground Coal Mine" (1980); reprinted in Douglas Harper and Helene Lawson, eds., *The Cultural Study of Work* (Lanham, MD: Rowman and Littlefield, 2003), 98, 101, 103, 105.

21. Revealing themselves to coworkers but not bosses were Juravich, *Chaos*, 141; Rollins, *Between Women*, 9–10, 15, 234–235 nn. 7, 18; Fink, *Cutting*, 9–10; and Steve Striffler, "Inside a Poultry-Processing Plant: An Ethnographer's Portrait," *Labor History* 43 (August 2002): 311. Amy Flowers acknowledged being a graduate student but not a researcher in *Fantasy Factory*, 19–20. The sociologist William E. Thompson, who worked in a meat-processing plant, called himself a "complete participant," using Raymond Gold's definition; however, Thompson was known by his fellow workers to

be a sociologist, and the latter even joked that he might write a book about them. Similarly, Charles Vaught, an undercover coal miner, called himself a complete participant, but he was called "professor" by various coworkers. William E. Thompson, "Hanging Tongues: A Sociological Encounter with the Assembly Line," *Qualitative Sociology* 6 (Fall 1983): 219; Raymond Gold, "Roles in Sociological Field Observations," *Social Forces* 36 (March 1958): 217, 219–220; Vaught and Smith, "Incorporation and Mechanical Solidarity," 98, 107–109. Undercover material was restricted to one chapter in the books by Fernández-Kelly, Fink, and Striffler.

22. Severyn Bruyn, *The Human Perspective in Sociology: The Methodology of Participant Observation* (Englewood Cliffs, NJ: Prentice-Hall, 1966), 15–16, rejects the undercover method. Ignoring it are Glenn Jacobs, ed., *The Participant Observer* (New York: George Braziller, 1970), and Michael Burawoy, *Ethnography Unbound: Power and Resistance in the Modern Metropolis* (Berkeley: University of California Press, 1991). Burawoy had criticized Donald Roy's undercover method in his *Manufacturing Consent: Changes in the Labor Process under Monopoly Capitalism* (Chicago: University of Chicago Press, 1979), 33–35. Howard M. Bahr and the former down-and-outer Theodore Caplow sent "eager" disguised participant observers into New York City's Bowery district for preliminary research, but no undercover personae were constructed or evidence presented in the published book: *Old Men, Drunk and Sober* (New York: NYU Press, 1974), 3.

23. See David A. Snow and Leon Anderson, *Down on Their Luck: A Study of Homeless Street People* (Berkeley: University of California Press, 1993), 25. Other aboveground studies included Mark Fleisher, *Beggars and Thieves: Lives of Urban Street Criminals* (Madison: University of Wisconsin Press, 1995), and Irene Glasser and Rae Bridgman, *Braving the Street: The Anthropology of Homelessness* (New York: Berghahn Books, 1999).

24. Richard Balzer, *Clockwork* (New York: Doubleday, 1976), ix, 2–3; William Kornblum, *Blue-Collar Community* (Chicago: University of Chicago Press, 1974), 17–18; Robin Leidner, *Fast Food, Fast Talk: Service Work and the Routinization of Everyday Life* (Berkeley: University of California Press, 1993), 15–16; Steven Peter Vallas, *Power in the Workplace: The Politics of Production at AT&T* (Albany: SUNY Press, 1993), 199–200; Kevin A. Yelvington, *Producing Power: Ethnicity, Gender, and Class in a Caribbean Workplace* (Philadelphia: Temple University Press, 1995), 6–7.

25. Pfeffer, *Working for Capitalism*, 6, 11–12. Pfeffer died in 2002 after a distinguished career as a lawyer at the Labor Department. According to his *Baltimore Sun* obituary, the political science department's negative vote resulted from their assessment of his book. Pfeffer was well known as a campus radical—his case provoked a major controversy among students and faculty—so other considerations may also have figured in the decision. Jacques Kelly, "Richard Pfeffer, 65, Professor, Advocate for Workers' Safety," *Baltimore Sun* (May 22, 2002), http://articles.baltimoresun.com/2002-05-22/

news/0205220118_1_pfeffer-hopkins-political-science-department (accessed August 20, 2010).

26. Rollins, *Between Women*, 15; Pfeffer, *Working for Capitali$m*, 9.

27. This story is summed up in Charlotte Allen, "Spies Like Us: When Sociologists Deceive Their Subjects," *Lingua Franca* 7 (November 1997): 30–39; Erikson and Gans are quoted on pp. 33 and 32, respectively. See also Kai Erikson, "A Comment on Disguised Observation in Sociology," *Social Problems* 14 (Spring 1967): 366–373, and Herbert Gans, "The Participant-Observer as a Human Being," in *Institutions and the Person: Papers Presented to Everett C. Hughes*, ed. Howard S. Becker (Chicago: Aldine, 1968), 309. For the revised codes, see the American Sociological Association Code of Ethics (Spring 1997), http://www2.asanet.org/members/ecoderev.html (accessed August 25, 2010); and the Code of Ethics of the American Anthropological Association (June 1998), http://www.aaanet.org/committees/ethics/ethcode.htm (accessed August 25, 2010). A similar debate proceeded in British sociology, with a similar outcome. See Roger Homan, "The Ethics of Covert Methods," and Martin Bulmer, "Comment on 'The Ethics of Covert Methods,'" *British Journal of Sociology* 31 (March 1980): 46–59, 59–65; and the Statement of Ethical Practice for the British Sociological Association (March 2002), http://www.britsoc.co.uk/equality/Statement+Ethical+Practice.htm (accessed August 25, 2010). The British also acknowledged the influence of the American Sociological Association's statement of principles.

28. Examples included Charles E. Lindblom, *Inquiry and Change: The Troubled Attempt to Understand and Shape Society* (New Haven: Yale University Press, 1990), and Bent Flyvbjerg, *Making Social Science Matter: Why Social Science Inquiry Fails and How It Can Succeed Again* (Cambridge: Cambridge University Press, 2001).

29. This summary paragraph draws on the following; many other examples could be listed. Science: Ehrenreich, *Nickel and Dimed*, 3–4. Rituals: Conover, *Rolling Nowhere*, 14–15. Frustrations: Davis, *If You Came*, 126; Ehrenreich, *Nickel and Dimed*, 101–102; Mitchell, "Passing as Welfare Recipient." Hustling: Collier, "Down and Out"; Coleman, "Diary." Skills: Juravich, *Chaos*, 50–55; Striffler, *Chicken*, 380; Ehrenreich, *Nickel and Dimed*, 193. Soldiering: Collier, "Down and Out"; Ehrenreich, *Nickel and Dimed*, 195. Multiple jobs: Ehrenreich, *Nickel and Dimed*, 32. Fellow workers: Striffler, *Chicken*, 310, 124–127; Coleman, *Blue Collar Journal*, 43; Juravich, *Chaos*, 15. Generosity: Davis, *If You Came*, 126–127. No sinister aura—an exception to this was the ideologically conservative writers, who emphasized that the poor were not just regular folks with mainstream social values who were enduring hard times: Olasky, *Tragedy*, 209; McMurry, "Hard Times," 19. Taking refuge: Coleman, *Blue Collar Journal*, 52; Conover, *Rolling Nowhere*, 213. Going native: Ehrenreich, *Nickel and Dimed*, 34, 166–169; Tichi, "Interview with Ehrenreich," 123; Fernández-Kelly, *For We Are Sold*, 128; Edward Fowler, *San´ya Blues: Laboring Life in Contemporary Tokyo* (Ithaca: Cornell University Press, 1996), 203. Not real: Fink, *Cutting*, 37; Striffler, *Chicken*, 133.

30. It is commonly suggested that a fading modernist culture and political economy gave way to postmodernism sometime during and after the 1960s: see Daniel Joseph Singal, "Towards a Definition of American Modernism," *American Quarterly* 39 (Spring 1987): 21–23; David Harvey, *The Condition of Postmodernity: An Enquiry into the Origins of Cultural Change* (Cambridge, MA: Blackwell, 1989). My reference to "postmodernity" is intended especially to echo the usage of the sociologist William DiFazio, who emphasizes the term's socioeconomic and political dimensions as they interact reciprocally with cultural conditions and forms: see his *Ordinary Poverty: A Little Food and Cold Storage* (Philadelphia: Temple University Press, 2006), 23–24. See also Jones on "postmodern poverty" in *The Dispossessed*, 269–292.

31. For fuller discussions of the distinction I employ between "difference" and "otherness," see Beth J. Singer, *Pragmatism, Rights, and Democracy* (New York: Fordham University Press, 1999), 83–85, and Etienne Balibar, "Difference, Otherness, Exclusion," *Parallax* 11 (January-March 2005): 19–34.

INDEX

Note: An 'n' following a page number indicates a footnote.

ABC News, 184

Addams, Jane, 16–17

African Americans: and "culture of poverty" discourse, 180; intelligence testing of, 63; and interracial relationships, 227n19; and Peters's undercover investigations-turned-theater productions, 96–102; presence of, in undercover narratives, 122–23; presence of, in WWII shipyards, 239n17; Williams's stereotyping of, 73. *See also Black Like Me* (Griffin); "Dock-wallopers" (Peters); *In the Land of Jim Crow* (Sprigle); racial issues; *Stevedore* (Peters)

Alcoholics Anonymous, 135

Allen, Harbor. *See* Peters, Paul

American Anthropological Association, 186

American Civil Liberties Union (ACLU), 53

American Sociological Association (ASA), 185–86

America's Mainspring and the Great Society: A Pick-and-Shovel Outlook (Williams), 177

Anderson, Nels: *The American Hobo*, 60; on *Boy and Girl Tramps of America* (Minehan), 89; and culture concept, 58–59; *The Hobo*, 47–48; on legitimacy of undercover investigations, 215n42; on slumming, 57–58; as undercover investigator, 56; working-class background of, 54–55

Anderson, Paul, 20

anti-Semitism. See *Gentleman's Agreement* (Hobson)

anxieties: about identity, 142; of middle class, 12–13, 79–80, 109, 146

Arendt, Hannah, 126

Atkinson, Brooks, 100–101

authenticity. *See* reality

Babcock, Fern, 52

Bain, Read, 58–59, 88–89

Baker, Ray Stannard, 153

Bakke, E. Wight, 112, 123–24, 229n29

Baldwin, Roger, 52–53, 208n126

"Banana Time" (Roy), 132

Banks, Elizabeth, 14, 18, 23, 196n20

Beard, Charles, 46

Beasley, Robert W., 84

Becker, Howard S., 134, 241–42n34

begging, 28, 204n79

Bensman, Joseph, 135–36

"Beyond Otherness" (Griffin), 172

Bingham, Alfred, 49, 52–53, 76–77

Black Is a Man (Roskolenko), 152

Black Like Me (film), 168, 255n81

Black Like Me (Griffin): authenticity of, 158–59; class issues in, 161–62, 165; compared to *In the Land of Jim Crow* (Sprigle), 155, 157–58, 160; as exploration of boundary crossing, 140; issues of identity in, 165, 168; mirror scene in, 165, 254n69; origins of, 253n51;

ABOUT THE AUTHOR

Mark Pittenger is Associate Professor of History at the University of Colorado, Boulder. He is the author of *American Socialists and Evolutionary Thought, 1870–1920*.